RWBCS

RWBCS

A GREAT
FLEET OF
SHIPS

THE CANADIAN FORTS & PARKS

A GREAT FLEET OF SHIPS

THE CANADIAN FORTS & PARKS

S.C. Heal

Vanwell Publishing Limited

St. Catharines, Ontario

Vanwell Publishing acknowledges the financial support of the Government of Canada through the book Publishing Industry Development Program for our publishing activities.

Cover: Courtesy of Wm. G. Hutcherson of Richmond, BC. Adapted from an original painting by W. Hardcastle.

Design: Linda Moroz-Irvine
Editor: Ken Macpherson

Vanwell Publishing Limited
1 Northrup Crescent
P.O. Box 2131
St. Catharines, Ontario L2R 7S2

Printed in Canada

04 03 02 01 00   5 4 3 2 1

Canadian Cataloguing in Publication Data

Heal, S.C. (Syd C.)
        A great fleet of ships : the Canadian forts & parks

Includes bibliographical references and index.
ISBN 1-55125-023-3

1. Merchant ships – Canada – History – 20th century. 2. Merchant marine – Canada – History – 20th century – . 3. Shipbuilding – Canada – History – 20th century. I. Title.

HE769.H415 1999   387.5'0971'0904   C99-931961-2

TABLE OF CONTENTS

ACKNOWLEDGEMENTS

A book like this would have been doubly hard, if not impossible, to put together at a point in history when the last Park or Fort Ship left the shipyards in 1946 and, in the form it now takes, without the contributions of a number of people whom I have named below.

In the fifty-odd intervening years, only one of the ships survives as a floating antique whose days must now be numbered. Of the many thousands of men who went to sea in the ships their ranks have drastically thinned as age has taken its toll.

My grateful thanks go to those named below whose cooperation has been of inestimable value in bringing this project to fruition.

George Conway-Brown of Blind Bay, BC, Lew Brewer of San José, California, Josh Jones of Rickmansworth, England, David Martin-Smith, Jan Drent and Jim Butterfield all of Victoria, BC, Olive Roeckner (Carroll) of Mirror Lake, BC, Dick Wilson and Jim Grey of Vancouver, BC, Bill Hutcherson and Peter Tull of Richmond, BC, Peter Kelly of Scarborough, ON, all of whom have contributed specially written material, or have allowed me to quote from previously published works, or use material supplied by them and appropriate to the text. Ian Stewart of Perth, Western Australia, the Vancouver Maritime Museum and the World Ship Society have been sources of photographic material in addition to my own collection. Photographs have come from a number of other sources which have been acknowledged with the photo.

Special thanks must go to George Conway-Brown for the research contribution he made to the geographical and historical names chosen for the ships and also his proofreading activities. Also I would like to remember the late John Hetherington who died in 1997. He was a great supporter of this project and it is with much personal regret on my part that he was never able to see the finished project. I know he would have approved of it.

Others to whom thanks are due are June Thompson of the North Vancouver Museum and Archives, the repository of the Burrard and Wallace collections, Len McCann of the Vancouver Maritime Museum, both of whom have been ready and willing at all times to open their files. Also Cec Woods custodian of the World Ship Society collection of photos at the Vancouver Maritime Museum, Roland Webb, formerly of Burrard Dry Dock Company, but now president of Todd Shipyards Corporation, Seattle, who along with George Conway-Brown provided copies of correspondence between shipmasters, chief engineers and others, and Burrard Dry Dock and West Coast Shipbuilders respectively. I am sure that other yards turned out equally excellent products and also had similar correspondence with the personnel aboard ships they built, but none has turned up in my researches. None of these letters is earthshaking, but they do in fact provide small, interesting excerpts of ship activity and the human interplay involved at that time.

I also wish to thank Clyde Jacobs, president of Pacific Commerce Line, Vancouver, Roland Webb of Todd Shipyards and Peter L. Wright of the Vancouver Arbitration Centre, author in his own right and a prominent consultant in the marine insurance industry. They read my manuscript material on matters dealing with ship chartering, shipbuilding, management and marine insurance. None of these subjects is treated as exhaustively as it would be in special textbooks, and all recognized that I was writing for a broad, rather than a highly specialized readership.

It has been a pleasure working with all the above named. To say the least it has been a struggle bringing this project to fruition. My own age and personal health have been factors. The first I can do nothing about, but happily health has improved and completion of this project has given me a fresh lease on life.

Finally I wish to thank my publishers, Vanwell Publishing Limited for their participation. As I had to give up my own publishing enterprise for the reasons stated in the previous paragraph, it was good news indeed when they agreed to take this project on and turn it into a reality.

S.C. Heal
Vancouver, BC
March, 1999

INTRODUCTION

This book is offered as the definitive memorial to a group of ships which have left behind nostalgic memories. Its purpose is not only to detail these Canadian-built ships, but also to show in some measure how they fitted into the larger-scale elements of history and the world's commerce. It was a Canadian Second World War achievement paralleling the shipbuilding program of the First World War, but in its ultimate execution it greatly exceeded the earlier program. It is a story of wartime shipbuilding, wartime ship operations and ship's crews, many of whom paid the ultimate price. It is also the story of postwar ship operations which eroded away the Canadian Merchant Navy as we knew it, in the glory days at the end of the Second World War. The CMN was ground to virtual and final extinction by the forces of politics, union action, operating economics and the realities of a rapidly changing world shipping scene.

A Great Fleet of Ships: The Canadian Forts and Parks is a follow-up to the author's *Conceived in War, Born in Peace: Canada's Deep Sea Merchant Marine*, a book which has been well received and, in the relatively limited specialist market for marine books, something of a best seller. That book had a number of limitations. One was that while its concept was broad in that it covered both World War shipbuilding programs, it was constrained by time and financial considerations. For that reason some aspects were not dealt with as fully as the author would have liked and that, in effect, now gives rise to this more specialized book.

Neither the first book nor the present volume has been assisted by subsidy of any sort from any source. It was sought in producing the first book, but the application was turned down, presumably because it lacked a broad enough historical appeal, a miscon-

Ocean Liberty. The first of 30 Ocean class North Sands ships to be completed at Bath Ironworks, Portland Maine yard. The ship was flying the Red Ensign from the signal mast which indicates that she was still technically the property of the builder before completion of trials and handover to the British government.   (Todd-Bath Iron Shipbuilding Corporation)

Fort St. James. The first North Sands ship to be built on the West Coast and the second from a Canadian yard. She was on trials in English Bay when this photo was taken. There was no Canadian-type cowl fitted to the funnel and the signal mast was mounted on top of the portside derrick post at No. 3 hatch. As history unfolded she became one of the longest-lived of the entire group, being on the Chinese register until 1991.

(North Vancouver Museum & Archives 27-2397)

Rupert Park. Returning from a trial run in English Bay, Vancouver. Net booms and anti-aircraft armament still await fitting, but as she was not completed until May 1945, there is some doubt if these items were ever installed. Of the Canadian oil/coal burner type, none of this class was transferred to the British.   (North Vancouver Museum & Archives 27-2298)

ception in my view as the shipbuilding program and the fleet it produced were of critical importance to the Allied war effort and probably, taking the shipyards collectively, represented the largest group industrial undertaking in Canada to that time, notwithstanding the aircraft, tanks and many other munitions of war we produced in great numbers.

This seems to arise from the official disinterest which has transmitted itself to war historians, who barely mention the Wartime Emergency Shipbuilding Program and Canadian merchant shipping, if at all. It is reflected in the lack of knowledge of or even interest in the vanished shipyards where thousands sweated and strained, where Canadian-built ships tasted saltwater and went to sea, often with hurriedly trained green crews who stepped into the emergency. There now seems little interest in passing on remembrances of this important historical heritage to today's generations.

Capping all this is the fact that successive Canadian governments have ignored the need for the maintenance of a Canadian merchant marine as a key part of a national maritime policy. Other than in wartime, we have never had any national shipping policy which could be described as anything better than a band-aid solution. Canadian governments, which can be so considerate of others when it suits their political purpose, should hang their heads in shame for the manner in which they have treated their Merchant Navy veterans. More often than not, they have been ignored in official and other war histories. The historians who have written the nation's history sometimes have seemed barely conscious that there ever was a shipping industry and a merchant navy manned by tens of thousands of Canadians, a considerable number of whom gave up their lives to torpedo, gunfire and mine, not only in Canadian-registered ships, but as crew aboard British and foreign vessels.

As a nation we are not alone in the process of deterioration. The once great British merchant navy, which during the war and in its aftermath included so many Canadian-built Fort ships, is a shadow of its former self. Take away P & O and what little remains of Cunard, now foreign controlled, and there is not much left. The American merchant navy has shrunk in a similar way, and in Western Europe only the merchant marines of Norway, Denmark, Holland, Greece, Germany and possibly Spain and Italy, have maintained significant positions in the rosters of world shipping. The usual answer is that it cannot be done without subsidies in our high-cost economy. However, Norway and Germany, both with high cost economies, have done it by removal of their traditionally rigid national flag and manning requirements. They and others have recognized that taxation policies and such factors as manning costs have contributed significantly to the creation of a world shipping industry, now based very strongly on flags of convenience and the employment of third world crews.

The Americans invented flags of convenience, the Greeks took early advantage of them, Oriental owners have made a fine art out of Liberian and Panamanian registry and even the British arch-oppo-

nents have had to accept the concept of a global shipping village where survival depends heavily on the bottom line and hardly at all on national pride. In the British case they lit on Bermuda, the Isle of Man and Gibraltar as flag of convenience registers. These moves have succeeded to some extent, one of the main beneficiaries being our own Canadian Pacific Limited. C.P. is now a very large factor in the North Atlantic container trade through several subsidiary operations. Other successful Canadian operators who have embraced the concept of the global shipping village are Canada Steamship Lines and FedNav Limited, both of Montreal.

The move to flags of convenience has grown parallel with traditional management yielding its function to lawyers, accountants and bankers more interested in international competition and the bottom line than in the concepts of national flags and old fashioned ideas about patriotism. Even the Japanese recognize the necessity to compete on this basis, and have switched substantial tonnages of their national shipping to Panama and Liberia. In the case of the Russians, Malta, Cyprus and minor flags from the West Indies have had particular appeal for similar reasons.

The world shipping scene has changed so much in the past fifty years as to be unrecognisable. The days when a multiplicity of national shipping lines served one route alone have gone forever. At the outbreak of the Second World War some ten British lines served British Columbia ports on a regular basis. An assortment of Scandinavian lines served the same purpose. In addition there were regular liner services under the US, German, French, Dutch, Italian and Japanese flags. With few exceptions almost all these owners are now simply a part of shipping history.

Today the concentration of so much of the world's shipowning capital is in the Orient. Where national flag carriers still exist in, for example, the container business, a given country may have only one such line based in the home country and even then most of its ships may be under flags of convenience. Examples include Britain's P & O, Denmark's Maersk Line, Holland's NedLloyd, Germany's Hapag-Lloyd and American President Line, or APL, of the US The latter is now controlled

Fort Bellingham. One of 32 Victory Class ships transferred to Britain. This ship was one of two lost by enemy action, in this case while on the Murmansk convoy run in January 1944.   (North Vancouver Museum & Archives 27-OS-29)

by Neptune Orient of Malaysia and P & O has now merged its container services with Nederland Lloyd of Holland in a full marriage rather than through a rearrangeable consortium. Canadian Pacific has regained its prime position on the North Atlantic by taking over rival CAST and the famous Lykes Lines of the US following financial troubles at both acquired companies, but this could not have been done if there had been a requirement to hoist the Canadian or British flags.

I have set out the foregoing to more conveniently isolate the Fort and Park ships as an historical phenomenon, the like of which we will never see again. They were wholly a product of the Second World War as also were their contemporaries, the great fleets of Liberties, Empires and other wartime classes.

In accounting for these ships, I have largely restricted myself to the two basic ocean-going types, the North Sands and its derivatives, the Canadian and Victory types, and the 4,700 ton Grey or Scandinavian type and its variations. As something of an afterthought I have added the six Great Lakes tankers that bore Park names, along with one oddment, *Riding Mountain Park,* a converted dredger, so that the complete Park fleet can be accounted for.

There are also three groups without which the accounting would be incomplete. These are the 60 Oceans built in the US but effectively full sisters of the North Sands ships built in Canada and a closely related part of the same tonnage replacement program initiated by the British Ministry of War Transport; the 90 North Sands ships financed and owned by the United States War Shipping Administration and bareboat chartered to the British

Ministry of War Transport; and the Victory and Canadian type ships which were built to British account as Fleet Maintenance ships or bareboated by the Canadian government to the British as supply auxiliaries.

On the subject of the maintenance ships, a Canadian reviewer once took me to task for including these ships in my book *Conceived in War, Born in Peace*. His reasoning was that the ships were built as warships and more correctly belonged in Navy histories. By all means they can be included in Navy histories if that is what another author in some other work wishes to do, but that does not disqualify them from honourable mention in this book. However, in that an author is entitled to explain his concept, in my opinion the link between the Navy maintenance ships and the merchant shipbuilding program is indisputable. They were sister ships in that they were basically Victory-type ships like all the other 10,000-tonners of the same design built on the same original North Sands hull. The propulsion machinery was the same and the profile was changed only in matters of detail in the design which emerged from the shipyards. To omit them for some fanciful reason would be like drawing the human body with one limb missing, and I make no apology for including them again. Apart from all else they were built in Canada, which is the common factor binding all these ships in what may be the last work pertaining to a key epochal event in Canadian maritime history. Some were completed as merchant ships and others became merchant ships following disposal, it seems inconsequential that they were laid down as warships.

As I wrote the first draft of this book efforts were being made to preserve the very last of all the Canadian-built hulls owned in Canada. This is HMCS *Cape Breton*, ex-HMS *Flamborough Head*, and for those who are interested in seeing the project succeed I am sure there is less concern about whether the ship sailed as a navy repair ship or a merchantman. The prime consideration is that one ship at least should be saved, and as it is the last in Canadian hands, it could also be added that it is a last chance to preserve something representative of a great national shipbuilding program. Since completing this book, the fate of *Cape Breton* has been settled. She is to be scuttled as an artificial reef off the BC coast, and will be the only remaining representative of the wartime program, accessible only to divers.

One final point concerns Chapters One and Five. It may be thought that I am straying away from the central theme of the Fort and Park story. However, keep in mind that this book is not simply a tabulated record of ships' names or statistical data. With the aid of contributors, I have added both romance and colour to lend background both to the human picture and to the lineage of these ships back to Britain where, as everyone should know, the designs originated. Ship design is always in a state of evolution and a major part of the evolution of the Forts and Parks derives from British shipbuilding traditions, ownership, management and commercial practices.

In connection with Chapter Five, one might ask what insurance has to do with the subject in hand? The answer is that it is as integral a part of ship operation as ship management and chartering. Whenever suitable I have injected the insurance dimension into the circumstances of losses and other matters. I offer this in the knowledge that this aspect of maritime commerce seldom receives any attention at the hands of maritime historians, in spite of its importance and the fact that it becomes a part of maritime history with every loss. The importance of this subject cannot be minimized (see end of Chapter 10), as it was the marine insurance industry which played the pivotal role in ridding the seas of old and rundown wartime shipping during the 1960s and 70s, which included most of the surviving Forts and Parks.

There are also personal perspectives in Chapters One and Five including sentimental links to the land of my birth. These in turn were tempered by my enormous affection for Canada long before I ever came to this country. My first sight of a Fort ship at anchor among a group of US Liberty ships, in 1942, in the River Mersey, immediately told me I was viewing something different. The later knowledge that she had been built in Canada gave me a sense of pride and even today, as I read accounts of the ships and view photographs, I feel a similar sense of pride tinged with nostalgia. Maybe the slight tingle I have is like the remnants of an old love affair that has never quite died.

Historical Perspectives

For an English schoolboy raised as I was in the vicinity of Liverpool, England, it was inevitable that one of the countries about which I gained early knowledge was Canada. This was the principal British port of embarkation for emigrants destined for North America. For many years it was the home port of two of the main carriers of passengers engaged in the St. Lawrence trade — White Star and Cunard. Both lines maintained regular sailings for East Coast Canadian ports up to the thirties when Cunard White Star Limited was created as part of the financing package when the merger of the two historic rivals was forced by the British Government in return for its guarantees which led to completion of the *Queen Mary*. It was the first major rationalization in North Atlantic passenger travel brought about by the depression and changing conditions prior to the war of 1939.

They were not alone, of course. Canadian Pacific of London, Donaldson Line of Glasgow and London-based Furness Withy also provided regular passenger service from Liverpool to Canada, the lat-

Montcalm. A pre-1939 photo of one of the Canadian Pacific "M" class passenger liners alongside the Liverpool landing stage. It was from this point that many tens of thousands of migrants from the British Isles and Western Europe sailed for a new life in Canada.

(S.C. Heal)

ter through its Liverpool-based Johnston Warren Line. In addition, several primarily cargo services operated from British ports, but Liverpool remained the principal port of embarkation for Canada-bound emigrants. Liverpool Landing Stage, a huge elongated floating raft secured to the shore by oversize girder structures and massive chains, could accommodate ocean liners sailing to many overseas destinations and regular coastal passenger services to such places as the Isle of Man, North Wales and Ireland.

A walk along the landing stage at lunchtime was an excursion for bored office clerks to smell the perfumes of the sea and the distinctive wafts of oil and coal smoke, and the tars and paints used around ships. There was the hustle and bustle of passengers and porters worrying about their luggage and every several minutes the lunging of a Mersey ferry from the Cheshire side. These ferry masters knew their stuff. As they say, they could land on a dime, precisely placed so that the side ramps would go down at their appointed spot without delay. Passengers would rush in a great horde off the vessel, while another group awaited their turn to board. Regardless of weather or the strong tides of the Mersey this routine went on inexorably. The Mersey ferries were totally reliable in all situations and had a safety record second to none.

That same landing stage, somewhat after the manner of big British railway stations, also displayed posters beckoning the passenger to Sunny Saskatchewan or a variety of other locations in Canada, all of which sought settlers. There were posters depicting beautiful girls picking perfect Okanagan apples or stooking wheat on the prairies. Many from my home area of Cheshire tried it and succeeded. Others were not so successful and I well remember a decent young man who worked for my father, who had sheepishly returned after his failure to make it on the prairies. To emigrate to Canada with few skills and little money in the depression years of the thirties, was indeed for many a one-way ticket to Hell.

A visit today to the Merseyside Maritime Museum, located in old multi-storied warehouses in the heart of Liverpool's oldest dockland area, reveals a wealth of history, with its own Canada Dock and the port's connections to Canada and the United States. It is difficult to disentangle the two, for the migrant route to one country might also well have been via the neighbour to the north or south. Liverpool drew a great many migrants from Continental Europe, who travelled from points in Eastern Europe and Scandinavia to catch an emigrant ship out of Liverpool or some other British port such as Avonmouth or Glasgow. There was a great deal of competition among the European passenger lines to grab their share of this lucrative traffic and their agency systems combed far and wide to obtain it for their own ships.

Norddeutscher Lloyd of Bremen, was perhaps the largest of all the European passenger carriers in the North Atlantic emigrant trade and there is no doubt that with its national rival, Hamburg-Amerika Line, the two had the biggest share up until the First World War if only because geography favoured them. With the American open door policy, migration from Germany and Central Europe was particularly heavy into the United States. Cunard and White Star also had a large slice of the American emigrant traffic, as the records at the Merseyside Museum attest, and lodging the hordes of people awaiting sailing day was a big business for scores of cheap hotels and flop houses within easy reach of the Liverpool Landing Stage.

The British lines had a virtual monopoly of the seaborne passenger traffic into Canada. The Canadian Pacific Railway, even though British-controlled and financed in its earlier days, was a distinctively Canadian enterprise based in Montreal. The CPR ran its ocean steamship services as a British concern, ships were built and registered in Britain and manned by British crews. Voyages started and ended at Liverpool — Montreal, Halifax or St. John, New Brunswick were the turnaround points, at least for the British crews.

There were good reasons for this. Manning has already been touched upon, but in addition all the other servicing needs of a shipowning industry were to be found in Britain in abundance. Shipping needed a variety of services: financing and building the ships, engine building, cheap coal, plentiful steel and shipbuilding materials, drydocks and a full range of repair facilities, ship chandlery and supplies of every description, not to mention the world's leading

Ferozapore. Typical of wooden sailing ships built on Canada's East Coast, this barque was launched from the yard of Joseph Cunard at Chatham, NB on Sept. 12, 1846. Of 955 gt, she was built for Michael Samuel of Miramichi and sold in 1847 to Belfast merchants. In 1864, the author's great-grandfather shipped out in this ship as second mate when owned by the Company of African Merchants, Liverpool. (Barlow Collection, Mariners Museum Newport News)

marine insurance market. These services were provided competitively right from the days of the industrial revolution and even the foreigners purchased a great many of their requirements in Britain, often including their ships.

Arguably management was paramount. This function with its expertise, defined need and saw opportunity, and it was in the quality of its judgement that progress in a given industry was made and the support of investment capital thus gained. British shipowners of the nineteenth century and up to the First World War were in every sense of the word true entrepreneurs, trail-blazers in fact, on a scale seldom seen in traditional industries before or since.

The slow communications of this era gave rise to a need for trusted and reliable agents in every port where a line called. It was around these agents, many of whom served a multiplicity of shipping lines, that a local shipping fraternity developed. Aside from the US and Japan the main shipowning countries of note were all European at the beginning of the twentieth century. Generally, shipping grew in those countries which had a major industrial base, such as Britain, Germany and Sweden. There were notable exceptions such as Greece and Norway, where the strong capabilities of their mariners and an ancient and strong identification with the sea as their way of earning a living, encouraged large shipowning industries which gained most of their freight earnings through serving the major industrial countries.

Canada had, of course, developed a shipping and shipbuilding industry of considerable size by the middle of the nineteenth century. Cheap and plentiful lumber on both coasts encouraged United Empire Loyalists to remove themselves from the new United States, or in the case of British Columbia, had encouraged a great variety of entrepreneurs to establish forest industries which remain the backbone of the BC economy. They joined new immigrants from Europe, at that time mostly Britain, who brought their skills with them. There was an earlier influence which was already well established in the form of the Québécois and Acadian settlers from the northern areas of France who were known for their wooden shipbuilding and fishing skills, as well as the early Scottish settlers who put down roots in coastal Nova Scotia, along with their traditions as boatbuilders and fishermen.

Ships built in the Maritimes were famous for their quality of design and construction even if, being built mostly of softwood, their lives would not be long. Such ships were often filled with lumber and dispatched to Britain for resale, frequently by auction, and a number of names which became famous in British shipping annals got their first start through acquisition of a Maritime or Quebec-built vessel.

But it was Quebec, most notably Montreal, which became the centre of early Canadian shipowning activity on any sort of an international scale. Halifax, it is true, had developed an early trade with the West Indies and the fact that it was ice-free in the winter created its attractions, but when passengers or cargo were discharged at that port it followed that there was a long and tedious train journey inland in order to reach the heartland of the country. When the St. Lawrence was open ships could travel right into the heartland. Montreal, as the country's main port and financial centre, was at the centre of it all.

Expatriate Britons were among the first shipping agents representing the interests of their British principals at Montreal and other Canadian East Coast ports. One has only to examine the names of the agencies to determine the lineage, but it was from these that the Montreal shipping market emerged. A true blue Canadian shipping enterprise out of Montreal was the Allen Line, founded by Scottish expatriates with their first steamer, appropriately named *Canadian,* in 1853. The Allen Line was to be one of the trio of Canadian-owned enterprises which flourished in the North Atlantic passenger trade, the other two being Canadian Pacific and the relatively short-lived Canadian Northern Steamships Royal Line. Like Canadian Pacific, Royal functioned as a British concern, managed from London, but used Avonmouth as its terminus. Like its larger competitor it was an arm of a railway, in this case the Canadian Northern Railway for which it was set up to act as a feeder to its parent.

To the disappointment of ship buffs of the period Allen was to eventually be absorbed into Canadian Pacific. The single surviving ship of the Royal Line, *Royal George,* followed the same fate when the Canadian Northern Railway became part of the newly formed Canadian National Railway. CN wanted no part in North Atlantic passenger steamship services so it was inevitable that the Royal Line should be sold to Cunard as an alternative to doing anything which would assist its great rival, Canadian Pacific.

On the West Coast the situation was a little different. Today, we hear talk of Cascadia, a region which is still a notion, mostly originating with American economists, and stretching from British Columbia, through Oregon and Washington into Northern California. Realistically this has always existed to some extent as commercial ties on the West Coast have often more strongly followed a north-south direction. It was only the building of an east-west transcontinental railway which assured British Columbia joining Confederation. Just as early gold-seekers and lumbermen mostly came up from the south, so also did shipping and marine insurance agencies whose principals, often British shipping concerns, saw San Francisco as the commercial capital of the entire Pacific coast from the Mexican border to Alaska.

Coastal shipping services had grown on both coasts, the Great Lakes, and important interior lakes like Winnipeg and Okanagan as settlement progressed. The coastal and lakes steamship lines were easily and quickly established by comparison with building railways or roads. As such they provided a nucleus from which trained personnel could be drawn to man merchant ships in both world wars.

Vancouver's early eminence as Canada's West Coast port was greatly enhanced by the dictates of geography. It was the logical base for Canadian Pacific's passenger services to the Orient and it was the turnaround port for services from Australia and New Zealand. All these services added lustre to Vancouver's position as a key link in the *All Red* route of Empire, whereby the Mother Country was connected to its main possessions around the world by globe-spanning routes functioning in opposite directions. The concept of *Empire* was in everyone's mind in those days and Britain above all wanted to protect its dominant position against the colonial interests of France, Russia, Holland, Japan and particularly Germany, its most aggressive rival. American competition was of a different nature. The Americans disclaimed imperialism, but it was American commercial imperialism which came to dominate the world's economy, particularly after the Second World War.

City of Victoria. Using First World War style standard tonnage built in their own yard, John Coughlan & Son, as the only deep sea tramp operator out of Vancouver, managed to successfully operate this vessel and her sister ship *City of Vancouver* in the lumber trade until 1936.
(Vancouver Maritime Museum)

It took the First World War to establish Vancouver's reputation as a centre in which steel ships could be built and deep sea shipowning could take hold as a local industry. This was also largely true of the East Coast.

In 1917, when Britain was in the direst peril as the result of successful German U-boat warfare against its shipping and losses which could not be readily replaced, it turned to the United States with its largely underemployed shipbuilding industry and huge steel-making capacity as a means to provide suitable replacement shipping. Before long, however, the United States was drawn into the war and the large tonnages of shipping earmarked for Britain were taken over by the United States before delivery could be made.

The other sources to which Britain turned were Hong Kong, China, Japan and Canada. The first two supplied a handful of vessels. Japan was a bigger supplier, but Canada was the one with the greatest potential, and as a result some 60 steel and a further 49 short-lived wooden vessels were supplied by Canadian yards to the British government. Not surprisingly after a period when shipping for Canadian exports was in increasingly short supply, the Canadian government decided to get into shipping on its own account. Some schooners had been built in BC yards for a syndicate backed by BC government legislation, but very soon a fleet of some 68 Canadian government steel cargo steamers came out of the yards on both coasts.

These ships formed the fleet of what became the Canadian Government Merchant Marine (CGMM), a concern which was more the creation of politicians than a soundly based commercial enterprise. In spite of this, it enjoyed some success in competition with private owners. However, by the time the last ships had been sold off to private owners in 1936, the venture into shipping had cost the Canadian taxpayer about 86 million dollars.

Very little private oceangoing shipping came into being under the Canadian flag after the First World

War. Furness Withy, with longstanding interests in Canada, had acquired the Quebec Steamship Company in 1919, but did not increase its fleet from the pool of postwar Canadian-built ships. Only two private Canadian companies acquired vessels from this fleet of war-built types. These were Forbes Corporation of Montreal which acquired one vessel and J. Coughlan & Son who built three vessels for their own account at their Vancouver Shipyard. The small Coughlan fleet was to be the only truly Vancouver-domiciled deep sea shipowner between the wars, in fact up to their demise in 1936, when a shipwreck left them with just one remaining vessel. The surviving ship was quickly sold and Coughlan retired from business.

When war broke out in 1939, Canada's deep sea fleet consisted of 37 vessels manned by 1,450 Canadian personnel. Canadian National and Imperial Oil were the biggest owners of deep sea ships flying the Canadian flag. Canadian Pacific maintained their coastal fleet under the Canadian flag, but had their entire fleet of deep sea ships under the British flag with the exception of the *Empress of Asia* and *Empress of Russia* which were registered in Vancouver. The three main foreign-trade ports of Halifax, Montreal and Vancouver had small shipping markets made up almost entirely of shipping agencies and branch offices.

Any notion that the Second World War would be short, fast and decisively in favour of the Allies was soon dispelled. German submarines were on station around the British Isles the day war was declared and within hours the first war loss was announced. She was the Donaldson liner *Athenia* sunk on September 3, 1939, by the German submarine *U 30*. One of the casualties was a stewardess from the Montreal area who became Canada's first merchant marine casualty of the war. Over the next several weeks the names of lost ships were released to the press. Of the next seven ships sunk between September 5 and 7, all but one was assisted to its grave by submarine gunfire, which gives an indication of the vulnerability of unarmed, unescorted merchantmen.

It was a war for which Canada was ill-prepared. There was a small navy and merchant marine but little shipbuilding capacity. The task ahead was enormous. By the time it was over the country had the largest shipyard capacity in the world after the US and Britain, the fourth largest merchant fleet and the third largest navy made up of hundreds of warships ranging from cruisers, destroyers and frigates through to corvettes, minesweepers and sundry small craft. This superiority was not to last long, particularly so far as the Canadian merchant navy was concerned. The decline took place over a period of time almost as short as that required for the buildup.

CHAPTER TWO

The War at Sea

Nothing illustrates better than dry statistics the precarious state of Allied shipping over a large part of the war and the dire necessity for emergency replacement programs to make good the enormous losses suffered by Britain and the Allied nations over much of the world. It was nowhere worse than in the North Atlantic theatre, where a determined offensive war was waged by the German submarine arm under the command of Admiral Karl Doënitz. Highly-trained and disciplined, working with excellent boats which were at the forefront of submarine technology, the U-boat crews should not be denied their own accolades for courage, no matter how they created mayhem on the surface.

The war at sea has been covered by many authors in a variety of ways in books published intermittently since the war. One of the best, relating to the merchant service, and possibly the most extensive in terms of actual ship details and the numbers of vessels covered is John Slader's impressive book *The Fourth Service,* published as recently as 1995. Slader, a British merchant navy officer during the war, suffered and survived no fewer than four sinkings by enemy action, thus acquiring a fund of direct experience which has given him an advantage over armchair historians. Slader came from a merchant navy family with a father, uncle and two brothers all serving at sea during the war, and that alone must be a record hardly likely to be repeated.

One of his ships was *Fort Fitzgerald,* a Vancouver-built North Sands type and one of the group of 90 financed and owned by the United States Maritime Commission and bareboated to the British Ministry of War Transport. Slader picked up this newly built ship from West Coast Shipbuilders, and was thus fully aware that these Canadian ships came from typical Canadian shipbuilders. His book details a considerable number of incidents involving Fort and Ocean ships. None of the Parks is detailed, as there were only four actual war losses out of the fleet operated by Park Steamship Company and of these, two were under British manning at the time and two were lost in Indian Ocean or South African waters well away from the central war zones. Canadian merchant service personnel suffered heavily with 1437 lost out of a total of some 15,000, but the losses were mainly in ships other than the Parks.

Other anecdotal accounts of individual ship losses and experiences follow in Chapters Six and Seven in this book, giving a fair idea of wartime conditions and experiences as they relate to individual ships and their crews. Details of all recorded losses involving Fort and Park ships are including in the individual ship histories contained in the fleet list.

It was a savage war, always fought without consideration for the comfort of the other side. Humanitarian considerations usually went by the board until the battle was over, and charges of atrocities were levelled by both sides. One German U-boat commander, Heinz Eck of *U 852* along with four other defendants from his crew, were sentenced to death and executed November 30, 1945, for their role in cold-bloodedly gunning down survivors of the Blue Funnel liner *Peleus* the previous year. Other crew members of the submarine received long prison sentences, all of which were subsequently commuted. The same could not be said for the Imperial Japanese Navy which is covered in a section of Chapter Six, when setting out details of the loss of *Fort Mumford.*

City of Benares. Of the 90 children on board as evacuees to Canada only 13 survived when the ship was torpedoed in mid-Atlantic. More than most wartime losses this incident brought home to the world the tragedy and horror of the war at sea.   (K.P. Lewis)

There were also some remarkable stories of humanity at its best. One such was the sinking of the Cunard White Star liner *Laconia* on September 12, 1942, 500 miles south of Cap Palmas, Liberia. With a crew of 692, 766 passengers and 1,793 Italian prisoners of war from North Africa, the ship was torpedoed by Korvettenkapitän Werner Hartenstein in *U 156*. The U-boat commander was so horrified by the damage wrought in torpedoing the liner that he called up other U-boats and an Italian submarine in an effort to get survivors at least close to shore and rescue. After checking with Admiral Doënitz, he had sent out an open language message to both sides calling for a short truce to enable rescue to proceed, but unfortunately it was not picked up by a US Liberator from Ascension Island which proceeded to bomb the assembled submarines and the collection of *Laconia* lifeboats. The rescue had to be called off. Loss of life was heavy with only 975 survivors. At the Nuremberg trials the bombing incident was cited as an Allied atrocity by the defence.

On the other side of the coin, the sinking of the Ellerman liner *City of Benares* on September 17, 1940, more than most sinkings, brought home to the public the horror of the battle of the convoys. In this case the ship was carrying evacuee children from Britain to Canada when she was sunk without warn-ing. Loss of life was heavy and most of the children died of exposure in the lifeboats after the ship was abandoned. This loss, which was fully publicized for propaganda purposes, put an end to the scheme for evacuating British children to safe overseas havens.

"Without warning" was a useful propaganda phrase which overlooked the fact that all participants with a submarine arm had been sinking their respective enemy merchant ships ever since the war began or, in the case of the Americans, since they entered the war. In fact anti-submarine weapons became so effective that the idea of a gentlemanly warning was a flashback to an earlier chivalrous era, as neither side gave any quarter. Survivors were rescued by both sides, often with the idea of taking a prisoner for intelligence purposes; nonetheless, many an unfortunate survivor was to drown or be killed in the heat of action.

In 1947 the British government released its official lists of merchant vessels lost by enemy action and, separately, those which suffered heavy damage and lived to fight again. Included in the list were all vessels under the British flag, i.e. those on United Kingdom, Dominion, Indian or Colonial registers, and vessels under Bareboat Charter or on requisition from other flags. This meant that all Canadian-registered vessels counted as British vessels.

Jasper Park. The scene at the launch, in Lauzon, Quebec, of Canada's first Park Steamship Company war loss. See separate account in Chapter 7.
(Davie Shipbuilding & Repair Co. Ltd.)

The total personnel casualties in the merchant ships, including fishing vessels, covered by the foregoing definition was 62,923.

United Kingdom	31,908
Royal Navy DEMS	2,713
Maritime Regiment Royal Artillery	1,222
United States	5,662
United States Navy Armed Guard	1,640
Canada	1,437
South Africa	182
Australia	109
New Zealand	72
Norway	4,795
Greece	2,000
Holland	1,914
Denmark	1,886
Belgium	893
Neutral Countries	6,500
Total	62,923

The numbers for the United Kingdom included Lascars, Chinese, Arabs and others engaged as crew in British ships. While Royal Navy DEMS gun crews sailing in merchant ships are included, the figures do not include navy personnel lost in escort vessels engaged in convoy protection duties.

The Table of Losses given here shows the number and gross tonnage of British, Allied and Neutral Merchant and Fishing vessels lost by enemy action through the same period. These figures would include American ships which were not subject to British control and those of Norway, which retained its independence as an Allied maritime power even though most of the time the ships were under British and sometimes later American direction after the US entered the war.

Little detail has been revealed of Soviet losses, and these are not included in the totals of Allied merchant ships quoted on the following page.

Merchant Ship Losses: British, Allied and Neutral

May 1940-May 1944

	Months	British	No. gross tons	Allied	No. gross tons	Neutral	No. gross tons	Total	No. gross tons
1940	May	31	82,429	26	134,078	20	56,712	77	273,219
	June	61	282,560	37	187,128	27	101,808	125	571,496
	July	64	271,056	14	48,239	20	62,672	98	381,967
	Aug	56	278,323	13	55,817	19	59,870	88	394,010
	Sept	62	324,030	19	79,181	9	39,423	90	442,634
	Oct	63	301,892	17	73,885	17	66,675	97	442,452
	Nov	73	303,682	13	47,685	5	24,731	91	376,098
	Dec	61	265,314	11	70,916	7	21,084	79	357,314
1941	Jan	44	209,394	30	107,692	1	2,962	75	320,048
	Feb	79	316,349	20	82,222	1	3,197	100	401,768
	March	98	366,847	32	138,307	9	32,339	139	537,493
	April	79	362,471	67	256,612	8	34,877	154	653,960
	May	96	387,303	24	98,559	6	14,201	126	500,063
	June	63	268,634	35	142,887	10	19,516	108	431,037
	July	36	95,465	6	23,994	1	1,516	43	120,975
	Aug	31	96,989	9	32,010	1	1,700	41	130,699
	Sept	61	215,207	13	47,950	9	22,595	83	285,752
	Oct	32	151,777	14	53,434	5	13,078	51	218,289
	Nov	29	91,352	4	6,260	1	6,600	34	104,212
	Dec	124	271,401	44	159,276	19	55,308	187	485,985
1942	Jan	38	146,274	65	259,135	3	14,498	106	419,907
	Feb	79	341,271	69	304,804	6	33,557	154	679,532
	March	107	276,312	158	531,214	8	26,638	273	834,164
	April	53	293,083	76	372,284	3	9,090	132	674,457
	May	58	258,273	86	410,382	7	36,395	151	705,050
	June	50	233,740	110	571,254	13	29,202	173	834,196
	July	43	232,718	74	350,473	11	34,922	128	618,113
	Aug	58	344,763	53	281,262	13	39,608	124	665,633
	Sept	50	274,952	52	266,265	12	26,110	114	567,327
	Oct	60	409,519	40	224,537	1	3,777	101	637,833
	Nov	75	469,493	57	329,308	2	8,953	134	807,754
	Dec	46	226,581	24	113,074	3	9,247	73	348,902
1943	Jan	19	98,096	24	143,358	7	19,905	50	261,359
	Feb	29	166,947	39	232,235	5	3,880	73	403,062
	March	62	384,914	53	303,284	5	5,191	120	693,389
	April	33	194,252	27	137,081	4	13,347	64	344,680
	May	31	146,496	26	151,299	1	1,633	58	299,428
	June	12	44,975	13	75,854	3	2,096	28	123,825
	July	30	187,759	26	166,231	5	11,408	61	365,398
	Aug	14	62,900	9	56,578	2	323	25	119,801
	Sept	12	60,541	15	94,010	2	1,868	29	156,419
	Oct	11	57,565	17	81,631	1	665	29	139,861
	Nov	15	61,593	12	82,696	2	102	29	144,391
	Dec	10	55,611	21	112,913	-	-	31	168,524
1944	Jan	16	67,112	9	62,115	1	1,408	26	130,635
	Feb	12	63,411	8	53,244	3	200	23	116,855
	March	10	49,637	14	104,964	1	3,359	25	157,960
	April	3	21,439	10	60,933	-	-	13	82,372
	May	5	27,297	-	-	-	-	5	27,297

Total ships
(May 1940-May 1944):

British	2,284	Gross tons	10,199,999
Allied	1,635	Gross tons	7,778,550
Neutral	317	Gross tons	979,146

Grand total   4,240   18,957,695

Total British, Allied and Neutral Ships sunk during the Second World War (September 1939-May 1945): 4,786. Gross tons: 21,194,000

CHAPTER THREE

The Concept of the Standard Ship

The concept of building ships in series originated with the design of groups of sister ships which as time went on tended to become larger in size and numbers built to the design. The concept went back to sailing ship days when certain yards such as Russell on the Clyde and Oswald Mordaunt at Southampton offered designs for three- and four-masted ships which came, with variations to suit individual owners, virtually off the same set of blueprints.

Prior to the First World War, William Doxford of Sunderland, England, came up with the design for the turret ship which enjoyed some popularity with both liner and tramp companies. Most of these ships were built between 1905 and 1912, by which time the design had become history. The turrets with their unusual hull design seemed to start a trend among individual yards to create new technical variations as designers strove to gain small operating and economic advantages. Such design variations included the trunk-deck ship, the Isherwood longitudinal-framed ship, the Arc-form ship and the Maier-form bow favoured in particular by Dutch and German owners,

Clan Lindsay. An example of the Doxford Turret Ship which gained popularity before WWI. Measurements varied, but in all other regards it was an early attempt to market a standard design. Advantages were great longitudinal strength and low Suez Canal dues because of low net tonnage.

(World Ship Society Photo Library)

New Mexico. The N-type standard ship was the ultimate in British prefabrication at the end of WWI. With a double bevelled, hard chine bilge, the two chines converged to a single chine at the bow, seen emerging from the water. A few of these ships gave good service into the post WWII period.   (S.C. Heal)

Invergordon. An N-type standard finished as a tanker. Note the all straight- framed angular construction and the similarity between the stern of this ship and *Encho Maru,* following. Speed and ease of construction were the objectives with this design. Good looks were not an issue.   (S.C. Heal)

the latter three dating from the 1920s. These design variations embodied a high degree of standardization, but did not usually result in a standard ship.

The idea of building large numbers of ships to a common design became well established during the First World War. Britain's losses of merchant shipping to a sustained U-boat campaign had reached the crisis point, so that by 1916 the idea of fast building of replacement tonnage was conceived as a wartime emergency project. Such projects were usually labelled emergency ship building programs, the name reflecting the extreme urgency which they sought to address.

Responding to government requirements, the famous Belfast yard of Harland & Wolff came forward with the design of the A and B class standard tramp. The first A-class ship, *War Shamrock,* was launched and ready for sea by August 1917. She was followed in large numbers by many sister ships from various yards. Also the British government expanded the emergency program designs to include refrigerator

ships and the fully prefabricated N-type ship, which was designed to allow the prefabrication of vessel sub-assemblies and component sections at locations well away from the building yard. This in itself was quite a feat as matching up rivetted components or sections with each other was far more difficult than dealing with similar all- welded sections.

The N-class (for National) was the first fully prefabricated design in the history of shipbuilding. What resulted was an extraordinary-looking vessel with straight angular frames throughout, a sheerless profile except for a slight upward incline near bow and stern which improved the appearance immensely. The decks lacked any camber. The stern was cut off with a flat triangular shell plate as is now common with ocean-going ships, and underwater the lines were those of a box with hard chines instead of rounded bilges all drawn to pinched-out ends at stem and stern. In spite of their ugliness they proved good functional ships, with several lines, including Union-

Encho Maru. These two views illustrate the Japanese answer to the Liberty ship. Thrown together as a desperate measure to overcome enormous merchant ship losses, about 150 of these ships were built from 1943 on, with two thirds lost. The survivors were largely rebuilt or improved after the war and formed the nucleus of the Japanese postwar merchant marine. Experience with N-type freighters acquired from the British inspired this design. (E.N. Hickling)

Castle and Elder Dempster, incorporating a number of units into their fleets. In fact some of the Elder Dempster ships gave such excellent service that they survived the Second World War before being replaced by modern units.

It is pure theory on the part of the author, but this design and the technology of simple fabrication it involved seems to have become the basis for the Japanese type-A standard freighter which was their equivalent of the Liberty ship in the Second World War. The Japanese acquired a number of N-type ships on the secondhand market between the wars and the similarities between the two designs seem to be more than pure coincidence.

With the entry of the United States into the First World War, a shipbuilding program in American yards, initiated by the British government acting through Cunard Line's New York Office, was taken over in its entirety by the US government and also greatly extended. The ships under construction were all of Norwegian or British design, suitably adapted to American conditions and techniques, but with

the adoption of the Hog Islanders a new era began in large-scale prefabrication, which in many ways would become the forerunner of the Second World War Liberty ship program.

The Hog Island ships were actually named for the American Shipbuilding Corporation yard at Hog Island, near Philadelphia, which was constructed for the express purpose of building the ships of this design. Some thought that the design had the name Hog Island bestowed on it because what resulted was a three-island design, straight-framed, without deck camber or longitudinal sheer, which gave the ships a distinctly hogged appearance similar to that of the British N-type.

Of conventional layout in superstructure and positioning of the holds, the Hog Island ships, like the Doxford turret ships, were no things of beauty, being ungainly looking vessels even to the extent that the stem tumbled inboard and the counter stern had a huge radius on it with a heavy built-up appearance. They were efficient ships which discharged their purpose very well however, and in the interwar

THE CONCEPT OF THE STANDARD SHIP

years they were operated on a number of American cargo liner routes. During the Second World War a number passed into British control and were retained in peacetime service until replacement ships of more modern design could be obtained.

With the end of the First World War many shipyards in Europe and North America closed forever. Typical were the Hog Island yard and the National Shipbuilding yards at locations on or near the Bristol Channel and the River Severn. Harland & Wolff had initiated the construction of N-class fully prefabricated standard ships at Belfast and other private yards, but the National yards had been laid out at enormous cost with the idea that they would turn these ships out in very large numbers. In reality they were starved both for skilled labour and for adequate material supplies, and to cap it all they were tied up by their own internal bureaucracies. It was a classic case of government in business and a private industry which ran rings round it. In the event, the ending of the war put a stop to the completion of any hulls other than those already covered by material acquisitions, or well advanced.

Following the war a number of yards made distinct marketing efforts with their shipyard prototypes. Some of the Dutch and German yards had success in this direction, cutting heavily into the prewar British trade of building for foreign owners. Sweden and Denmark also built a great deal of high class, mostly diesel tonnage of both cargo liner and tramp types for their own account as well as the Norwegians. The Gotaverken and Burmeister & Wain diesel engines from Sweden and Denmark became household names in shipping circles.

Like the Scandinavians, the Dutch, Germans and Italians pinned great hope on the diesel engine and developed a strong national presence, offering exceptional products under the names of M.A.N., Werkspoor and Fiat, along with the Swiss Sulzer. In general these European yards incorporated considerable standardization into their shipyard prototype designs, although it is doubtful that they could be called standard ships in the sense of the wartime designs which are the subject of this book. Aggressive marketing saw these European yards make progress while many of their competitors fell by the wayside, for the interwar years were generally not easy for world shipbuilders or operators. The patchwork of good and bad years through the twenties culminated in the 1929 Wall Street crash and the depression of the thirties which hit all countries in some degree.

Several British yards did relatively well given the times. The Scottish, Northern Irish and the yards of Northwest England tended to concentrate on high-class tonnage — warships, passenger liners, cargo and refrigerated liners, and tankers. The lowly tramp, the work horse of the seas, was more likely

Barnaby. The American government shipbuilding program of WWI produced this prefabricated design, known as the Hog Island ship, built at the yard of that name near Philadelphia. Like the N-type, straight framed without deck camber, they were successful ships in spite of their ungainly lines. This ship, built as *Quistconck,* was the first in a lengthy succession of sister ships.   (Frank Barr)

to be built on the English or Scottish East coast on such rivers as the Tyne, Tees and Wear and it was these yards which were hardest hit by the depression conditions of the 1920s and 30s. There was so much wartime standard tramp tonnage available that owners in many cases chose to re-equip their fleets from this pool of shipping and defer new construction for as long as possible. In the case of the American merchant fleet, these ships were laid up in large numbers for many years in freshwater anchorages only to taste saltwater again when the Second World War came and a large fleet was transferred to Britain, in the ships for bases deal, to help make up her heavy war losses.

Canada had also built a fleet of emergency-type standard ships, mostly by adopting US Shipping Board designs which had clearly originated from Britain or Norway. These were over and above the fleet built for Britain. They came into being because wartime conditions and shipping shortages over which Canada had little control had affected our overseas trade. Initially the justification, which was valid enough, was that it was necessary for Canadian control over sufficient shipping to ensure, in large measure, independence of our shipping needs from those of Britain. In the postwar period this fleet was vested in the Canadian Government Merchant Marine (CGMM). Its history is described in *Conceived in War, Born in Peace.*

Arguably, the most notable British east coast Yard was Doxford of Sunderland. The well-known Doxford "Economy" diesel tramp became a standard within the shipping industry. The first Economies came out in the early 1920s greatly assisted by the Doxford diesel, the only large diesel originating from British designs and carrying a proprietary name of international stature. Actually the internationally known and respected Economy series, according to the shipping journal, *Fairplay,* really started with the diesel trampship *Yngaren,* built by Doxford for Transatlantic Rederi A/b of Gothenburg, Sweden, although they did not start using the term "Economy" until world shipbuilding was coming out of the depression in the early 1930s. By that time marketing tools took on extra significance as the world's shipbuilding industry fought for whatever orders could be developed.

Other diesels were built in Britain, but they were for small craft or were entirely built by engine builders like North Eastern under license from European engine builders, the most notable probably being Sulzer and Burmeister & Wain.

The Doxford diesel was particularly appropriate for the tramp designs which came out of the East Coast British yards. However the diesel tramp did not make headway with British owners as it had with the Scandinavians. High quality, economically attractive bunker coal was available in abundance throughout Britain and Welsh steaming coal from the South Wales coalfields was rated the best in the world. In fact a major tramp cargo was coal from Wales and North East England for delivery to overseas depots in order to fuel the needs of the large British and foreign fleet of coal burners, as well as numerous foreign railways. Britain had no oil industry such as today's North Sea oil and coal was cheap. The first cost of steamers was lower than that of diesel ships even though the diesels produced operating economies over the life of a ship which made them more cost-effective in the long term.

The depression of the early 1930s produced some novel plans for reviving British shipbuilding and simultaneously helping British shipowners. "Scrap and Build" became the first of two significant programs. Under this scheme owners could scrap one ton of overage deadweight tonnage for one new in order to obtain low cost finance from the British Government. The second program was a low interest, high ratio loan plan which did not require a previous undertaking to scrap old tonnage. The program was particularly attractive to the liner companies, some of which took advantage of it to launch replacement programs where scrapping would inevitably follow, liner services being more geared to the demand on their routes than the amorphous tramp market with its worldwide sensitivity to slumps and trade cycles. The idea was that the rapidly aging British fleet, which had seen few additions of new tonnage since 1929, could be renewed at the same time as life was breathed back into ailing shipyards. Some of the shipyards were woefully out of date and, as in the wake of the First World War, there were more candidates for permanent retirement. This mention is necessarily brief, but a notable book on the subject is *Scrap & Build,* by D.C.E. Burrell.

THE CONCEPT OF THE STANDARD SHIP

Among the survivors were the brace of East Coast yards most identified with forward thinking and design technology in the development of the tramp, the type on which they mostly depended for the bulk of their business. Doxford has been named, but other respected names included Irvine's Shipbuilding, Short Brothers, S.B. Austin, John Readhead, Bartram, William Gray, Joseph L. Thompson, John Crown, Furness S.B. Co., Sir J. Laing and Wm. Pickersgill, all of which were active shipbuilders through World War II.

The Scrap and Build and Shipping Loan programs also achieved the return of some confidence. Many of the British lay-up sites such as certain Scottish lochs, the Tyne and the River Fal in Cornwall, saw a reduction in the volume of laid-up tonnage as old ships went to the scrap yards. New, up-to-date ships resulted in a more competitive position for British shipowners in the export lumber trades of BC and the US northwest. Some of the new ships departed but little from the old split-profile steam tramp, the main improvements being in propulsion machinery, a slow increase in average deadweight tonnage and speed, improved accommodation and cargo handling gear. The split profile, brought about by the need to provide bunkers adjacent to the boiler room as well as hatches to service them, remained in vogue even for motorships, where there was really very little need for such a layout. With number three hatch situated between the bridge and engineroom, there was some loss of efficiency which was well demonstrated when the Liberty came in with its long sweep of uninterrupted deck space forward of the bridge, save only for the mast housings. This was not new for this type of hull as the Doxford "Economy" had adopted a similar layout for its 1936 series, but reverted to the split profile by 1938.

This reversion was probably brought about at the insistence of Greek owners, who were well used to it through their operations of ex-British coal burners and felt more comfortable with the design. Also there was the traditional antipathy between engineroom and deck officers, where once again tradition probably had something to do with the choice of design. It has even been suggested that No. 3 hatch was the "parade ground" in the eyes of some, where crews could be paraded to be addressed by the captain, particularly when there was labour strife on board.

No review would be complete without a reference to what the United States was doing with its fleet replacement program which got under way in 1935. Five exceptional new standard designs were adopted. These were the C1, C2 and C3 cargo ship designs and the T2 turbo-electric tanker, all of which were followed by the Victory type, an exceptional vessel much favoured by European liner operators after the war. During the ten-year period of building these types, they were to take several forms and all found favour with US operators on what they called their strategic trade routes. The smallest was the C1 which was turned out with steam and diesel alternative propulsion. The profile was not dissimilar to the wartime Liberty ship with an island structure amidship and clear cargo carrying decks fore and aft. Thirteen of these ships were transferred to the British Navy and gave wonderful service as Infantry Landing ships (LSI) in Europe and South East Asia.

Canadian Importer. Built from a basic British design, Canada's contribution to WWI standard ship production was highly significant for a country with such a small industrial base. This was one of five similar designs in different size categories.

(Vancouver Maritime Museum)

The C2 came out in more forms than the others and had the advantage of a very long operating capability, as the comparative table below shows. For this reason many saw service with the US Navy in various auxiliary capacities during the Pacific War. The C3 turned out to be an excellent platform for the pocket aircraft carriers so useful in convoy work in both major theatres. When the war started none of these vessels were available to the British but by the time the US

Siranger ex Cape River. The C1-type was also the first of the USMC standard designs from the late 1930's. Fast and handy sized, a dozen served as Infantry Landing ships (LSI) with British amphibious operations in Europe and South East Asia.   (Vancouver Maritime Museum)

entered the war they had a high-speed fleet of merchantmen drawn from these classes which enabled them to quickly create a large fleet of naval auxiliaries.

All of these standard classes which made up the bulk of the larger American-built ships in this period, outside of the Liberty and Victory ship programs, had the advantage of high speed. The Americans favoured turbines or turbo-electric drive and the diesel did not make the same inroads as it did in Europe. At that time there was really only one indigenous heavy-duty marine diesel manufactured in the US This was the Nordberg, many units of which were placed into the C1 class of ship and the small coastal type freighter, the C1MAV1 class. It was really the postwar changes of the American railroads that launched the diesel into the American market on such a large scale, making General Motors and Caterpillar into household names for marine as well as railroad and other industrial uses.

When war came in 1939, all of the British East Coast yards had largely full order books. The first moves toward standardization came when the government, in order to conserve steel and materials, required modifications of new ships on order, but not at an advanced stage of construction. Two sources of additional tonnage were the acquisition, previously mentioned, of War Shipping Board vessels transferred from the US Maritime Commission and some captured German vessels, most of which had been caught with the outbreak of war in Allied ports or had been prevented from scuttling on the high seas following interception by warships.

Ventura. This representative of the C2-type was previously *USS Todd*, a fast attack transport that was one of many inducted into the US Navy for service in the Pacific War. The C2 had a greater range than any of the other American standard types, plus high speed.   (S.C. Heal)

With mounting submarine and magnetic mine losses the next move was to encourage the design of new standard ships based on shipyard prototypes. Two such designs which grew out of shipyard prototypes were the well-tested North Sands, which was representative of a relatively common group of East Coast tramps.

Almdijk. Speed and greater size made the C3 type standard ship ideal for conversion to escort aircraft carriers. This one served as HMS *Hunter.* The Royal Navy operated 17 of this type while the RCN had two.　(S.C. Heal)

Wolverine State . An unusual design for the period, the C4-types appeared mostly as troopers and hospital ships. Some, including this ship built in 1945 as *Marine Runner,* were converted to cargo ships after the war.　(Vancouver Maritime Museum)

This design came out of the Joseph L. Thompson North Sands shipyard at Sunderland. The second was the 4,700-ton *Scandinavian* from the William Gray shipyard at West Hartlepool. This was another well-tested design particularly suitable for deck loading of lumber with unimpeded fore and aft welldecks for deck cargo. The type was popular in the Baltic, St. Lawrence and North Russian lumber trades, and larger versions were developed by several Norwegian and Danish owners in the North Pacific lumber trades.

The North Sands and Scandinavian ships were the prototypes for the Canadian shipbuilding pro-grams. The types never had the opportunity of fully showing off their versatility as the need did not really arise. The North Sands were amended to produce the Canadian and Victory types, which are dealt with in the next chapter, and the Victory in turn showed its capability when turned out in substantial numbers as Royal Navy maintenance ships and as tankers. There were even plans drawn up to convert some of the Victories to troopships as happened with some of the US Liberty and Victory types, but the need for this never arose.

Esso Cardiff. The American T2 turbo-electric was the largest class of standard tanker ever built and one of the most successful. Built as *Halls of Montezuma,* this ship became a unit in Esso's British tanker fleet.   (Frank Barr)

Jalamanjari. A typical Liberty ship, first cousin to the Canadian Forts and Parks, operated by Scindia S.N. Company, leaving Birkenhead for Bombay. Loaded on deck are four locomotives with tenders bound for the Indian railways. Somewhat unusually, the engine room ventilators clustered around the funnel have been extended to funnel height which probably indicated the need for improved ventilation in the extreme heat of the Indian Coast.   (Frank Barr)

California ex Drew Victory. The American Victory ship was a distinctively different ship to the Canadian Victory. Slightly larger than the Liberty ship, some of the class had a designed speed of 17 knots and the rest could make 15 knots. Deliveries started in 1944 and continued after the Liberty was phased out. They made popular cargo liners after the war.   (S.C. Heal)

Mandasor ex Empire Malacca. Typical of several classes of British wartime standard ships, this ship was of the partially fabricated B type. With an unusually large No. 3 hold and extra large hatches the type was specially developed for carrying heavy oversize military cargo such as tanks.

(John Clarkson)

Drakensberg Castle ex Empire Allenby. An example of the largest class of British standards. Known as the Fast 15-knot cargo type, they had a deadweight tonnage of 12,000 tons and among other considerations they were built with a view to early postwar cargo liner service. Several British lines were licensed to build examples for their own account before the war ended including Canadian Pacific which built four and purchased two from the British Government.
(S.C. Heal)

A British-Built North Sands Ship. The Newcastle tramp shipping company, Allan, Black & Co. ordered this ship as *Thistlemuir.* Except for fitting out details, these ships were built off the same set of plans as the Oceans and North Sands ships. She is seen here as the Panamanian *Nunez de Balboa.*

(W.H. Young and L.A. Sawyer)

CHAPTER FOUR

The Ocean, Fort and Park Programs

During the nation's history there have been booms in shipbuilding and ship operations followed by busts which could be better described as wipeouts. The first was the wooden shipbuilding boom in the middle years of the nineteenth century, described in Chapter One.

The second and third boom periods were generated by the special conditions of the First and Second World Wars. If there had been no wars there would have been no shipbuilding boom such as history has witnessed, but with the realities of each war, different but positive approaches were adopted to sustain the merchant navies which came into being.

The end of the First World War saw a fleet being created under the guise of the Canadian Government Merchant Marine which started off with high hopes and much optimism. The war demonstrated that there were good and valid reasons why Canada should have control of its own merchant marine, but as with all wartime emergency fleets the ships were built more with a view to expediency and the emergency at hand, than to the longer-term considerations of efficient peacetime service and operating economics. The good and valid reasons referred to, which probably reflected the official jingoistic explanation, arose when the external trade of Canada was manifestly being affected by the shortage of shipping occasioned by the war. Having become dependent on British shipping for most of its needs, Canada found itself in a badly compromised position through having no control of its own shipping.

Ocean Courage, fresh from the builder's yard and flying the red ensign as a British crew takes delivery. This ship became a war loss.
(Todd- Bath Shipbuilding Corp)

Fort Ville Marie, shown here as *Makalla* of the Brocklebank Line. This ship had three distinctions; she was the first of the Canadian Forts and Parks built on the East Coast; the very first in Canada and the only ship in the entire program that had a full ship's life in the management and ownership of one shipping company, Brocklebank. She was affectionately nicknamed "Vile Mary."   (John Clarkson)

Laying the keel. High tide bathes the keel of a Fort or Park ship whose double bottom takes shape among a forest of scaffolding.   (Burrard Collection)

Another side to this program was put forth in an article in *Shipping and Railway World*, of May 1918, in which the Hon. C.C. Ballantyne, Minister of Marine & Fisheries explained his government's plans. According to Ballantyne, because of the nature of the emergency he simply gave orders to the steel shipbuilding yards that, as their building berths became available following completion of orders from the Imperial Munitions Board of Great Britain, they should simply carry on with further ships of the same type. It is easy to render judgements in hindsight, but two circumstances should have alerted Ballantyne to exercise caution. First, by 1918 the worst of the submarine war was over and second, Britain placed no fresh contracts in probable recognition of this fact. Here again we have an example of muddled planning, or the complete lack of it, when government goes into business. The political thinkers of the day gave their reason for continuation of the program as the need to create "jobs for the boys" when they returned from the front. Was this to be achieved by creating steel boxes and putting engines in them?

Alternatively, with proper planning backed by genuine knowledge and experience, a superior vessel should have been in the planning stage which might have given the CGMM a better chance of competing in peacetime conditions.

The CGMM enjoyed some degree of success, but it faded out with the sale of its last ships by 1936. A fairly extensive account of this shipping enterprise and the two others that grew out of the First World War are contained in *Conceived in*

War, Born in Peace. A further source is *Asian Dream,* by Mackay, which gives considerable attention to CGMM's efforts to develop a commercial shipping network internationally.

The fact that some of the steel shipbuilding yards involved in the First World War program remained substantially in being was to stand the country in good stead when the Second World War program got underway, a fact that should be borne in mind when considering the Fort program later in this chapter.

The problem with all wartime emergency fleets is that at the end of hostilities the large number of ships built creates a huge bubble in supply and this takes time for the market to absorb without overly depressing freight rates and accelerating a slump. The entire pattern of trade changes almost overnight as cargoes are cut off as fast as possible, but it takes longer to return to peacetime patterns of trade. After World War I, the availability of relief cargoes helped maintain a level of relative prosperity until about 1920 when the market collapsed, doing much damage to the tramp shipping industry. This hit the CGMM like everyone else and a number of their

ships were sold at substantially less than building cost, as they were selling into a depressed market. The fact that after World War II the market avoided a massive collapse was probably due to the huge volume of postwar relief cargoes. Most of Europe and much of the Far East had been laid waste, and the need to rebuild was spread over a longer period and involved far greater volume.

The other contingency is that the victors in some ways enjoy a pyrrhic victory. They not only have built up a huge fleet of wartime standard ships of which governments are only too anxious to divest themselves, so that the burden on the taxpayer can be reduced, but they may also have inherited a large fleet of ex-enemy vessels by way of wartime reparations. The vanquished on the other hand may have lost their merchant navy, but subject to the ability to finance and rebuild, they may then be in a better position to build a new fleet of modern vessels, which in turn can become a very competitive factor against the victor's fleet.

These were the relative positions of Britain and Germany after the First World War. Germany was

Looking towards the stern. Gear sits on double bottom frames as 'tween-deck beams are fitted in a Fort or Park ship.
(Burrard Collection)

Late afternoon sun streams through the structure towards stem and bow sections. The visible deck beam would be at about the position of the future collision bulkhead.   (Burrard Collection)

forcibly deprived of almost its entire merchant navy through reparations and, even though political and business conditions were in severe straits, the country's merchant marine was able to revitalize itself through the 1920s by buying modern secondhand tonnage, much of it being ships that Germany had been forced to turn over as reparations, as well as to build a fleet of modern highly competitive ships. When war came again Germany possessed an important fleet of modern ships with a fairly low average age. Britain on the other hand was saddled with a far older fleet in terms of average years, which she was only able to thin out with the blood-letting of the depression of the 1930s.

Fortunately with the aid of the "Scrap and Build" program and a second low-cost financing scheme (see Chapter Three), both initiated by the British government, there was a resurgence of ship building in Britain with new modern designs finding great favour with progressive shipowners. Even though the North Sands ships were direct descendants of a design which had been evolving since the last century, it was not until about 1910 that the design of the modern coal-burning tramp became established and was adopted by British and foreign owners alike.

This was a five-hatch vessel with two holds forward of the bridge, two abaft the engine room and one between the bridge and engine room accommodation. The North Sands was the design of Joseph L. Thompson & Sons Limited, of the North Sands shipyard at Sunderland, England, which was probably arrived at in the shipbuilding boom of the late 1930s when Thompson was able to offer it, or a variation on the design, as a shipyard prototype to its shipowner clients. The ship was not unique, in fact many British yards offered similar designs which, while not exact sister ships, were certainly close relatives. This may be an important point in recognizing the considerable popularity of the Fort and Park ships of which the vast majority found ready buyers among foreign owners.

The two important variants on the North Sands, the Victory and Canadian evolved, probably in Canada, in order to effect improvements in fuelling, boiler and accommodations on the original design. We do not know who initiated this development, but it seems probable that the initiative came from Park Steamships, who by that time had had experience with the coal-burning North Sands and had found them wanting on the trade routes to the southern hemisphere. Oil bunkers could be taken on far more economically at San Pedro, California and Aruba in the Netherlands Antilles when on voyages which took them to the southern hemisphere or when returning. Features of design are discussed more fully when describing the North Sands and its variants later in this chapter.

The other imported design, the so-called Grey or Scandinavian was equally the product of a lengthy evolution. In Canada the design was usually referred to by the original builder's name, William Grey & Co. Limited of West Hartlepool, not far from Thompson's North Sands yard. In Britain the 38 ships built to the Grey prototype were called the Scandinavian type. Such ships had been built for the Baltic and North Russian lumber trade for decades, and had found particular favour with Scandinavian owners who required long unencumbered decks for cargoes of lumber.

The two designs plus one Canadian design for a small Lakes tanker are the subject of the more specific descriptions which follow in this chapter. Inclusion of the six vessels in this last class means that all ships with Park names will have been covered except for *Riding Mountain Park,* an oddity and a converted dredger outside of any standard class.

The wartime history of the Canadian shipbuilding effort has been covered in considerable detail in a limited number of books which are listed in the bibliography. The pathfinder authors were Mitchell and Sawyer in 1966, followed by Heal in 1992 who also gave considerable coverage to the First World War shipbuilding program. These books dealt quite fully with the ships involved.

Reid in 1990, Halford in 1995, Fraser and Martin-Smith in 1997 also covered the subject with, among other historical data, valuable insights into the manning, training of crews, labour issues and working conditions, as well as the frustrations that all experienced or were able to pass along at secondhand from their contributors.

In addition there have been a small number of published books explaining the labour union point of view. Generally they have covered a broader horizon than that pertaining strictly to Canadian shipbuilding and management, and the factors they present have been taken more fully into account in later chapters dealing with disposal of the ships and ongoing operations in the peacetime trampship market.

There are also a number of privately published works by Hill Wilson, Peter Tull, William Hutcherson, Max Reid and William Cowling. Many of these were put together as labours of love for a very limited circle of readers or for family reasons. They incorporate much interesting material, some of which has been drawn upon in this book.

These books collectively cover virtually all the available historical data on Canada's wartime merchant navy. Details of each have been provided in the bibliography.

The National Archives in Ottawa holds a treasure house of unsorted material, but there is insufficient time or interest, or funding available to pay someone to sort and classify the material.

The Beginnings of the Program

In September 1940, R.C. Thompson of the venerable east coast shipbuilder, J.L. Thompson & Sons Limited of Sunderland, and Harry Hunter, marine engineer, were invited by the British Admiralty to proceed to the United States as part of a Technical Merchant Shipbuilding Mission. They left Britain in the Cunard liner *Scythia* on September 21, 1940, a little over one year after the breaking out of war in Europe. In New York they met William Bennett, Principal Surveyor for *Lloyd's Register* of Shipping for the US and Canada, J.S. Heck, Principal Engineer Surveyor for *Lloyd's Register*, New York, and R.R. Powell, an Assistant Secretary at the Admiralty who was to act as the Mission Secretary. John Robson, of the Department of Merchant Shipbuilding at the Admiralty, joined the Mission in New York in February 1941.

According to Admiral Emery S. Land, Chairman of the US Maritime Commission, Mr. Thompson was followed by Sir Arthur Salter who arrived in October of 1940, on behalf of the British government, with ten million pounds sterling and authority to build and purchase new ships.

The object of the mission was to obtain at the earliest possible time, merchant tonnage at the rate of 60 vessels per annum of the 10,000-ton deadweight tramp type. This might be seen as the spark that led to the biggest shipbuilding program in history. The order for 60 Ocean class vessels built to the original Empire Liberty design, in essence the first North Sands ship, was placed with two new American yards. This led in turn to the order for the first 26 vessels placed with three Canadian yards. Even before these orders were started, the North Sands prototype had been taken by the New York firm of naval architects, Gibbs & Cox, on behalf of the United States Maritime Commission, and modified into the Liberty ship. All told 2,710 Liberties were actually constructed and, when the 60 Oceans and a final total of 353 Fort and Park North Sands in their original and variant designs, including the Royal Navy maintenance ship program, were factored in, the total came to 3,123 ships built in North America. Thompson's small output of 24 from their North Sands shipyard brought the grand total to 3,147, a record that will never be repeated.

For Thompson and his colleagues, initiating this program turned out to be quite an achievement. The Americans wanted to help, but all existing yards with the potential to build ships for Britain were fully booked with naval and merchant ship construction. The massive building to meet both the US Navy requirements and the merchant marine replacement programs had started in earnest in 1937 and had kept the existing American yards busy ever since.

Thompson and his colleagues visited most of the larger shipbuilding facilities and engine builders on all three coasts and accumulated a great deal of comparative data. Perhaps one of the most important features was that when war broke out in 1939 the number of unemployed in the US alone was 12 million, plus a comparable number percentage-wise in Canada. This was a manpower reserve which was to prove very important in the rapid change from a peacetime to a wartime economy in both countries. To this could be added the fact that for the first time American and Canadian yards also employed women in large numbers, many of them in heavy jobs alongside the men.

No such reserve existed in Britain where the country had been on a war footing for two years prior to the start of the Emergency Shipbuilding Programs in North America. While manpower was plentiful in Canada and the US however, it was untrained and there simply was neither the time nor the facilities to create the long-term apprenticeship programs which in Britain had created the pool of highly skilled tradesmen. The situation was probably better in the US than in Canada as it was possible to spread the skilled people further in creating the management, supervisors and foremen to lead the raw labour force in the new shipyards which were to come into being.

In Canada, while some of the yards which were to participate in the emergency shipbuilding program already existed, Davie and Canadian Vickers were the only ones completely established. On the west coast, Burrard had one slipway but immediately set about adding more on its eastern boundary. Victoria Machinery Depot, Yarrows, Prince Rupert Dry Dock and West Coast Shipbuilders needed a great deal of work to make them suitable to participate in the program. In the east coast/great lakes region similar conditions applied. Collingwood at Collingwood, ON had already been a builder in the First World War. Foundation Maritime at Pictou was a new yard, as was Marine Industries at Sorel. Two new wartime yards came into being, namely United at Montreal and Burrard's South yard in Vancouver, but closed as soon as war work had been completed.

The labour infrastructure had to be expanded, as the industry had largely survived on the smaller volume of repair work available. To make up shortages of management-level people, a number of skilled personnel were brought over from Britain to strengthen the Canadian yards. This was a repeat of what had happened in the First World War. Differences in British practice and American were noteworthy. American yards had turned to large-scale welding with a minimum of rivetting, but in order to obtain the economies offered by large-scale prefabrication, more ground was needed than was commonly available in most British yards and, for that matter, in many of the older longer established east coast yards in the United States.

Welding saved weight in the elimination of plate overlaps and the considerable weight of the rivets themselves, and offered the advantage of a smoother underwater skin and therefore minimal surface friction. This also brought about economy in fuel consumption and a lesser horsepower requirement to move the same weight and volume. In some instances damage to shell plating could also be more easily repaired than replacement of rivetted plates.

Its disadvantages showed up in practice when a number of all-welded ships broke up at sea or devel-

Bridge wing support plate stands proud as a component of the upper bridge is swung into place. Meanwhile fitters swarm over the bridge structure as they put the ship together like a constructor set.   (Burrard Collection)

Before the hard hat era a fitter works on a scuttle aboard Burrard Hull # 131 which became *Fort Halkett* and a war loss.   (Burrard Collection)

Stern frames rise as a sister ship fits out astern. Burrard's floating dock can be seen to the right.   (Burrard Collection)

oped major fractures. In one instance an all-welded T2 tanker, *Schenectady*, snapped in two while fitting out at the builder's yard. Quality of steel, welding and atmospheric temperatures, welding techniques, and adequate training of operators were all shown to be factors which had to be improved.

Taking into account the foregoing deficiencies of welding, proponents of rivetting claimed that a stronger hull with the ability to flex better than an all-welded hull produced a superior vessel. There may have been some support in practice for this contention as, among Liberty ships, 95 major fractures had extended into the hull frames. Twenty of these sustained complete fractures of the strength deck and of these five broke in two. There is no recorded instance of a Canadian-built Fort or Park, with their largely rivetted hulls, breaking up or suffering a critical fracture while at sea. The only precedents for rivetted ships of similar design breaking completely under the most severe stress are *Anglo-Australian* in 1937 and *Hopestar*, in 1947. Both ships disappeared without trace, but the subsequent enquiries found that an identified prior weakness, or a structural change, had been found or undertaken prior to the loss.

A limited survey of former seagoing personnel indicates only one known fracture, in the deck of *Tecumseh Park* right at the most critical stress point in this design, namely in the vicinity of number three hatch. This crack did not evidently extend across to or down the shell plating. For another example of the inherent strength

The Final Test. Paravane gear is in place and net booms are lowered with anti-torpedo nets doing their job of protection aboard a ship in Esquimalt Roads, built at Victoria Machinery Depot.

(Hill Wilson Collection)

of the Canadian-built ships, consider the account of *Green Hill Park,* in Chapter Eight, where following the explosions which were the consequences of a very severe fire, beaching in an open roadstead with an enormous volume of water inside the vessel, the two halves even though badly cracked from maindeck to bilge did not part company. It is a reasonable proposition that a welded ship of the period would have succumbed to far worse structural damage. In spite of this comparison of ships built in wartime conditions, welding, using much improved techniques, has now gained universal acceptance and has superseded rivetting in steel ship construction.

The British Mission found that a comparison between an American built vessel, mainly welded, and a British ship mainly rivetted, produced some interesting results. Such a vessel in the US initially required 1.2 million man hours on the first ship but after seven cycles (a cycle being the time required to build one ship from keel-laying to completion), this came down to 3- to 400,000 man hours. The figure did not include bitumastic, upholstery or the supply of such items as ventilators which were provided by sub-contractors. The total of man hours involved was about twice that required for a comparable vessel built in Britain. That probably proved surprising when it was likely the opinion of many people that welding offered time savings which could not be equalled by rivetting. When the same ships were built in Canada the commencement figure was sim-

ilarly high, but this was greatly improved as the yards quickly developed greater efficiency.

Two considerations became apparent. Because of a far higher percentage of unskilled labour, even in relatively key jobs, the British plans had to be expanded into a vastly greater number of working drawings to suit North American conditions, which included a lower average standard of skilled labour. This applied to propulsion and auxiliary machinery as well. British custom, based on a highly skilled labour force, left much to individual yard practice and cut down greatly on the need for working drawings.

Secondly, while the British Ministry of War Transport developed a number of standard designs from tramps down to a whole range of small craft, they were more inclined to leave certain yards to build to their own prototype designs. For this reason British yards seemed to produce ships built to a profusion of designs and while this was technically true, the variation between a 10,000-ton tramp built in one yard and the same product of another yard was usually small. This system would probably not have worked if adopted in North American yards where standardization was carried to the furthest feasible extreme thus ensuring the best productivity from the less skilled workforces available.

With American yards fully engaged on naval and merchant shipbuilding, this left the British mission with only one option. That option was the construction of two new shipyards, one at Portland,

Nipiwan Park. The effect of a torpedo can be readily appreciated in this photo. The torpedo probably hit the starboard side in the cargo tanks ahead of the bridge. The explosion broke off the forepart and threw the bridge over towards the port side. As the next illustration shows the vessel had to be greatly rebuilt, but because of an intact engine room and engines it was evidently worth the cost and trouble.   (Ken Macpherson Collection)

Nipiwan Park. The forward half of this 3,600-ton Lakes type tanker sank following torpedoing. Rebuilding with a new fore half, bridge and engine was deemed worthwhile as these handy tankers were evidently in short supply.   (Milne, German & Gilmore)

Hollywood Actress Barbara Stanwyck makes an appearance at West Coast Shipbuilders, Vancouver yard. Seen with his back to the camera welcoming Ms Stanwyck is the late William McLaren, general manager of the yard and one of the great figures in Canadian shipbuilding. The Hollywood star was making a trip to promote the sale of war bonds. (G. Conway-Brown Collection)

Maine and the other near San Francisco, at Richmond, California.

Each yard was thus able to complete its contract with the British ahead of time, and then immediately turn over to building Liberty ships without a break when the Ocean program was completed. Other than the heavy adoption of welding and the elimination of the tumblehome in the American-built Oceans they stayed with the original North Sands design.

Canadian Vickers, through what appeared to be superhuman effort was determined to complete the first vessel, *Fort Ville Marie,* before the end of 1941. This it achieved by moving the ship down river ahead of the freezeup, loading a cargo and doing final touch-up work in Britain. The first west coast vessel, *Fort St. James,* was completed 39 days later.

Most people who take an interest in merchant shipping are aware that war historians have given little attention to the enormous effort put out by Canada, in building and operating a huge merchant fleet, in addition to many warships of various types, as a part of our contribution to the overall war effort. The following brief table gives some idea of how the floodgate of new merchant shipping poured forth, all within a timeframe of something over three months. Once launched the tide of new ships did not let up until the war had been won. Truly, it was a mighty effort and Mr. Richard Thompson and his cohorts may have had little idea what his plans for a North Sands ship would lead to when he set sail from Liverpool in the *Scythia* on September 21, 1940.

RELEVANT DATES FOR THE FIRST SHIPS IN THE MAIN CLASSES

	Oceans	Liberties	N/Sands (EC)	N/Sands (WC)
Contract date	20/12/40	01/41	01/41	01/41
Keel Laying date	14/04/41	30/04/41	?	23/04/41
Launching date	16/08/41	27/09/41	?	15/10/41
Delivery date	10/41	30/12/41	21/12/41	29/01/42

The Ship Types

North Sands/Ocean type

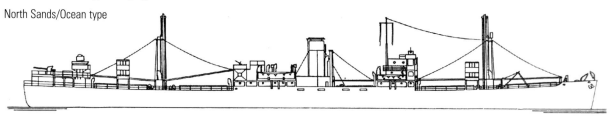

THE NORTH SANDS/OCEAN TYPES

Dimensions and specifications:

Length between perpendiculars	425.0 ft
Length overall (variable to 2 ft)	440.0 ft*
Moulded breadth	57.2 ft
Moulded depth	34.9 ft
Gross tonnage	7,167 tons
Deadweight tonnage	10,500 tons
Speed	10 $\frac{1}{2}$ knots

T expansion cal 24 $\frac{1}{2}$", 37", 70" x 48" stroke

Three Scotch boilers.

*Overall length varied by as much as three feet less than this in certain ships.

This was a design which came close to the peak of development in the typical British coal-burning tramp. It was directly descended from the original three-island design of the latter thirty years of the nineteenth century. In its original concept it was a four-hatch vessel with coal bunkers ahead of the boilers and bunker hatches in recesses in the midships accommodation.

As the size of the ships increased and improvements developed the midships island was extended, the bridge structure moved forward and a smaller No. 3 hold developed ahead of the bunkers. The layout became common from early in this century until the end of the coal-burner period. It placed Nos. 1 and 2 holds and hatches ahead of the accommodation, No. 3 hatch between the midships accommodation occupied by the engineers and the bridge structure, but with the bulkhead between Nos. 2 and 3 holds situated in such a way that a fairly large part of No. 3 'tween-deck and the lower hold were under the bridge structure.

This design, while usually ascribed to British evolutionary development, was widely adopted by the rest of the world and therefore did not remain uniquely British. It was even utilized in a great many diesel tramps under various flags where the only justification was that it was a tested and traditional design.

When the plans were taken to the United States and Canada, the Americans in particular immediately started a process of redesign to better adapt it to American construction practice. The 60 Ocean type ships were amended to suit an almost all-welded construction as described elsewhere in this chapter, the biggest design change being that of eliminating the tumblehome in the original British design. Following the British plans exactly, the Canadian-built Fort and Park ships retained the feature of tumblehome which, to the expert eye, did give them a slightly altered appearance from the Oceans. Maximum beam at the waterline remained unaltered, but it did decrease the Canadian-built ships' main deck measurement by possibly six inches.

Tumblehome occurs when the sides of the vessel's hull inclines inward from the vertical, towards the centre line. The artist's rendering depicts this feature in *Weston Park*, seen on the dustjacket of this book. Walton in *Know Your Own Ship* defines tumblehome as being "the amount the ship narrows at amidships above the waterline to the uppermost deck."

In the eighteenth century tumblehome probably reached its peak of greatest development. The so-called "Wooden Walls" of Nelson's day incorporated extreme tumblehome so that the maximum width could be developed at the waterline in order to accommodate the enormous weight of heavy iron guns on up to three decks. Without this tumblehome, the weight of a full broadside would have been sufficient to send the ship onto its beam ends, so it was not only a matter of additional weight-carrying capacity, but also stability.

By narrowing the decks from the waterline up, metacentric height was reduced, and the righting moment following a list caused by an outside force such as wave action was improved, righting moment being the point at which a ship begins to recover from a list.

In older designs of steamships in the nineteenth century, beam was sacrificed for the long fine hull lines which promoted speed with the lower-powered engines then developed. Tumblehome assisted stability and righting moment, but as engines increased in power, the beam of ships likewise increased and thus carrying capacity was improved. Tumblehome was not abandoned but its need was greatly reduced.

British and European practice tended to hang onto tumblehome for another practical reason which had to do with reducing the possibility of stressing the main deck at its junction with the shell plating when a ship was against a dock, as would happen when the vessel listed for any reason, say in loading. In many European ports it was common practice to allow a vessel berthed alongside to dry out at low water. To avoid the ship falling over steps were taken to have her lean inboard against the dock, where tumblehome created a safety factor.

In American practice the elimination of deck camber and tumblehome, particularly in the Hog Islander design of the First World War, produced a vessel of near perfect box section which still handled to satisfaction in most conditions. This feature was then abandoned in the several C-type designs of the 1930s. Among other factors it made for less complicated construction, given the less experienced nature of wartime shipyard supervision and labour. Entire sub-assemblies normally constructed vertically could be assembled on a flat surface and lifted into place in large sections.

From the North Sands design the Americans also evolved the Liberty ship. Most shipping experts would likely agree that the Liberty was an improvement on the North Sands. With a larger forepeak saltwater ballast tank and two deep tanks in No. 1 lower hold, this combination provided better ballasting when the ship was in light condition. A perennial problem with all of the Canadian-built ships was the lack of sufficient water ballast capability forward to hold the ship's head down, which was the prime reason why in certain ballast conditions the North Sands type became very difficult to manage. The forepart of the ship acted like a sail in storm conditions when a high wind on either bow could cause the vessel to slew off course. If the conditions were extreme enough the ship could become unmanageable. This was probably the primary contributing cause of the loss of *Westbank Park*, detailed in Chapter 7.

By the 1960s the split profile type of ship was virtually extinct. Even though it was developed to accommodate the more efficient stowage of coal fuel, the type persisted even in many modern motor vessels of the period. However, experience with the Liberty ship demonstrated a number of improvements. One was that No. 3 hold was full size, unimpeded by cross bunkers which took up additional space, and that full access was available without the need to stow cargo under the bridge structure as in the split profile design of the North Sands. The other feature was that the long unimpeded deck space forward of the bridge over Nos. 1, 2 and 3 hatches made for better on-deck stowage of lumber cargoes. Sundry improvements of this nature contributed to an increased deadweight capacity of about 500 tons when compared to the North Sands type.

North Sands and Victory Tankers

Dimensions and specifications remained the same as with the types' dry cargo versions. The main difference was that tanks were installed in the cargo holds and all usual piping and pumping details common to tankers added. These ships could load 10,000 barrels of oil per hour for a total capacity of 62,000 barrels.

The Victory and Canadian Types

Dimensions and specifications remained the same as the North Sands design with some exceptions. These two types were simply improved North Sands ships. The Victory, the first of the two, was an oil burner. Two watertube boilers were substituted for the original three Scotch boilers. With the elimination of coal-loading hatches, the boat deck amidships was extended forward, enabling all four

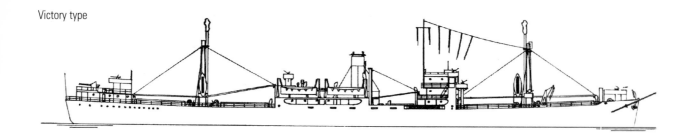

Victory type

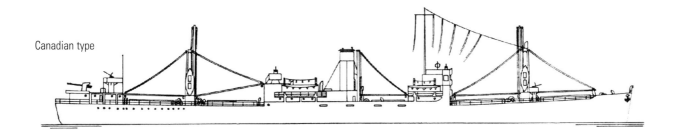

Canadian type

lifeboats to be mounted on the same boat deck, thus removing the original two smaller lifeboats from the Captain's bridge deck.

Because of concerns about oil fuel supplies the second type, the Canadian, had coal bunkers and alternate oil fuel capacity installed, but there was a reversion to the original three Scotch boilers of the North Sands type. Also the accommodation plan largely reverted to the North Sands plan, as did the mounting of the lifeboats.

THE GREY OR SCANDINAVIAN TYPE

Dimensions and specifications:

Length between perpendiculars	315.5 ft
Length overall	328.0 ft
Moulded breadth	46.5 ft
Moulded depth	34.9 ft
Gross tonnage	2,875 tons
Gross tonnage (Dominion type only)	2,960 tons
Deadweight tonnage	4,700 tons
Speed	10 knots

T expansion cal 20", 31", 55" x 39" stroke

Two single ended Scotch boilers

Most of these ships came out according to the original builder's plan. Two variations were built: the first, the Revised, had altered derrick arrangements and some improvements in accommodation. The second, known as the Dominion, had 'tween-decks fitted to suit them better for Canadian National Steamships' West Indies service in which they were employed for some years after the war.

THE 3,600-TON GREAT LAKES TYPE TANKER

Dimensions and specifications:

Length between perpendiculars	251.5 ft
Length overall	259.0 ft
Moulded breadth	44.0 ft
Moulded depth	-
Gross tonnage	2,400 tons
Deadweight tonnage	3,600 tons
Speed	10 knots

Oil engines 28 CSA 6 cyl by Dominion Eng. Works.

Of the Canadian war-built ships above the size of tugs, this ship had three distinctions. It was the only

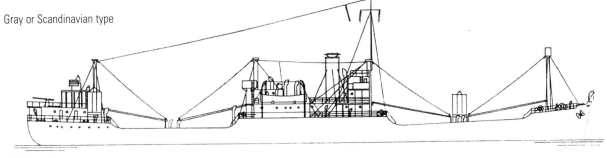

Gray or Scandinavian type

4,700-ton dwt

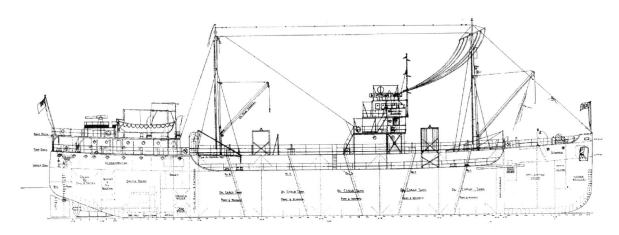

Profile plan view of the standard trunk-decked 3,600-ton Lakes type tanker. (Milne German & Gilmore)

one to be all-welded and it was a wholly Canadian design. It was the largest of the war-built standard types built in Canada to be fitted with diesel engines.

The well known Montreal naval architects, Milne, Gilmore & German followed Great Lakes practice, but gave the design the full capability of serving the Great Lakes and Atlantic Seaboard with voyages down the American coast and into the Caribbean to ports on the north coast of South America when occasion arose.

Statistical Data - The Output from Canadian Shipyards

ANALYSIS OF SHIPBUILDING CONTRACTS

Classes Included:
North Sands and Victory ships for Bareboat Charter to Britain.
North Sands, Victory and Canadian ships operated by Park Steamship Company.
Tankers of North Sands and Victory types.
Store ships of Victory and Canadian types chartered to Britain as part of the Fleet Train.
Royal Navy Victory type Maintenance ships built for British Account.
Grey or Scandinavian type ships operated by Park Steamship Company.
Lakes tankers operated by Park Steamship Company.

Classes Excepted:

"B" and "C" type standard coasters and tug classes.

One tanker converted from a Public Works dredger, *Riding Mountain Park*.

All naval construction except as noted above.

Abbreviations:

N/S = North Sands, V = Victory, C = Canadian

G/S = Grey/Scandinavian, L/T = Lakes Tanker.

	Forts		Parks			Store		RN	Park		Yard
	N/S	V	N/S	V	C	V	C	V	G/S	L/T	total
West Coast											
Burrard North	24	10	1	7	3	4	-	6	-	-	55
Burrard South	25	7	-	10	3	4	-	5	-	-	54
North Van/PacDD	24	7	2	14	3	-	-	5	-	-	55
Prince Rupert	5	2	1	3	2	-	-	-	-	-	13
Victoria M.D.	8	-	1	8[1]	2	1	-	-	-	-	20
West Coast S/B	20	6	2	18[2]	3	-	-	5	-	-	54
Yarrows	2	-	-	-	-	-	-	-	-	-	2
TOTAL	108	32	7	60	16	9	0	21	0	0	253
East Coast and Great Lakes											
Canadian Vickers	6[3]	-	-	-	-	-	-	-	-	-	6
Collingwood	-	-	-	-	-	-	-	-	-	3	3
Davie SB & Rep	10	-	9	-	-	-	-	-	7[4]	-	26
Foundation	-	-	-	-	-	-	-	-	24[5]	-	24
Marine Indust	15	-	12	-	3	-	-	-	-	3	33
Moreton Eng & DD	-	-	-	-	-	-	-	-	4[6]	-	4
St John DD	-	-	-	-	-	-	-	-	8[7]	-	8
United Ship	17	-	16	-	9	-	3	-	-	-	45
TOTAL	48	0	37	0	12	0	3	0	43	6	149
GRAND TOTAL	156	32	44	60	28	9	3	21	43	6	402

Notes:

1. Canadian Vickers completed one North Sands type as a tanker.

2. Victoria Machinery Depot completed five Victory types as tankers.

3. West Coast Shipbuilders completed seven Victory types as tankers.

4. Davie Shipbuilding & Repairs completed two ships as "Revised" variants and two as "Dominion" variants.

5. Foundation Maritime completed four ships as "Revised" variants and two as "Dominion" variants. One ship, *Hector Park*, is included in the above totals although she was bareboated to the British Ministry of War Transport as *Camp Debert*.

6. Morton Eng. built none of the original basic design, but completed two ships as "Revised" variants and two as "Dominion" variants.

7. St. John Dry Dock completed two ships as "Revised" variants.

The total number of ships bearing a Park name was 183. Marine and war losses totalled 7 ships, thus leaving 176 ships available for disposal.

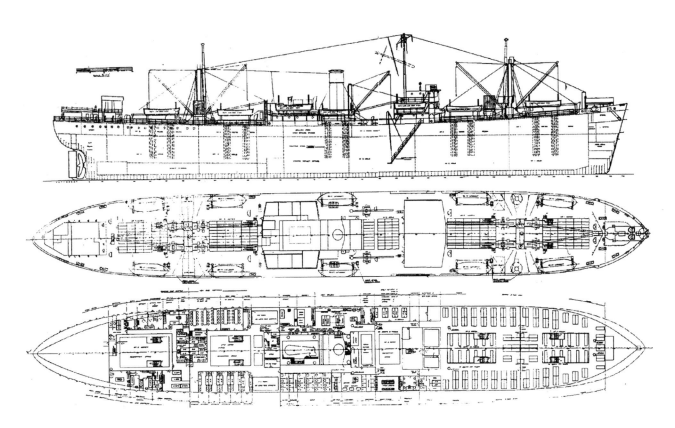

The Ship that Never Was. A design prepared in Canada for conversion of Fort ships to troopers for the assault on Europe. Ten extra lifeboats and rearrangement of the fore and aft upper 'tween-decks, connected by through trunks were allowed for. Stairways were set through hatches providing access to the lower holds which contained more berthing. The designers indicated that none were refitted to their design although a number of Forts were converted in England to another, but probably similar design.

(Milne German & Gilmore)

CHAPTER FIVE

Marine Insurance and the War Risks Market

ew people who are not directly engaged in it fully realize the importance and function of the marine insurance industry in the coverage of goods moved by sea and the ships that do the carrying. It has given security to ship and cargo owners since the first crude arrangements at sharing the risk with others, by receiving from them a token or premium to assume their proportion of the risk. The originators were the Phoenician merchants of the Levant in the Eastern Mediterranean before the birth of Christ, and by stages it became a primary component of world commerce as we know it today.

In the 1940s, the London marine insurance market, of which Lloyd's is by far the best known traditional and historical component, also comprised many insurance companies, large and small, mostly British-owned, but with some foreign companies also represented. Over a hundred of these companies belonged to the Institute of London Underwriters. The mix between Lloyd's and the Institute companies has probably changed little except that it is now more international in nature and many of the old names have disappeared as a result of major reorganizations and realignments in the world's insurance markets. The same drive to expansion and the economics of scale which have been apparent in many modern commercial fields have not left the marine insurance business unaffected.

I left school in 1942 and hoped to join the merchant navy in the very worst year of the war at sea. Not surprisingly, parental intervention killed that idea, so a year later I joined the Royal Navy at the tender age of 17. In the intervening period I worked as a junior clerk for the Thames & Mersey Marine Insurance Company in Liverpool. The T & M shared wartime offices with the British & Foreign Marine Insurance Company, its sister company in the giant Royal-Liverpool group, at their evacuated office located at Hoylake, Cheshire, which also happened to be my birthplace. Working in the Statistics department was an eye opener for a callow, inexperienced, but ship-crazy youth who thought of shipping in terms of what could be seen at the docks, in the river or in photographs. It was an introduction to a wartime economy, a vastly different situation from peacetime.

It took some time to understand the complex workings of a marine insurance market that was now geared to war. One of my first jobs was to make proper note, for statistical purposes, of all paid claims on cargo losses. The date, the vessel's name, the cargo involved, the type of loss, and the amount paid out had to be recorded according to a certain routine. Familiar vessel names showed as well as others quite unfamiliar. One such which I knew well was the *Politician,* a T & J Harrison liner which ran ashore on the island of Eriskay, off the Scottish coast with a large cargo of export whisky. This was a typical wartime marine loss caused by the blackout of all lighthouses, lightships and lightbouys.

This event inspired a whimsical book, *Tight Little Island,* by Compton Mackenzie and a popular and funny movie called *Whisky Galore,* but entertainment aside, the loss cost the British

Convoys on a Collision Course. Both ships sank when *Bodnant* (5,300 gt/1919), upper photo and *City of Bedford* (6,402 gt/1924), collided when convoys on opposite tracks came too close to each other.   (John Clarkson)

Whisky Galore. Due to wartime blackout conditions *Politician* (7,939 gt/1923) ran ashore on the Scottish Isle of Eriskay with 275,000 bottles of Scotch whisky among her cargo, of which 20,000 found their way into the hands of the islanders. The Customs dynamited the rest of the cargo in place in the ship. The island's only pub is named "The Politician" in memory of the celebrated event.   (John Clarkson)

marine insurance market a lot of money in paid claims. The H & M market paid out on the ship itself as she was in every sense a marine total loss. The British & Foreign and Thames & Mersey companies underwrote a large part of the Scotch whisky export business, but the risk would have been spread around by reinsurance, particularly in the Liverpool marine market, as the companies centred there, which included the B & F and T & M, tended to keep as much business as they could close to home as the principle of reciprocity helped everyone. Scotch whisky was one of the few major exports the British could still supply to the outside world to obtain foreign currency, but as the war drew on, it became more important to grow cereals for human and animal consumption than to use it for distilled spirits.

Two other ship names showed up which meant little to me at that time. The formation of the Crown corporation, Park Steamship Company Limited, while no doubt well publicized in Canada, had little impact in wartime Britain. The first, *Jasper*

Park, was the first Park ship lost by enemy action. The ship was carrying a large cargo of the new Indian tea crop and it was this cargo that concerned the two insurance companies. It was a war loss and would have normally been absorbed by the British government war risks insurance, but this also provided an example of an exception for special reasons to that general rule, about which more later.

The second was *Gatineau Park,* although the amounts involved were much smaller. As I recall this vessel had declared a General Average following a marine accident or heavy weather damage which resulted in a jettison of deck cargo, possibly lumber on deck, or heavy or oversize munitions such as aircraft or tanks. In the circumstances this was not a war loss.

A General Average is declared following some sacrifice such as jettisoning cargo, or the engagement of tugs to pull off a stranded vessel in order to mitigate accruing loss as would inevitably occur if the vessel remained aground. General Average means that the loss of one interest, such as jettisoned cargo to save the ship, and remaining cargo is averaged in

Fort Camosun. This ship had the rare distinction of being torpedoed on two different occasions and surviving both to see further service. The photo shows her on her maiden voyage following the first torpedoing off the Washington Coast. The crosstrees were extended for net booms but the usual clamps are not in place which perhaps indicates that the fitting of the booms was done later.   (Vancouver Maritime Museum)

a general way across all interests, i.e the ship itself, remaining cargo and the freight, all of which through their insurance make a rateable contribution to the loss of the owner of the jettisoned cargo or the costs of a tow by way of salvaging a vessel to avoid greater loss.

When war was declared the British government, with the experiences of the First World War still quite fresh, was quick off the mark with new Ministries covering Munitions, Food & Supply and War Transport, and a host of new regulations which controlled foodstuffs, commodities, basic raw materials including oil, together with shipping and all other forms of transport. Rationing was quickly introduced as the war changed the flow of goods, and vast industries which had been doing business in well-established ways for decades suddenly found themselves doing the bidding of others in entirely different ways. The alternative was to close shop for the duration, and notices to that effect were not uncommon on office doors and in shop windows. They were almost like "gone fishing" notices except that no one knew when and if they would ever reopen.

The Ministries initiated numerous programs which involved private businesspeople. War Transport appointed established shipping companies as managers to take care of day-to-day management functions for captured enemy ships and the new ships which would pour from the shipyards including those transferred from the US and Canada.

In the early period of the war the Ministry of Food & Supply quickly brought into effect a host of new regulations, the first and foremost in the experience of the common citizen being food, clothing and gasoline rationing. To accomplish this industry had to be reorganized on a war footing. For example, all lumber and wood products came under the control of the Timber Controller, an office staffed by experienced former employers and employees from major timber importers. Timber Control was a part of the giant Ministry of Food and Supply.

Insurance markets also went to war. War Risks, in peacetime provided in the private insurance market, was taken over bodily by the government. Government or its agencies were to give the orders regardless of private misgivings of the shipowners, so it was fair that they should cover the risk. Every new hull under construction in a shipyard had to be covered from keel-laying to delivery, as the new construction was at the risk of the shipbuilder until the vessel was completed, but Builder's Risk as it was termed was still covered in the private market. This applied equally in Canada once her shipbuilding industry got into gear. The markets which would logically have looked after placing Builder's Risk insurance on new tonnage were in Montreal, Toronto and Vancouver. Every agency and branch office capable of providing some capacity to the market, found itself inundated with new business placed by such brokers as Marsh & MacLennan, Dale & Company, Macaulay Nicolls & Maitland, and Osborn & Lange.

"Capacity" is a word almost special to the insurance industry. In effect it means — given the financial strength of the insurance carrier and its policy on acceptance of risks — the percentage of the insurance cover, measured in money, but expressed usually as a percentage of the total value it could assume by way of insured risk on a given vessel.

Once the ship was completed and turned over, Builder's Risk insurance would terminate and Hull and Machinery (H & M) insurance against marine perils, appropriate to an operating ship, would take over. This would in all likelihood find its way to a different insurance market. In the case of Park Steamship Company, if as an owner the company was a regular commercial business owned in the private sector, a new vessel would normally be added to its fleet policy for H & M and additionally insured for a type of legal liability insurance known as Protection & Indemnity (P & I). However, Park was not a private owner, and it seems certain, followed the practice of self-insurance adopted by most governments in bearing any loss as a charge against its revenue. In other words it carried the risk itself on the basis that the premium it would otherwise have paid would have represented the value of one or two of its ships each year.

Likewise, there is no ascertainable record as to whether P & I was carried by Park Steamship, because in this instance the potential for extensive third party claims might well have exceeded the value of a ship. There is no record of the extent to which P & I insurance was called into play, if at all, in the case of *Green Hill Park* or *Fort Stikine,* but the potential value of P & I insurance was demonstrated as the property of others was affected.

The best-known example of a self-insured fleet was Alfred Holt's Blue Funnel Line of Liverpool, often called Holt's Navy on account of the meticulous way in which the fleet was managed and the standards and specifications it maintained for its ships and operating personnel. Its captains and managers had the strictest instructions to take no short cuts and avoid all potential loss-making situations. The end result was that from the beginning of this century to the time when it eventually retired from the shipping business in the early 1980s, Holt only had three marine losses. It put aside to its insurance reserve each year an amount deemed equivalent to the annual insurance premium, but as the reserve grew to greater proportions, the percentage it had to set aside was proportionately less in order to maintain a stable reserve fund for insurance losses.

The collision while in convoy of two ships, the *Bodnant* and *City of Bedford* is described in *The Elder Dempster Fleet History* by Cowden and Duffy:

Bodnant (Elder Dempster Lines) sailed from Hull on December 28, 1940 bound for Freetown and Lagos, via Methil and Oban, having a crew of 52 (including two gunners) 10 passengers and 1,150 tons of government stores.

She was in a convoy of about 30 vessels in nine columns of three or four each, distances between columns being five cables and that between ships in column, two cables. The *Bodnant* was leading ship in the starboard column.

On the night of December 29, 1940 the convoy was proceeding into the North Atlantic at a speed of nine knots course of South 76 deg. West true. The following day, at 0900 BST in about 62 deg. North, 21 deg. West, 280 miles south of Ireland, the weather conditions were very dark, the wind being a moderate gale from the South East and there was a rough and heavy swell. No lights were exhibited, but the loom of the vessel in the first column on the port beam of the *Bodnant* could just be observed.

The Chief Officer (D. Haigh) was in charge of the bridge with a helmsman at the wheel, one seaman on lookout, and two passengers, one on each wing, also on lookout on the lower bridge. At 0920 hours he observed right ahead and at a distance of four to five cables the shape of a vessel whose navigation lights were switched on immediately after the Chief Officer sighted her.

The lights were two sidelights and the fore-masthead light. They were bright and from their position the oncoming vessel appeared to be on an exactly opposite course.

It would appear that this vessel (the *City of Bedford*, Ellerman Lines) switched on her lights, having seen the *Bodnant* almost at the same moment that the *Bodnant* saw her.

The Chief Officer, who was at the starboard side of the wheelhouse immediately ordered the helm hard-a-starboard, sounded a short blast on the whistle and stepped into the wheelhouse and switched on the navigation lights using the dimmer switch. He then left the wheelhouse and found Captain Harding who had at that time been taking breakfast in his cabin, standing at the top of the starboard ladder, asking "what's up?"

No sound was heard from the *City of Bedford* but she was altering course to port rapidly, shutting out her red light. The *Bodnant* gave another short blast on her whistle without response from the *City of Bedford*.

The interval between the two blasts was apparently 30 seconds and when the second blast was given, the distance between the two vessels was about two cables. At the same time, Captain Harding rang the telegraph full ahead, a double ring, and repeated the order hard-a-starboard.

The *City of Bedford* continued to go to port and the vessels collided; the point of impact being the *City of Bedford's* starboard side between the fo'c'sle and the foremast and the *Bodnant's* stem. The blow was a heavy one and the *Bodnant* seemed to ride over the *City of Bedford* as if she were on the crest of a wave and the *City of Bedford* in the trough. The *Bodnant* was a near light ship with only 1,150 tons of cargo, whereas the *City of Bedford* was low in the water and appeared to be heavily laden. The two vessels fell together the bows of each being close together as far (aft) as the foremasts. They then drifted apart and cleared one another.

About the time of the collision lights appeared abeam, those lights being in some cases from vessels forming the *Bodnant's* convoy and in others in the convoy of which the *City of Bedford* was a part. The two convoys were proceeding on almost directly opposite courses and presumably they were making the same speed of nine knots. The two vessels would therefore, be meeting at a combined speed of 18 knots — 1,800 ft. per minute, that is four cables = 2,400 ft. — 80 seconds.

Both vessels suffered considerable damage, with the result that some hours afterwards they both foundered.

Apart from a clear error in dates, as it is not possible that a vessel travelling at nine knots could leave Hull on December 28, call at Methil and Oban and be 280 miles south of Iceland to founder two days later on December 30, this is an interesting example of the hazards of sailing in convoy, particularly before the introduction of radar.

An interesting sidelight is revealed in Duncan Haws' book *Merchant Fleets: Ellerman Lines,* when he comments on the loss of the *City of Bedford:*

> Lost.... when two convoys came too close to each other. No lives were lost but $7^{1}/_{2}$ million rifle cartridges went down; the largest munitions loss in the war to that date. Winston Churchill was 'greatly distressed' and demanded to know why all the ammunition was in one ship. He laid down that, in future, such loads be spread over sufficient vessels to ensure the safe arrival of 'sufficient of the weapons without which we cannot wage war'.

In retrospect that seems to have been an elementary application of the principle of spreading the risk.

The next major insurance carried in wartime was War Risks Insurance. This covered the Hull & Machinery against the risks of act of war by the enemy. The delineation between a marine risk and a war risk was often quite hazy, as we have seen in the *Bodnant* case cited above. Victor Dover in *Handbook of Marine Insurance* quotes the case of *Athel Line v. Liverpool and London War Risks Association (1945)*, in which a ship acting under a wartime directive came to anchor and as the tide went down settled on a rock causing bottom damage. Liverpool and London was a government agency set up to handle war risks insurance on behalf of the government.

Following the example of the *Bodnant/City of Bedford* case one might have thought that *Athel Line* would have been settled as a marine claim, but evidently this was not the case, as it was stated in the subsequent legal action, that but for the circumstances of war, the ship would not have been there. One might sense some confusion when comparing the two cases, but the difference appears to be that in the *Bodnant/City of Bedford* case both ships were going about their legitimate mercantile business even though, in the strain of wartime circumstances, they were sailing in separate convoys on opposite tracks. In *Athel Line's* case the ship responded to a specific directive, probably from a Director of Naval Operations, as DNO's controlled most merchant shipping activities in their given area of command under wartime conditions. Since a war loss would normally be defined as the consequence of a warlike action of the enemy, or as the result of inadvertent 'friendly fire', it seems that *Athel Line* suggests some very special circumstances which Dover has not explained. Otherwise, the argument could have differed little from the case of *Fort Stikine,* discussed in Chapter Six.

In peacetime, War Risk insurance has always been provided by the private insurance market and is transacted along with Strikes, Riot and Civil Commotion insurance (SR&CC). One might ask what war risks occur in peacetime? Occasionally international shipping is imperiled, in some event like the Iraq/Iran war, or the Spanish Civil War of 1936-39 when foreign, non-Spanish shipping was exposed to the acts of the opposing sides. War risk rates can escalate rapidly according to the insurance underwriters' assessment of the degree of risk.

In the Second World War matters took a different course regarding the risks of war. All shipping fell under government control or direction as did all essential imported cargo, as already outlined. About the only exceptions would be harbour service craft such as dredgers, ship-berthing tugs, pilotage vessels and fishing vessels below a certain size, these being usually small inshore craft which filled their role perfectly as they were still able to land essential food. With cargo shipments British exports fell off rapidly so that whisky exported under permit would be one of the few consistent exports. Privately owned ships, which at the outset of war represented the total merchant fleet, were quickly augmented by enemy prize ships and the start of a war shipbuilding emergency program. British yards started to deliver "Empire" named ships of Liberty ship-equivalent size and others for British Ministry of War Transport account in 1940. The Canadian Fort and American Ocean programs commenced deliveries in 1941, but by 1942 the stream of these ships, now joined and swollen by the American Liberties, were pouring from the shipyards of each country in prodigious numbers.

Dover comments at considerable length on War Risks insurance and here lies the clue as to why the war risk was assumed, in the case of *Jasper Park,* by the private insurance market rather than by government insurance. The ship was engaged to carry a substantial shipment of the Indian tea crop for the North American market. This tea was loaded f.o.b. at Calcutta, but British Government War Risk insurance would not have been available for the purpose of insuring non-government cargo on a cross voyage. If the consignees were in, say, Montreal or New York they would have had to accept the exposure to war risks and arrange insurance in the private insurance market accordingly. That explains why eventually the proportion of the claim accepted by the British & Foreign and Thames & Mersey companies found its way, via their American or Canadian agencies, back to the statistics department in Hoylake where the author worked in early 1943. If the tea had been consigned to Britain I would not have heard anything about the loss because the Government War Risks would have picked it up.

A final note concerns the mode of compensating the owners of ships lost from war causes. The whole or a substantial part of the value of these ships was held in a special government account for settlement following the war. It obviously avoided an owner profiting from windfall gains following a loss due to war, but placed him in a strong position with often substantial credits held to his account which could be liquidated by purchasing government-owned tonnage as soon as it became available. Large, well-established lines like Clan, Ellerman, Harrison, Royal Mail and Furness Withy were able to re-equip their fleets almost overnight so that normal trade patterns could be re-established without delay while they awaited the delivery of replacement postwar ships of a superior specification to the wartime ships. This would not apply to most Canadian owners who, with the exception of prewar fleets such as Canadian Pacific, Canadian National, British-American and Imperial Oil, only became established following the war.

Some Definitions of Loss

Throughout this book there are instances of several different types of total or other loss, which are explained here.

A *Total Loss* occurs when a ship or its cargo or both are irretrievably lost through sinking, stranding, collision or fire, or is so badly damaged as to be beyond repair. A *Constructive Total Loss* occurs when the cost of repair of a damaged vessel exceeds the amount insured when a vessel is insured, or exceeds the fair market value when uninsured. An example of the latter was *Green Hill Park*.

A *Compromised* or *Arranged Total Loss* arises when a vessel suffers extensive damage, but is unlikely to reach the insured or fair market value limit required

to define it as a constructive total loss. In this case the underwriters may agree to pay out the estimated amount of the claim and allow the owner to keep the wreck. Typically this could arise when damage occurs to a very old vessel nearing the end of its economic life. The question then becomes why repair a ship that is approaching the scrapping stage? In effect, by paying out the claim the underwriters are leaving the decision as to disposal of the ship to the owner. An example was *Silver Star Park,* described in Chapter Seven. The ship was not old, but would have joined the fleet of wartime ships available for disposal in an oversupplied market. She was not described in official records as a total or constructive total loss as she was probably not beyond economic repair, but as she was not insured it became a matter of Park Steamship deciding that they would dispose of her without further investment and write her off as an arranged total loss.

A *General Average* occurs if, following a loss, there is a sacrifice of one or more interests, i.e. the hull and machinery, the cargo or the freight earned are sacrificed for the common good in order to forestall further loss. Examples include the cost of towing off following a stranding, the jettisoning of cargo to lighten ship following a stranding, and the cost of towing following a mishap at sea.

A *Particular Average* means in effect a partial loss. A particular average is confined to the interest insured and is of a fortuitous nature. A ship hits a dock and sustains shellplate damage, a cargo is lost while loading or unloading, are both examples.

Subrogation occurs when underwriters of shipowners having paid out a loss on a damaged ship or cargo then seek under their powers of subrogation to sell the damaged cargo to recover part of the loss or go after a third party who might have been the cause of the loss.

CHAPTER SIX

Bareboat to Britain

The term "bareboat" refers to a form of charter which the word actually describes quite well. Under a bareboat, or as it is sometimes termed a "demise" charter, the owner, sometimes referred to as the disponant owner, supplies the ship, with such expendable supplies as remain on board, at fair value. The charterer supplies or equips the vessel with all needed fuel, chandlery, hardware, paint and other expendable supplies including crew victualling, plus of course the necessary crew.

Under a bareboat charter the rate of hire is based at a certain rate per deadweight ton on summer freeboard. The duration of the charter is usually fairly long-term, probably in excess of two years and commonly for five to seven years, to correspond with the amortization of a ship's mortgage. The fact that in certain periods the vessel may only be loaded to her winter loadline does not affect the charter hire rate and as a rule, charter hire is settled per calendar month, payable in advance.

When the ship is returned to the owner a reverse adjustment is made for fuel and expendable supplies which may remain on board at the end of the charter. With some items such as standing and running rigging, cargo gear, anchors and mooring lines, what was on the ship at delivery is replaced with like quality and kind at redelivery, as failure to maintain these items to standard could result in the vessel being deemed unseaworthy.

The one matter which a prudent owner could be expected to attend to was basic Hull and Machinery, and Protection and Indemnity insurance, the cost of which would be factored into the charter hire rate.

Awaiting her date with the water. *Fort Sturgeon*, allocated for bareboat charter to Britain. There was probably very little ceremony on that overcast day. (BC Archives, E-00676)

These are the essential elements of a commercial bareboat charter, one of several forms of charter transacted in the world shipping markets on a daily basis (See Chapter Twelve for an explanation of other types of charter). Given the speculative nature of shipping, bareboat or a common time charter was also regarded as the most secure form of employment available to a trampship owner, when his ship was chartered out to a first-class liner operator at a satisfatory rate. Because it was

Fort Sturgeon. The North Sands Forts were popular with the London Greeks. When this photo was taken the ship was under the management of Dalhousie Steam and Motorship Company and then quickly passed into the ownership of Counties Ship Management, which had more of the type in their fleet than any other owner.   (Ian Stewart Collection)

Fort Stikine. This Prince Rupert-built vessel was at the centre of the Bombay catastrophe which killed or injured thousands in April, 1944. The earlier ships were evidently sent to sea without bow guns or anti-aircraft guns abreast of the main mast. She was not fitted with paravane gear or net booms.   (Wm. Hutcherson Collection)

secure it had the disadvantage of diminishing the owner's return when voyage charter rates were high, as the charterer could recharter the vessel in the spot market and reap a sizeable profit over his committment to pay the owner his agreed guaranteed rate.

It was also the most convenient instrument for handling the large fleet of Fort ships turned over to the British by the Government of Canada through its agency, Wartime Merchant Shipping Limited, or those ships chartered in the same way

by the US War Shipping Administration which included 200 Liberty ships and the 90 Forts built in Canada but sold to the United States Government. It did not include the first two Forts built and delivered, as these were purchased by the British along with the 60 Oceans, noted in Chapter Four, as was the original intent when the British Merchant Shipbuilding Mission came to North America.

It should be noted that the 90 Forts sold to the US was wholly a financing transaction. Britain was

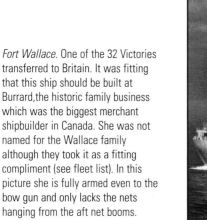

Fort Wallace. One of the 32 Victories transferred to Britain. It was fitting that this ship should be built at Burrard, the historic family business which was the biggest merchant shipbuilder in Canada. She was not named for the Wallace family although they took it as a fitting compliment (see fleet list). In this picture she is fully armed even to the bow gun and only lacks the nets hanging from the aft net booms.

(Vancouver Maritime Museum)

already financially strained as it gave its maximum to its own survival. It had stood alone with the Dominions against the Axis onslaught and had even diverted precious resources to the USSR following Germany's invasion of that country. Britain's payment to Canada for new ships obviously created a problem for both countries which led to the Hyde Park Declaration, so named for the location of President Roosevelt's summer home in upper New York State. Of the 90, some had already appeared in *Lloyd's Register* of 1941-42, as being owned by the "Dominion of Canada" so that in the next issue they were listed as being owned by the United States War Shipping Administration. The actual inscription was "Ministry of War Transport under bareboat charter from the W.S.A." After the war a few were disposed of to foreign owners, but the balance of the survivors went into long term layup at one of the American layup sites until sold to the shipbreakers.

What the British government paid by way of a charter hire rate is not known, but the spirit of lease lend as devised by the government of President Rooosevelt, was to get the weapons of war into the hands of America's allies, more as an act of strategic generosity than one of commercial realism. Realism took over when it came to securing legal title to the benefactor's property and for this reason the Fort ships built in Canada, with the two exceptions noted, and turned over to Britain remained the property of Canada and were so registered.

Remember also, the process of turning the ships over to the British was a government-to-government transaction and it is equally likely that the entire matter of charter hire was dealt with as a simple accounting transaction where the process of debits and credits from one nation to the other was dealt with in a running account. Many standard commercial practices were abandoned in the stress of the times. It was more important to the Allied war effort to work the ships and a greater consideration might have been the ability to man the vessel with a competent crew, one thing Britain never seemed to run out of.

That can be attributed to the excellence of their training schemes plus a long tradition of "going to sea" in what was then the world's largest merchant navy, a leadership position unchallenged over several centuries. Fully 20 per cent of the boys in the author's graduating class at high school were destined to go to sea in the Royal or British Merchant Navies, and in some communities this may well have been far higher. To these could be added Chinese, Lascars from the Bengal area and Arabs from East Africa and elsewhere, who in one way or another bolstered crews and were generally well thought of by shipowners.

British officers trained in two floating training ships, *Worcester* and *Conway,* plus the Pangbourne Nautical school. Additionally, many lines had apprenticeship schemes by which a youth could leave school having achieved the requisite education level and be apprenticed, under indentures, as

Fort Boise. This photo shows the ship leaving for her trial trip. One of the 32 Victories she was one of four that were lost while still owned by the Dominion of Canada. See later story.

(Wm. Hutcherson Collection)

a deck officer. Engineers apprenticed at one of many industrial establishments before shipping out at the lowest rank of officer engineers. There was no equivalent apprenticeship scheme afloat, as with deck officers. The Marconi Company trained wireless operators who essentially remained under their control, as Marconi not only supplied the radio equipment, but also the operators.

For seamen there were also a number of training schools, some of which were designed to take "wayward" boys who had come from poverty-stricken circumstances. One such was *Vindicatrix*, a training ship located at Bristol. They did a course lasting six weeks and then shipped out as ordinary seamen.

With the large output of ships from the Canadian shipyards, the matter of crewing was a continuous headache. Manning pools existed on both coasts which through force of circumstances often had to settle for virtually untrained personnel. Wireless schools turned out good wireless operators in Vancouver and elsewhere, and St. Margaret's School at Hubbards, NS educated officer cadets in a course of training that lasted 13 weeks before they were sent afloat to Park Steamship vessels. At the same school there was a similar training program for young men who declined to take the upper deck route. These youngsters either by choice or by qualification chose to become seamen instead. Some Canadian captains and ship officers had had no association

with the sea since the First World War or, in some instances, somewhat later in the heyday of the Canadian Government Merchant Marine.

Otherwise they had served time in Canadian Pacific and Canadian National ocean and coastal ships, the small fleet of the Coughlan Line of Vancouver, Great Lakes vessels or tankers of Imperial Oil and other oil companies. Another source was Canadians who had served or trained with British lines sailing to Canada, which were open to taking a percentage of Canadian youth into their apprenticeship schemes. A full description of the background to Canadian manning needs and the Canadian training scheme at St. Margarets School, Hubbards, Nova Scotia is contained in an exceptional book, *A School of Seamen: A Pride of Ships,* by Hill Wilson.

Evidence probably exists among unsorted papers at the National Archives, but one suspects that with the large number of ships launched with Fort names, but renamed with Park names during the fitting-out process, it was sometimes a hit and miss proposition as to which flag a ship sailed under, often determined quite late in the day. We don't know what the determining factor was as to whether a given ship remained in Canada or was sent to the British, but it does seem very likely that the matter of manning might have been a determining factor in some instances.

The memoirs of the late Captain Trevor Bridges set out in *Across Far Distant Horizons,*

(Heal) tell of the case of the two ships bearing the name *Mount Robson Park*. It was an unusual transaction in which the earlier ship, a North Sands vessel, had been built with this name. Later, a new Victory ship had been named *Fort Miami* and was on the point of delivery from its builder in Vancouver. In what became a double renaming, the *Fort Miami* became the second *Mount Robson Park,* and the older *Mount Robson Park* became the second *Fort Miami*. The British crew sent out to stand by the new ships must have been chagrined to find that instead of a brand new Victory, they were to take over an older North Sands which had suffered quite badly from engine trouble on her last trip to the Antipodes. Captain Bridges was very complimentary about his new command and had no regrets about giving up the older ship.

Crews for the Fort ships were assembled in Britain and sent over by passenger liner to stand by a new ship under construction on the east or west coast. The British practice was to appoint a manager, invariably a well known British liner or trampship company. The management firm would then take responsibility for booking a passage across the Atlantic and seeing that the crew arrived at their destination. Usually the British company had an agent or could find one at Vancouver, Montreal or another port who would see to necessary ship's business, dispatching her on the maiden voyage to Britain.

The ship would be registered in *Lloyd's Register of Ships* with the description, for example, "Ministry of War Transport under bareboat charter from the Dominion of Canada (owners)(XYZ Shipping Company, Managers)." This description made a clear statement about the underlying ownership and the relationship of the Ministry of War Transport and the nominated manager. The manager had no say in the selection of cargoes or the routing, destination, or employment of the vessel. His sole role was to deal with day-to-day management matters such as manning, victualling, supplies and other ship's business, and that is where his duty ended. Managers once appointed seldom changed, provided they remained capable, unless they went out of business. The *Lloyd's Register* notation was accurate and in researches only two instances of a change of management was found when the firm sold out to another shipping company.

It was not the practice of the Canadian government to insure government property, including its ships. The same practice existed in Britain and the United States, faced with handling even larger inventories of government property. A loss was a direct charge against revenue derived from taxation in one form or another, which supports the contention that "the taxpayer, sooner or later, pays for everything."

Once the ship had been transferred to Britain she came under British articles, and to all intents and purposes everything to do with her future use and employment was out of the hands of any Canadian government agency. When the war ended steps were taken to reclaim and dispose of all the Canadian-owned Forts (their story is taken up again in Chapter Nine).

The fleet of Ocean ships purchased by Britain is listed below. An asterisk after the ship's name denotes a war or marine total loss, of which there were 17.

Built by Todd-Bath Iron Shipbuilding Corp. at Portland, Maine:

Ocean Angel	*Ocean Liberty*
Ocean Athlete	*Ocean Might**
Ocean Courier	*Ocean Merchant*
*Ocean Courage**	*Ocean Messenger*
*Ocean Crusader**	*Ocean Peace**
Ocean Faith	*Ocean Pilgrim*
Ocean Fame	*Ocean Pride*
*Ocean Freedom**	*Ocean Rider*
Ocean Gallant	*Ocean Seaman**
Ocean Glory	*Ocean Stranger*
Ocean Gypsy	*Ocean Strength*
*Ocean Honour**	*Ocean Trader*
Ocean Hope	*Ocean Traveller*
*Ocean Hunter**	*Ocean Wanderer*
*Ocean Justice**	*Ocean Wayfarer*

Built by Permanente Metals Corporation, later renamed Todd-California Shipbuilding Corp. at Richmond, California:

Ocean Vagabond*	Ocean Vigil
Ocean Vagrant	Ocean Vigour
Ocean Valentine	Ocean Viking*
Ocean Valley	Ocean Vintage*
Ocean Valour	Ocean Virtue
Ocean Vanity	Ocean Viscount
Ocean Vanguard*	Ocean Vision
Ocean Vanquisher	Ocean Vista
Ocean Vengeance	Ocean Victory
Ocean Venture*	Ocean Voice*
Ocean Venus*	Ocean Volga
Ocean Verity	Ocean Volunteer
Ocean Vesper	Ocean Voyager*
Ocean Vestal	Ocean Vulcan
Ocean Viceroy	

The following were significant partial losses resulting from enemy action. One (#) was lost later and is also noted above.

Ocean Courier	Ocean Vanquisher
Ocean Rider	Ocean Viceroy
Ocean Vagabond#	Ocean Volga

The 90 North Sands ships transferred to US ownership under the Hyde Park Declaration are listed below. An asterisk (*) following the ship's name indicates a war or marine total loss. There were 22 total losses from among this group:

Fort Abitibi,	Fort La Maune*
Fort Acton	Fort La Montée*
Fort a la Corne*	Fort La Reine*
Fort Alexandria	Fort La Trait
Fort Ann	Fort Lawrence
Fort Augustus	Fort Liard
Fort Babine*	Fort Livingston
Fort Battle River*	Fort Longueuil*
Fort Bourbon	Fort Louisbourg
Fort Brule	Fort Maurepas
Fort Buckingham*	Fort McLeod*
Fort Camosun	Fort McLoughlin
Fort Cataraqui	Fort McMurray
Fort Cedar Lake*	Fort Meductic
Fort Chambly	Fort Mumford*
Fort Charnisay	Fort Nipigon
Fort Chilcotin*	Fort Norman
Fort Chipewyan	Fort Nashwaak
Fort Churchill	Fort Paskoyac
Fort Concord*	Fort Pelly*
Fort Confidence*	Fort Pembina
Fort Drew	Fort Pine
Fort Douglas	Fort Pitt
Fort Ellice	Fort Poplar
Fort Fairford	Fort Qu'appelle*
Fort Finlay	Fort Rae
Fort Fitzgerald*	Fort Rampart*
Fort Fork	Fort Reliance
Fort Franklin*	Fort Remy
Fort Fraser	Fort Rupert
Fort Frederick	Fort Senneville
Fort Frobisher	Fort Simpson
Fort Gaspereau	Fort Slave
Fort George	Fort Souris
Fort Gibraltar	Fort Stager
Fort Good Hope*	Fort Steele
Fort Grahame	Fort Stikine*
Fort Halkett*	Fort St. François
Fort Howe*	Fort Tadoussac
Fort Hudson's Hope	Fort Thompson
Fort Jasper	Fort Tremblant
Fort Jemseg*	Fort Vermillion
Fort Kootenay	Fort Walsh
Fort Lac La Ronge*	Fort Wedderburne
Fort Lajoie	Fort Yale*

The following were significant partial losses resulting from enemy action. Two (#) were lost later and are also noted above:

Fort Babine#	Fort Lac la Ronge#
Fort Camosun	Fort Louisbourg
Fort Drew	Fort Norman
Fort Lajoie	Fort Paskoyac

A total of 63 North Sands ships were transferred to Britain under bareboat charter, two were purchased outright (#) and a further four were transferred from Park Steamship and renamed as Forts. A total of five (*) of these ships were lost by war or marine total loss:

Fort Aklavik
Fort Albany
Fort Ash
Fort Assiniboine
Fort Athabaska*
Fort Beauséjour
Fort Bedford
Fort Bell
Fort Brandon
Fort Brunswick
Fort Buffalo
Fort Cadotte
Fort Capot River
Fort Caribou
Fort Carillon
Fort Carlton
Fort Chesterfield
Fort Connolly
Fort Coulonge
Fort Covington
Fort Crevier*
Fort Cumberland
Fort Dauphin
Fort Dease Lake
Fort Enterprise
Fort Erie
Fort Espérance
Fort Fidler
Fort Frontenac
Fort Glenlyon
Fort Glenora
Fort Gloucester
Fort Grant

Fort Grouard
Fort Henley
Fort La Cloche
Fort La Prairie
Fort La Tour
Fort Lennox
Fort Maisonneuve*
Fort Mattagami
Fort McPherson
Fort Michipicoten
Fort Mingan
Fort Missanabie*
Fort Moose
Fort Musquarro
Fort Nakasley
Fort Norfolk*
Fort Nottingham
Fort Pic
Fort Richelieu
Fort Romaine
Fort Rouille
Fort St. James#
Fort St. Joseph
Fort St. Paul
Fort St, Regis
Fort Sturgeon
Fort Ticonderoga
Fort Turtle
Fort Verchères
Fort Ville Marie#
Fort Wellington
Fort Wrigley

Fort Highfield ex-Yoho Park
Fort Miami ex-Mount Robson Park
Fort Nisqually ex-Kootenay Park
Fort Spokane ex-Mohawk Park

The following were significant partial losses from enemy action:

Fort Fidler
Fort Gloucester
Fort McPherson

The following 32 Victories were transferred to Britain under bareboat charter. Two were lost by enemy action and two by marine loss. One ship, Fort Colville, was classified as an Air Stores Issuing Ship as part of the Fleet Train:

Fort Aspin
Fort Astoria
Fort Bellingham*
Fort Biloxi
Fort Boise*
Fort Brisebois
Fort Clatsop
Fort Columbia
Fort Crèvecoeur
Fort Dearborn
Fort Hall
Fort Island
Fort Kaskaskia
Fort Kullyspell
Fort La Baye
Fort La Have

Fort Machault
Fort Marin
Fort Massac*
Fort Orleans
Fort Panmure
Fort Perrot
Fort Prudhomme
Fort Sakisdac
Fort Saleesh
Fort St. Antoine
Fort St. Croix
Fort St. Nicholas*
Fort Venango
Fort Wallace
Fort Yukon

Fort Colville

The following were significant partial losses:

Fort Dearborn
Fort Kaskaskia
Fort La Baye
Fort Perrot

The Bari Disaster;
The Loss of *Fort Athabaska*; Damage to *Fort Lajoie*

On December 2, 1943, there occurred the greatest single loss of shipping, other than in certain convoy actions, sustained by the Allies as the result of offensive action by the Germans. Sicily had been conquered and now British, Canadian and American forces were fighting their way up the Italian peninsula. As ports and other facilities were secured they were turned to Allied advantage.

One such was the port of Bari on the east side of the peninsula, looking out onto the Adriatic sea. It was a measure of the fact that the Germans still had lots of sting left when their bombers were able to attack and do such destruction to the shipping crowded into the port. The disaster was intensified by the fact that the Allies, always in anticipation of the Germans resorting to chemical warfare, maintained stocks of gas as a deterrent against enemy action.

Few could forget the horrors of the First World War when mustard and phosgene gases were first used by the Germans in an effort to break the stalemate in Northern France. It took the British and French by surprise for their troops in most instances did not even have gas masks, but their response was prompt. They were able to retaliate with gas attacks of their own as well as quickly put together a crude gas mask. As a result chemical warfare was quickly checkmated and never reached its best potential in WWI nor was it resorted to by either side in WWII, although the threat was always assumed to be present. Hitler himself is said to have suffered from Allied gas attacks as a soldier in WWI so it was perhaps fortunate that he had had first-hand experience.

One of the ships present was the US Liberty ship *John Harvey*, whose cargo included several hundred tons of mustard gas shells. She was also one of some 37 freighters or warships at anchor or tied up within the harbour. Of these 17 were totally lost and a further six severely damaged. Of the total losses no less than five were US Liberty ships, with one other severely damaged. So far as is known all the shipping in the harbour was Allied. Among them were *Fort Athabaska*, carrying two captured German glider bombs destined for North Africa and Allied analysis, and *Fort Lajoie*.

Fort Athabaska was ready to sail when the German attack commenced. Other than the glider bombs her cargo consisted mainly of several hundred bags of mail. Unfortunately she caught fire when the nearby Liberty ship *Joseph Wheeler* blew up. When the fire reached the glider bombs the heat detonated them and her fate was sealed. The resultant explosions were devastating for the ship and crew. Two were killed and a further 44 were missing presumed killed within the ship or drowned when seeking to escape into the water. There were only ten survivors accounted for.

Fort Lajoie fared somewhat better. She was also anchored in the harbour awaiting a convoy when *John Harvey* blew up. An illumination flare dropped by a German airplane landed in one of the Oerlikon tubs and started a fire while red-hot flying debris landed on the ship and started more fires, one in No. 4 hold where it ignited waste dunnage and another which set fire to the lower bridge. All hatches were blown off and hatch tarpaulins ripped to shreds.

An ammunition box landed on the ship, cut through a deck at number four and fell into the hold. A 100-pound anvil from another ship put a big dent into the deck. Two-pound live shells were found in the boiler lagging but as they did not explode there was no damage done to the boilers.

Despite the terrible damage inflicted on *Fort Lajoie*, the crew did not abandon. Lifeboats had sustained damage in any event, but they fought the fires and waited for the action going on all around them to die down. Casualties were one killed with eight injured.

The explosion in *John Harvey* released a large amount of mustard gas which spread across the water and into the town, causing many casualties. The ship sinkings were listed as follows:

US	John Bascom
	John L. Motley
	Joseph Wheeler
	John L. Harvey
	Samuel Tilden
British	Testbank
	Lars Kruse
	Fort Athabaska
	Devon Coast
Norwegian	Lom
	Bollsta
	Norlom
Italian	Barletta
	Frosinone
	Cassala
Polish	Puck
	Lwow

The following were damaged but not sunk:

US	Lyman Abbott
British	Christa
	Fort Lajoie
	Brittany Coast
Dutch	Odysseus
Norwegian	Vest

The Bombay Explosion:
The Loss of *Fort Stikine* and *Fort Crevier*

Many aspects of ship operations pass in wartime which would never be permitted in peacetime. One such was the manner in which cargoes were sometimes handled and stowed, and the case of *Fort Stikine* was a classic example.

The Bombay explosion took place during the afternoon of Friday, April 14, 1944. A friend of the author was a fairly near witness to the events that followed. Able Seaman Ron Richardson, RN was on temporary naval staff at the shore base after recuperating from an illness. Richardson said that word of the fire in a freighter at Bombay Docks had reached him like many others, but no one seemed alarmed, as fires at the docks were fairly commonplace and always seemed to be handled in a satisfactory way.

When the ship's forepart exploded there was a massive fall of debris which peppered his neighbourhood, but when the second explosion followed some time later there could be no doubt that a massive disaster had occurred. Bits of hot torn metal and all manner of debris rained down and did a lot of damage even though the navy depot was located a mile or more from the site of the explosion. When he was ordered out with other navy personnel to help with disaster relief, it was to see a scene of the most total destruction that could be imagined. Buildings were flattened, their remains on fire and thousands were dead in a city which even then teemed with so much humanity that any disaster would take a serious toll.

Fort Stikine, a standard North Sands ship built at Prince Rupert, BC had left the Port of Liverpool in February 1944 for Karachi and Bombay. Her cargo was a range of typical munitions — bombs, shells, torpedoes, rockets and magnesium used for making incendiaries — a total of 1,400 tons. Aircraft were crated on deck. Partial discharge at Karachi was followed by the loading of 9000 bales of cotton, thousands of drums of lubricating oil, scrap metal, rice, sulphur, fish meal and resin. There was even an attempt to load 750 drums of turpentine on top of the coal in the bunkers, but this was refused even though the ship was already a potential floating powder keg.

The ship arrived at Bombay on April 12th and fully 24 hours after being placed alongside in Victoria Dock unloading commenced, even though a priority certificate had been issued, given that she had three categories of explosives in her manifest and the quicker they could be unloaded the better.

Aboard *Fort Crevier*, a sister ship berthed at least two ship lengths away, crew saw smoke spiralling out of *Fort Stikine's* ventilators, as did people aboard the steamer *Iran*. An inspector on the dock also noticed that something was amiss, but one has to wonder what the ship's own officers and crew were up to. Was everyone aboard asleep? By the time some fire equipment arrived alongside it was obvious that the ship was well and truly on fire.

By then it was probably already too late to save the ship. Some 32 hoses poured a thousand tons of water into the seat of the fire in No. 2 hold, but at 3:45 pm the explosives caught fire. Minutes later a sheet of flame shot up and the ship became a blazing inferno. At 4:05 pm the ship exploded with a deafening noise. Flaming drums, white-hot shards of metal and burning cotton poured down on ships in Victoria Dock, dockside sheds and the city, spreading death and destruction in their path.

The explosion created a tidal wave sufficient to lift the Indian-owned freighter *Jalapadma* across No. 2 shed. High and dry, she broke her back. Under the dense clouds of smoke eleven other vessels were on fire and four had already sunk. Other ships were aground or listing and dockside installations like gates, bridges, warehouses and sheds were in ruins, destroyed totally or on fire. The dock roads and railways were a tangled mass of wreckage. Where the forepart of *Fort Stikine* had blown up and sunk there was a huge crater in the berth.

The aft section of the ship was still afloat but blazing furiously. There were still close to 800 tons of explosives stowed aft and 35 minutes later this exploded with a force even greater than the first. This created a new crater so that No. 1 berth was

now totally destroyed. The ship had been carrying a large consignment of gold bars worth at that time over a million pounds sterling. Able Seaman Richardson related that some of these bars were found three and four miles away from the site of the explosion. Naturally there was a great hunt for any of the gold and no doubt a sizeable proportion was found and never turned in.

Fires broke out in sheds and oil installations in a radius of one mile from the site of the explosion. Thousands died or were injured and the loss of shelter caused great hardship for many survivors. The magnitude of the disaster was simply beyond the capability of the city of Bombay or any city to manage. It was probably the largest single disaster of its type on the Allied side during the war and ranked close to the largest ever, prior to the nuclear age, the Halifax Explosion of 1917.

The result could have been far worse. The damage spread to the nearby Princes Dock, but at the Alexandra Dock there were another three munition ships and a loaded tanker, which fortunately were not involved in the disaster. In this case, the theory is that the most likely cause of the fire was to be found in the recently loaded cargo of cotton, as cotton is known to be subject to spontaneous combustion.

Of the various vessels sunk or still afloat but badly damaged the following were designated total or constructive total losses:

Baroda	3205/11	British India S.N. UK
Fort Crevier	7131/43	MOWT Jos. Robinson & Sons UK
Fort Stikine	7142/42	MOWT Port Line Ltd. UK
General Van der Heijden	1213/28	Konink. Paketvaart Maats. Holl.
General Van Swieten	1300/28	Konink. Paketvaart Maats. Holl.
Graciosa	1773/17	Skibs A/S Fjeld, Norway
Iran	5704/19	Iran S.S. Co. (Wallem & Co.) Panama.
Jalapadma	3935/29	Scindia S.N. Co. India
Kingyuan	2653/21	China Nav. Co. UK
Rod el Farag	6842/10	Soc. Misr. Navigation, Egypt
Tinombo	872/30	Konink. Paketvaart Maats. Holl

When the author was in Bombay eight months after the event very little damage was visible. A massive clean-up, repair and salvage operation was mounted which might normally have taken several years to complete. The docks were all fully functional and such wreckage as that of *Jalapadma* had long since been broken up on the spot and removed. The recoverable wreckage from *Fort Stikine* was mainly the forepart of the ship which had sunk and lower sections of the hull which had not been rended in the explosions. The dock had to be drained in order to get at the huge volume of wreckage from this and other ships as well as dockside installations which had fallen into the water.

Fort Crevier never sailed again. She was beyond repair economically so was written off as a constructive total loss. She was used as a floating grain storage hulk at Bombay and broken up shortly after the war.

IMPLICATIONS FOR INSURANCE

In marine insurance terms, a comparison between the Bari and Bombay disasters demonstrates the essential difference between war losses and marine loss. Bari was a war loss while Bombay would have been processed as a marine loss. War losses would be covered by government insurance while marine losses would have fallen on Lloyd's and the insurance company markets. The significant difference between the two is that Bari followed a deliberate warlike act on the part of the Luftwaffe in attacking the shipping berthed in the harbour at Bari. In the case of Bombay there was no aggressive act on the part of any enemy, despite the fact that the ship and its cargo would never have existed but for the war. It could also be said that she would not have been in Bombay, but for the need to build up armaments for the coming offensive against Japan, but it still ranked as a marine loss by fire and explosion, as the proximity of an enemy conducting warlike acts was missing.

Another point of interest is that the Dutch KPM company lost no less than three vessels in the blast. When the invasion of the Dutch East Indies took place many inter-island trading vessels owned by Dutch companies escaped to Australia and India. Prior to the surrender of Japan, Dutch shipping of this type was always in evidence throughout South East Asia in almost every port that one could visit.

Conflagrations at Algiers: The Loss of *Fort Confidence* and *Fort La Montée*

Of all the ships built in Canada during the Second World War none sustained more losses on a percentage basis than the group of North Sands ships which were transferred to Britain. No fewer than 27 were officially listed as war losses, and of the marine losses a further four were engaged in warlike pursuits when fire or explosion overtook them and brought about their destruction. The four were *Fort Stikine, Fort Crevier, Fort Confidence* and *Fort La Montée.*

By the time the events that destroyed the last two vessels occurred, Algiers had been in Allied hands for some time and the invasion of Italy was well under way. However, there were concerns about the work of saboteurs. The Norwegian steam tramp *Bjorkhaug* had been part of the Allied offensive codenamed "Torch" which had seen the invasion of North Africa in late 1942.

Slader in *The Fourth Service* describes the sequence of events that overtook Algiers in the summer of 1943:

> *Bjorkhaug* was a steamship of 3200dwt, built in 1919 that functioned as a supply

and ammunition vessel. On July 16, 1943 she was loading a mixed cargo of scrap steel, empty shells and German and Italian land-mines. The latter were said to be "not dangerous," but at 1525 hrs. there was a huge explosion that blew away the entire forepart of the vessel. The aft section of the vessel remained afloat, but the midship section was partly submerged. Seven wounded were brought to the hospital, but all those members of the crew who had been in the ship's forward section lost their lives, as well as Captain Sandvik and two British Navy officers who had been in the captain's living quarters. In addition to Captain Sandvik eight crew members lost their lives. There was considerable devastation ashore from the explosion and from several explosions and fires on shore around the vessel and in the harbour area which caused the deaths of some 1,000 people, mostly Arab dock workers. Another Norwegian vessel, *Lysaker V*, was moored nearby and escaped the effects of the explosion, but was threatened by a dangerous fire. The first mate, assisted by British officers, managed to get hold of a tug and succeeded in towing *Lysaker V* away from the quay to safety.

Meanwhile, *Fort Confidence* was loading gasoline in drums for the use of the Allied armies engaged in the conquest of Italy. The published reports are scanty, mostly confined to two-line entries in *Lloyd's Confidential Index*. On July 16, this ship also caught fire, presumably following the explosion in *Bjorkhaug*. So far as can be discerned *Fort Confidence* was totally burned out. After the wreck had cooled down she was removed to a nearby beach where she lay until cut up for scrap. Presumably it was burning gasoline from this ship which threatened *Lysaker V.*

On August 4, in an unrelated incident fire broke out in *Fort La Montée*. Among her cargo was a large consignment of phosphorus, a dangerous substance at any time, which self-ignites when exposed to air.

To carry the substance successfully as cargo it would have to be stowed in hermetically sealed canisters or drums. When it is exposed to air it glows as it oxidises, and burns with the explosive flare of an ignited match. What started the fire is unknown. It might have been a drum dropped or sprung in handling which then self-ignited. Sabotage was not ruled out, but was unproven. Regardless of cause, once a fire like this took hold it would have been very difficult to control.

The ship was moved out into the bay, and it was fortunate that this precaution was taken, otherwise the consequences could have been far more horrendous, but nothing could quell the blaze. A massive explosion then occurred which completely split the ship's foredeck and part of her hull. The British destroyer *Arrow* which was standing by sustained serious damage, and ships slightly farther away were hit by flying debris, including the hospital ship *Amarapoora*.

Fort La Montée burned for days despite shellfire from a British submarine in an effort to sink the ship, which eventually succeeded, but over 100 lives were lost in the ship and in *Arrow.*

These events did not rank with either the Bari or Bombay disasters in their magnitude, and the consequences could have been far worse. What mitigated the scope of the second Algiers disaster was moving *Fort La Montée* into the outer anchorage. Even though it probably made firefighting more difficult, it did reduce exposure. In hindsight it would have been better to have scuttled the ship once fire took hold in the phosphorus cargo, as at the outset there appeared to be plenty of time to do so. Had this taken place it seems probable that *Fort La Montée* could have been raised and returned to service.

Bari was too sudden and devastating to take mitigating action. In the case of Bombay, there was not enough time to move the burning ship through tidal locks and into the outer harbour. Even if there had been time, it was a gamble which few would have been prepared to face.

The Loss of *Fort Mumford*

Fort Mumford left Canada never to return, for she was a casualty on her maiden voyage. Loading war supplies for the Mediterranean, she left Vancouver for Lyttleton, New Zealand, completed loading there and made for Colombo where she took on bunkers on March 15, 1943. From there she departed for Aden, but on the 20th she was torpedoed by the Japanese submarine *I 27*. The exact position of her sinking has never been established as there was only one survivor, a DEMS rating who had the good fortune to be picked up by an Indian dhow engaged in the trade to the east coast of Africa. Otherwise we may never have known of the fate of *Fort Mumford.*

The fate of the rest of the crew can only be surmised, but on the record it seems probable that they were machine-gunned upon abandoning ship. Even though so little is known about the loss of *Fort Mumford,* her short life and tragic end sets off a train of events which carries a sort of justice of its own.

Commander Fukumura, of *I 27,* like a number of other Japanese submariners had a particularly bad record. Machine-gunning of crews from sunken ships was fairly commonplace and there are a number of instances recorded by Slader in *The Fourth Service.* That Fukumura was a killer was well confirmed when, still in command of *I 27,* he torpedoed the British Liberty ship *Sambridge* in about the same latitude as the *Fort Mumford.* He machine-gunned the survivors in their lifeboat and rafts and took the second officer on board and landed him at Penang. The master of *Sambridge,* in his survivor's report to the Admiralty, described Fukumura's action as "an act of deliberate terrorism." Fukumura and *I 27* completed his record as a scourge of the sea when he torpedoed the liner *Khedive Ishmael* on February 24th, 1944. The liner was actually Egyptian-owned, but was under the management of the British India Line. The sinking was one of the worst in the British merchant shipping history of the Second World War. Lives lost totalled 1383 including 137 of her 183 crew. Those saved consisted of 201 men and 6 women. The submerged *I 27* hid underneath the survivors swimming or floundering for their lives in the water. The ship

had gone under in 36 seconds so there was no time to launch boats and passing ships in the convoy could do little to help.

One of the convoy escorts was HMS *Petard* under Commander Rupert Egan, who was to earn the distinction of sinking a submarine from all three of the Axis navies. The cries of help from those in the water turned to screams of horror as *Petard* raced among them and released her depth charges, but in war the destruction of an enemy took precedence over rescuing survivors. Inhuman though it was, the other side of the coin indicated that a surviving submarine could sink more ships with further loss of life.

The other escort, the destroyer *Paladin,* actually had boats over the side attempting rescue when *Petard* made her first run. On the third run *I 27* was forced to the surface but she still had lots of fight in her. Her gun crew made a dash for the 5-inch gun, but were shot down as they did so. *Paladin* made a run at the submarine and rammed her, doing considerable damage to herself. In the end it was a torpedo from *Petard* that finally destroyed the Japanese submarine and put an end to the life of one of the worst criminals in any navy.

Commander Egan was so distraught over the enormity of the *Khedive Ishmael* disaster and the loss of life among survivors following his successful attack on Fukumura that he eventually committed suicide. As for the bad record of the Japanese navy submarines, John Slader, who himself survived no less than four torpedoings, has this to say in *The Fourth Service:*

> During the UN trials of Japanese criminals (May 1946 to November 1948) 5,500 were accused of killing, torturing or otherwise ill-treating Allied servicemen and civilians. Some 4,450 were found guilty. A thousand suffered execution by hanging, yet the deaths of the men who lost their lives after abandoning ship went almost unnoticed and unavenged. Fifty years later the controversy continues. It is difficult to understand why, unlike the Germans and

the Italians, the Japanese, members of a maritime nation, ignored the bond of comradeship which has existed for centuries during times of peace and war between seamen of different nationalities. The barbaric behaviour shown by certain Japanese mariners would not have been tolerated by the German High Command. Indeed in the main, German U-boat and surface raider commanders were helpful to those seamen, who, through no fault of their own, found themselves at the mercy of the elements.

The Germans were not quite as blameless as the above may suggest. Harsh conditions for prisoners aboard a German ship were not unknown, as the *Altmark* incident bears out. However, there was only one incident involving survivors being machine-gunned from a U-boat. That is detailed in Chapter Two in the matter of Heinz Eck and his command, *U 852,* and the sinking of the Alfred Holt liner *Peleus.*

The Loss by Mine of *Fort Maisonneuve*

Prepared from documents and material supplied by Josh Jones of Rickmansworth, England. Mr. Jones was the son of the late Captain John Jones, in command of Fort Maisonneuve at the time of her loss.

The circumstances of the loss of *Fort Maisonneuve* are outlined in the convoy escort's laconic message:

```
FROM:    Commanding Officer, HMS "MENDIP"
DATE:    17th December, 1944 No. 2/2
TO:      The Captain 'D' 21st Destroyer Flotilla
MINING OF S.S. "FORT MAISONNEUVE" IN CONVOY T.A.M.18
```

The following report of mining and sinking of S.S. "Fort Maisonneuve" in convoy T.A.M. 18 is submitted.

2. Convoy was in single line ahead, speed four knots, visibility one mile. Convoy consisted of 16 ships spread over about six miles, "Mendip" was astern of rear ship.

3. At 1310 while passing N.F. 14 buoy, a stranded wreck was sighted on starboard bow. It was thought at first that this was from a previous convoy as there was no smoke coming from it and survivors and wreckage had almost drifted out of sight. The nameboard revealed that it belonged to our convoy, and that it was the "Fort Maisonneuve" who had been about six ships ahead of "Mendip" in the line. No signal had been made on R/T and no explosion had been heard on Asdics. I was informed by an ML that the ship had been mined at 1234.

4. Survivors were picked up by MLs, and wounded were transferred to "Mendip". The wreck was fixed and a signal made both on R/T to S.O.

Escort and Commodore, and by W/T to Naval Officer-in-charge, Antwerp etc. List of survivors retained in "Mendip" was passed to NOIC, Antwerp.

5. The radio operator of "Fort Maisonneuve" reported that he tried to transmit a signal on R/T but could not get it through.

6. It is suggested that Masters be informed that if they see a ship mined and are in doubt as to whether the occurrence has been observed by an escort, they should transmit a signal on R/T or if not fitted for transmission, should pass a signal down the line until it reaches a ship that is so fitted.

7. If this had occurred at night, it seems quite possible that it would have passed unnoticed with subsequent heavy loss of life and potential danger to other shipping.

(signed) F.D. Davey
Lieutenant in Command

Fort Maisonneuve left New York in convoy bound for Antwerp. Aboard she had 602 tons of ammunition and other explosives, 69 tons of naval ordnance supplies, 955 tons of vehicles and road-building equipment, 4585 tons of flour and 31 tons of canteen and medical supplies and equipment. For newly liberated Antwerp's military requirements and the need to feed the population and repair installations this was a very important cargo.

In the great sweep of the British and Canadian armies which more or less paralleled the north European coast as the Allies swept into the heartland of Germany, securing Antwerp was a critical strategic objective. It had not been bombed with the intensity of many of the Northern French ports and had not been a base for U-boats and minor German warships which had been such a scourge in the English Channel. It was therefore in relatively undamaged condition and fell quickly enough to the advancing Allies.

This was not the case with the river Schelde which had been extensively mined by the Germans. The entrance to the Wester Schelde is marked by the town and port of Vlissingen, otherwise known as Flushing, on the north bank and the town of Breskens on the south bank. *Fort Maisonneuve* had been mined off the village of Cadzand near the Belgian-Dutch frontier. The Schelde flows through

Dutch territory until it reaches the head of the broad estuary where it touches a very small Belgian waterfront which secures the mouth of the upper Schelde, where shipping proceeds upriver to the port of Antwerp.

There is no information as to the type of mine sown at this site by the Germans, but as the effectiveness of magnetic mines had largely been nullified by degaussing gear used on Allied ships, it is assumed that it was the standard contact type. The point of contact was evidently aft, probably either in No. 4 or 5 holds, as mentioned in the official *London Gazette* of August 14, 1945 when announcing the award of the British Empire Medal to Hassan Ismail, Donkeyman, aboard *Fort Maisonneuve:*

The S.S. "Fort Maisonneuve" was in convoy when she was severely damaged by a mine. The ship settled rapidly by the stern and touched bottom about ten minutes later. The crew was ordered into the boats but the Master and Donkeyman remained on the damaged ship with two injured men. In response to a call for volunteers, four of the crew returned on board and a careful search was then made for further survivors. The injured were helped to a launch which came alongside. The ship was then abandoned.

Donkeyman Ismail displayed great gallantry and courage and was outstanding throughout. He refused to leave the ship with the remainder of the crew and stayed on board to assist the master and the injured.

In the list of commendations for brave conduct that followed mention was also made of "Captain John Alun Jones, Master 'Fort Maisonneuve'."

A number of the engine room crew were Arabs of whom two were lost along with two British deck crew. A further six suffered severe injuries, but almost every other man aboard suffered some degree of more minor injury. A telegram to the Admiralty from the Naval authorities in Ostend gave a list of numbers taken on board HM ships *Mendip* and *Cottesmore* and landed at Terneuzen or Ostend.

From that point on *Fort Maisonneuve* lay on her bed of silt in the river, a hazard to navigation for 18 years, mostly forgotten by the rest of the world, until the following article appeared in *Lloyd's List & Shipping Gazette* of May 25, 1962:

SALVAGE CONTRACT FOR DUTCH FIRM

Removal of Four Wrecks from West Scheldt River

AMSTERDAM

The salvage firm Van der Akker, Flushing have acquired a contract with the Dept. of Waterways in Holland for the removal of four shipwrecks in the River Scheldt-West Scheldt. They are the British cargo vessel *Fort Maisonneuve*, (7128 tons gross) mined three kilometres off Cadzand in December, 1944, the *Funch of Phoenix*, of unknown nationality, lying in the South Sloe since 1879, a Belgian dredger in Wielingin Fairway off Cadzand, and the British vessel *Edward Dawson*, which sank off Zoutelande in 1911.

The removal of the *Fort Maisonneuve* may be dangerous.

Bound for the liberated port of Antwerp, she carried bulldozers and roadbuilding machines, along with some 4500 tons of flour and a few hundred tons of explosives. The position of the shipwreck, lying at a depth of over 20 metres has been accurately charted. She broke in three parts when running on to a mine; the middle section lies at a depth of 24 metres, the fore and aft parts, however, have some parts pointing up to less than 14 metres under water.

UTMOST CARE NEEDED

It will be necessary to remove about 10 per cent of the hull in addition to the upper structure. The job is listed to take 550 calendar days, but working will on average only be possible in one out of three days and the utmost care will be required in view of the explosives in the afterpart.

The suggestion that the ship broke into three parts as a result of the mining is doubtful. These ships were strongly built and there is no record of one of them breaking up in this manner following an internal explosion, a severe stranding or any other war or marine event. The probable explanation is that after settling on the bottom, severe tidal scouring action would have undermined her with every tide and eventually brought about the breaking of the hull. In 18 years much would have happened to the three parts as they lay on the bottom and this is indicated from the salvage company's plan, a reproduction of which accompanies this account.

The break at the fore end of No.4 hatch might have been accelerated by the weakening in the hull caused by the mine. The break at the fore end of No.3 hatch was probably caused by tidal action as the entire midsection containing the boiler and engine room compartments were lying at an acute angle compared to the rest of the hull. The fore and stern sections were lying over to port and the mid-section over to starboard.

Akker's contract called for the remains to be lowered to 16 metres at Low Low Water Spring tides. The job started on January 1st 1961 and was completed to a depth of 16 metres at LLWS on December 18th, 1963. It was made more difficult by the fact that the wreck was in open waters and thus affected by weather conditions which at times could be severe. Also because of the danger posed by the explosives in the cargo charges had to be set off after the salvage vessel was 1800-2000 metres away. Sometimes cargo was ignited and parts of the vessel came above the surface with explosions.

Thus ended the history of *Fort Maisonneuve* some 20 years after her completion at United Shipyards, Montreal in May 1943.

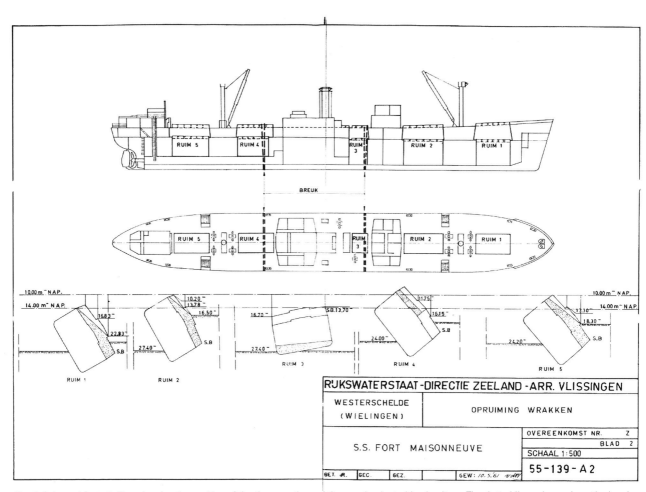

Dutch Salvage Master's Plan showing the position of the three sections of the wreck prior to blowing it up. The dotted lines show where the breaks occured in the hull. "Ruim" means "hold".

The Loss of *Fort Boise*

Contributed by Peter T. Kelly, Scarborough, ON

I first signed on the *Fort Boise* on May 23, 1946, as an able seaman. We sailed to Naples, Italy and to Valetta, Malta, and returned to Halifax July 20, 1946. Our bosun signed off the ship in Halifax and before we sailed again I was promoted to take his place.

From Halifax we were sent to Baltimore, Md. where we picked up a load of coal for Botwood, Nfld. We were ten days in Botwood discharging the coal and taking on a cargo of zinc concentrate which was consigned to northern France. On leaving Botwood we were supposed to pick up 500 tons of cargo at St. Pierre, then proceed to Halifax before sailing for France.

Early on the morning of August 23, 1946 we steamed slowly through fog, two miles off St. Pierre. On the bridge, Captain McLean and Chief Officer Solowan peered through the mist searching for the pilot boat carrying the pilot who was to take us through the treacherous harbour entrance. They never found it.

Shortly after 7 am I stepped out of my quarters on the boat deck, when suddenly I was thrown off balance. The ship stopped dead as if she had silently run into a brick wall. I heard her engines stop for a moment, then they reversed and ran full astern for several minutes, during which the ship shuddered violently like a dying animal. Then the ship's engines stopped and she lay still. The fog pressed down. Water lapped gently at the ship's side. Not another sound could be heard. *Fort Boise* was hard aground.

Within a very short time Captain McLean, through the company's agent in St. Pierre, requested Foundation Maritime in Halifax to come to our rescue. They dispatched the salvage tug *Foundation Franklin*, but we knew it would take two days steaming time for the *Franklin* to reach us. In the meantime, Captain McLean requested the assistance of a small tug from St. Pierre, hoping she could pull us off the rocks. For safety's sake, most of the crew were sent ashore, leaving only a skeleton crew aboard. We dropped a kedge anchor with a heavy insurance wire shackled to it, on to the tug's stern, paid out the wire as she steamed away, then made the wire fast on the after bitts. The little tug tried to move us, but we didn't budge. That afternoon, the crew members who had been sent ashore came back aboard.

After 48 hours, *Foundation Franklin* arrived and I cannot praise her crew enough, not only for their seamanship but also for their courage and bravery. Her salvage crew worked along with our deck crew to lighten the ship by jettisoning cargo overside.

By the fourth day of the stranding the weather worsened and we were not yet ready to be towed off. As darkness fell that night, the *Franklin* crew members returned to their tug which stood by us on the dark, heaving sea. Our 40 crew members were all aboard *Fort Boise* as the wind and waves mounted a violent attack on us. The two starboard side lifeboats were smashed to pulpwood by giant waves battering the stricken ship. Water poured into the hold through gashes in her side where she had hit the rocks. By 9 pm the engine room began to fill up like a giant swimming pool. The firemen barely had time to douse her fires and shut down the boilers to prevent an explosion, before abandoning the engine room. The lights went out as the generator was shut down and *Fort Boise,* crippled and pummelled by the furious storm, was now in total darkness.

Unfortunately, at this point, someone panicked and yelled, "Lifeboats!" Several men began lowering one of the two remaining boats on the port side. Sixteen men scrambled into it as it was being lowered, and were almost dumped into the heaving seas. They managed to pull clear of the ship's side without being smashed to bits and we lost sight of them in the dark. The captain signalled the *Franklin.* Her crew turned on a huge searchlight and swept the surging sea until they spotted the lifeboat, pitching and tossing out of control because no one was in command.

The *Franklin* edged in towards the rocks. Risking everything, the lives of all her crew and the tug itself, she skirted the hidden rocks beneath the surface and

Fort Boise. This sequence of three pictures shows the ship after her stranding on the Island of St. Pierre. Here she lies following the storm with her back broken. An effort was made to lighten ship by jettisoning cargo overside.

(Peter Kelly Collection)

Fort Boise. Close-up of the hull fracture in number three hold. The stern section had already sunk by some eight feet. Prior to the break she evidently had steam and could work some cargo. Note the extra accommodation which was added to the captain's bridge deck. The original monkey island was enclosed and a new monkey island placed on top of it.

(Peter Kelly Collection)

Fort Boise. Montreal appears on the stern as the port of registry. While the Fort names were reserved for British ships, the 28 returned Victories were not given Park names as all were quickly disposed of to private owners. Here she lies abandoned, soon to break up and sink. The distinctive Canadian-designed cowl on top of the funnel can be seen. Many private owners did not like it and removed this fitting as soon as they could.

(Peter Kelly Collection)

picked up our men. Then, slowly, she backed off again and stood by us in the raging seas.

Finally, an hour later, with all hope gone, Captain McLean gave the order for the rest of us to abandon ship. We lowered the last remaining lifeboat and 20 of us scrambled into it, with Chief Officer Solowan in charge. Captain McLean, Third Officer Drummond, Chief Engineer Hall and Radio Officer Dufresne elected to stay aboard.

We pulled away from the stricken *Fort Boise* into the impenetrable darkness. By now the frenzied boiling seas were too violent for the *Franklin* to risk coming in again. We could only hope that we could reach her. But it was not to be. We soon lost sight of her. All night we worked the oars, to keep the boat's bow into the wind so we would not be swamped. All night we baled furiously to keep the boat from filling with water. All night Mr. Solowan sat at the tiller and yelled through the screaming of the storm, "Row." "Row." "Row." If he had stopped, we would have stopped. He saved our lives and almost lost his voice.

In the morning, the seas subsided and through the lingering fog came a fishing smack and towed us into St. Pierre where we learned the fate of the four men who had elected to stay aboard ship.

At midnight, with a rending crash of twisted metal, *Fort Boise* broke her back. She had cracked in two across her beam roughly at the fore end of number 3 hatch. Although she was still held fast on the rocks, the four men lowered a life raft in a desperate attempt to save themselves, because they were sure the ship was breaking up completely. The raft, of course could not be controlled or steered. The storm swept it onto the rocky beach on the island of St. Pierre, killing Captain McLean and Chief Engineer Hall. Drummond and Dufresne, knocked unconscious, came to lying on the beach, and in the morning found their way to the town of St. Pierre. Captain McLean's body was returned to his home in England and Mr. Hall's body was returned to his wife's home in Montreal. Hall was only 27 when he died.

Ironically, *Fort Boise* was still sitting on the rocks with the break through her mid-section that morning when we came ashore. She looked like a bold wet hen clinging tenaciously to her nest after a rainstorm. Had we known she would have remained on her perch and if we had stuck with her through the night, two tragic deaths would have been avoided. But such are the vagaries of a seagoing life.

Four of us remained on St. Pierre for three weeks after the rest of the crew had shipped back to the Canadian mainland via Sidney, NS Chief Officer Solowan, the ship's donkeyman, Able Seaman Jimmy Burke and myself made three trips back to *Fort Boise*. Mr. Solowan completed a report for the shipping company, describing the ship as "a total constructive loss*." We salvaged as much of the crew's gear as we could, then we also returned to the mainland.

---

*The term "Total Constructive Loss" while commonly used is not correct. It is actually "Constructive Total Loss" which is a marine insurance term applicable when the cost of actual or potential salvage and repairs exceeds the insured value of the vessel.
An enquiry by Mr. Kelly to Montship Lines in 1957, brought the confirmation from Vice-president, J.S. Anderson, that the ship broke up and sank shortly after grounding. There was no salvage as she went to the bottom before salvors could deal with the wreck.

North to Archangel: *Fort Astoria*

This vessel was West Coast Shipbuilders Limited's Hull No. 123, launched May 21, 1943. She was finished to become the first Victory type cargo ship built by this yard. Captain T.L. Blair took command of the ship at the builder's yard in July, 1943 and these were his comments when contacted in 1945:

```
    These ships have done a very fine job of work and the people
responsible for their construction deserve the highest praise
possible for a good job in the shortest time, to help the Old
Country.
    After departing the West Coast yard, we loaded lumber at New
Westminster and Tacoma and ran to Europe via Panama and New
York. At the latter point we grounded, but did not dry dock till
reaching England where it was found that a few bottom plates
were waved. Next trip took us to Archangel with guns and tanks
but, while assembling the convoy at Loch Ewe, we dragged our
anchor, fouling another ship which carried away the two port
lifeboats. We returned with a load of Russian lumber to the Old
Country. Following voyages included war materials from Scotland
to Sicily; several shuttles between Italy and North Africa; Aden
for bunkers, ballast to Calcutta; tea and jute from Calcutta;
cotton and general cargo to Manchester, ballast to Liverpool;
RAF equipment and personnel for the Pacific, and now we are
bound for Singapore.
    I have tried to give you an outline of what your good ship
has accomplished and, considering the things we have had to do
(in the way of mooring alongside a sunken ship for a wharf and
going alongside a waterboat half our own length, etc.), I
consider we have been exceptionally fortunate to escape with
just a few minor dents.
    The damage done by the grounding is not really noticeable,
the plates have all gone back into shape. There is only the
chief officer and myself left of the original crew and we would
both wish to be remembered to Mr. McLaren and his son whom I
worried quite a lot, in a friendly way, during the ship's
construction. Long may you be able to turn out ships equally as
good as this one.

                        Yours etc
                        T.L. Blair
                        S.S. Fort Astoria
                        3 October, 1945
```

Success to your Company, Gentlemen: *Fort Bedford*

This letter, dated three days later than the actual delivery date, was passed to Mr. Robertson, head of the engineering department at Burrard Dry Dock. It is in complete contrast to that of another chief engineer, quoted later. *Fort Bedford* was hull No. 161 at the North Vancouver yard of Burrard, the 18th North Sands ship to be launched there, and the 37th in terms of total output including the output of the company's south yard in Vancouver.

```
Gentlemen,
   It gives me great pleasure to inform you that I am very
pleased indeed with the work that has been carried out in the
Engine Dept. of the above vessel.
   Everyone has given me every assistance and have been most
helpful and courteous. I hope that everything will be
satisfactory when we arrive home (UK) and I will be only too
pleased to, not only show them, but to tell them, that Canada in
general and the Burrard Company in particular are doing their
very best.
   Success to your company, Gentlemen.

                    Ralph C. Annison
                    S.S. Fort Bedford
                    Chief Engineer
```

A Reminder of the Past: *Fort Brandon*

Requests for photos of ships from the builders were fairly common, but not all ships lent themselves to launching or completion photos if the weather was overcast or rainy, which was frequently the case on the BC coast. The shipyards did however have a number of good photos of each class of ship and often these served the purpose very well as each ship was virtually a duplicate of others before or since. This request was from the City Clerk, a lawyer, with City Hall, Brandon.

Fort Brandon was the next-to-last North Sands type ship to leave Burrard Dry Dock Company before the company turned over to building the Victory type ships.

```
Dear Sirs,
    The City Council has recently received a letter from somewhere
in the Mediterranean written by D.B. Davis, master of the ship
Fort Brandon, advising that the ship was named in commemoration
of the historic site a few miles east of Brandon where was
located a Hudson Bay trading post called Fort Brandon.
    The City of Brandon gets its name from this old trading post
and there is therefore a direct association between the City of
Brandon and the good ship Fort Brandon.
    I have therefore been directed by the Mayor and Council to
write to your company and express the appreciation of the
Council and citizens of this city. If it is customary it would
also be appreciated if you could send a plaque or picture of the
ship Fort Brandon, which will be exhibited in a public place so
that citizens of this City can be reminded that the ship is in
service and its valiant officers and crew are fighting our
battles on the seven seas.

                        Yours very truly
                        G.A. Hall
                        City Clerk
```

I Regret that for Security Reasons: *Fort Brisebois*

```
Jas. Robertson, Esq          21, April, 1944
Burrard Drydock Co.
N. Vancouver, BC
```

Dear Sir,

   It is with the greatest pleasure that I write to you at this
time giving a brief report on the performance of the above
vessel.

   We have had a very trouble free and comfortable passage, and
I state that I was agreeably surprised at the way this vessel
maintained her speed with such reasonable consumption of fuel,
which I am sure will compare favourably with any of your vessels
of this class. I regret that for security reasons I am unable to
quote figures, but you will no doubt receive them from the
Ministry of War Transport in Vancouver.

   This performance was entirely due to the help and assistance
I received from Mr. Baillie, of Lloyd's Register and Mr. Sid
Long, your chief engineer. By putting their liberal advice into
practice, I found things went along very smoothly, and no
trouble was experienced.

   I will be grateful if you will convey to those gentlemen my
sincere thanks and also my kindest regards to Miss Kennedy.

   In closing I thank Burrard's and all who work there for this
very fine vessel, and I assure you that if I am ever asked to
come over for another, I shall do so with the greatest of
pleasure. So wishing you God's speed — my kindest regards, I am
Sir,

```
               Yours faithfully
               W. Renwick Adam
               Chief Engineer
```

Understandings of security varied greatly, but to refuse to reveal daily fuel consumption seems to have been stretching matters, particularly as Burrard had already built a number of comparable vessels and probable already knew what to expect. Some respondents only identified their vessel by its yard number which seems to have been a more reasonable precaution. *Fort Brisebois* was hull No. 204 and a Victory type ship.

Nothing Worked Except the Funnel: *Fort Cadotte*

This ship was Hull No. 159 in the Burrard sequence. The following letter is addressed to "Shamus," believed to have been the writer's pet name for Mr. James Robertson. The name indicates a warm, but probably spirited friendship between the signatory, a Scottish engineer, and Mr. Robertson. Today the engineer would have been called a nitpicker. Once again Alberta coal comes in for criticism. It seems evident, too, that the engineers gave help to the firemen. This might have been because of the poor coal and the need to burn more of it, but the writer also refers to sickness.

21st April, 1943

Dear Shamus,

   Just a wee note with no excuses this time. You will have heard from other sources, how we have got on, sort of fair to middling (Tyneside), might have been worse and could have been much better. Not too bad considering, but quite a bit of it came out of the Chief Engineer's skin. The Alberta coal was filthy, it has heat in it but it takes some getting out and about 2½ hours of the watch is taken up in heaving ashes. They ought to "stuff it" grain by grain. Seriously though, it would not be too bad if there were only some lumps to get the fires away. It actually takes about 1½ hours to build up the clean fire to anything like decent working order and we have loads of trouble with the trimming. We have 5 trainee firemen out of 12 and 3 of the others are "lead swingers" so it has been a lively time for the engineers. Do not pay too much attention to the figures given for "consumption" as I have not been able to keep the bunkers as I should have liked them, but I have shovelled more coal than I have done for a 'ellofatime.

   It's a pity they (the North Sands ships) are not all oil fuel and we might have done something. By the way I had a grand time in Vancouver and want to return. How about it?

   I have not very much to say about the job, two main check valve covers gave out, the feed heater joints and the main condenser door joints would not hold Alberta coal and numerous other joints had to be hardened up. We had the air pump out in Alberni because of a rattle, the after bilge pump suction valves came adrift. We had to stop to harden up the low pressure slipper guides and this is now 20/1000" slack. The high pressure is also kicking up a bit of a din. The starboard feed pump chamber is in a badly scored state. Taking it all in all, it might have been worse!

   I'm not satisfied with the superheat we are getting as there is only about 540 degrees average with mixing valves shut and

```
all auxiliaries on superheat. The feed heater also leaves a lot
to be desired. Cheerio, I'll be seeing you.
                          Yours truly
                          Alan Nairn


    P.S. What I said about the propeller in Vancouver still holds
good. Someone wants to remeasure the pitch as continuous
negative slip would appear to me to be absurd.
```

Someone penned the following notation on the bottom of the letter: "I guess the funnel was O.K. as he doesn't mention it!"

VI Flying Bombs and a Torpedo: *Fort Gloucester*

Most letters dealing with a ship's performance were received by the shipbuilders from captains and chief engineers. In this instance the ship's manager on behalf of the Ministry of War Transport, Messrs. W.A. Souter & Co. Ltd. of Newcastle, England, responded with an unusually detailed history of *Fort Gloucester*. Souter was a well-known and respected tramp operator in business until the 1980s. The ship was awaiting repairs in 1944, after her torpedoing when the managers were contacted by the builders.

```
West Coast Shipbuilders
Vancouver, BC


Dear Sirs,
   This ship was torpedoed in the English Channel when returning
from North France where she had discharged a cargo for the
invasion forces. There was no loss of life. The torpedo struck
in No. 3 hold and water entered both No. 2 hold and the engine
room. She remained afloat and was towed to the Thames, where
she was beached. A drydock was not immediately available, but
when she was docked it was found that the engine room and
boiler room, including generators, were covered with a heavy
deposit of mud and the damage was severe — there being a gaping
hole on both sides of No. 3 hold.
   Engines, boilers and generators were thoroughly cleaned and
temporary repairs made with bolted plates and various forms of
strengthening. She then proceeded under her own power to the
Tyne. Repairs, when started are estimated to take three months.
```

Regarding the war experiences of this ship, we have relied upon the reports of Mr. A.C.S. Oliver, chief engineer from August 1943 to August 1944. He says the ship's first cargo was discharged in London and then she was detailed for service in the Middle East. She took on a number of Canadian troops at Sunderland and proceeded in convoy to Malta, arriving just in time to see the first units of the Italian fleet surrendering. She discharged in Sicily. For the next ten months she shuttled regularly between North African, Sicilian and Italian mainland ports carrying troops, stores, tanks, munitions and petrol.

During the whole of this period, the ship behaved splendidly. We were never delayed, loading or discharging cargo through failure of deck machinery. The main engines and boilers were everything that could be desired, running sweetly and never giving a moment's trouble. Ports visited in this period were Syracuse, Augusta, Naples, Brindisi, Taranto, Bari, Alexandria, Bone and Bizerta. Troops carried included Italian, British, Canadian, New Zealand, Australian, South African, Indian and Polish.

The Gloucester then loaded phosphates for London, where the crew was paid off and the ship drydocked to be fitted for "Special Operations" which proved to be the invasion of Europe. A new volunteer crew was signed on, among them being many of the old crew.

While loading in London the first V1 flying bombs appeared, and when ready for sea, one of these bombs landed 20 feet from the ship's bow and damaged the deckwork and bridge. After speedy repairs the ship sailed for Normandy. Although hounded by E-boats, she arrived at her allotted beachhead, anchored close inshore and discharged cargo into lighters. She returned to London for another cargo with flying bombs coming thick and heavy. Quickly loaded, she again left for Normandy and discharged her cargo. It was on the return voyage that she was torpedoed, at 3 a.m. on 18 August, 1944.

Yours etc.
W.A. Souter & Co. Ltd.
Newcastle-on-Tyne

The Alberta Coal Won't Cake: *Fort Caribou*

The thermal capacity and steaming qualities of coal varied the world over. There had been a steady demand for Vancouver Island coal for ship bunkering purposes since coal was first mined there. But presumably the demand for this coal on the North Sands type ships then being turned out by West Coast yards could not always be met. Alberta coal was probably mined by a different method using large boring-type coal cutters which ensured that the coal would be produced as a small granular product containing a lot of dust.

5th June, 1943

Mr. J. Robertson
Burrard Shipbuilding Yard
North Vancouver, BC

Dear Sir,

As promised I am writing to let you know of this other of your new ships.

Our average speed down has proved to be 10.5 knots on a consumption of 35 tons per day. The weather the whole way has been ideal, with light winds and slight seas and we should have done much better, but owing to the very poor steaming qualities of the Alberta coal supplied it has proved impossible. The coal is so small it will not cake and drops through the bars, requires $2^1/_2$ to 3 inches of fan and there is a high percentage of ash — 21 per cent, or nearly $7^1/_2$ tons per day. The tubes are blown every second night, nevertheless, the steam goes back, sometimes to 130 lbs. Our average is only 175 lbs for the passage.

The firemen are a fairly average lot and could keep steam with decent coal. I am not impressed by the chief engineer. He means well, but is out of his depth here.

We are beginning to settle down in our new ship and I trust she will be a lucky one.

Please give my sincere regards to Mr. Blackie and accept the same yourself. I trust to see you all again in the not too distant future. I remain,

Yours truly,
P.W. Sutherland
Master

A Letter of Thanks From the Chief: *Fort Dease Lake*

Thank-you letters were the commonest type of correspondence received by the shipyards. Here a chief engineer couches his letter in plain, straightforward, courteous English.

```
Mr. James Robertson                    May, 1943
Burrard Dry Dock Co.
N. Vancouver, BC


Dear Mr. Robertson,
   A few lines to let you know how the job has behaved to date.
Well, it is a pleasure to be able to say that everything has
gone well so far and we have had no major troubles of any kind.
I am very pleased with, and proud of the ship, and congratulate
the builders and all concerned. There is only one item not quite
satisfactory, that is the low pressure top end brasses. We have
adjusted them twice since taking over and once again they are
knocking like "L". They seemingly are soft and wear quickly. I
intend to fit the spares at the first opportunity. This is not a
big item, but it's all I can find to grouse about!
   I must thank yourself and staff for the help given us at
Vancouver, and I hope to return some day and look you up. In
the meantime we will do our best to get "over there" and deliver
the goods.

               With kind regards,
               Sincerely yours
               George S. Lee
               Chief Engineer
```

Under Heavy Attack: *Fort Glenora*

This ship, Hull No. 119 at West Coast Shipbuilders, like many others of the Forts served well and steadily as a typical workhorse. This optimistic letter indicates a master who was confident and happy with his ship. Just maybe, if ships have a soul and some think they do, *Fort Glenora* was just as confident and happy with her master. Captain Arundell took over command of the ship at Barry Dock, South Wales following her maiden voyage.

Fort Glenora is one of my favourites, as I find her a very good seaworthy ship and one that is excellent to handle. I am probably a little superstitious but she seems a very lucky ship.

The Glenora made her second voyage to North Africa and, after discharging, did six trips between Egypt and the Italian war fronts, carrying tanks, vehicles and troops, the latter including New Zealanders, Polish, South Africans, Indian and British. Then to Sierra Leone to load with ore for Cardiff. This was a trying trip for we were under heavy air and submarine attack, but managed to get through without being hit.

Then came a full cargo of reconstruction material for Archangel, again under heavy attack. We returned with a cargo of pit props for Newcastle. Next a load of shells, stores, bombs, tanks etc. from Sunderland to Italy, discharging at Reggio which at that time, was only six miles from the enemy front. [After that] we took on a cargo of ore for Newport, Monmouthshire. Following, were commercial cargo to Cochin and Bombay; ballast to the River Plate to load foodstuff for England but, during loading, orders came to prepare the ship for the invasion of Malaya, but V-J arrived. It was decided, however, to complete the schedule and the Glenora was the first ship to enter Port Swettenham, Malaya, after the Japanese capitulation. Then to Madras and Sumatra.

In her short, but splendid career, Fort Glenora has been in every battle front from North Russia through the Mediterranean to the Far East. I don't blame you for having an interest in such a fine ship as I must say that I have spent two and a half very happy years in her.

Captain G. Arundell
S.S. Fort Glenora
Calcutta, India
25 October, 1945

David Spencer's Bread Kept Well: *Fort Halkett*

Hull No. 150 was built at Burrard Dry Dock's South Yard. This whimsical, profusely mellifluous letter from the master of *Fort Halkett*, was written just seven and a half months before she was torpedoed, SE of Pernambuco, Brazil, Aug 6, 1943.

```
Clarence Wallace, Esq.                    22, December, 1942
Director
The Burrard Dry Dock Company Ltd.
North Vancouver, BC
```

Dear Sir,

The Good Book says, "It is more blessed to give than receive, -Cast thy bread upon the waters, etc" and here am I at the receiving end, so to speak, rubbing my hands in glee and blessed contentment and, bidding all benevolent folk welcome to every benefit their liberal giving entitles them.

To your kind curly-haired yard superintendent, Mr. Robertson, the most agreeable person one could meet, in fact so much of a gentleman that he would not even disagree with his mother-in-law, the writer suggests some thanks were due to the builders of this fine vessel.

But the writer being modest and reticent refrained from incommoding you by calling at your office, where his eyes undoubtedly would have expressed his thanks better than mumbled words, so writing must be resorted to.

Writing however, means work and there is nothing more abominable than work to a merchant navy man at present.

Now kind Sir, I beg leave to thank you most heartily for this grand ship, for the library supplied us, for the picture framed, for the trial luncheon, afternoon tea, refreshments and cigars and all other things known and unknown.

For our wonderful, air-conditioned provision store, stocked with an abundance of good eats like David Spencer's, [now a part of Eaton's] whose paper-wrapped bread supplied at Vancouver kept soft, good and wholesome for 14 days, for the most lavish supply of stationary, office equipment, charts, books and instruments.

For the friendliness extended me by your knowing office engineer superintendent Mr. Blackie, for the nice lunch, sheaf of "lettuce" and for warm wishes concerning ship, her crew and my humble self.

Indeed this is a grand boat, good for 11 knots loaded and probably more. Here are some performance figures.

```
Cape Beale to Panama Examination Station:
17 days, 14 hours and 09 minutes
Distance 4,095 miles, Av. Speed 9.7 knots
Zigzagging not allowed for
Daily coal consumption 33 to 34 tons
```

Soundings reveal no leaks in tanks and bilges, but a leak was found in the after peak where a hole had been left in the brass drainpipe. On the main deck on the starboard side abreast of the galley there is no deck scupper, but luckily enough Mr. Robertson gave us one on the port side so at least one side of the deck gets drained.

The chief engineer is very much troubled with the feed pump, he has had it all apart twice and to-day states he would need a new pump. Luckily he has more than one pump.

I wish you all the compliments of the season.

> Yours very gratefully
> O. Paulsen
> Master/S.S. Fort Halkett

Torpedoed off Normandy: *Fort Kaskaskia*

There were two short hauls which employed substantial numbers of the Fort ships while the need lasted. These were North Africa to Sicily and then Italy, and southern UK ports to Normandy. So little credit has been given in war histories to these ships and their crews, for their constant devotion to duty, when they repeatedly went back into the dangers of the front line to supply the Allied armies. *Fort Kaskaskia*, a Victory-type ship, was no exception as her master's report attests.

```
    The officers and crew of the S.S. Fort Kaskaskia are
extremely pleased with the way the accommodation has been fitted
out and, in their opinion she is a very fine ship.
    The Kaskaskia made her first voyage, in the Pacific, without
mishap and was then detailed to take part in the invasion of
France, taking troops and motor transport to Normandy beaches.
She made six successive trips to the beaches. On one of these
she took over part of the 2nd Canadian Division and I can assure
you, your boys were very pleased that a Canadian-built ship
landed them on the shores of France.
    Returning from Normandy on July 31, 1944, the Kaskaskia was
torpedoed by a German E-boat. The torpedo struck right in line
with the divisional bulkhead between No. 2 and No. 3 holds on
the port side, exploding in the hold and causing great damage.
The two holds filled up to 'tweendeck level and one of the
portable hatch beams went right through the engine room
bulkhead, through the starboard settling tank and out the ship's
side. Fortunately it was possible to keep the engine room dry
and she steamed at four knots in this condition to a safe
anchorage in England.
    Repairs were carried out by the Swan-Hunter yard on the Tyne.
Forty-nine new plates were fitted and half of No.2 and No.3
bulkheads were renewed. New fore and aft bulkheads were fitted
in this region.
    Those who built Fort Kaskaskia can be justly proud of the
part she played in helping us all to Victory. Kind regards to
all those at West Coast Shipbuilders Ltd., from all those on
board. I send personal greetings to Mr. McLaren and "Lang mae
his lum reek."

                    Captain V. Scott
                    S.S. Fort Kaskaskia
                    Newcastle, New South Wales
```

Shuttling in the Mediterranean: *Fort Maurepas*

This North Sands type vessel, fifth in sequence at West Coast Shipbuilders, evidently led a trouble-free, constantly exciting, dangerous, but charmed life throughout the war. The master's report follows.

> The interest you are taking in vessels built [at your yard] is very much appreciated. A ship becomes almost like a human being to those whose duties it is to control her destinies against the furies of the elements. To find a fellow interest on the part of builders is as pleasing as it is unusual. However, you are, after all, the mother of the dear old girl, while I am merely the anxious husband.
>
> Fort Maurepas first loaded lead, zinc, salmon and lumber in Canada for Manchester and then shuttled between Mediterranean ports with guns, ammunition and food. She took part in the landings on Sicily and was in the thick of it at Syracuse, where considerable damage was sustained by shrapnel and the explosion of an ammunition ship nearby. Repairs were made at Malta and completed in September, 1943, so she was able to take part in the 'fierce onslaught at Salerno.'
>
> After more shuttling, the Maurepas loaded iron ore at Freetown for London. Transferred to the Sea Transport Service, a cargo was taken on at Tilbury for Italy, during the voyage the ship survived several air and U-boat attacks. Thence to Baltimore, USA, for a full cargo of military stores, planes, explosives and foodstuffs for Karachi, India.
>
> There followed a lone trip, without convoy, from Bombay to Rio de Janeiro, via Durban and Cape Town, with many alarms and anxious moments. Thankfully, there was no contact with the enemy.
>
> From Rio to Freetown and Cardiff; to St. John's Newfoundland and back to London just in time to take part in V-E Day celebrations. Then Fort Maurepas was the first ship to cross the Atlantic without convoy, but we nearly came to grief on an iceberg. However, we managed to steer clear of the darn thing by a mere 100 feet and arrived at Montreal unscathed. We were fortunate to arrive in New York just in time for V-J Day celebrations.
>
> Thus, after six long and hard years of war and deeply conscious of many a lost shipmate, we humbly thank God for our own deliverance and now look forward with heartfelt relief to once again sailing the seas in safety and peace.
>
> Captain J.F. Champion
> S.S. Fort Maurepas

When a Locomotive Enters the Saloon: *Fort Slave*

The weather conditions could be atrocious for any ship, but when ships are trying to keep station in convoy, often with unusual and heavy deckloads, the conditions could indeed be frightful. Fortunately in this instance the ship that was affected by a runaway locomotive was not *Fort Slave*. This ship was actually commanded by two brothers, one in succession to the other, and both make their comments. Captain R. Storm took command at Hull, England and was master from August 1943 to July 1945.

At Hull we loaded for North Africa with tanks, ammunition and army stores. While loading, we had a near miss from a bomb that damaged the upper deck structure. From Italy we proceeded to Philadelphia in ballast to load steel and lumber for Hull. Then to Sunderland to load for North Russia, experiencing very bad weather near Iceland. The Slave came through with nothing worse than damage to a boat deck and fittings and one of the tanks came adrift, but several other vessels had to return to England. One Liberty vessel was fractured, another had a locomotive through the saloon and quite a number of ships lost lifeboats. Only about two thirds of the convoy continued the voyage beyond Iceland. Submarines were encountered at North Cape but only three vessels were lost. The Slave delivered her cargo at Archangel and returned to Leith with lumber.

At Leith the vessel was fitted out for "special operations". The aft 'tweendecks were fitted to carry 600 troops and all holds were ballasted and floored ready for vehicles. On D-Day, 500 troops and 150 vehicles were taken on at Tilbury and three days later they were safely landed on Normandy beaches. In all, eight trips were made from the Thames to the beaches during the landings. Fort Slave experienced a little of everything, E-boat attacks, shelling in Dover Strait, other vessels nearby blown up by mines and near misses by flying bombs.

In August the Slave was sent to the Tyne to have extra fittings removed and bow damage repaired, and by December, she was taking stores to the continent for civilian relief.

I trust it will give you and the men who built her, much satisfaction to know that Fort Slave has emerged unscathed, after playing a worthy part in the European war zone. Her running efficiency has been a tribute to West Coast Shipbuilders, as at no time were there any major difficulties experienced beyond normal repairs.

Captain R. Storm
S.S. Fort Slave

Captain Raymond Storm took command of the ship in July 1945, and he responded with these comments:

```
    From my own experience of the ship I find her very
satisfactory, quite sound in both hull and engines and I do not
think there has been any structural fault in her. For a ship
built under war conditions, she shows a very high standard of
workmanship with very sound fittings.

                         Captain Raymond Storm
                         S.S. Fort Slave
                         H.E. Mundy & Co. Ltd.
                         London Agents
```

A More Formal Response: *Fort Wallace*

This ship was a Victory type built in North Vancouver. Evidently she was trouble-free in all regards. Quoting from a letter received from Lambert Brothers Ltd., London, the managers appointed by the British Ministry of War Transport, prominent Vancouver shipping manager, Mr. F.C. Garde was pleased to pass their comments along to Burrard Dry Dock Co.

```
                                           May 23, 1944


Dear Sirs,
                        S.S. Fort Wallace

    In connection with the above vessel built in your yards and
turned over to Messrs. Lambert Brothers for operation, we
thought you might be interested in the following extract from a
letter dated April 2nd:
        "The vessel has arrived here safely after an uneventful
        voyage with no stoppages or troubles of any kind. Both
        Captain James and Mr. Foster and the other engineers
        are very pleased with her, as also is our
        superintendent who has made a preliminary examination.
        She certainly appears a fine ship."

                      Yours truly
            EMPIRE SHIPPING COMPANY LIMITED

                        "F.C. Garde"
                        Manager
```

CHAPTER SEVEN

The Park Steamship Company Limited

T he Park Steamship Company was incorporated by the Canadian government in 1942 as a Crown corporation. Its stated purposes were to own, manage and operate ships allocated to it for the purposes of the war. It gave the Canadian government a more focussed role in the control and allocation of its shipping, which certainly could not be assured once ships had been transferred to Britain, as happened with all the Fort ships.

Many of the Park ships were launched with Fort names, as if the intended purpose was to transfer them to Britain, but as noted in Chapter 6, this did not always happen, and a Park name was then allocated. Once a ship was completed for Park Steamship, the practice at all times was to allocate management to a shipping company or agency with an established reputation in the shipping business. Thus in Vancouver, for example, Anglo-Canadian, Empire Shipping, North Pacific Shipping and

Canada Shipping Corporation, all of whom represented different lines at Vancouver before the war, had ships allocated to them. Their own businesses had differed considerably, from liner agency representation to tramp chartering work, but after the war the four came together in forming the largest west coast company, Western Canada Steamships Limited. The shipping subsidiaries of MacMillan & Bloedel and the Seaboard organizations, Canadian Transport and Seaboard Shipping, managed certain ships, as did Johnson Walton Steamships Ltd. and Kerr Steamship Agencies.

On the east coast Canadian Pacific and I.H. Mathers Ltd. of Halifax, and the long established Canadian subsidiaries of the British companies — Furness Withy and Elder Dempster among others — were also allocated ships, but they remained Canadian Park vessels and were not mixed in any way with the large fleets of owned and managed

Stanley Park. After management by Elder Dempster, this ship like the majority of the North Sands coalburners went to companies dominated by London-based Greeks. The liner companies wanted Victory or Canadian type oil-fired ships and quickly re-equipped with these superior vessels as soon as the Park fleet became available for purchase. (S.C. Heal)

ships which the parent companies ran from their British headquarters. In a similar way Canadian-Australasian Line, a concern based in New Zealand and controlled jointly by Canadian Pacific and the giant P & O Line, had ships allocated to them which they managed from Vancouver in the Transpacific trades to Australia and New Zealand.

The thirteen 10,000-ton tankers had allocated managers such as Imperial Oil, British American Oil and Shell Oil, which saw to their employment, mostly in the oil trade from South America to ports around the Caribbean and to the east coast of Canada. Whereas management allocations of the Fort ships were easy to record, as the British practice was to note the manager of the individual ships in *Lloyd's Register*, Park Steamship (so far as can be determined) never officially announced the name of the allocated manager, so the mention of managers above is neither exhaustive nor specific. We merely know that certain companies, if they had the ability and infrastructure available, took on management functions.

As with the British, the Canadian managers had responsibility for hiring crews from the manning pools and finding suitable officers, which was often not easy, as well as looking after supplying the ships with all necessary fuel, stores and supplies. They had little if any control over the routing of the vessel or the allocation of cargo, as war materials had preference at all times. However, it is believed that they did in reality have more control over surplus space than their British counterparts since Canada had a net outflow of cargoes, particularly lumber, grain, fertilizers and metals which were in continuous demand, and finding space was probably easier as the Park Ships were not engaged in the total war which employed many of the Fort ships from the time of North Africa, Italy and through Normandy and beyond.

An examination of the manifest of *Green Hill Park*, at the time of her explosion and fire, tends to bear this supposition out. There was certainly plenty of war materiel on board, but much of the cargo was normal commercial or civilian in nature, which

Mission Park. A Victory type takes to the water following a perfect launch at Victoria Machinery Depot in 1944.   (BC Archives F-09704)

THE PARK STEAMSHIP COMPANY LIMITED

Earlscourt Park. A West Coast Victory type, managed from Vancouver. Even before the Japanese war ended, ships unlikely to find themselves in a Far Eastern war zone were being stripped of armaments. Except for the bridge gun positions, all gun tubs, the stern and bow guns and net booms have gone. One wonders why the life rafts remained.

(World Ship Society)

Brentwood Bay Park.
Of the Victory ships built by Victoria Machinery Depot, five including this ship were completed as tankers.

(BC Archives H-05386)

Leaside Park, the subject of a light-hearted story in this chapter about running low of fuel at Labuan, North Borneo. The ship is painted in the colours of Park Steamship Company pending disposal to Western Canada Steamships.

(Ian Stewart Collection)

Arlington Beach Park. A dead ship awaiting a tow in the North Pacific. Built as a Victory tanker, all but two of the twelve sister ships and one North Sands tanker were converted to dry cargo ships after the war. Suspended between big waves with less flotation amidships puts a considerable strain on a hull, particularly when the weight of engines, boilers and bunkers are taken into account and weight is not evenly distributed. This can result in a broken back.

(Rob Sheret)

Arlington Beach Park. Now named *Mills Trader*, the broken-down vessel appears to be sliding downhill towards the stern of a Seaspan tug readying itself to rig a towline for a tow into Vancouver.

(Rob Sheret)

Eglinton Park. Park Steamship Company had six of these handy-sized Lakes tankers built which were managed by oil companies. The ship appears to be fresh out of the builder's yard, but half a century later the prominent trunk deck over the cargo tanks seems unnecessary. Carrying the main deck out to the extremities and eliminating the trunk would have created more deadweight capacity for little extra cost and some small increase in draft.

(Milne, German & Gilmore)

Cypress Hills Park. Liferafts and guns are all in place aboard this brand-new Victory tanker. Note the heavy-duty pipeline and gate valve for stern loading or discharge. The torpedo nets appear to be in place, ahead of the liferafts ready to hoist to the head end of the boom.   (BC Archives F-09702)

Seven Oaks Park. By July 1945, the merchant ship-building program was almost at an end. This ship was the last from Victoria and only one, *Gaspesian Park*, remained for completion at Prince Rupert. Any other remaining were for the Royal Navy and the Fleet Train. This was launching day with runners crew standing by and spectators waiting on the dock.   (BC Archives F-09699)

suggests that her manager had considerable leeway in the booking of cargo for Australian consignees. Return voyages to Canada also saw much civilian-type cargo being carried as the space was available. For example *Beaton Park* on her return maiden voyage carried coal to Montevideo from South Africa and then loaded among other cargo a large consignment of hides from Montevideo to Los Angeles. Obviously, the hides were being acquired for the manufacture of leather which could have been for military boots or civilian purposes. Likewise *Mount Robson Park* (1) returned with raw sugar from Suva consigned to BC Sugar at Vancouver, while *Mount Robson Park* (2) was diverted on her return trip from Australia with grain for Peru and from there the ship loaded concentrates for American consignees in the Columbia River. These were all typical trades in which the steamship agencies at Vancouver had considerable experience.

In general Park vessels were somewhat less exposed to the hazards of war than the Fort vessels. An examination of the official British list of all British and Commonwealth war losses, which included many instances of torpedoings, bombings, minings, etc. resulting in partial losses of the vessels, contains no Park ship. Fort and Ocean names appeared frequently on the other hand (see Chapter Six), reflecting the hard nature of the warfare in which they were engaged.

There was an exception to this observation in the case of a number of the 4,700-ton vessels. In all, 14 were transferred temporarily to British articles for employment in the Normandy campaign. The ships with their long cargo booms and relatively shallow draft were ideal for beaching on the long flat beaches of Normandy, where between tides, discharge of cargo could be undertaken directly into vehicles driven out across the sand. Two of this group, *Avondale Park* and *Taber Park* became war losses, and are detailed later in this chapter.

Tipperary Park. Spray breaks over lumber cargo on deck. The view towards foremast and bow was taken from the bridge while in a rolling Pacific sea in 1944.   (E.K.(Ted) Bain)

Tipperary Park. Foaming water from a boisterous sea runs along the main deck to flush overside through a washport with the next roll of the ship. A safety catwalk is in place rigged from the boat deck to the lower bridge deck as a precaution against heavy seas which could flood these flush-decked vessels with an enormous volume of water. View from aft side of the bridge takes in the port lifeboats which are rigged outboard.   (E.K.(Ted) Bain)

The lesser exposure to the war zones was not a matter of policy to shelter the Canadian ships. Instead, they were logically and heavily employed on two vital routes, one from North America to Australia, New Zealand and Fiji, with cross-trades to the West Coast of South America and the other to South and East Africa, India and Ceylon via the Cape, with cross-trades to Argentina, Uruguay and Paraguay.

On the Australasian route there were no Park ship losses, although at one time there were plenty of indications that the Japanese advance into the Solomons, which was turned back at Guadalcanal, would have interfered in a very serious way with this vital route. It would then have been more difficult to prevent Australia and New Zealand from being isolated. On the second route there had been considerable German U-boat activity with the larger long-range Type IX submarines. It was on this route that *Jasper Park* and *Point Pleasant Park* were lost to submarine attacks.

Ships returning from these routes found that they were often diverted to South American ports to load return cargo, as in the above examples, after delivering South African coal in the cross-trades to Uruguay or Argentina, or Australian grain or flour to the east coast of South America. Coal was one of the few bulk cargoes available to returning ships from South Africa, and at the time South American railways and power stations depended heavily on imported coal. Their most usual supplier had been South Wales, but with the extra demands of the British war effort, there had been a reduction in coal exports from the British Isles.

When the war ended Park Steamship Company had a total of 176 vessels on its books, which the Canadian government had determined to dispose of as quickly as possible. Four vessels had been lost from enemy action and three were classified as total or constructive total losses. *Silver Star Park,* was an arranged total loss, having suffered sufficiently serious damage to be written off by Park as not being worth the major repair job required.

The war losses were: *Avondale Park, Jasper Park, Taber Park, Point Pleasant Park.*

The only partial loss from war causes that can be found was *Nipiwan Park.*

In this case the entire forward half of the vessel was lost, as the result of torpedo attack, but the ship was evidently deemed worth repairing, possibly on account of the fact that her type, a handy sized Lakes tanker, was in short supply.

The marine losses were: *Green Hill Park, Mount Douglas Park, Silver Star Park, Westbank Park.*

After the war, the fleet was disposed of as rapidly as possible. At the end of 1947 War Assets Corporation announced that the entire fleet had been sold, but this was not quite true as the remaining 28 Park North Sands ships were turned over to the British Ministry of War Transport, for sale or for time chartering to British operators. By dealing with these ships in this way, it enabled Park Steamship Company to be wound up, ownership of the vessels being then vested in the Canadian Maritime Commission. This was probably a more convenient arrangement, with the vessels' ultimate sale being on behalf of the Canadian Maritime Commission which had absorbed Park Steamship Company in 1948.

Tipperary Park. Looking aft from bridge at a point almost on the centre line of the ship. Aft netbooms can be seen with the funnel superimposed between. A variety of cowl ventilators surround the funnel with one small mushroom ventilator visible to starboard of the galley coal bunker with the galley stovepipe in front of the funnel. The ladder gains access to the top of the funnel under the cowl. The fitting high on the starboard side of the funnel is rigging for an aerial, while the steam-organ pipe whistle is to be seen above the stovepipe.   (E.K.(Ted) Bain)

The Voyages and Final Loss of *Mount Douglas Park*

Contributed by the late John Hetherington, MM of Vancouver, BC

In March of 1943 I was in Glasgow, Scotland having just obtained my Chief Officer's certificate of competency. I contacted Canada House in London and arranged a transfer from the British Manning Pool to its Canadian counterpart. Being a Canadian national, born in Vancouver, the British had no choice but to release me to control of the Canadian Manning Pool. Canada House arranged my passage from Liverpool to Halifax. On May 8, 1943, I married my fiancée in Montreal and boarded the train

for home, spending the first four nights of our honeymoon in the lower berth of a Pullman.

On June 11, 1943, I signed on as second mate of the brand new North Sands freighter *Mount Douglas Park,* under the management of Canadian Transport Company, the shipping arm of H.R. MacMillan. The ship was lying at her builder's, the False Creek yard of West Coast Shipbuilders. We loaded a full cargo of 5,500,000 fbm of random length loose lumber, which included 900,000 fbm on deck stowage, which seemed like a lot until one compares it with modern bulk carriers which can stow the full cargo of a North Sands ship on deck alone.

After four solid years of North Atlantic convoy work, I was excited to learn that we were slated to make several voyages to Australia, travelling independently. After loading lumber at Vancouver and Chemainus, followed by coal bunkers at Union Bay, we completed our lumber cargo at the old dock in Cowichan Bay. Our 'tweendeck space was packed with picrite and amenol, both high explosives from James Bay, a fact I was able to conceal from my wife. She and I were able to spend a couple of days together at the old Buena Vista Hotel, now long gone, at Cowichan Bay, thanks to an understanding "Old Man". He was ancient to me then but was several years younger than I am now.

The Navy in its wisdom routed us to Sydney by way of Port Lyttleton, New Zealand, for coal bunkers. On the way across the Tasman Sea we streamed and tested our submarine nets. This was a slightly hair-raising experience for our green crew.

After a slow discharge in Sydney and Melbourne we steamed along the South Coast to Port Adelaide for a full cargo of 9,500 tons of sacked wheat for Callao, Peru. The stevedores in Adelaide referred to lumber ships from the West Coast of North America as "Oregon boats", because the Douglas fir that we exported was marketed locally as "Oregon pine." Marking off lengths of lumber for sorting purposes was done with ropeyarn and whitewash.

After discharge of the Australian sacked wheat we loaded lead and zinc concentrates for the Tacoma Smelter. The Australia, Peru, Puget Sound/BC triangle was particularly lucrative for H.R. MacMillan Export Company. Steaming times were long on each leg of the journey. Typically it took 29 days from Vancouver to Australia, Australia to Peru required 31 days, Peru to Vancouver 21 days, but each leg involved a full freight-earning cargo.

After completing two such round trips in *Mount Douglas Park,* I left this ship to join *Tecumseh Park* as chief mate.

AUTHOR'S NOTE: Unfortunately there is no known archival collection for the period of about three years, 1946-1949, when Canadian Transport functioned as a manager of Park Steamship vessels and as a shipowner. More broadly, these would have dealt with the intricacies and details of ship operations in the years while Canadian Transport was owned by, and functioned as the ship management and chartering arm of H.R. MacMillan Export Company or its successors.

Mount Douglas Park was one of 28 remaining Park Steamship Company North Sands vessels which were turned over to the British Ministry of War Transport in exchange for the return of the surviving 28 Victory ships that had been bareboated to the British during the war. The British managers appointed by the MOWT under their standard management contract were Hall Brothers Limited of Newcastle-on-Tyne, one of the smaller but well respected British tramp companies. Hall Brothers sent out a British crew to Vancouver to take over from Canadian Transport and fix the vessel for the first voyage under their management. There is no record of the voyage charter into which the new managers entered, so conjecture now plays a part.

As she had been under the management of Canadian Transport Ltd. and bearing in mind that they were thoroughly familiar with her, it is quite probable that her first employment was to load a lumber cargo for H.R. MacMillan Export Company for Singapore and Indian ports, and it would have been from Singapore that the vessel proceeded through the Straits of Malacca. Following discharge of the last of her lumber cargo Hall Brothers would have planned to place the ship into general tramping in keeping with their regular business.

No one aboard would have thought that this was to be the ship's last voyage as she came out of the Northern end of Malacca Strait to go ashore on Preparis Shoal in the Andaman Islands on August 19, 1946. However, an attempt has been made to fix more precisely a position for the wreck, taking into account Canadian Transport's trading pattern for its ships. While the war was in progress, the first two voyages on a triangular run, Vancouver/Australia and New Zealand/Peru with return to Vancouver were typical.

Once the war was over the Canadian Transport ships ranged farther afield, as will be confirmed by Captain Hetherington's account of the round-the-world voyage of *Harmac Victoria* later in this chapter. In 1946 Canadian Transport acquired six, ex-Park Steamship vessels, four of the oil-fired Victory type and two of the Canadian type, which could be optionally fired by coal or oil. None of the Vancouver owners were to purchase any of the coal-burning North Sands vessels, and undoubtedly *Mount Douglas Park* was slated for return to Park Steamship as the newly purchased ships were integrated into the fleet. They were not necessarily available for immediate service as there is evidence that considerable refitting was done to the vessels with new longer booms and some rearrangement of accommodation etc, as happened with *Harmac Vancouver, ex-Cromwell Park* which is detailed in Chapter 12.

By her wreck position 14.48N, 93.43E, it seems reasonable to suppose that *Mount Douglas Park* was on a voyage from Singapore to Calcutta or vice-versa, as this route would have taken the ship through either the North or South Preparis channels. These channels were separated by the Preparis Islets which formed the top of a reef of the same name roughly midway between the Coco Islands to the south and the southwest tip of Burma. The Coco Islands are really a part of the Andaman chain as also is the Preparis group, but carry the different name as they are, like the Preparis group, Burmese territory.

The light on Great Coco Island is what a ship would have been guided by if taking the South Channel route. The Preparis Islands did not have a light but the reef has a considerable extremity to north and south. The presumption is that the master chose the North Channel route to save a few miles, whereas the South Channel route would have been the better choice as the islands to the south were fairly high and the light on Great Coco was a positive factor. As the monsoon season was in full bore, *Mount Douglas Park* was also probably hampered by poor visibility and miscalculated her proximity to the north end of Preparis Reef. In the event she cut a little too close and went aground, August 19, 1946 at the position given above. Whether there was any attempt at lightening the vessel and towing her off the reef or whether there was any post-loss salvage is not known. According to crew records at the time of the ship's last sailing from Vancouver earlier in 1946, the master was 26 and the chief mate 24 years of age.

The Loss of *Jasper Park*

Contributed by Jim Butterfield, Lt-Commander, RCN(Ret'd), of Victoria, BC.

On returning to Canada after the war, Second Mate Jim Butterfield joined the RCNR. He was appointed to HMCS *North Bay* as navigating officer and spent the last two years of the war on the mid-ocean convoy runs from Newfoundland to the UK. After the war he transferred to the RCN, retiring with the rank of Lieutenant-Commander in 1967 after a rewarding naval career. In 1987 after 20 more years of sea service he retired once again from the British Columbia Ferries where he had been senior master on the Northern service from Vancouver Island to Prince Rupert and the Queen Charlotte Islands.

The North Sands type steamer *Jasper Park,* was under the management of Furness Withy (Canada) Ltd out of Montreal and under the command of Captain Malcolm Buchanan, a Scotsman and a resident of Vancouver. The ship sailed in convoy from Halifax for the United Kingdom, on September 29, 1942, with a wartime general cargo which was duly discharged at Liverpool.

A full cargo of miscellaneous war supplies for India was loaded and the ship was routed in convoy, via Freetown, West Africa. However, before clearing Western Approaches, an attack by the Luftwaffe caused some anxiety with several near misses, so the convoy route was changed to proceed to Halifax where it arrived early in January, 1943. Several personnel changes took place aboard *Jasper Park* at that time, among them the chief officer and second officer. The new chief officer was a Dane from the Merchant Navy manning pool. As the new second officer, I was a replacement for Charles Brown, who had joined *Bowness Park.* I was from Vancouver and had served my time for second mate with the Canadian Pacific Empress liners.

The ship sailed again in convoy on January 16, a day that began quietly as the convoy formed up. By noon it had begun to blow and by 1400 hours, a full gale and high seas were responsible for the complete dispersal of all the ships in the convoy. *Jasper Park* made great efforts to remain afloat and limped through the Cape Cod Ship Canal to find a safe haven in Hoboken, NJ where she remained for three weeks making repairs. Among other problems an 18-inch seam had opened in the hull under a boiler, and as a wartime expedient. the double bottom tank was filled with cement without having to discharge cargo.

At the human level, the new chief officer who had joined the same morning as me, while at Halifax, was acquainting himself with his new ship before relieving the bridge for his watch at 1600 hours. It is believed that he stepped out on deck at the wrong moment, having probably come up the escape hatch from the steering compartment. The flush weather deck, covered with ice and snow was being raked by heavy seas and it is presumed that he lost his balance and went overboard. All that was ever known of the incident for certain was the finding of his cap frozen hard up under the deck of the port side of the after docking bridge. A young man: it was indeed one of the tragedies of war. None of his shipmates had a chance to say hello, or to enjoy a meal or a smoke together.

The replacement for the chief officer was George Cookson, like me, an "old Conway," who had survived the First World War, and had lived for many years in Canada. He had returned to sea to do his bit for World War Two. We were to learn that he was a cousin of Anthony Eden, a fact of which he was justly proud, and at age 19 he had been a mate of a large wool clipper to Australia. The third mate was Joseph Drapeau, a former St. Lawrence River pilot, who had already lost one ship under him in a convoy on the North Russia run to Murmansk. The senior engineers were Furness Withy company men as was the chief steward. The senior radio officer was Al Davis from Beamsville, Ontario. Altogether the crew numbered 46 men, including the three DEMS gunners.

Jasper Park sailed from New York the third week in February, 1943. She proceeded independently most of the way. We arrived in Calcutta, the final port of discharge, early in May. The homeward journey was begun towards the end of the month having loaded a small quantity of jute, plus chests of tea loaded at Madras, Colombo and Cochin on the Malabar coast. The latter port was cleared on June 22, and again we proceeded independently, this time for Durban, South Africa.

On July 5th, a matter of 13 days later, *Jasper Park* was some 640 miles south of Madagascar, when the story of the few final days commences. It was the normal practice for the 'crowsnest' lookout up on the foremast to report to the watch officer on the bridge after handing over to his relief. On this occasion a bright-eyed Canadian lad named Jack Sharkey reported at 1600 hours that he had been watching a vessel on a steady bearing, hull down on the port bow, making intermittent small puffs of smoke. From his higher position he was certain that he was looking at a positive submarine sighting. The sub, if that was what it was, was underway on the surface running on her diesel power.

There was never a clearer afternoon at sea and indeed from time to time the smoke could be seen from the level of the bridge, which information was duly reported to Captain Buchanan. Arrived on the bridge, however, the master was unable to see the submarine and the report was disregarded. Some hours later on this very dark night, the seaman lookout on the first watch (2000-2400 hours) reported sighting a torpedo track close in crossing the bow from port to starboard, followed a few minutes later by an explosion off to starboard. When this man called me at 2345 hours for the middle watch (midnight to 0400 hours), he told what had transpired and advised me to be sure to wear my lifejacket. This good man had had the misfortune to be in several Royal Navy ships which had been lost to enemy action, resulting in his discharge on medical grounds. He had, of course, reported the above circumstances to the officer of the watch who could not corroborate anything that had happened. I was given to understand that the captain had been informed, but again, given the source of this "sighting," it was considered too unreliable and was again disregarded. At approximately 1110 hours (ship's time) in the morning, *Jasper Park* was hit by two torpedoes.

At this time the chief officer and myself were overhauling the deep sea sounding machine on the starboard side of the weatherdeck, just forward of the break of the bridge superstructure. I have a confused impression of suddenly becoming a part of a loud explosion. Seconds later, regaining full consciousness, I found myself just inside and hanging on to the port side bulwark guardrail — a quantum lateral displacement across the upper deck of approximately 65 feet. Mr. Cookson too was thrown about and was later found to have five broken ribs in addition to other injuries. The first torpedo hit the starboard side just forward of where we had been working, abeam of No. 2 hold and the second torpedo struck further aft, abeam of the boiler and engine room, killing the fourth engineer, a fine young Englishman, and six firemen on watch below.

Jasper Park's back was broken and both lifeboats on the starboard side reduced to matchwood by the explosion. The submarine captain's war diary was later found to agree with the ship's sinking position as given in the attack report, i.e. 32 degrees, 52' South and 42 degrees, 15' East. I was to learn later that the ship's guns had been reported as being unusable, the starboard Oerlikon on the bridge having been shattered by the explosion and the training ring of the 4-inch gun aft was jammed. After the attack the ship's code books were reported as being disposed of in the official manner.

By the time I had worked my way aft, the two port lifeboats had already been manned by the surviving crew and lowered to the water. With the possibility of being underway in open boats in the days ahead, I recovered my sextant and Norrie's Tables from the bridge and checked my position. Returning to the embarkation ladder, I called out, "Pretend this sextant is a baby, and be sure to catch it!". This was, of course, too much to hope for and the box containing the sextant was smashed on hitting the bottom of the boat. However, the instrument survived and is still in my possession in good working order in its original repaired box, defying the accepted axiom that a sextant is a delicate precison instrument.

The one surviving member of *Jasper Park's* crew who was inadvertently left behind until it was too late was Jasper, the ship's mascot. A wire-haired terrier, he knew his shipmates so well he had the "hot bunk routine" worked out to perfection, i.e. he would shift his sleeping arrangements from the bunk of the seaman just coming off watch to the bunk of the seaman just going on watch with uncannily accurate timing and he could climb vertical ladders with extraordinary skill.

Jasper Park took about fifty minutes to sink, but while she was going down the boats pulled clear of the ship and set about relieving the rafts of their emergency rations, provisions and fresh water. These rafts were stowed in special fittings on the fore and mainmast shrouds, that broke loose as the ship was sinking. While this was being carried out, the submarine was seen surfacing in the midst of hundreds of chests of tea which had floated free when the ship's hatches burst.

The submarine was *U 177* whose captain ordered us alongside. I scrambled on to the casing with a bow line from where I fended our boat off to prevent damage and contemplated the dismal possibility of a trip to France as a guest of the German government. The captain, Kapitän-Leutnant (Lieutenant-Commander) Robert Gysae, asked in halting but adequate English about the ship's identity, tonnage and her destination. He also asked if anyone had been badly injured. From his war diary we were later to learn he was not particularly impressed by the survivors as, "there were mostly deadbeats" in the two boats. Somewhere in the German Admiralty archives film footage exists which was taken from the conning tower, which could doubtless confirm this statement, as not one of the surviving crew in the boats could really be said to be looking their best. They were dressed in various bits of working clothing within an hour of losing their ship. One cannot forego the chance to comment that *Jasper Park's* only positive action on July 5th, was to be present when the good news (quite unbeknown to us), was received that the submarine captain was promoted Kapitän-Leutnant. By all accounts he was a fine officer.

On pulling clear of the submarine, the boats made sail and course was set for the African coast.

During the night the wind came up and the temperature went down so it was quite cold. When we cast off from the submarine the survivors were asked to surrender any matches, cigarettes, knives and possible candies about their person, to the coxswain in the sternsheets for equal sharing as might be required later on. This proved to be unnecessary as we were greeted by the welcome sight of two Australian destroyers, *Quickmatch* and *Quiberon,* the next afternoon. They took on board the survivors from both boats and continued north to escort a troop convoy, returning to Durban some days later.

After several days on the beach and a trip in the deluxe Blue Train to Cape Town, via Johannesburg, *Jasper Park's* crew were returned to the UK in the flagship of the Shaw Savill & Albion Line, *Dominion Monarch.* From the UK the Canadian members of the crew were later embarked in *Cavina,* a banana carrier of Elders & Fyffes Lines. We sailed for Halifax with Convoy ONS 18, in September, 1943. During this crossing the Canadian destroyer *St. Croix* and the two smaller RN escorts, *Polyanthus* and *Itchen* were lost, as well as six merchant ships.

Kapitän-Leutnant Gysae went on to sink the American Liberty ship, *William Ogden,* on July 10, 1943. He eventually returned to France after a six-month patrol, during which six Allied merchant ships with a total tonnage of 47,000 gross tons had been sunk. His performance and daring were commended by the German Flag Officer (submarines) and he went ashore to command a U-boat training flotilla on the Baltic. He survived the war but remained a prisoner until 1947.

Captain Malcolm Buchanan was given command of another Park ship and once again had Mr. George Cookson as his chief officer.

Summary of Report from the War Diary of Kapitän-Leutnant Robert Gysae, Commanding Officer of U 177, concerning the sinking of *Jasper Park*. Translated from the German by Jan Drent, Commdr. RCN (Rtd).

U 177 was one of the large 1800-ton Type IXD submarines with a displacement more than twice that of Type VII, the type most commonly deployed in the Battle of the North Atlantic. These large submarines had an endurance of 23,700 miles which enabled them to roam as far as the Indian Ocean. By early July, *U 177* had been at sea for just over three months. At the beginning of the month she operated within sight of the southeast coast of Madagascar and then moved steadily south.

Kapitän-Leutnant Gysae was 32 years old. He had been a member of the 1931 Naval Academy intake and had been in submarines since 1940. Gysae had commanded a type VIIC before taking over *U 177* on commissioning in March 1942. He was an 'ace' having been awarded the Knight's Cross in December 1941 and Oak Leaves in May 1943.

When conditions permitted, *U 177* flew her Bachsteize, a helicopter kite which carried an observer aloft as high as 150 metres. The submarine first sighted *Jasper Park's* funnel smoke at 1240 on July 5, 1943, and then stalked the target for almost 22 hours before sinking her the following forenoon. In fact the commanding officer started to position himself ahead on the surface for an attack as soon as he sighted the freighter. The submarine's war diary noted that the coal-burning *Jasper Park* was belching smoke copiously. The positioning manoeuvre took some four hours and by that time the C.O. had decided that it was growing too dark and he dived for a twilight attack.

However, it proved impossible to see enough of *Jasper Park* through the periscope and *U 177's* passive sonar broke down so this attack was also broken off. The submarine surfaced and positioned herself for another attempt. Two torpedoes were fired at 2125 (2225 ship's time) from a range of approximately 1,000 metres. One track was seen to be making directly for the target but missed. The other torpedo was a dud and sank soon after leaving its tube. Later that watch a radio message was received promoting the commanding officer to Kapitän-Leutnant.

U 177 again attempted to position herself ahead for an attack on the surface during darkness, but was unsuccessful. Eventually it was decided that the sea was too calm to avoid detection while closing.

At daylight on July 6, it was calm and clear with a slight swell. The submarine dived at 0857 for a submerged attack and fired a spread of three torpedoes at 1005 (0810 GMT). The submarine was keeping German time, the ship's time in *Jasper Park* was 1105. The periscope was immediately housed because the sea was so flat, but the hits were heard in the boat. Gysae raised his periscope and established that the freighter had been hit twice forward. The victim's torpedoing report was then heard by *U 177's* radio and the submariners noted that the position given coincided with their navigational plot.

The ship was to sink by the bow and her boats were at water level, but when she had not disappeared almost an hour later Kapitän-Leutnent fired a *coup de grace* after satisfying himself that there were no further survivors on board. He then surfaced at 1118 for a gun action, but heard loud sinking and breaking-up noises, so he closed the ship's lifeboats instead, observing tea chests from burst hatches floating in the sea as the ship was sinking.

AUTHOR'S NOTE: Captain Buchanan could have been termed a character. Now long dead, he is not forgotten by those surviving who sailed with him. Long on boorishness and short on good manners, he evidently combined arrogance with stubbornness in his dealings with juniors whom he usually regarded as inferiors. He is remembered in two more accounts of events in this chapter. He also appears in print in the prewar account of voyages in the steamship *City of Vancouver*, in the book *Full Line, Full Away* by James E. Wilson and S.C. Heal.

It is easy to be critical in hindsight, but Captain Buchanan's disregard of two warnings of possible impending U-boat activity against his ship seem inexcusable. The ship was provided with anti-torpedo nets, which were not used, and had standard merchant ship armaments, none of which guaranteed her

safety. She could have also been placed on a zig-zag course and the crew at least alerted. In the hands of a more determined master the ship might have given a better account of herself. Clearly, any warning from a lookout, no matter how tenuous, must be taken into account by the officer of the watch and anyone else, including the captain, who bears responsibility, but the lookout's word should not be dismissed by the master, as evidently happened.

The U-boat commander commented on the heavy smoke given off by *Jasper Park*, and the fact that this was what first alerted the submarine to her presence over the horizon. This was probably unavoidable as the ship last coaled at Colombo where large stocks of Bengali coal were available. This coal was well known for its dirty burning qualities, lower thermal capacity and a tendency to give off tell-tale heavy smoke. It was used regardless because it was cheap and available, and ships in regular Indian trade had grates fitted which better utilized the coal.

Kapitän-Leutnant Gysae was clearly a careful, painstaking officer who was not going to take any chances even with an unescorted merchant ship. The expenditure of five torpedoes in two attacks seems a high price to pay for one merchant ship, although admittedly the first two were evidently faulty. There is a mention in the war diary of administering the *coup de grâce* to the sinking ship which presumably referred to a sixth torpedo. Mr. Butterfield has no recollection of hearing or seeing the explosion of a further torpedo while the crew sat in the boats. The submarine was then going to surface to use her deck gun, but this proved unnecessary as the noise of the ship breaking up as it went down was apparent.

A final point: seven ships of 47,000 gross tons total in a six-month cruise seems to be a very low yield. However, it should be kept in mind that these long-distance submarines operated as far east as Penang in Malaya, and mainly attacked the substantial number of unescorted ships in the Indian Ocean and South Atlantic. Troop convoys were to be found between Australia, South Africa and the Middle East through Suez. The pickings could be few and far between for single ships and might well have involved widespread cruising to find prey. It was clearly a different war to that involving the many large convoys crossing the North Atlantic.

The Loss of *Taber Park* and *Avondale Park*

The author is indebted to Fraser McKee and Robert Darlington for permission to quote the details on these two war losses from their book, *The Canadian Naval Chronicle.*

The Gray/Scandinavian 4,700-ton sister ships *Taber Park* and *Avondale Park* were among 14 of this class which were taken up under charter by the British Ministry of War Transport for the invasion of Normandy. There was a role for handy-sized ships such as these. With their relatively shallow draft they could be taken in on a tide and allowed to dry out close inshore, where cargo could be loaded into wheeled or tracked vehicles using the ship's gear.

As the war in Northern Europe progressed they proved useful reducing the congestion at the country's major ports, as they could be turned around at smaller British ports. They could also use the many smaller ports on the North European coast which were not readily available to the bigger classes of ships.

Even though the ships were manned by British crews, they were evidently not transferred to British registry with management passing to individual British shipping companies, as occurred with the Fort ships. The chartering arrangements appeared to have been conventional time charters, but with the British undertaking manning. Who actually undertook management is not recorded as it was not the practice of the registered owner, the Park Steamship Company, or the time charterer, the British Ministry of War Transport, to undertake direct management of the ships owned by them or under their control. It seems logical to suppose that actual management was handled by British companies prominent in the European coastal trades, such as The Clyde Shipping Company Limited, Coast Lines Limited, General Steam Navigation Company Limited, Stephenson Clarke Companies Limited, Constants (South Wales) Limited and William Cory & Sons.

Following Normandy, the ships were employed in almost any trade suitable for short-seas trading. Both ships had sailed on their last voyages from Methil on the East Coast of Scotland, roughly midway between Edinburgh and Dundee. While there is no note of the cargo being carried in each instance, Methil was an outlet for coal from the Fifeshire coalfield, so it can be assumed that both were carrying full cargoes of coal. McKee and Darlington report as follows:

> *Taber Park* was sunk when in coastal convoy FS-1753, Methil to the Thames. In March of 1945, in a last ditch effort, the German Navy sent out two groups of miniature *Seehund* two-man-crew U-boats designated Type XXVIIB. They were true U-boats, unlike many of their counterparts in the Kleinkampverband that were little more than manned torpedoes. They were to sink nine merchantmen between January and 28 April, when their operations ceased. *Taber Park* was one of these unfortunate nine. The crew was British, and twenty-four crew and four DEMS gunners were killed; only four were saved. Some sources indicate the ship was mined, but Kleinkampverband records are quite clear, for that crew reached home safely to report.

The date of loss for *Taber Park* was March 13, 1945. *Avondale Park* was lost May 7, 1945. McKee and Darlington reported on this latter vessel's loss in the following terms:

> *Avondale Park* was the last British ship to be sunk in World War II, two miles southeast of May Island in the Firth of Forth. In convoy EN-91, bound from Methil for Belfast, she sailed during the 7th and was torpedoed at 2240 that evening by *U 2336*, sinking by the stern within ten minutes. Although fitted with a 4-inch gun and five Oerlikons, *Avondale Park* was unable to use them as the U-boat or her torpedo tracks were not seen. The torpedo hit on the starboard side between the engineroom and No. 3 hold, destroying the starboard lifeboat. Rafts were released but some jammed in their rails. Of the 39 British crew, four RN DEMS gunners and three Maritime Regiment RA gunners, the chief engineer and one donkeyman were lost. Survivors were picked up by a convoy escort.

The war ended two days later.

Some Captains I Have Known

Contributed by Bill Hutcherson, Wireless Operator, Richmond BC

Although I served in only five Park ships, these same vessels were commanded by ten different captains. Even though my job as wireless operator placed me in close contact with the captain, I find it remarkable that of the ten different men, only four come readily to mind. Frank MacQuarrie is remembered for his down-to-earth ways and his booming voice; Frank Stewart for his drinking habits, and in my view his incompetence; J. Stott for his impatience and lack of courtesy and Charles Alltree, as a gentleman and a complete master mariner. The other six remain faceless and un-noteworthy, not for a lack of competence, but probably because of aloofness.

It seems to have been a fact that in many ships the man in command regarded it as a point of weakness if he showed understanding, courtesy, friendliness, or anything else which might have been typed as the milk of human kindness. Some shut themselves up on the bridge as if they occupied a fortress against their own officers and crews, only appearing when they must for noon sights and usually at mealtimes. What they did with their time when shut away was always a good question. The worst performers in this regard were those of the so-called "old school." The younger, newer skippers had usually been brought up in a different and broader tradition who saw us young "upstarts" as being closer to them in age and for them fraternization was the rule rather than the exception.

Charles Alltree alone will forever stand out as a seaman's skipper — the type in whom you could place the fullest trust, in his ability to bring both ship and crew safely home, while at the same time being able to enjoy his genuine friendliness. You always knew who was in command and no one I ever knew tried to take advantage of his outgoing attitude.

Captain Charles Alltree.
An old tradition was observed aboard many ships when, for Christmas dinner, the officers waited on the sailors. Here Captain Alltree, full of good cheer, dispenses a tot to one of the deckhands, aboard *Lake Sicamous, ex-Weston Park*.
(Wm. Hutcherson)

Incidents on a Voyage: Refuelling *Leaside Park*

Contributed by Dick Wilson, M.M., of Vancouver, BC

I was chief mate at the time in early 1946 when *Leaside Park* left Vancouver bound for Singapore, via Manila in the Philippines, and Labuan, North Borneo, with a full cargo of relief supplies. The late Captain Alf Hailey was in command. After leaving Manila we passed down the slow steamer passage skirting the north coast of Palawan and thence North Borneo. The voyage was uneventful except that on arrival at Labuan we knew we were short of fuel and without bunkering facilities at Victoria, the port and capital of Labuan, we could have been in some trouble.

Actually it was only a short hop across the mouth of the Gulf of Brunei to the Shell oilfields at Miri, but whether they could supply us or even if they were back in production at that time I do not recall. It was and still is a fact that royalties from this immensely productive oilfield have made the Sultan of Brunei one of the richest men in the world.

On enquiry we found that there was a small coastal tanker beached inshore having evidently been run aground by the Japanese in their hurry to evacuate the place which had been subject to much Allied bombing of both the town and Japanese shipping in the area. In fact everything had been flattened, the only building to survive being a church. We were told that the tanker was loaded with oil, which was the case when we opened the tank tops, but how much was water and how much oil was the next question.

Being an old tanker man I coated a sounding rod with syrup and got a clear reading on the oil and water levels when we dipped. I found that there was about two feet of water at the bottom of each tank and the rest was good bunker oil. In the meantime our engineers found that the General Motors (Jimmy) diesels with which she was fitted could be started. With these providing power to her pump we were able to clear the water from the bottom of the tanks so that the vessel actually floated free.

A nearby US Navy tug offered a hand and put a huge coir towing hawser onto the tanker and placed her alongside *Leaside Park*. When the Japanese abandoned the tanker they burned off all the valves. This created a problem for us. How were we to make a connection and pump off oil into our own tanks? Not expecting anyone to do any more than I was capable of, I waded into the tanks which were quite small, and with oil up to my armpits and armed with a heavy pipe wrench I managed to open the valves so that the pump suction could deliver all the oil we could take to our ship, which was refuelled at no cost to anyone.

The little tanker was interesting. The GMC engines indicated she might be of American origin perhaps having fallen into the hands of the Japanese when the Philippines was captured by them. The US Navy tug was the biggest vessel in the harbour and her captain appeared to be in charge of everything although the place was still then a British possession. I asked if we could remove the tanker's engines and take them with us. He replied that he had a better idea and would sell us two brand-new Jimmy diesels that had never been unpacked from the crates.

I replied that I had no money so he suggested I might be able to trade for liquor. I said, "Leave it with me, I'll see what I can do." I spoke with Captain Hailey who had two 40 oz. bottles of Seagrams V.O. he could spare. With these the trade was done and the two new diesels were loaded on board and stowed below, still in their packing cases and with all the original sealings still in place.

With one for the captain and one for me, the sequel to the story ended in North Vancouver. The customs came aboard and pointed to the diesels. I told them they had been brought back for repair. That satisfied them so after all formalities were complete I found a buyer for my diesel at a very good price. What Captain Hailey did with his I never did find out.

Friendly Rivalry: *Beaton Park* and *Winnipegosis Park*

Contributed by David Martin-Smith, M.M., retired BC Coast Pilot of Victoria, BC

The *Beaton* and the *Winnie*, as they were popularly known, were not only sister ships in every respect, but had been completed about three weeks apart at the end of 1943. The first was a product of Burrard Dry Dock Company, North Vancouver and had been launched as *Fort Mackinac*, and the second was built at Prince Rupert Dry Dock Company as *Fort Aspin*. There was an even closer connection as many of the components used in the Prince Rupert ships were supplied from Burrard's own manufacturing facilities. Burrard itself was the biggest merchant shipbuilder in Canada with two yards of its own and connections with Yarrows in Victoria. As such it helped some of the smaller yards.

Both ships left Vancouver within days of each other destined for a virtually identical maiden voyage, through Panama, around the Cape of Good Hope to South African ports and then across the South Atlantic to Montevideo and Buenos Aires. From South Africa they then went southabout, around the southern tip of South America and up the West Coast of the American continents and back to Vancouver. We sailed independently from Vancouver to Panama and then joined a smaller convoy from there to reach a common convoy assembly point at Trinidad where we joined an American convoy.

The Trinidad convoy conference, made up of US Navy officers, ship masters, some second mates like myself as the ship's navigator, and the senior wireless operator in our case, proceeded ashore. Here we met Captain Ritchie of the *Winnie*, her chief wireless operator and the DEMS gunnery officer, a navy sub-lieutenant. Ritchie conveyed an icy reaction when we were introduced which was a little puzzling considering I had never met him before, but then on the other hand I was hardly surprised as his response was typical of many masters of the old school when being introduced to lowly colonial upstart mates of junior age.

After the conference adjourned, the two masters, Buchanan and Ritchie, left the rest of us to our own devices as we were to stay ashore overnight, rejoining our anchored ships in the morning. We spent a convivial evening together and were then boarded overnight in a barracks-like building. As we had entered the tropics and warm-weather watchkeeping on the upper bridge, it became a great temptation to strip down to minimum clothing to catch some sun. I thought little of it as it seemed sensible to be comfortable, but after leaving Trinidad I received a large rocket from our good captain who forbade further sunning while on watch. I soon found out the reason for Ritchie's chilly response when introduced at Trinidad and recalled seeing two figures on her bridge watching our ship very closely through binoculars which occasionally reflected the sun. Ritchie, in the manner of a school telltale had regaled Buchanan with the results of his binocular watching of our ship. To say the very least, this unwarranted obtrusiveness, this relentless piece of meddling and gossip by another ship's master of a similar blend to ours rates as the only piece of such nonsense I was ever to run across in 46 years at sea.

When the convoy dispersed off Cape Recife, Brazil, *Beaton Park* and *Winnipegosis Park* were on their own and both ships made for their first South African port of discharge. We crisscrossed each other's tracks but finally loaded coal for Montevideo and made our way independently across the South Atlantic, always with the *Winnie* a little ahead of us.

After discharge we made our way to Buenos Aires to load linseed and compressed animal products for San Pedro. The *Winnie* was loading for Los Angeles at the same time, after Captain Ritchie had arranged an unauthorized drydocking and bottom cleaning. Captain Buchanan presumably took the view that he had no authorization for such work and we returned to our home port with all the weed we had collected on the round voyage. We proceeded south into Magellan Straits and came across the *Winnie* at anchor waiting for the weather to improve. It was like a goad to Captain Ritchie who, seeing us pass him, upped anchor and showed that he was determined to make it back to Vancouver before we did. With a clean bottom this was not hard to do.

After discharge of both ships at San Pedro, we made our way back to Vancouver in ballast for the final leg. Somehow word of a troubled voyage had leaked back to Vancouver and Buchanan lost his command. The *Beaton* had not been a happy ship so far as I was concerned, but with friends aboard *Winnie* and learning also that Captain Ritchie would not be sailing in her for her second voyage, I signed on as second mate. Ritchie was replaced by Captain "Wild Bill" W.P. Rion, a far more compatible master who had my respect. When Mr. Haines, the chief officer had to be taken off in South Africa with sickness I was offered the job of chief officer at the tender age of 21. In those days advancement was rapid if one was the right man in the right place at the right time.

Captain Martin-Smith's account of the maiden voyage of Beaton Park *is told in his own inimitable style in his book* South to the Southern Capes: The Maiden Voyage of the S.S. Beaton Park, *possibly the only published and detailed account of the travels and travails of a Canadian-flag merchant ship in the Second World War.*

Captain Bligh of *Beaton Park*

Contributed by David Martin-Smith, M.M., retired BC Coast Pilot, of Victoria BC

There are masters and there are masters. All have to know their calling as otherwise they would not last long, but there the similarity ended. My captain aboard *Beaton Park* was Captain Malcolm Buchanan, a man from the old school who at best treated everyone with a suspicious neutrality or at worst with a boorish rudeness which might have been more commonplace in an earlier age when the master of a ship was indeed master of all he surveyed, with a Godlike power, regardless of fairness, human consideration or good manners.

I knew little of his early life. It was never something he referred to. I did know that he had served as master in Coughlan ships out of Vancouver, being master of their last ship, *City of Vancouver*, and evidently was held in high esteem by old Mr. John Coughlan, who entrusted his children and their cousins to his care when they sailed as passengers in company ships with a view to gaining some knowledge of the world. That was to his credit, but might also have been indicative of his assessment of what was good for his own hide. After all Coughlan was his boss and the underlings below him were his vassals and this perhaps gave rise to a chameleon-like personality.

From the time we left Vancouver to our return from a maiden trip to South Africa and Argentina, life was one long litany of conflict and disturbance, particularly between Buchanan and myself. I had shipped out as second mate, my second appointment to this rank, at the tender age of 21 after service in the ancient Carpenter line freighter *Lansing*, and freighters of the Kingsley Navigation Company and others. Following this voyage in *Beaton Park*, I was to sail in a fair number of deep sea and coastal ships until I became a BC coast pilot, but never was I to be exposed to a floating three-ring circus such as existed aboard this ship.

One typical example concerned the chief and second stewards who had a love-tryst going on between them. To say the very least it created a bad atmosphere and at best was the subject of ribald jokes. To keep our captain's blind eye turned in their direction the two lavished all sorts of special attention to his gourmet tastes, making sure that he had a good supply of specially prepared treats delivered to his cabin each evening. In the meantime the night duty officers had to make do with the leavings, particularly when it came to a rotten chicken carcass left out for the port duty night watchkeepers. The galley and pantry were locked to everyone except the two stewards, by order of the captain, which only served to heighten the bad feeling further.

By this time I was fed up with this one-sided situation as were most of the rest of us. Regrettably, Chief Officer Cookson was of little help, as even though he was a true gentleman, he was also totally loyal to the man in command. While Cookson could see the injustice of it all he was not about to become a second Mr. Christian and lead a modern-day version of *Mutiny on the Bounty*, or should I say the *Beaton*.

The second engineer and myself harboured similar resentments so on the rotten chicken night we barged into the stewards' cabin. The second steward had abandoned his own cabin and moved in with the chief, somewhat like a favourite concubine. The engineer and myself had armed ourselves with a dispenser of molasses which we had managed to lay our hands on. As we went into their cabin there were the two of them clenched together. What with their shrieking and our threats of one sort or another we poured the molasses all over them.

The next morning there was hell to pay. Like a defiant innocent I was brought before the captain who had difficulty in finding words to describe his anger, disgust and a host of other things. If he was expecting a quiet and subservient wrongdoer to meekly stand before him with head bowed he was mistaken. I let him have it with both barrels, verbally that is, and told him in the strongest, firmest words I could find without forgetting our relative positions, just what I thought of him, and his mode of command. I took the wind out of his sails when I asked to be relieved of my duties as second mate and to be transferred to seaman rank. I was so angered and so fed up with the state of affairs aboard ship that I was quite serious and was not setting up a bluff.

Bluff or not, it called our captain's bluff with his dire threats of action so strong that it would have destroyed my career. The matter died down almost as quickly as it came to a head. Peace was restored, with the captain ultimately taking no action and giving me a V.G. on my discharge. It turned out to be not so good for him as both he and the ship's agents had their connection severed with the good ship *Beaton Park* at the conclusion of the voyage at Vancouver. In my case I could have signed on for a second voyage, but with sour memories I thought better of it and joined *Winnipegosis Park* for her second voyage. The good old *Winnie* turned out to be a far happier ship.

Meeting *Belwoods Park*

Contributed by Olive Carroll, Wireless Operator, Mirror Lake, BC

Following graduation from radio school in Vancouver I worked a brief stint as a shore-based operator with the Canadian Department of Transport. The Canadian merchant navy did not employ women afloat so a number of Canadian girls followed the lead of the pioneer, Fern Blodgett of Ontario, who had shipped out as wireless operator in June of 1941 in a Norwegian ship, m/v *Mosdale*.

Fern spent the rest of the war in this ship carrying food supplies to Britain, married the ship's master, Captain Gerner Sunde, and settled in Norway. She led the way for the rest of us and perhaps a dozen or so Canadian girls served in Norwegian ships as wireless operators. I visited Fern in Norway on the 50th anniversary of the day she signed aboard *Mosdale*. It was June 13th and a Friday. She had reason to remember a date like that!

Eventually an opportunity arose for me to ship out as a wireless operator aboard the Norwegian m/v *Siranger* of the Westfal-Larsen Line, an opportunity

I had longed for ever since starting my training.

The episode I am now recalling saw our ship moored alongside a Canadian-built vessel, the steamship *Belwoods Park* at the river port of San Lorenzo, Argentina. She was loading wheat for Haifa, Israel, while we loaded the same cargo for Gothenburg, Sweden.

Hoping to meet with fellow Canadians it was with some surprise that I found a British crew instead. The ship was under bareboat charter to the British Ministry of Transport and had been sub-chartered to the South American Saint Line of Cardiff. She was one of a group of Park Steamship North Sands ships which had been turned over to the British 'en bloc' following the war and had not been given the customary 'Fort' name.

Her good-looking wireless operator, Tom Dalzell, welcomed me aboard and after exchanging notes as fellow operators he introduced me to the captain and the other officers who were a delightful and friendly crowd. I gathered that the British official attitude to women serving aboard ship was much the same as the Canadian, although it became far more liberal later. Having a woman aboard as a fellow professional was something of a new experience for them and they made a great fuss of me. Captain Maughns, a charming white-haired Scot of 49, promptly conferred the more feminine "Sparklets" on me and that remained my nickname during the entire interlude with *Belwoods Park*.

The atmosphere aboard this ship was warm and without any visible strain and I think credit was due to the captain, a very social man, who made an effort to get on well with everyone. It was quite in contrast to our current captain aboard *Siranger*. His personality and attitude cast a pall over everything.

The officers of *Belwoods Park* threw a party for me one night and of course our chief mate, Mr. Danielsen, who could smell a party a mile away, invited himself along, as my chaperon, I suppose. I had never needed one aboard *Siranger*, so why I would need one now was a good question.

Belwoods Park was due to sail ahead of us and as she passed us at our berth, I waved to them and all officers aboard and in view, responded. I had been invited to sail down river with them and pick up *Siranger* at Buenos Aires. It was a nice idea, but I could see that it might lead to difficulties with the Argentine authorities. However, I did stay in touch by radio with Tom Dalzell who passed along a great deal of useful information about the North Sea as the ship had not been there before and we were in need of knowledge concerning certain navigational matters and aids.

Captain Maughns sent me the jolliest message before we lost radio contact. It read:

> Olive, *Siranger* — Wot'cher Sparklets! Did you know that every plane and every bus from Rosario to Baires between 27th March and 4th April was met by a mournful little man hoping to keep a date with a certain Sparklets he finally sailed away with his heart in his mouth and tears in his eyes forgotten but not forgetting.

Such was the humour of men (and women) at sea.

Ms. Carroll's account of her fascinating four years of service with the Norwegian merchant navy is told in her book *Deep Sea Sparks: A Canadian Girl in the Norwegian Merchant Navy.*

THE PARK STEAMSHIP COMPANY LIMITED

Rained Out for a Meeting Aboard *Aspen Park*

S.C. Heal

My first introduction to a Canadian merchant ship was a frustrating experience. It concerned *Aspen Park*, then newly painted in the attractive colours of Western Canada Steamship Company and lying at anchor in Hong Kong Harbour, a short distance from the cross-harbour route of the Star ferry. The ferry ran between Kowloon and Victoria, the town on Hong Kong Island and the seat of government and commercial power in the colony.

I had crossed over the previous day and had noticed *Aspen Park* and her sister ship *Garden Park*, at anchor about six ship-lengths further to the north. I had never seen these ship colours before the afternoon of that day and for that matter had not heard of Western Canada Steamships, so both vessels while being clearly Canadian Victory type ships were a mystery to me, but not for long.

That evening I visited the officers' club in the Gloucester Hotel to slake my thirst. It was a favourite watering hole for service and merchant navy officers. I stood at the bar and heard two Canadian voices behind me. After an exchange of pleasantries they invited me to join them. They were both wearing radio officers' epaulettes on their shoulders and in the process of swopping yarns it came out that they were off *Aspen Park*. They told me a fair amount about their ship and that Western Canada was one of the recently established new shipowners based in Vancouver. In the process one of them identified himself as the ship's carpenter. He readily admitted he had borrowed the radio officer's epaulettes to gain admission because as a petty officer he would otherwise not have a right of admission. Both men were from Vancouver and when I told them of my plans to settle in Vancouver after discharge from the Royal Navy we became firm pals.

I was invited to visit the ship the following day and was asked to meet their liberty boat at a certain pier at 2 pm. On my way over from Kowloon a rainstorm came on with tropical intensity. As I came off the ferry it was to step into streets which were flooded and like everyone else I sought whatever shelter I could until it had blown over. By the time I reached the pier the *Aspen Park's* boat was halfway back to the ship. Sometime that night the ship sailed and that was the last time I was to see her.

Ten years later I was the owner of a home on Capilano Road, in North Vancouver. I was driving home on a spring evening when a similar downpour to that in Hong Kong came on. As I turned the corner into my street I noticed a figure standing at the bus stop looking like a drowned rat. I could hardly pass him by so stopped the car and invited him to accept a lift. We each looked at the other thinking he looked familiar. I was the first to remember. He was Mr. Robson, the carpenter off *Aspen Park*.

Robson had left the sea and was just completing a new house on Capilano Road about a mile further up from mine. I visited him once more before he sold the house and moved down to Arizona. I still see the house when I'm in the neighbourhood and think of the visit we nearly had aboard *Aspen Park* 52 years ago.

It seems that Western Canada Steamships stripped many of the ships they acquired of their wartime gear and armaments, and repainted them before renaming took place. This might have been because they held them nominally on a bareboat charter from Park Steamship Company with option to buy. They had to find over ten million dollars of purchase money, a large amount to place into a shipping investment in those days. This covered 20 ships in the initial purchase at about a half million dollars a ship. It is known that the Bank of Montreal and Wood Gundy Limited, the securities firm, handled the financing for the original group of founding shareholders, the four local shipping agencies who started the company.

Upon renaming, *Aspen Park* became *Lake Athabasca* and *Garden Park* became *Lake Cowichan*. Captain Hill Wilson of Victoria, BC pointed out to me that my memory was faulty as in an earlier version of this story I had it that the carpenter, Mr. Robson, was off *Garden Park*. In fact I had over a period of 50 plus years switched the names of the ships. The ship I was supposed to visit was *Aspen Park* and then-Cadet Wilson had received instructions to pick me up. After waiting around for several minutes he gave up and returned to his ship.

Carrier of Navy Fuel: *Arlington Beach Park*

One North Sands ship and twelve Victories saw service as tankers. A coal-burning tanker seems in retrospect to have been the result of muddled planning, although she came out about a year before the oil-burning Victory type was developed. The Victories were built exclusively on the West Coast and of the twelve tankers, five were entrusted to Victoria Machinery Depot Company Limited and seven to West Coast Shipbuilders Limited. This report contains some interesting suggestions from M.B. Kean, a master who obviously studied the economies of messing and food handling, as well as the shortcomings of painting ship in the West Coast climate.

I take great pleasure in replying to your letter of the 8th instant, [1945]. I regard it as a most commendable gesture for shipbuilders to enquire as to how their ships are meeting requirements after so many years and months in commission.

In compliance with your request I shall endeavour to give you a brief outline of the work performed by the ship, and my opinion of her qualities generally during the period of which I have had the honour to have been in command.

On November 8, 1944, I was appointed master of this ship, relieving Captain Treweek, O.B.E.. Since that date we have been engaged for the most part in the Caribbean Sea on a shuttle service between Aruba and Curaçao, NWI and Cristóbal, Panama Canal Zone, supplying special navy fuel for the war effort.

The average full cargo capacity is 62,000 barrels, and one cargo a week was maintained up to V-E day. Since then we have been making round trips from Portland, Maine, in ballast to Beaumont, Galveston and Houston, Texas, taking full cargoes of special navy fuel to ports in the Panama Canal Zone. From there we went to Cartagena, Colombia to load crude oil for Portland, Maine, to feed the pipeline from that port to Montreal.

During all this work a perfect schedule was maintained and our arrivals and departures all worked according to plan. Naturally I feel rather proud of this accomplishment and it was achieved by the fact that the ship averaged 11.5 knots loaded, and 12.5 knots in ballast on 23 tons of bunker fuel averaging about 71 revs.

Throughout this time, the machinery was always ready when required. There has not been one stop for repairs or adjustment during a run and repairs in port at the termination of a voyage have been just about all. As a seaboat I should say she is as near to perfection as can be attained. I was provided an excellent opportunity of proving this while caught in a tropical hurricane on June 27. It was a terrible gale while it lasted, accompanied with heavy seas. She handled it admirably and came through it all without damage except for the usual loss of glassware and crockery. Her performance on that occasion was just one of those events which endears a ship to its crew. Her qualities of handling and manoeuvring leave nothing to be desired. When adequately ballasted she handles like a towboat.

With reference to the accommodation I can only say it is very good indeed. I have recommended an alteration in the messing

THE PARK STEAMSHIP COMPANY LIMITED

arrangement to make a messroom out of the forward starboard
rooms of the engineroom deckhouse. In other words, the space on
the starboard side opposite to the Chief Engineer's quarters on
the port side. This would be close to the galley, and the
firemen and seamen could be served by plate service instead of
carrying food 250 feet to the extreme aft end of the ship. This,
in my opinion, would eliminate one mess steward and save 30 per
cent on food, as under the present system, food is carried to
aft messrooms in large containers and what is left over is
always wasted overside.

The only bad feature I can report is the impossibility of
coping with the rust situation. Notwithstanding persistent
chipping and painting, the rust will come back to the surface
through everything. Why the scientists and men of the type and
brains to invent the atomic bomb cannot invent some ingredient
or alloy to put in the molten metal to eliminate rust, is a
thing I cannot understand.

The writer is dangerously near the retiring age. I have spent
45 years at sea, 35 of them as master. I have commanded many
ships in my time, of all types and qualities.

In conclusion, in order to answer your question, how do I
like my ship?, I cannot do better than add that for my few
remaining years of service I would ask nothing better than to
end my career, if possible, on the Arlington Beach Park.

To summarize on her qualities, I can cheerfully use the old
sailor's expression, "Keep her clear of the rocks and she'll
bring you home."

M.B.Kean,
Master
S.S. Arlington Beach Park

16,000 Miles–27,000 Tons: *Mewata Park*

Mewata Park broke no records, but in the way her master describes both mileage and tonnage there is a sense of pride in a job well done. In every sense the wartime standard ships were built to be expendable, but not as expendable as the original concept of the Liberty ship, which would have met its job description if it only managed to deliver one vital cargo from the US to Britain and was then sunk, destroyed or scrapped. As matters developed following the war many of the wartime standards, including the Forts and Parks, lived for a full ship life of 20-30 years giving continuous good service throughout.

June 1, 1944

Burrard Dry Dock Company Ltd.
Vancouver, BC

Gentlemen,
  I had the honour to work in your shipyard last year and I
have now the pleasure of writing to let you know I have
travelled 16,000 miles, in Hull No. 198.
  This vessel has done some excellent work and I am proud to be
in command of her. Everything has worked fine and the ship has
not lost one minute or hurt a pound of cargo of the 27,000 tons
she has carried. It is a good performance for a new ship.
  Our Chief Engineer makes the same report and the crew (mostly
local boys) like their ship.
  We have no other option but to congratulate you all on your
excellent work, and wish you good luck and good launchings.

        Sincerely yours,
        William Wood, Master
        Mewata Park

Voyaging up a Jungle River: *Moose Mountain Park*

From such records as exist, it appears that the primary function of the 13 tanker conversions of Victory and North Sands ships was to ensure that Canada's main sources of crude oil from the Caribbean areas were not disrupted by wartime needs in other areas of the world. This they did successfully by making certain that the Portland, Maine end of the pipeline to the Montreal area refineries was never allowed to go dry. Here Captain Sydney P. Chapman gives his report to West Coast Shipbuilders.

On the run from Vancouver to the oil areas of South America, fire broke out near Cristóbal, but the damage done was to the shins of the Captain, who ran against a winch in the darkness.

Arriving at Port-of-Spain, a swarthy pilot in white uniform climbed aboard, and guided the ship for forty miles upriver through steaming noisy jungle, to the oil dock at Carapito. Here the ship was turned around by the simple expedient of shoving the bow into the mud and tangled undergrowth of the river bank and allowing her forward momentum to swing her stern around in the desired direction. Next, an even dozen of haphazardly uniformed Spanish-speaking officials descended upon the ship in a manner that can best be described as 'locust-like'. The process of cementing friendly relations with this delegation all but exhausted the supplies in the ship's bonded liquor stores.

Crude oil was pumped into the ship's tanks at 10,000 barrels per hour, the total cargo being 62,000 barrels. The Moose then pulled out for Portland, Maine.

Although considerable difficulty was experienced by some ships in the convoy in maintaining proper distances from ships in line ahead or either side of them, the Moose had no such difficulty due to the extreme sensitivity of the throttle, which enabled the engineers to increase or reduce the speed of the ship at will, to within one half of a revolution of the propeller per minute. This quality was the subject of many approving remarks by deck officers and engineers in this convoy and on all subsequent convoy voyages.

The Moose continued this same trip during the remainder of the war, and returned to Canada in September, 1945, for drydocking and removal of armaments, this being done at Halifax. She was then painted in peacetime colours of black hull, white upperworks and red funnel with black top, and is now making the run between Portland and Covenas, Colombia, with the regularity of a West Vancouver ferry.

Four of the original crew of 40 remain. They think they have been fortunate to serve aboard such a ship as Moose Mountain Park, and they are reluctant to give up a good berth.

Captain Sydney P. Chapman
Moose Mountain Park
25 November, 1945

Mistaken for the Pilot Boat: *Mount Bruce Park*

This vessel was the first of the seven Victory tankers completed by West Coast Shipbuilders Limited at Vancouver. She was placed under the management of British-American Oil Company Limited, of Toronto. Like most of her sisters she was heavily engaged in the shuttle service to and from the Caribbean oil areas to keep the Portland-Montreal pipeline full. The response to West Coast came from the company's marine manager, who obviously took an enthusiastic interest in the ship and her crew.

The Mount Bruce Park is a fine substantial ship, and a great credit to West Coast Shipbuilders Ltd. With Portland, Maine, as her home base, the Bruce made ten trips to Venezuela and one to Texas City. We are particularly proud of her master, Captain Donald M. Murphy and her original crew all of whom were taken from Great Lakes boats owned by B-A Oil.

On her first voyage [after leaving the builder's yard] the ship ran into bad weather off the Farillon Islands, but she rode out the gale and barely moved a dish from the table. On the second voyage Mount Bruce Park was the "Commodore vessel" of a 21-ship convoy. The port of Carapito, Venezuela, visited on the third voyage, is 45 miles up the San Juan River and, while the river is deep, it is so narrow that it is frequently possible to jump ashore from the ship. Officers on the bridge had to be alert to avoid being knocked down by overhanging trees. On the return trip, bad weather was encountered off Cape Hatteras and the ship took an awful beating, the starboard motor lifeboat and davits being carried away. After the fourth voyage the ship drydocked at New York for painting and repair.

On voyage No. 8, the record shows that an average of 11.07 knots was attained, with more than 12 knots some days. Voyage No. 9 was undertaken without convoy, but a hurricane struck near Norfolk, Virginia, which beached a nearby tanker and two destroyers. Although the wind reached a velocity of 90 miles per hour, Mount Bruce Park rode it out successfully with both anchors and eight shackles of chain down and the engine working at full or half speed ahead with the ship steered to prevent dragging too badly. On this trip out of Cartagena the vessel was damaged in collision with a large Norwegian tanker which had mistaken our "pride and joy" for the pilot boat!

A member of the crew was lost on voyage 10. In very heavy weather a door leading to the crew's quarters stove in and flooded the cabins. While shoring up the broken door an A.B. was washed overboard and never seen again. The storm lasted three days — the waves reaching over the crowsnest. The ship steered well even though hove-to.

Captain W.G. Smith
Manager, Marine Department
B-A Oil Co. Ltd.
Toronto, Ontario

Collision and Fire off New Bedford: *Silver Star Park*

On April 12, 1945 this ship was in collision with another vessel off New Bedford, Massachusetts, which resulted in 16 crew fatalities and extensive structural damage. Towed to New Jersey for repairs, she was then disposed of from the Park fleet.

For all practical purposes *Silver Star Park* was a constructive or "arranged" total loss following her collision and the subsequent devastating fire. As noted in Chapter 5, the Park Steamship Company did not insure its vessels in common with the practice on other government property. The question faced by Park at the time concerned whether the vessel could be economically repaired and placed back in service, or whether the cost of repairs would have exceeded the vessel's fair market value. No matter how the numbers may have been added up, it seems certain that Park did not feel it to be worth the time and trouble to repair the ship and, as with *Green Hill Park*, she was offered for sale on an "as is, where is" basis. She became a Brazilian Navy vessel and was one of the only two of this group to spend all her service life as a tanker.

The collision report received by West Coast Shipbuilders follows. There was no indication as to its origin, but it seems to be an excerpt from a marine surveyor's or Lloyd's agent's report.

The *Silver Star Park* was run down by a ship called the *Mangore*, being struck on the port bow just abaft the collision bulkhead, at an angle of about 45 degrees. The colliding vessel penetrated to the magazine which exploded, setting fire to the oil released from No. 1 port tank. Some of this oil was showered all over the ship by the impact and the balance ran out and caught fire all around the ship, especially the port side.

The heat set off the after magazine which in turn, set fire to the after accommodation. The bridge house is completely destroyed by fire and is very badly buckled over. The engineers' quarters, etc. are also totally burned out.

There is however no damage to any of the winches or to hatches and hatch coamings. In fact the paint on them has not been damaged.

The ship discharged 95 per cent of her cargo of Venezuelan crude oil with her own equipment after the fire burned out.

Her lifeboats and rafts were totally consumed. The engine and pump rooms were not affected in any way and the hull from the 28-foot waterline is perfect.

The repair means taking off about 20 feet of the bow down to the 30-foot waterline. This is because it was drawn back by the impact and slightly set up. The first two strakes on the entire port side have also to be renewed as they are corrugated by the heat. The deck on the after crew's quarters has also to be renewed as it is buckled due to the fire in the crews quarters. When on drydock, however, the hull did not show the slightest sign of distortion.

Work has been started and is expected to take 90 days.

CHAPTER EIGHT

The *Green Hill Park* Disaster

PART I
Her Last Voyage and the Explosion

The narrative of events is contributed by George Conway-Brown, a retired Air Force officer, now resident at Blind Bay, BC. Mr. Conway-Brown was an ordinary seaman, age 16 when the events he relates took place. He sailed with *Green Hill Park* on her last globe-girdling voyage and was an eyewitness to the fateful disaster of March 6, 1945.

My merchant navy career path leading to the *Green Hill Park* disaster commenced in 1942, about midway through the war. I had just turned 14 and I landed my first real job, working for the Union Steamship Company of BC out of Vancouver. My first ship was the S.S. *Catala*, a 1476-ton passenger-cargo ship that ran from Vancouver to Alaska, serving various ports en route, including the air base at Bella Bella, Prince Rupert, and several others. It was an exciting time for me as a teenager, because the ship was operating under wartime conditions, including radio silence, black-out during hours of darknesss and it was painted wartime grey. We even carried a navy gunner, armed with a Lewis gun, to provide very questionable protection against Japanese submarines.

The following year, in 1943, I was again employed by Union Steamship as a crew member aboard the steamships *Lady Pam*, *Lady Cecilia* and *Cassiar*. The latter was running from Vancouver to the Queen Charlotte Islands when I heard of a ship signing on crew for Australia. I went to the Shipping Master's office in Vancouver where I was approached by a tall man dressed in a business suit and wearing

a fedora hat. He asked if I had any experience. I told him about working for the Union Steamship Company and he signed me up immediately as a crew member in *Green Hill Park*. He did not even question my age. I had just turned 16. I discovered later that the man in the hat was the ship's captain and he was desperate to enlist a full crew. Subsequently, I learned that his extensive experience at sea included years in sailing ships, before the steam engine swept them from the sea.

I joined *Green Hill Park* at the Burrard Dry Dock shipyard in North Vancouver, where she was in drydock receiving underwater repairs and maintenance. This ship had been built at Burrard Dry Dock in 1943 at a cost of $1.6 million and she had already made one ocean voyage. She was owned by the Park Steamship Company, a Crown corporation, and the ship's agent was the Canada Shipping Company with offices in the Marine Building, Vancouver.

The only training I received was in gunnery, a very short course given by the Royal Canadian Navy on the operations of the 20mm Oerlikon gun and the 0.5 Browning machine gun, the primary anti-aircraft armament fitted on the Park Steamship vessels. For practice, we fired at a drogue that was towed by an RCAF Anson aircraft at a gunnery range off the coast of either Sea Island or Lulu Island, near Vancouver. After each exercise, the drogue was dropped for inspection. It usually survived with only minor wounds, and very few bullet holes. On the ship my actual combat role was the position of loader with the 4-inch gun crew, manning the main armament that was fitted at the stern of the vessel. I seem to recall that the shells weighed about 40 pounds each and my job was to stuff them into the breech. The gun crew positions required more training and higher skill levels. Those of gun layer, gun trainer, and breach operator were all positions manned by navy DEMS crews.

When we sailed from Vancouver, we paused off William Head, just south of Victoria to load ammunition. A Navy lieutenant came aboard and tested our guns. We then made our way to San Pedro, California, to take on fuel. As often happened, we did not have the opportunity to go ashore. We set out to cross the Pacific Ocean alone, but took the usual wartime precautions such as operating under strict radio silence, blackout during hours of darkness and sometimes we streamed out our steel anti-torpedo nets.

Dragging these nets through the water reduced our speed from about ten down to eight knots. Periodically our normal routines were interrupted by emergency exercises when called to action stations. For a brief time we would create quite a commotion and a lot of racket by firing at some unfortunate enemy target that the ship's carpenter had constructed from scrap canvas and lumber and thrown overboard.

Green Hill Park was armed with six independent 20mm Oerlikon anti-aircraft guns, one 4-inch surface gun at the stern and a single 12-pounder gun at the bow. We also had an anti-aircraft multiple rocket-launcher fitted above and just forward of the 4-inch gun deck at the stern of the ship. I don't know how effective the rockets were in scaring off attacking enemy aircraft, but they were extremely effective in scaring hell out of the 4-inch gun crew just below. The unconditional surrender would have taken place right on *Green Hill Park's* gun deck, instead of aboard the battleship *Missouri* in Tokyo harbour much later. All it would have taken was the threat of a certain RCNVR petty officer to fire his rockets.

Green Hill Park carried a standard wartime crew. There was a captain and three deck officers normally referred to as mates, five engineers, three wireless officers, two officer apprentices, a chief steward and

The raging fire in *Green Hill Park* has already reached No. 1 hold. A scow lying alongside No. 3 is ablaze in its lumber cargo, no doubt ignited by burning debris from the explosions. The Canadian Pacific coal bunkering hulk is in the foreground. (G. Conway-Brown collection)

a messing staff of five, three galley staff, ten seamen, six firemen, three oilers, a bosun, a ship's carpenter, a donkeyman and eight navy DEMS gunners for a total of 53. Occasionally we carried additional personnel, because there were few passenger liners operating during the war and even fewer airlines. I recall seeing more sailing ships than airliners. We saw some multi-engined flying boats off the coast of Africa once, serving a neutral country. For our trip from Vancouver to Australia, we carried several airmen of the Royal Australian Air Force, taking them home following completion of aircrew training in Canada, under the British Commonwealth Air Training Plan. These airmen assisted us as lookouts during our Pacific crossing.

We arrived in Australia without incident after a crossing time of 30 days. In Sydney Harbour we shared a berth with the USS *Boise*, a Brooklyn Class

In the foreground, lazy steam from a CPR locomotive curls up while a range of vintage motor cars remains parked, with unconcerned citizens watching or walking by. The coal hulk has been removed. Meanwhile, debris smokes where it has fallen on the roof of the Canadian Pacific pier B and arrangements are under way to tow *Bowness Park* clear from her berth lying astern of the blazing ship.

(G. Conway-Brown Collection)

cruiser that had seen a lot of action in some of the major battles of the Pacific war. This warship is quite prominent now in US Navy history books. The bridge of *Boise* was decorated with small Japanese flags, representing many aircraft shot down and there were many small painted silhouettes of Japanese shipping sunk. When we arrived in Hobart, Tasmania, we shared a berth with a US submarine that had earned some rest and recuperation time. The submarine crew told some fascinating stories.

As we made our way to Fremantle, Western Australia, Japanese submarine activity in the area led us to take refuge in a coastal bay, where we remained until it was thought safe to proceed. At Fremantle, we formed a convoy with several other ships for our crossing of the Indian Ocean to Colombo, Ceylon (now Sri Lanka). Captain Wright was the most senior captain, consequently he became the convoy commodore and *Green Hill Park*, the lead ship. Our escorts were destroyers of the Royal Australian Navy. The crossing to Ceylon was successful and uneventful, but at that time there were many stories of shipping losses in both the Indian and Pacific Oceans. These days were undoubtedly the "finest hour" for *Green Hill Park*.

Wherever we went during the war, we were reminded that Canadians had an identity crisis. We called ourselves "Canadian", and the port authorities around the world simply said there was no such thing as a Canadian citizen so they recorded us as British. At that time there was still a British Empire. The search for our true identity became the subject for lively discussions among the crew, and the best spokesman in the *Green Hill Park* was the chief officer who held the view that Canada was truly part of the Empire. The opposite view was held by the chief engineer who saw us as being more closely tied to the United States. This became a main subject for debate while *Green Hill Park* made her way around the world as porpoises played at the bow, flying fish crashed on our decks and albatrosses flew overhead. The debate eventually led to a real crisis.

From Colombo we proceeded to Cochin, India, a port on the Malabar coast, not far from the southernmost tip of India. It was one of the first places in India to have a white settlement. This was, without doubt, the most romantic, idyllic and unreal place we ever visited, at least that was how it appeared to us from our ship at anchor, before we stepped ashore. The tropical sunrises and sunsets were beautiful and we watched little brown men on small, quaint local sailing craft, casting their nets into the sea to catch fish. On shore were swarms of men and women, moving about amongst the palm trees, and the buildings appeared to be mostly native huts. India even after partition is a country made up of an enormous number of ethnicities, religions and a rigid caste system. The local inhabitants were mostly Tamils,a very dark small-boned type who occupied much of South India and were descended from an ancient race called the Dravidians.

When we were cleared to enter the harbour, we discovered a different city of Cochin. The completely protected harbour did not offer us a berth, so we tied up at buoys and our cargo of Australian wheat was to be removed manually. The Tamil coolies carried sacks of wheat on their heads to lighters and barges that tied up alongside. This was a monumental task, because we carried 10,000 tons of cargo. The harbour was filled with Royal Navy fighting ships, including an aircraft carrier, all being assembled for the assault on Japan's South East Asian Empire. When we were cleared to go ashore, the only water taxis available were small rowboats operated by the local natives. They actually fought each other for our business, competition was so keen. On one occasion, I witnessed a knife fight between two water taxi operators.

When we stepped ashore, we were finally greeted by the real Cochin. The most lasting memory I retain is of the many smells that we encountered as we walked along the streets. There appeared to be no sewer system, as raw sewage ran along the streets in the gutters. There was thus a constant foul smell in the streets. From almost every flimsy house, hut, or building, a contrasting sweet smell emerged, as the people burned incense. The sweet smells and the foul odours mingled with those of cooking food to form some strange combinations. Although there

were motor vehicles operated by white people, the colonial masters who drove recklessly through the masses of people in the narrow cobblestone streets, visitors like ourselves had only one means of transportation, the rickshaw, pulled by a Tamil.

When we discovered the facilities used by the British colonial officials and servicemen, we saw quite another side of Cochin and colonial India. There was a club, restaurant and theatre, all located in a "white" part of the city. The servants were all Indians dressed smartly in white tunics, colourful sashes and many wore turbans. Air conditioning inside the buildings was supplied by neatly uniformed brown boys, who pulled on long ropes that moved large paddle fans overhead, to create a breeze in the hot evening air. I do not recall seeing any electric fans. As a matter of fact, I don't recall there being any electricity in the native sections of the city, because the house lamps at night were oil lamps.

After discharging our cargo at Cochin we proceeded to Cape Town, South Africa. This modern city was in sharp contrast to the very primitive city of Cochin we left behind. But in Cape Town, perhaps it was the *Green Hill Park* crew who could be called primitive. We all went ashore, in various small groups, but we seemed to end up as a large group in the Delmonico Club, a palatial restaurant and bar establishment. It was frequented by the white population and the soldiers, sailors and merchant seamen from many nations. Most of the clients were involved in some way with the war and many were preparing for the onslaught against Japan. The club offered the very best in food, drinks and facilities. White linen tablecloths covered the tables, the staff

The blazing ship is towed astern, clear of the dock. Open flames can be seen issuing from No. 2 hold while No. 2 starboard lifeboat blazes and No. 4 is already smoking. The starboard side shell plating over No. 3 'tween-deck has peeled back like a banana following the series of explosions.

(G. Conway-Brown Collection)

As the ship is towed to the outer harbour the fireboat rides alongside always pouring more water into the ship. No. 1 port side lifeboat has burned to its keel, while a monitor jets water into the open side of No. 3 'tween-deck. With both sides blown out a weak point has developed which would have seen the vessel break in two in any kind of rough sea.

(Versatile Pacific Shipyards)

were all Indian, dressed in white tunics with some sporting coloured turbans. Each wore a colour-coded sash or cummerbund around his waist, the colour indicating if he was a food or liquor waiter. On the main floor of the club, a very formal string orchestra played classical music for the patrons. The restaurant extended upwards into dining balconies that overlooked the main floor.

Into this very classy establishment came the *Green Hill Park* crew and they tended to congregate on the main floor. The chief officer and the chief engineer were seated at a central table and they were in uniform. The chief engineer had four gold rings on his sleeves and the chief officer had three. After a few drinks, they resumed their usual Canadian identity discussion. It was basically repeating well-entrenched views favouring either British or American affiliation for Canada. In a place swarming with the servicemen and merchant seamen of both nations, and similar clients from many other nations, who had strong views on the subject, this discussion proved to be the ignition for an increasingly explosive mixture.

The two *Green Hill Park* officers progressed from a simple discussion to a heated debate. Patrons of the club gathered around the table, lining up, as if taking sides. Faces alternated with smiles and frowns as *Green Hill Park's* finest took their best shots in the debate. Many in the audience perhaps thought that

here were two senior naval officers, extending a wartime conflict ashore. It was quite clearly the British against the Americans, but the two Canadians were struggling with the fuse.

There is some confusion as to what happened next. The argument stopped abruptly and the fight was on. It was basically a conflict of British uniforms against American and they were fighting over Canada, much like the War of 1812. It was a war within a war. Merchant seamen in civilian clothes entered the battle for whichever side they chose and it became difficult to distinguish friend from foe. Tables and glasses were smashed to the floor. Chairs became weapons. The most surprising thing about this war was that it had live background theme music, for the string orchestra continued to play and the battle was fought to the strains of "Jealousy."

As the fighting intensified, reinforcements for both sides poured into the club from the streets outside, and as many of the new combatants entered the fray, they just picked up a chair to smash over any convenient opponent as an opening declaration of war. The orchestra played on and they kept repeating "Jealousy." Contestants on both sides forgot their common conflict with Germany and Japan and this critical battle for a Canadian identity consumed most of the Allied war effort in Cape Town that night. Perhaps there were greater battles fought during World War II, but for me, the battle of the

Delmonico Club in Cape Town was the most fiercely fought battle that I witnessed. Right at the centre of the conflict was a rather serene Canadian merchant ship from Vancouver, *Green Hill Park* and her gallant crew, but no one won.

Eventually, navy shore patrol and army military police units for both sides arrived and brought the conflict to a halt. A hostile truce was declared. The Delmonico Club was a battlefield in ruins. I don't recall any fatalities, but quite possibly there may have been a few violins or cellos that never played "Jealousy" again. For the combatants, there were many black eyes and cuts and bruises that needed attention. Aboard *Green Hill Park* our second officer, Mr. Colin Wilson of Vancouver, performed the duties of ship's doctor.

There was one permanent change that resulted from this incident. Our chief officer and chief engineer never again discussed the topic of our Canadian identity. In fact I don't recall that they ever discussed anything again. The officers' dining saloon became more like a monastery, wherein the monks had taken vows of silence and meals became very quiet affairs.

Even today, whenever I hear the strains of "Jealousy," a smile creeps across my face, as I remember *Green Hill Park*, her gallant crew and their greatest battle of World War II. It really was a splendid fight, but it did nothing to resolve the Canadian identity problem.

We left the battlefield of Cape Town for the more peaceful war zone of the Atlantic Ocean, where there were only German submarines to contend with. Proceeding up the Congo River our next port of call was Boma, followed by Matadi, both in the Belgian Congo (now Zaire), These jungle places provided us with a unique insight into colonial Africa. Small schooners, owned by white Europeans with black crews, traded goods between the jungle communities up and down the Congo River. The Belgians were firmly in control and their harsh methods quite clearly led to the violent uprisings later when the native population seized independence. Boma was then just a village, but it was the only place I ever visited where labour was undertaken by prisoners in striped suits, chained together by shackles on their ankles. These black prisoners smashed rocks and used rakes and shovels to improve the roads in Boma under the watchful supervision of armed guards. Quite surpris-

ingly to me, the prisoners seemed rather happy and cheerful, as they joked among themselves, even though I did not understand their language.

Ashore in Boma were warning signs in a language I could not read, erected where there was a patch of bush or jungle. I presumed they warned of snakes and other wild creatures that might be dangerous. At night, the lights of houses and buildings that were completely closed in by screens, illuminated a multitude of insects, lizards and other creepy creatures that crawled on the outside of the screens.

At Matadi, the upper limit of ship navigation on the Congo River, we almost ran our ship aground while turning her around. *Green Hill Park* was caught sideways in the river current, out of control and heading for the riverbank. Quick thinking by the captain on the bridge, the chief officer who was at the bow, or the ship's carpenter who controlled the anchor windlass, saved the day. One of the anchors was released, it caught hold on the river bottom and the ship swung away from shore.

Our next port of call was Takoradi on the Gold Coast. Here we found the black population, which was under British colonial control, rather hostile. On one occasion, a gang of young blacks wanted to beat my head in with stones, because my skin was white. I had to bluff my way through the incident to escape unhurt.

Green Hill Park then crossed the Atlantic Ocean towards the Panama Canal. We paused at Port-of-Spain, Trinidad, and then we had a brief shore leave at Cristobal-Colon at the Caribbean end of the canal. Our remaining ports of call were San Francisco and Portland, Oregon. We returned to Vancouver towards the end of February, about nine months after our departure.

At the conclusion of our circumnavigation of the world aboard *Green Hill Park*, I had already missed so much schooling, that I decided to remain at sea until the end of the war. I did not leave the ship, but merely moved to new quarters. Many of the crew spent a few days ashore, visiting their families, while others simply went back to work, as the ship was loaded once again with cargo bound for Australia. This time the cargo included military aircraft for the Royal Australian Air Force, a large load of lumber, tinplate and newsprint. The general cargo was placed in Number 3 hold and it consisted of 50 barrels of whisky, 8 tons of pyrotechnic flares, 120 tons of sodium chlorate packed in about 2000 steel drums, and tons of mustard pickles. The sodium chlorate drums were placed in the 'tween-deck stowage. It was placed there so that it could be reached more easily than if it were deep in the hold.

On the morning of March 6, 1945, Victor Moore, age 17, of Newton, Surrey BC and I were the two seamen who were given the task of replacing the emergency rations and equipment in the ship's four lifeboats and four liferafts. We completed our work a few minutes before noon and went aft for lunch in the seamen's mess, joining several other crew members there. We each poured a bowl of soup, started lunch, but we never finished it.

We heard a commotion on deck and someone shouted, "Fire at Number 3 hatch!" Because the seamen are the firefighters on a ship, we responded immediately. We ran forward to man the fire hoses, but fortunately for us, the ship exploded before we reached Number 3 hold. If we had responded more quickly, we could have arrived just in time for the first blast and been added to the death toll. A series of four or five closely spaced explosions followed while the deck of the ship sprang up and down with each detonation. The hull vibrations were much like a guitar string that had been plucked, and their amplitude interfered with walking. I recall feeling the explosions more than hearing them. With each blast, the sky filled with debris, parts of the ship, fragments of cargo and I thought I saw bodies flying through the air. A Vancouver newspaper report that night quoted one observer who claimed he had seen "A man, his clothes aflame, blown up in the air, and that he had fallen back into the flaming ship."

Immediately, the debris and chunks of metal rained down on the ship and I ran for cover under the closest upper steel deck that offered protection from falling objects. The steel plating of the ship's sides had peeled back, as if opened by some giant can-opener. The entire bridge structure collapsed back into the gaping hole that had seconds before been Number 3 hold. When the blasts subsided, I ran with several other crew members, longshoremen and Burrard shipyard maintenance workers, to the stern of the ship to get as far as possible from the midships section.

The gun deck above our heads provided good protection from the debris that was raining down. The fire then spread quickly through the holds and cargo decks beneath us, and it ignited the lumber barges that were tied up alongside the ship. We looked to the dock for a means of escape, but none was apparent.

There were a few miracles for *Green Hill Park* that day. Captain Wright was ashore for a brief rest period and in relief was Captain Harold J. Vince of Vancouver. The relief captain was in the master's cabin within the bridge structure when the first blast occurred, placing him very near the centre of the explosion. His clothing caught fire in the inferno, but he escaped with his life and only minor burns.

The new chief officer, Alan P. Horsfield, was in the officer's dining saloon when notified of the fire, and he went outside to see that crew members and longshoremen were attempting to extinguish the fire with a fire extinguisher and three fire-hoses. He must then have entered the hold to determine the exact nature of the fire, because third officer Stuart S. McKenzie of Vancouver was on deck at Number 3 hold and later recounted, "The first officer had no sooner jumped out of the hold, than it seemed to blow all to hell." I think it safe to say that both these officers received some miraculous help from somewhere that day. McKenzie added, "The first explosion wasn't bad. It was the second and the third explosions that were real humdingers. The second explosion blew the side of the ship out."

Seaman Don Smith of Vancouver, age 17, was at Number 3 hatch laying out a fire-hose when the first blast occurred. He ran forward and later expressed surprise that he did not recall seeing anyone else around him. A second blast threw him against a bulkhead and he picked himself up, resuming his flight toward the bow. He then went over the side and as he attempted to slide down a rope, his hands went numb and he fell into the water. Someone fished him out and the next thing he remembered was waking up in a bed in St. Paul's Hospital.

Seaman Alfred Coombs of Vancouver, age 17, was between the galley and Number 3 hatch when the first blast threw him against the side of the galley. He picked himself up and ran towards the bow as the explosions continued. He jumped over the side and clung to a stowed anchor. Then he grabbed a rope and slipped into the water when another crew member fell on top of him and they both went under. He surfaced into a dense mess of driftwood and oil and swam to an oily breakwater log that was chained to the dock. Falling debris from the explosions forced him to take shelter behind a piling. Rescuers on the dock threw him a line and hauled him up. He felt numb, started to walk and when his legs failed him, he staggered and was caught by a city fireman. They removed his clothes, wrapped him in a blanket and then an ambulance took him to St. Paul's Hospital.

Chief cook Jules Lantchier of Vancouver, age 46, was working in the galley at the time of the first blast. He ran out on deck and then went over the side of the ship by rope to the dock. At first, he thought that he had not been injured, but a few minutes later he developed severe internal pains. He was taken to St. Paul's in "fair" condition with shock and internal injuries. He was the most severely injured of all the surviving crew members.

Able seaman Frank Syms of Winnipeg, one of the DEMS gunners on board that day, was in the galley at the time of the first blast. He was most fortunate to escape through a hatch, uninjured.

Seen from the top of Siwash Rock on the west side of Stanley Park, *Green Hill Park* now rests on a sandy bottom, safe for the moment while the fire burns itself out. Fireboats alongside had to maintain forward way to overcome the thrust of the jets of water against the ship.
(BC Archives E-039735)

Percy Churchill of North Vancouver was aboard *Green Hill Park* doing maintenance work for Burrard Dry Dock that day. He described his experience at Number 3 hatch this way. "The blast ripped both sides out of her like paper. I felt the ship sink and rise again. I was right over Number 3 hatch when she blew. I went up in the air and landed on my feet running."

Mac George of Vancouver, our ship's bosun, was just stepping ashore. He was blown into the water and later rescued by a harbour craft.

Seaman R.L. Ramsey of Vancouver was rushing towards Number 3 hatch with full pressure on a fire-

hose when he was hit by the first blast. He then retreated to the stern.

Officer cadet William Mundie of Vancouver, age 20, was on duty in the midships section that day. He escaped serious injury to become a leading witness in the subsequent investigation and court hearings. He was lucky that day, but unlucky a year later when he drowned off Africa while serving in *Lakeside Park*.

Messman Joe Kielek described his impressions with these words, "I saw the fire and told the mate. We tried to get some water on her before she went up. Then I ran aft and slid down a hawser. When I was on it the big blast went and I was thrown into the water. Some men got me up a rope at the end of the pier."

A newspaper reporter later said of Joe, "A soaked blonde man was led to the new first aid post, wrapped in blankets and handed a cup of coffee."

Longshoreman J.W. Nesbitt of Vancouver reported: "About seven men who were attempting to reach the deck and safety by sliding down a hawser were blown into the water." He slid down the same hawser himself, after the blast subsided.

Norman Wiles, a Vancouver truck driver who was inside the saloon at the time of the explosions, was rather modest in his assessment of the blasts, in stating, "They weren't bad, but they knocked me to the floor."

Seaman Ernest May of Saint John, N.B., said, "There were about seven men in the seamen's mess, starting lunch, just before the explosions. We noticed smoke and thought it was a small fire. No alarm had been given. One of the boys went up and had a look. He came running back and told us the ship was all ablaze. Everyone made a dash for the door."

Seaman William Matthews was admitted to Vancouver General Hospital suffering from shock.

Fireman Pat Lowcay of Sidney, BC was off shift and asleep in the crew quarters. He said, "The noise and the jolt woke me up, I packed my clothes in 12 seconds flat and got out on deck."

Donkeyman Robert Anderson of Vancouver and oiler Fred Jones of Cape Breton Island, NS both managed to escape to the dock without injury.

Messmen Bob Crane and C.P. Wilson, both of New Westminster, were preparing lunch in two separate mess pantries when the blast hit. They both ran to the stern. Others who gathered there were F. Odale of Powell River, a fireman I believe, W.J. Wilson of Shawville, Quebec and Frank Westcott of Edmonton, an oiler.

Seaman James McIlvenie of Australia was ashore that morning and was returning to the ship for lunch. As he descended the CPR viaduct steps, the shock wave hit him. He went to the dock to see his ship burn. His only remark to another onlooker was, "She was a fine ship."

There were not enough miracles available that day. Eight men perished and scores were injured. At first it was thought that nine men had been killed, because one body was shattered into pieces and erroneously counted as two people. Six of the eight victims were longshoremen, most of their bodies were unrecognizable and were recovered in the hold. The crew victims were chief steward Don Munn of Vancouver, age 54, and messman Julius Kun, age 41, who was new to the crew. He was a native of Hungary, a returned soldier and a new resident of Vancouver. They were both in the lower bridge structure, probably the pantry area which faced Number 3 hatch. They must have been killed instantly.

The fatalities would have been much greater, if the disaster had occurred at any other time of the working day. Most of the crew and longshoremen had left work a few minutes before noon with the blasts starting about one minute before noon. We were scattered to our various messes for lunch. All but the officer's dining saloon were well removed from the blast site.

Tied up astern of *Green Hill Park* was the S.S. *Bowness Park*, a sister ship and another product of Burrard Dry Dock. The crew of this ship had the best view of the disaster and all that happened. A newspaper report stated that it was the navy tugboat HMCS *Glendevon* that pulled *Bowness Park* out into the harbor to safety.

Parts of *Green Hill Park* and fragments of her cargo were spread far and wide. A roll of blazing fabric landed hundreds of feet away across the CPR dock, on board S.S. *Princess Joan*, and started a fire there. This was one of the Canadian Pacific ships that provided a link with Victoria before BC Ferries were established. Some of the cargo debris was recovered from as far away as Lumberman's Arch in Stanley Park, a mile or more away. One reporter described the explosions by saying, "They sent flares soaring into the sky in an awesome display of grim fireworks."

Much of the debris thrown upward was on fire and some of the flares had ignited. Burning debris fell on the floating gasoline stations in Coal Harbour and the attendants had to rush to extinguish these fires. Harry Miller of the Shell fuel barge had a white linen tablecloth from *Green Hill Park's* dining saloon come down on his station. Some of the flares had parachutes that had opened and one such burning flare drifted into the trees of Stanley Park.

The *Vancouver Sun* newspaper described the explosion with these words that day: "Like an earth-

The bridge structure can be seen collapsed into No. 3 hold. Somewhat incongruously, the keel and stern frame of No. 4 lifeboat sit on its chocks where water arrested the fire. The liferafts abreast of the foremast evidently burned where they rested on their skids. (BC Archives E-03974)

quake, today's blast shook office buildings savagely and sent tenants hurrying to the streets for safety. Thousands of windows were shattered in downtown Vancouver and up to one mile away."

The *Province* newspaper reported, "Heaviest damage was between Burrard and Richards Streets, along Hastings, Pender, Howe, Hornby and Granville, but extended from the dock area at Burrard Street east to Victory Square." All of the windows were blown out of some Hastings Street buildings. That evening the *Vancouver Sun* reported, "Broken glass strewing the streets from the 400 block on West Pender as far as Thurlow and from the waterfront up to Dunsmuir, whole office blocks with scarcely a window left intact, was the picture today."

An interesting observation in the *Province* read, "The explosion taught Vancouver people what Europeans learned long ago from bombing raids — to shun windows. Workers in downtown stores and offices rushed to windows on hearing the first blast. The second blast deluged many of them with shattered glass and caused numerous injuries."

Back at the ship, at the height of the explosions, the rivets popping from the ship's steel plating became missiles, which were reported initially in

error as ammunition and tracer bullets. The *Vancouver Sun* described the sight with these words, "Vancouver waterfront in the vicinity of the CPR docks today looked nothing less than a scene from war-torn Europe." The cargo of mustard pickles had splattered ship, dock and the waterfront area. It would be an understatement to say that at the waterfront in downtown Vancouver that day, mustard pickles were on everyone's lunch menu.

One of the smaller miracles that day came to us in the form of a navy harbour craft that just happened to be passing by, enroute to the North Shore. It was the 50-foot *Andamara*, operated by Able Seaman Neil MacMillan. Within minutes, this boat was under *Green Hill Park's* stern, ropes were thrown down and twenty of us slid down on to the rescue vessel's deck. As we pulled away we could see a surviving longshoreman standing on a burning lumber scow, surrounded by flames, right below and outboard of Number 3 hold. He appeared perfectly calm, as if waiting for a bus, but he could have been in shock. If he had been in that location only minutes before, the steel plating of the ship's side that opened up must have blown right over him, within inches of hitting his head. We went in and rescued him, but how he survived right at the centre of the explosion is still a miracle to me.

In my rush to abandon ship, I had no time to take any personal belongings. The boat dropped us off at a nearby dock and returned to rescue others. I stood there, watching my ship burn, without a cent in my pockets and nothing but the dirty clothes on my back. Many other crew members had the same experience of becoming destitute suddenly, without money to make a phone call, to buy bus fare, or to buy a drink. I then walked across the city, across the Cambie Street Bridge, to West Coast Shipbuilders on False Creek where my father worked, to let him know that I had survived.

As *Green Hill Park* was exploding the tugboat *R.F.M.*, owned by Marpole Towing, was entering Coal Harbour, under Captain Harry Jones. The captain quickly dropped his tow and proceeded over to the burning ship to move the ship from the dock. Three of the freighter's crew went back on board to secure the tugboat's towing line to the bitts at the stern. They were chief officer Alan Horsfield, third officer Stuart S. McKenzie and fireman Clarence Martin of Winnipeg. The third officer on the last voyage of *Green Hill Park* was Norman Ouellette who observed the eruption and smoke from some blocks away in the city. He rushed to the dock and then provided the necessary knowledge and assistance in supervising the release of the ship's mooring lines. Some 40 minutes after the first explosion *Green Hill Park* was being towed clear of the dock. *R.F.M.* was then joined and assisted by the navy tug *Glendevon* and another navy vessel named *Squamish*.

The ordeal of Horsfield, McKenzie and Martin on the burning ship lasted another four hours. The fires below made the steel decks too hot for them to venture more than 20 feet from the stern. They were eventually taken off by the police boat *Teco II*.

The North Vancouver fire barge *Louisa* quickly responded to the emergency and was soon available to escort the burning ship from the harbour. The Vancouver fire boat *J.H. Carlisle*, under the command of Captain Joe McInnis, was berthed in False Creek and she also responded quickly. The *J.H. Carlisle* met *Green Hill Park* and her entourage of escorting tugboats just inside the harbour as they all approached the Lions Gate Bridge, but she had difficulty in getting alongside due to strong tidal cur-

rents and the several small craft present which became obstructions.

After clearing Lion's Gate Bridge, *R.F.M.* attempted to beach *Green Hill Park* on shoals near the mouth of the Capilano River. Strong tidal currents foiled this attempt, as the ship would not ground securely. The tugboats then pulled for English Bay where they successfully grounded the ship near Siwash Rock off Stanley Park.

The stern was then secured with an anchor. The fire boat *J.H. Carlisle* and the fire barge *Louisa* were then made fast to the ship and poured water into the burning ship's holds with all their capacity. Thirty hours after the explosions, fires were still burning in the forward holds. She burned for two more days.

Even after *Green Hill Park* was grounded at Siwash Rock, naval authorities considered her a constant danger and threat for further explosions. There was also the possibility of her breaking up and becoming a permanent wreck off Stanley Park. A decision was taken to tow her out to deep water, where she could be scuttled. At the time this was attempted, the fire boats had pumped some thousands of tons of water into her holds which fastened her too securely to the bottom. The tugboats were unable to break her loose. The miracles of that day even extended to saving *Green Hill Park* from a deep-water grave.

The day following the disaster, a Vancouver newspaper offered this comment about the character of the burned ship: "All through the explosions and subsequent fire the *Green Hill Park* was properly dressed. Her merchant navy red ensign still flew from the stern." That was something that most of us didn't even notice.

Concerning the damage to ship and cargo, on March 7, 1945, a Vancouver newspaper made these observations: "Down in the holds where the cargo can be seen are rolls of newsprint floating in black water, shattered glass jars, their pickle contents spread in a thick coating all around, Number 2 hold is just a burned-out mass of debris, all that remains of 12 planes, which, according to one of the crew, had been stowed there." What had started as a small fire which was only apparent as a whiff of smoke, within five minutes became a series of massive explosions and a fire that destroyed and gutted Number 1, 2 and 3 holds.

Nothing remained of the 120 tons of sodium chlo-

Months later the ship sits on the chocks in Burrard's floating dock. Work is starting on cutting away wreckage so that rebuilding can proceed on behalf of the ship's new owners, New York Greeks who, considering that it took close to 18 months to rebuild the ship, probably had no bargain. (Versatile Pacific Shipyards)

rate cargo, except twisted wreckage that had been almost 2000 steel drums containing the chemical. The head of one drum had landed hundreds of feet away, at the end of Pier A. Some pieces were blown through the steel bulkhead that previously separated Number 2 and 3 holds. Most of the drums had been reduced to "pieces smaller than your hand." The only debris remaining in Number 3 hold from the 50 barrels of whisky was the bottom of one barrel.

The day following the disaster I reported to the Canada Shipping Company offices, our Vancouver agent, in the Marine Building near the site of the explosion. Norman Ouellette and Vic Moore also reported at the same time. We were met by Captain Wright, who seemed very pleased to see us, because the company was trying to account for missing members. We had been listed as possible casualties. Two other missing crew members were eventually found as overnight guests in the Vancouver city jail. The newspaper reporter who published this information tactfully neglected to give their names.

Mr. Ouellette, Vic Moore and I were sent back aboard the ship to collect all the personal belongings

of the crew. We were taken by vehicle and then by boat to the wreck off Siwash Rock. We filled and labelled about 50 bags of personal effects. While aboard the ship, we went through the rubble of the midships section, looking for anything that might be personal property. Although we did not locate any bodies, some of the casualties were still there, to be discovered later.

Green Hill Park was pulled free of her Siwash Rock beach on March 13, 1945, as high tide approached. There was great concern about the ship breaking up, because a giant crack extended down her starboard side, almost to the waterline at Number 3 hold. Three powerful tugboats pulled her free. They were the CPR *Kyuquot* under Captain Leslie Anderson and Pacific Salvage Company's *Salvage Queen* and *Salvage Princess*.

Under the direction of William Jordan, the burned-out ship was dislodged successfully from the beach at Siwash Rock and moved to a safe berth in Vancouver harbour. There were many investigations into the disaster. In general the conclusion was that a barrel of whisky had been broached and a careless smoker had ignited the fumes. The flames probably ignited the pyrotechnics and the sodium chlorate followed. I myself was questioned by an RCMP plainclothes investigator who was seeking to determine if the cause was sabotage. As Sherlock Holmes was attempting to solve the case of the missing mustard pickles by blaming the demon whiskey, I found my mind wandering. I deduced that perhaps the same culprit, whisky, may have been responsible for the other *Green Hill Park* eruption back at the Delmonico Club in Cape Town on her recently completed voyage. I thought it best to keep my detective conclusions to myself.

When I arrived back in Vancouver in October 1945, after my second voyage, this one in *Lakeside Park*, I immediately returned to Queen Elizabeth High School, in North Surrey, BC I was then 17 years old and starting grade 11. A Vancouver newspaper heard of my wartime adventures and published the story under the title of, "Why George was Late for School." Although such a note was never sent to the school, if it had been, it might have been worded like this:

Dear Teacher,

Please excuse George for being late for school. Some time ago, for summer employment, he obtained a job on a ship bound for Australia. The ship did not return because there was a war going on. Also, his ship did not move very fast, particularly when the anti-torpedo nets were out, or when it was in convoy. He also had to go a long distance, because he sailed around the world twice. He almost didn't return at all, due to some incidents, particularly when his ship blew up and he was almost killed. He had to learn how to use naval guns and do many things that used up so much of his time, that he missed a lot of school.

Yours truly,
A. Parent

Now who would believe a dumb excuse like that? It is even more ridiculous than, "A dog ate my homework."

Today, half a century and more later, whenever I visit Canada Place on the Vancouver waterfront, my thoughts are similar to the emotions and thoughts expressed in the poem, "The Rhyme of the Ancient Mariner." I see a grey ghost of a ship lying there, and it looks like my ship, *Green Hill Park*, fitted out and loading cargo for another exciting voyage to the Pacific Ocean and unknown destinations beyond. I see familiar faces in the phantom crew. They appear so young now. I recall hearing violins playing "Jealousy." The aircraft in Number 2 hold would have been used in the war. The whisky in Number 3 would have been served in bars and pubs across Australia. There would have been tons of mustard pickles there for lunch.

I know it is only an illusion, but the vision is so clear that it seems like it all happened yesterday.

PART II
Survey, Insurance and Legal Aspects
An analysis by the Author

Inevitably when a disaster of this magnitude occurs it sets off a whole range of processes which seek, in retrospect, to reassess the risk, determine responsibility, compensate loss — human and otherwise — and finally to clean up the financial and material losses in a variety of ways. Major disasters attract the attention of the lay press so long as there is any element of public interest, which usually means human loss, excitement, suspicions and similar factors. The specialist shipping press, which is much more objective, usually confines itself to the facts, which may take some time to become fully apparent and often are only finally settled in court.

In terms of compensation marine insurance in several forms seeks to apportion the loss in financial terms. The process involves paying out those losses which can be compensated and denying those which are spurious, irrelevant or, in simple terms had not been properly covered before the loss.

The cornerstone of processing the *Green Hill Park* loss was established when Lloyd's Agency at Vancouver, acting on behalf of insurance underwriters and/or the Park Steamship Company (the legal owner of the vessel in right of Canada), and the ship operator and agent (Canada Shipping Company), collectively engaged the Salvage Association through its appointed surveyor to conduct the survey described in the above heading. The Salvage Association's printed caveat was clearly set out in the report:

> In accepting this report or certificate it is agreed that the extent of the obligation of this Association with respect thereto is limited to furnishing a surveyor believed to be competent, and in the making of this report or certificate the surveyor is acting on behalf of the person requesting the same, and no liability shall attach to this association for the accuracy thereof.

The Salvage Association has considerable powers, in the sense that it can give direction to events which naturally follow after a loss. These can include removal of wreck and disposal of damaged property, for example. The Salvage Association's handling of a case such as *Green Hill Park*, provides a solid baseline to the process. It is from their report that marine insurance underwriters reach their basis of settlement, and protection and indemnity underwriters will determine the degree of the owner's, manager's or charterer's liability and compensate them in terms of P & I insurance. Lawyers involved in litigation, or a public enquiry, may also use the report as evidence in court action, as the report stands as effective, disinterested third party testimony by a professional expert.

There were many interests involved and many losses to be categorized. Cargo, other than government-owned cargo, would have been insured. We know the ship itself was not insured by Park Steamship Company, although legal liability aspects for third party losses might have been covered by a form of P & I Insurance, but of this there is no record. There was damage to surrounding property near the explosion site, but there were also many cases of glass breakage consequent upon the explosion and what these amounted to is now pure conjecture. It is assumed that property owners or their insurers would have claimed against the Park Steamship Company, but how the claims were compensated is not known. There would also have been a number of loss of life and personal injury claims as well as loss of personal effects and it is assumed that Park Steamship would have dealt with these quite fully.

The word "adjust" is an insurance term which in effect means to investigate, negotiate and present a settlement of all the varied aspects of the loss. For example, had the overall loss been a general average, meaning a mutual pooling of the loss as described in Chapter 5, the loss would have been allocated in a different way to the various underwriters involved.

The average adjuster in this case was the late Mr. H.E. Tom Warkman, then employed in this role by Lloyd's Agency, Vancouver, BC. He described the material aspects of the loss in his preamble, and set out a dated sequence of all pertinent events including meetings with others and those they represented. He then detailed the various negotiations he undertook with the owners of the ship and contractors, such as tugboat and salvage companies which provided some of the most important of the services involved in moving and securing the ship outside the harbour. He agreed and delegated supervision of the discharge of damaged cargo, recovering the lumber in Number 5 hold which only suffered water damage and was highly salvable at little loss, and then generally saw to making the ship safe for return to the inner harbour. As part of the adjustment, Warkman detailed the cargo down to its smallest items and named the shippers in each case.

Although much of the cargo would have been shipped against letters of credit, it is unlikely that title to individual parcels would have already passed to consignees. Regardless of this detail, Warkman was safe in staying with shippers in his descriptive material because he would have had access to the ship's manifest and bills of lading, through the ship's agent. He thus established the names of all shippers as the beneficial owners of cargo, which would have been the case prior to transfer of title by way of a normal trade transaction accompanying the letter of credit.

There was a small general average, in this case possibly through the engagement of shore and tugboat services to mitigate overall loss by towing the vessel to safety. That is not clear, as while Warkman estimated general average to represent a sum of $25,000, a very small amount in view of the overall value of the ship and cargo prior to the loss, he gave no details of what was allocated to the general average or how he arrived at his estimate. The general average was allowed for and an estimate made solely for reserve purposes. Undoubtedly the general average would have been relatively easy and quick to draw once all the parameters of the case had been established through the survey report.

In any event the master of the ship would have sworn his protest as almost his first act following the disaster, thus paving the way for a general average adjustment to be drawn up. There is now no ascertainable record of who drew the general average, if any, or its details. The bulk of the cargo loss ranked as either a total loss of goods, which was the case with almost all the cargo, or a partial loss, termed in marine insurance as a "particular average," which appears to have been the case only with water-damaged lumber in No. 5 hold. In any event Warkman was empowered to dispose of cargo by sale to salvage dealers or by public bid, which is what he actually did.

In the case of the vessel, she was a constructive total loss, as it was quickly established that the cost of repair, plus her value as she lay in damaged condition which was probably no more than scrap value, exceeded what she was worth on the market as a well found-operating vessel. In arriving at this conclusion it should be remembered that not only would there be a heavy direct cost to rebuilding, but also there would be substantial costs in preparing the vessel for rebuilding which included all the cutting away and removal of damaged material plus the time and expense of tying up a valuable dry dock for several months.

The negotiations and deliberations between a number of parties with an interest in the care and ultimate disposal of the ship were intensive rather than lengthy as there were time-sensitive details that had to be worked out. Just as the decision was made to move the burning wreck out of the harbour, so also was it necessary to consider the possibility of the ship becoming a broken wreck at her beaching site off Stanley Park. The decision to tow her off and scuttle her in deep water was frustrated by the fact that she had so much additional deadweight in her

since beaching, because of the water which had been pumped into her. The ship sat until a better alternative was reached, as after all it took time to clear out the damaged cargo and pump the water out so that she could be refloated.

The explosion had already weakened her hull structure, as much longitudinal strength was lost with her sides blown out at least down to the 'tween-deck level, right at the critical point of greatest potential weakness in any ship of her type, i.e. the midships section at No. 3 hold. While she had been beached at Siwash Rock, off Stanley Park, on a sandy level bottom with good support of her underbody, cracks had developed in the shell plating which extended from and below the area of the explosion damage and at No. 2 hold. It was at No. 2 and 3 holds that the subsequent fire reached its greatest intensity, as can be seen from the accompanying photos where the entire bridge structure over the bulkhead separating these two holds has collapsed into No. 3 hold.

Although Warkman expressed no concern in the matter it seems that no one could tell how the ship would stand up to bad weather and the possibility that her very presence on the beach would gradually alter the underwater topography and cause further damage if the supportive ground was eroded away.

Warkman and the representatives of the owners, the National Harbour Board and the salvage company had to reach additional decisions. If they were not going to scuttle Green Hill Park in deep water, with the possibility she would break in two while being towed to the scuttling site, where would they put the damaged hulk? Agreement was reached to berth her at Lapointe pier while a better site was located. The National Harbours Board was only too anxious to get her away from a pier needed for loading war cargoes. The Board was equally worried that if she sank at her berth this could cause serious dislocation while the wreck was refloated or broken up in situ.

By April 12, while cleanup and discharge continued it became apparent that the hull was in serious trouble. Cracks on both sides now extended down to the bilge strake and it was suggested that the ship had more or less broken in two. The two halves did not part, however, being kept together, it would seem, by the structure of the double bottom.

THE GREEN HILL PARK DISASTER

Burrard Dry Dock would not place her in their dry dock, the only one of sufficient capacity outside of Esquimalt's graving dock, unless she was strengthened sufficiently to permit further movement across the harbour.

Eventually Warkman negotiated a tidal wet berth offshore from the Evans Coleman installation in North Vancouver, and here she lay for a period of time until she was offered for sale by the War Assets Corporation on an "as is, where is" basis.

Cargo matters, including the disposal of damaged, saleable cargo were placed by Warkman in the hands of the Board of Marine Underwriters of San Francisco, who maintained a survey office in Vancouver, well used to handling cargo categories of loss.

The cargo upon disposal realized $65,073.60. There is no suggestion of the value of the cargo in undamaged condition, but at a guess the amounts realized might have amounted to 10 per cent of the total value as shipped. The hull was estimated to be worth $160,000, again about 10 per cent of the contracted new-building cost, as it lay in its damaged condition when offered for sale. The more essential matter was to arrive at an assessment of market value for the ship in undamaged condition at the time of future disposal, as it would be upon this value that a final determination would be made by a buyer as to whether the ship was worth repairing or would simply be cut up at a local scrapyard. This function was beyond the scope of Warkman's survey.

The total charge for services rendered following the explosion was $1,308.50. Charges after release from the ship's English Bay grounding site and for discharge came to $38,987.07. There were other ancillary expenses, including the cost of the survey, which brought the grand total of expenditures up to $50,295.57.

Looking back over 50 years it is interesting to see the almost minuscule figures involved when looking over contractors and tugboat bills. Part of an adjuster's role is to scrutinize all bills and bargain them down if justified. Most bills for services were adjudged "fair and reasonable" by Warkman. A few bills were disputed, including those of Marpole Towing and Evans Coleman & Evans, the Vancouver building supply firm. In the case of Marpole, their tugboat *R.F.M.* was instrumental in towing the burning freighter out from the dock although credit for this act was given by the local newspapers to the navy tug, *Glendevon*.

The *R.F.M.* was a steamer, probably burning coal at that time and likely with a crew of at least 7, and yet she presented a bill for $750.00 which included an amount for damage sustained. Mr. Warkman negotiated the bill down to about $650.50 as he considered the $250,00 sought for repairs excessive. At this distance in time and allowing for inflation, the Marpole bill seems very small indeed. In the case of Evans, Coleman & Evans Ltd. who presented a bill subsequent to the sale of the vessel for $3,250 for allowing the ship to be beached on their waterfront at their North Vancouver property, Mr. Warkman pared the bill down to $750.00. Without imputing anything to either, it is coincidental that Marpole Towing was a subsidiary of Evans, Coleman & Evans.

One of the biggest bills was that of Pacific Salvage Company, who had used their equipment to pump out the vessel, plus their three tugs to remove the vessel from English Bay to a safe berth in Vancouver Harbour. This bill was reduced from $50,000 to $32,500 after much negotiation. There is, of course, always the chance of some degree of opportunism on the part of salvors, contractors and towboat companies, if only to be sure that they are well compensated. However, the final settlement demonstrates the value of a surveyor or average adjuster and an impartial organization in reaching negotiated settlements, thus saving much money. The bill for the Salvage Association's work, which would have been largely made up of Mr. Warkman's salary, overhead and expenses, came to a final total of $3,474.42

PART III
The Inquest

Whenever a disaster occurs, particularly one where the public interest is thought to be at stake, or more probably where the politicians see some form of political advantage, a clamour goes up for an enquiry. This can take several forms: a parliamentary committee, a government appointed commission or a judicial enquiry headed by a highly knowledgeable legal personage.

The case of the *Green Hill Park* disaster was no exception. The International Longshoremen's and Warehousemen's Union (ILWU) and the Canadian Seamen's Union (CSU) were among the first to register loud protestations as they drew attention to lax shiploading and port management practices. At this distance in time the best account of the proceedings is that of John Stanton, well-known and now retired Vancouver labour lawyer, who represented the unions at the hearings which followed. I am indebted to Mr. Stanton for the public availability of his account which was published in *The Northern Mariner* and *Beaver* magazines in 1991.

British Columbia had known major sinkings and fire disasters on the its coast before, but a massive ship explosion which brought back memories of the 1917 Halifax disaster and the Bombay explosion of the previous year stirred great public response. Both the Halifax and Bombay tragedies had been on a massive scale and far outweighed the severity of the Vancouver explosion, although the Vancouver event could have been on a vastly greater scale if the three explosions had occurred simultaneously, in one single explosion with its potential for greater concentrated strength.(It will perhaps be remembered that Conway-Brown, in his account, considers there were more than three explosions based on the convulsions of the deck that he experienced, but to an onlooker further away some of these probably ran together in terms of the noise given off.) On that day Vancouver was far luckier that most people appreciated at the time.

The mayor of Vancouver and the Attorney-General of British Columbia made immediate demands for a full and open enquiry. There were concerns that a heavy veil of secrecy would be pulled down over the whole affair, perhaps on the grounds of wartime security. The unions found ready allies among the media, not normally friendly, who gave prominence to a number of questions which they perceived as being the core issues. Why had those in charge of loading the ship failed to observe safety regulations? Why were explosives and inflammable cargo stowed together, contrary to good stowage practice, and why were no warnings of the dangers involved posted or issued?

Ottawa's response was prompt. The government appointed three qualified former shipping men as a Commission of Enquiry. The central figure was Justice Sidney Smith, former sea captain, marine lawyer and Liberal politician, and one whose disarming blandness and Scottish burr hid his native canniness and an iron will. Justice Smith was not a man with whom one trifled. His two fellow commissioners were Captain Samuel Robinson and Steamship Inspector Hugh Robinson, who were unrelated and were both retired.

Stanton regarded it as fortunate that Ottawa appointed Dugald Donaghy, a dynamic, non-establishment lawyer to act as counsel at the enquiry. Donaghy worked long and hard to prepare for the two-part hearings, the first of which was to be held in secret. The unions instructed Stanton to cooperate with Donaghy and according to the former they worked well together.

Stanton gathered, as one would expect, all the evidence he could, and concluded that some companies, government agencies and the Port Warden of Vancouver were extremely slipshod in the way they treated their responsibility for the safety of ships, cargoes and men, a fact that was born out by Tom Warkman's factual findings in his survey report. Stanton's description and summary of events agreed in its essentials with George Conway-Brown's eyewitness account and Warkman's dispassionate chronological sequence of events. Warkman allocated no blame as that was not his mandate. It was the purpose of the commission headed by Justice Smith to deal with this aspect.

From this point on Stanton's account often reflects the cleavage which exists between organized labour and the management establishment. Following a brief description of the Park Steamship Company which operated 176 of the almost 400 merchant ships built in Canada during the war, Stanton singles out Ernest Farquehar Riddle for special attention. Riddle was Park's general manager and like many another so-called "Captain of Industry" he had been called to Ottawa at the princely salary of $1.00 per year. Known as dollar-a-year men, they included some of the most illustrious and successful business and professional men in the country and they were able to bring their knowledge, experience and connections to the government executive suite at a time when there was a major shortage of experienced executives to fill many roles, particularly those positions in the apparatus of government. It was in fact little different in the shipyards and afloat, and as a result a great many experienced British men were brought over to fill these essential positions although, not being wealthy, they were not dollar-a-year men.

Riddle, along with prominent lawyer Sherwood Lett and grain broker D.E. Harris, was an owner and director of Canada Shipping Company Limited, one of several Vancouver-based shipping agencies that assumed management functions for individual Park Steamship vessels. Riddle's giving a contract to operate, manage and control *Green Hill Park* to his own company suggested a conflict of interest to Stanton, but it was hard for prominent people handling commercial contracts not to run across their own companies in the ordinary course of government business, and possibly there were some abuses based on the functions of the "old boy network" which have since led politicians to be guided by stricter rules.

However, the argument falls a little flat when one considers that Canada Shipping Company, so far as was known contained a pool of professional expertise that was of value to the war effort. Management structures are not created on a whim. The generally accepted process in Canada, in Britain and the United States was to use whatever was available to its fullest extent. Governments are not noted for being the best managers of private industry and bureaucracy does not often equate with efficiency, as has been demonstrated on countless occasions. In Britain and the United States established ship managers who themselves usually owned tonnage of their own, ended the war often with huge fleets of government-owned tonnage under their control. Why

should it have been any different in Canada? When the boss goes to Ottawa at a dollar a year, why should his volunteer effort place him or his company in a prejudiced position?

Less than three weeks after the disaster the commission's secret first phase was over and then the public hearings began. No explanation for the purpose of the secret sessions has been offered in Stanton's account, beyond the implication that there was some "stage management" needed before going public, and on the face of it Stanton might well have been right. The Ministry of Transport named 22 individuals as parties. Three were senior personnel from Canada Shipping, two from Empire Stevedoring, the loading contractors and two from Canadian Pacific Railway, the owners of the pier. Six of the ship's officers, four longshoremen and five others, including the Port Warden, Captain Carl R. Bissett, were also named. The Unions and the National Harbours Board became active parties by voluntary appearance. Watching briefs were held by the Shipping Federation, the employers' organization, and the Canadian Merchant Service Guild, the union for ships' officers.

There were some notable omissions from the named parties which were significant because only parties could be punished. Stanton suggests that if there was to be a coverup this was where to look for it. One non-party was Captain John A. Wright, master of *Green Hill Park*, who was to be found "gravely in default." Why the master of the ship should be excused was a mystery, as normally he is the officer who would take the ultimate responsibility in any matter to do with safety of passengers, crew, cargo and the ship. This has been the tradition of the sea and ships for centuries.

In a private note, Conway-Brown told the author that Captain Wright lost a much-loved daughter a week before the accident, which may have imposed some additional strain on him. Also the fact that the ship was in the technical control of the relief master, Harold Vince, at the time of the disaster was not mentioned by Stanton and evidently had no impact on the commissioners.

Two other non-parties were Ernest Riddle and his company, Canada Shipping, and as Stanton notes this was particularly strange because three of Canada Shipping's senior men were found blameworthy. Final responsibility as to who would be named as parties and who would not, lay with the Minister of Transport, a Liberal politician. If this is so, then one would have to wonder if the process of justice was tampered with in the interests of political expediency. Perhaps this was the main reason for the first phase being held in secret. Justice Smith knew the political process very well and as Stanton suggests, was aware of what the establishment would or would not accept, although it is difficult to understand the possible implication that Riddle was responsible in some way for the disaster by allocating the management contract for *Green Hill Park* to his own company.

The battery of lawyers on the case evidently impressed Stanton, as they were for the most part the bluebloods of British Columbia's legal profession, the exceptions being Dugald Donaghy and Stanton himself. Four later became judges, and one a future Lieutenant-Governor. Another, J.V. Clyne, became a leading industrialist as head of MacMillan & Bloedel whose transport subsidiary, Canadian Transport, also operated a fleet of former Park ships in the years immediately after the war and was one of the managers by allocation from Park Steamship. That statement, of course, has no bearing on the case in hand, but illustrates the point that Park chose any company which had the needed management capability and willingness to handle its ships.

The commission identified 27 questions to which it needed answers. All were straightforward and made whitewashing of any of the parties joined in the action difficult. The unions identified the five biggest issues of interest to them as:

(1) How was dangerous cargo packed, labelled and stowed?

(2) Were sufficient instructions issued by Canada Shipping to the ship's officers, the longshoremen and their employer, to take precautions against fire and explosion?

(3) Were all, or any, of those involved in loading fully aware of the danger of the cargo?

(4) What caused the fire, explosions and loss of life?

(5) Was anyone careless, incompetent or lax, and if so who?

In the hearings several so-called "expert" people acquitted themselves poorly or at least inadequately. There is little doubt that the explosive qualities of sodium chlorate were either not understood or were ignored despite warnings, among them one from the British Ministry of War Transport, which complained of poor loading practices at Canadian ports and insisted that dangerous cargoes be properly handled and not contravene British rules, as after all their concern was that an explosion could just as easily happen in unloading at a destination as it could at a loading point. One only had to consider the Bombay explosion and *Fort Stikine* to support that point, although in that case the ship was not loaded in Canada.

The British "Notice to Shipowners and Ship Masters re Carriage of Dangerous Goods in Ships" stated that:

(1) Not more than ten tons of sodium chlorate must be allowed in any one hold;

(2) Sodium chlorate must be stowed away from explosives (such as flares), with the ship's engine room compartment separating them;

(3) Sodium chlorate must be stowed away from any combustible material.

From this it will be seen that the arrangements aboard *Green Hill Park* failed on all scores. In fact the danger was multiplied manyfold with explosive flares, sodium chlorate and the tempting inflammable whisky all in the one hold. Questioning revealed that both the manager of Canada Shipping and the company's supercargo also failed to comprehend the nature of the British advisory or to be guided by it.

Demonstrating some bias, Stanton describes Kenneth Montgomery, Canada Shipping's manager, as being in his job to "enrich" Riddle. Perhaps it would be better to say that in capitalism every manager of a business has a duty to make money. It is the lubricant by which his business survives and prospers — or fails if it loses enough money. In any business there must be a delegation of duties. It is certainly better if people understand each other's jobs, but there has to be a person who takes ultimate responsibility, be he captain of a ship, or head of a firm. The commission declared among its findings:

> Mr. Montgomery contended that as head of the firm he could not be expected to attend to details....But this was not a detail, it was a matter of prime importance in the business of a shipping company ....the safe carriage of cargoes .... We are unable to see that Mr. Montgomery can be cleared of fault.

Alexander Galt, marine superintendent for Canada Shipping Company was likewise indifferent to the British warning. He testified that he might have filed the advisory away, he wasn't sure. Galt had been a supercargo himself and should have known that sodium chlorate was dangerous. Under questioning from Dugald Donaghy, Galt was asked why he had not so advised his supercargo, Charles Heward, to which he responded that the latter should have known about sodium chlorate. If Galt himself knew about it, he certainly did not pass his knowledge along and it was quite wrong of him to assume that others would automatically know. Galt claimed that the only space available for stowage of the sodium chlorate was in No. 3 'tween-deck, whereas the ship's loading plan, prepared by Heward on Galt's instructions showed that there was plenty of available unused space in Nos. 4 and 5 'tween-decks.

The Canadian Pacific Railway whose boxcars delivered the sodium chlorate drums to the ship's side understood the nature of the material very well and even though only a few of the drums were yellow-tagged to indicate their hazardous nature, the railway saw to it that the boxcars were held on a siding at its yards at Coquitlam until they were required alongside the ship. The warning this implied was not passed on to anyone else.

If the commission was unimpressed by Galt's performance, the same applied to Heward. Heward claimed he had no idea that sodium chlorate was dangerous and that the CPR had sided the boxcars carrying the material at Coquitlam for that reason. He prepared the detailed loading plan and Galt approved it without paying further attention to the cargo or its stowage. Heward left copies of the loading plan for Captain Wright and First Officer Alan Horsfield, but had no discussion with either of them and assumed that they had approved the plan. The commission stated that while they had considerable sympathy for Mr. Heward, in that it seemed obvious that responsibility was placed by his seniors onto his shoulders and, while they were satisfied that he had done his best for this cargo, his best was not good enough.

Chief Officer Horsfield had authority to overrule the loading plan as presented, but did not do so as he was not aware that the ship was loading dangerous cargo. As for his punishment, the commission had the power to suspend his certificate, but decided not to even though he was clearly in breach of his duties. They pointed out that Horsfield had demonstrated gallant conduct after the explosions in exposing himself to danger and taking charge of unberthing the vessel so that she could be towed out into the stream. Added to this they saw the injustice of dealing with Horsfield's certificate when they were powerless to deal with that of Captain John Wright.

Captain Wright's position was that, as a non-party to the hearings, like Riddle and Canada Shipping Company Ltd., he was out of reach of the commission in terms of possible punishment. However, he volunteered a strange story to the commission. He claimed to have spent many hours studying the cargo list and loading plan and two books on stowage, to find that sodium chlorate was a dangerous substance. He overlooked a warning that this substance must not be stowed with combustibles or other explosives, and wrongly decided that the chlorate could be stowed with the flares (not to mention the whisky, inviting longshoremen to breach containers and sample the product).

If he had left his testimony at that and taken the criticism that inevitably followed he might have been far wiser. Instead he told the commission of a plan he had to watch No. 3 'tween-deck very carefully while at sea. If fire broke out he would order the crew to abandon ship, after which he and a few officers would close all apertures and then douse the fire with steam. To quote Stanton, "The officers were then to take to the boats and observe the results from a safe distance. That a captain could concoct such a plan showed a lively imagination, but the commission was far from enthusiastic." That left unanswered the consequences of a heavy sea running and having difficulties in launching boats.

The commissioners' comments were very damaging:

Captain Wright was fully alive to the potential danger....but we are unable to accept his evidence at face value ....[If he was so apprehensive] as to contemplate....such extreme measures....at sea, he should have taken steps to mitigate the danger....but he did nothing.

As for the suggestion of Wright and Montgomery, that wartime needs sometimes displaced good practice, the commission thought, "such a proposition has only to be stated to be refuted." The commissioners could not acquit Captain Wright of default, and his indifference to the nature and stowage of the cargo constituted a grave delinquency. They rejected outright his reason for putting all the inflammable cargo into No.3 'tween-deck so that everything would be accessible during the voyage.

It was obvious that the commissioners had no sympathy for the issue of wartime expediency. Other wartime accidents were the result of bad stowage, bad ship management and bad pilotage, and there might have been some excuse for this when taking into account the nature of wartime pressures. For example, when Britain's ports were at times under daily bombing attack, there was an inevitable attitude of "get the ship loaded (or unloaded) and get her out." Shortcuts in cargo handling and stowage were probably inevitable, but it is doubtful if the same pressure existed in the Port of Vancouver when loading a ship bound for Australia.

All through the war there had been constant traffic between Vancouver and Australia and New Zealand. Ships on the route could be kept well south of any Pacific war zone and Japanese submarines generally favoured the waters of their far-flung new "empire" or the Indian Ocean where they still had aggressive opportunities. Incursions, if any, into waters through which *Green Hill Park* was to travel were few and far between. The only exception involving a casualty appears to have been *Fort Camosun*, newly built at Victoria and on her maiden voyage. She was torpedoed near Cape Flattery by a Japanese submarine in the only such incident in local waters, but fortunately this vessel was able to return to port for repairs and to live another day.

The Port Warden, retired Captain Carl R. Bissett, was also taken to task. His job was to certify certain ships as being fit and ready for sea following loading. He inspected the loading in No. 3 and pronounced himself satisfied. He claimed to have consulted two books on stowage and found that they confirmed his position on the subject. Later when these books were examined they were found to say exactly the opposite of what Bisset claimed.

Several theories as to the cause of the explosions were advanced by witnesses. They ranged from sabotage to an incendiary bomb, spontaneous combustion and friction. None were sustainable and were rejected by the commissioners. Their attention was given to what was considered the most obvious cause — the whisky was leaking or had been broached and fumes had been ignited either by a cigarette or a match. Once this fire took hold, fed by more leaking whisky, the flames spread rapidly and within minutes the hold was a conflagration, igniting the sodium chlorate and the flares.

The last man out of the hold was union witness George Sickavish, who barely escaped with his life. The employers, such as Empire Stevedoring, the firm engaged to load the ship, spoke of the difficulty of getting longshoremen to stop smoking. Sickavish told of a recent union meeting where it was decided that anyone who smoked in a ship's hold would be fined $100, a substantial enough fine at that time, guaranteed to hurt. Percy Cavanagh, who was working on deck that day could see into the hold and was satisfied that he saw no one smoking — many of the men working below came up on deck to smoke. Six other men corroborated Cavanagh's statement, two others remained non-committal.

The commissioners did not think they were getting the whole story, just as they obviously felt they were getting close to the real cause of the fire. The explosion needed little conjecture, following on as the natural result of the fire. After much questioning and sometimes evasive answers, the commission held that "a lighted match carelessly dropped by a longshoreman" into spilled whisky was the true cause:

In coming to this conclusion we have kept before us the fact that there was no direct evidence that whisky had spilled, and none that a lighted match had been dropped. But....we are irresistibly drawn to that conclusion. There is no other rational conclusion....There is no evidence that the spilling of the whisky was by broaching, yet we think....such was the case. While we appreciate that it is almost impossible to load a general cargo like this without some damage in the course of loading yet we think that the whisky barrels....were stowed in sound condition. They had not very far to go from the wharf....they would not be damaged in that short journey. If that is so, broaching was the cause of the spilling.

Stanton's narrative jumped to the defence of the union members. He stated that the last conclusion was unreasonable, with no supporting evidence. All it takes is for a winch driver to drop a fragile load a small distance instead of letting it down gently. If the commissioners' conclusions are based on intelligent conjecture after all other reasons have been eliminated — and they virtually say as much — Stanton's own suggestion is equally conjectural.

To reach their conclusion the commission inferred that there was a passageway giving access to the whisky, that whisky was broached and spilled; and that one man lit a match, dropped it and ignited the fumes. Their line of reasoning relied heavily on evidence that a jacket had been found with rubber hot water bottles sewn inside and lunch pails with soldered compartments for liquids were found in No. 2 and 3 'tween-decks:

> Those utensils were there for the express purpose of carrying away pilfered whisky. They could have had no other purpose. They were direct evidence of preparation to this end and no explanation was forthcoming [to refute this].

In 1980 a 91-year old retired longshoreman told Vancouver news reporter Chuck Davis what he had learned from another longshoreman in 1957 when the two men were in hospital. The other man did not expect to live. He told his friend that a narrow passage had indeed been cleared back to the liquor. Taking turns, men took a drink or filled a bottle. Whisky was spilled and one man, already a little intoxicated, lit a match because he could not see well. The dying man kept his own counsel for 12 years. Davis's informant guarded the secret for another 23.

The commissioners concluded that fault lay not only with Montgomery, Galt, Wright, Bissett and Horsfield, but also with one or more longshoremen working in No. 3 'tween-deck. They were guilty of wrongful acts and defaults which contributed to the *Green Hill Park* disaster and must be censured.

Stanton's narrative returns to the attack on the matter of the non-parties and it is certainly hard to understand how Chief Officer Horsfield was named and Captain Wright was excused. There seems little logic in this and maybe Stanton was right when he suggested that for whatever reason the Department of Transport wanted to be kind to him. Certainly the commissioners had adequate time to consider Captain Wright's role in their earlier secret deliberations. As they were to say later they considered Wright to have been blameworthy on the basis of evidence that came out, and would have dealt with his certificate had they had the power.

However, Stanton focusses much of the blame on the Canada Shipping Company and Ernest Riddle, its major shareholder and general manager of Park Steamships, absent in Ottawa most of the time. It seems reasonable to suggest that if Riddle should have been joined, so also should the unions as organizations, unable and perhaps unwilling to control their members and their bad habits which led to the fire. There is no intent here to whitewash the role of the capitalist who happened to own a shipping company, but it could be said of Riddle that he was just as helpless to control events in Vancouver from Ottawa, as the union bosses were in Toronto. The fact that he awarded a contract to manage one or more ships is irrelevant in the events that overtook *Green Hill Park*, and Stanton's singling out of this fact smacks of the ideological rather than the hard-headed business decisions which had to be made to keep the ships managed and moving.

Stanton concludes with some theorizing on the whole process of disposal of government-owned ships which while useful, smacks of ideology of a type that is more properly answered in Chapter 11.

John Stanton's highly readable account was published in the *Northern Mariner* and *Beaver* magazines, in 1991. The author acknowledges the value of both articles, but has been largely guided overall by the official original accounts of the commissioners conducting the enquiry which are on file with the Vancouver Maritime Museum, to whom thanks are due.

CHAPTER NINE

The Last Voyage and Loss of *Westbank Park*

Contributed by Lew Brewer of San Jose, California, who was a wireless
operator aboard the ship during her final voyage and loss.

July 3, 1945, was a cool and damp day as the
Canadian freighter *Westbank Park* left Port Alberni,
British Columbia. The ship was fully laden with
general cargo and lumber taken on at Vancouver,
New Westminster, and Fraser Mills, and topped off
with a deck-load of lumber at Port Alberni. After
clearing Alberni Canal the pilot was disembarked off
Cape Beale and the ship turned south for the
Panama Canal.

This was the third voyage of *Westbank Park*.
Captain George Wallwork had taken command of
the vessel at the commencement of her second voyage, after having served as master of various ships for
two and a half years. He had been loaned to the
Canadian Government by the United Kingdom
Ministry of War Transport to help fill the need for
experienced senior deck officers on Canadian ships.
He was thirty-four years old at the time of this voyage, and when not at sea called Freshfield Lanes,
Lancashire, England, his home.

Among the crew of forty-nine there were twenty-
six new faces for this voyage. The new crewmen were
the chief and second mate, chief, second, third, and
fourth engineers, the bosun, carpenter, and donkeyman, two able seamen, two ordinary seamen, three
greasers, four fireman/water tenders, the second steward, two messmen, two messboys, and the galleyboy.
All four DEMS (Defensively Equipped Merchant
Ships) gunners were new to the *Westbank Park*.

The weather on July 3 may have been dreary, but
not so the crew's spirits. With Newport in the
United Kingdom being the outgoing destination it
meant that the latter half of this portion of the voyage would be in modified peacetime conditions. At
this time the ship's crew could not envision the strife
and misfortune that was to accompany the vessel
and finally lead to her destruction.

Some of the wartime conditions required of merchant ships travelling in the Atlantic after VE Day
were relaxed. Blackout curtains were no longer
required, nor the need to use porthole windscoops.
The restriction against a vessel "blowing tubes" during daylight was lifted and there was very little likelihood of a need for zigzag navigation, which resulted in the annoying "change course" alarm buzzer.
From a radio operator's perspective it meant some
relief from the restrictive BAMS (Broadcast All
Merchant Ships) procedures.

As the ship travelled south the weather warmed
progressively, as did the mood of the crew who were
contemplating going ashore at Panama. Any crew
member who had previously been ashore there, and
had visited Panama City, had many a listener hanging on to his every word while he extolled the mer-
its of such night spots as Kelley's Bar and Sloppy
Joe's. The likelihood of this shore leave was very
small as wartime conditions still prevailed, but it did
not stop a sailor from dreaming.

On July 19 *Westbank Park* rounded Punta Mala and entered the Gulf Of Panama for the approach to the Canal Zone. She steamed by a long line of vessels awaiting clearance to pass through the canal, and secured at Balboa. As so often happened in those times shore leave was not granted.

The ship passed through the canal on July 20, 1945. If you were one of the radio operators in the ship it meant an eight hour "excused from duty," so to speak, as United States military personnel took over various ship's operations during the canal transit. One of these was radio communications. Another significant change was the stationing of armed guards at the telegraph in the wheelhouse and engineroom. Their purpose was to ensure that the pilot's directives to the engineroom were carried out as ordered, thus lessening the possibility of sabotage.

It was also during the transit that the first indication of dissension arose between the deck crew and Chief Mate John Ridley. Some of the crew were required to work the ship's winches during their off-hours and expected to be paid overtime. However, the chief mate misinterpreted the agreement between the Seamens Union and Park Steamship Co., and refused their request.

The passage through the warm waters of the Caribbean was very pleasant and uneventful with the ship arriving at Aruba, Dutch West Indies, on July 23. Some of the off-duty crewmen were able to make use of the beautiful sandy beach adjacent to the pier, but in the days to follow suffered from the resultant sunburn. The ship passed through the Windward Passage, separating Cuba from

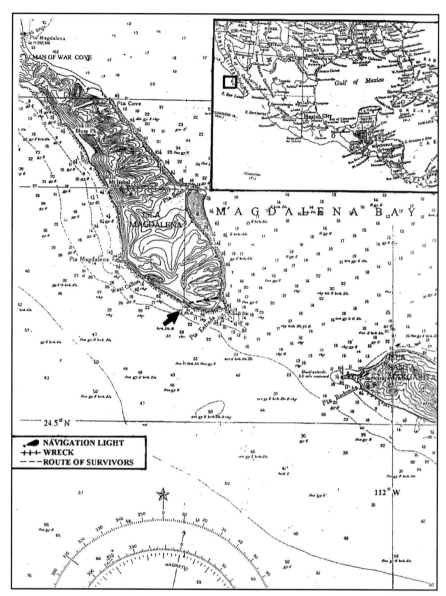

Map showing location of the wreck near the south end of the Baja California Peninsula.
(Lewis R. Brewer)

Hispaniola, and into the Atlantic arriving at Newport, Monmouthshire, on the Bristol Channel on August 8, 1945.

The arrival of the ship at Newport meant the return to their homeland for six of the crew in addition to Captain Wallwork. The ship's carpenter, Ken Wilkinson, called Newport his home, Third Officer Jim Surrey was from Hull, Able Seaman Stanley Haigh was from Aston, near Birmingham, and Gerald Wright, second engineer, lived at Thornton Heath. Two officers, Chief Engineer Emmanuel Bell, and Chief Steward Charlie Hunter, were from Scotland.

Discharging cargo at Newport became a lengthy undertaking. Soon after the ship arrived in the

Every master's nightmare. With both anchors down, *Westbank Park* leans precariously to port.

United Kingdom a nationwide dockyard worker's strike took place, shutting down all unloading operations. Further delays occurred when it was decided to bring in British Army personnel to move cargo, and again during the VJ Day celebrations.

During this time of delays, with the soldier's lack of ship handling experience, and their own uncertain future in peacetime, a tense atmosphere began to be felt by many of the ship's personnel. Apart from that, there was a growing feeling of nationalism among the Canadians. This feeling was generated by the fact that there were many non-Canadian senior officers aboard Canadian-flagged ships, and *Westbank Park* was by no means an exception to this situation. Adding fuel to this unsettled atmosphere was the contention that British crew members were being granted leave, but Canadians were not.

It was in this atmosphere that another difficulty arose between the deck crew and the chief mate. The crew questioned the validity of Mr. Ridley's order to replace a pier-mounted gangway with the ship's accommodation ladder, and to remove hatch covers. The deck crew's representative stated that there were uncertainties regarding duties to be carried out by ship's personnel or the dock workers. The seamen resumed work after being told by Captain Wallwork that the Custom of the Port required the ship's crew

to remove hatch covers. They were also warned that the local authorities would be called in should they not comply.

A similar action followed on August 18 when the crew refused to remove a hatch cover and replace covers on two unloaded holds. Because of this action Captain Wallwork felt that the union agreement with Park Steamship Co. had been broken. Some time later three or four of the deck crew agreed to prepare the hatches. It was on this date that the deck crew's representative reported to the master that they were unable to work with Mr. Ridley.

Two verbal charges were levied by the deck crew against the chief mate, one specific and the other implied. The specific charge pertained to the removal of approximately eighty gallons of lifeboat motor gasoline for transport ashore. Two unofficial reports were made regarding this action, one to Second Engineer Gerald Wright (who was responsible for maintaining the lifeboats) and the other to Mr. Ridley. Both of the individuals who reported this action were told to mind their own business.

The implied charge pertained to an incident that occurred while the deck crew were painting the ship's side immediately below the overboard discharge pipe from the officer's head. A sign had been placed in the bathroom warning of "Men Working Over Side," but someone flushed the toilet, resulting in the painters being inundated. There were few witnesses to this, other than the deck crew, but no one could specifically identify who did the flushing. The seamen were quite certain who it was.

On August 29, because some of the deck crew were ashore without authorization, and also because of the statement by the seamen's representative that they could not work with the chief mate, Captain Wallwork summoned the deck crew to the bridge. He read Part 3 of the Canada Shipping Act, which pertained to regulations for maintaining discipline. Despite the reading of the regulations the crew refused to work that day and again were mustered before the master.

They were informed, because of disobeying Mr. Ridley's order to work, that they were "off pay" as of that date, and would remain so until work resumed. In addition, shore leave during working hours was cancelled, as were all cash advances.

In order to accomplish necessary deck work Captain Wallwork instructed the chief mate to appoint Cadet Bruce Campbell as temporary bosun, and that he be assisted by the carpenter and four DEMS personnel, David Redden, Clifford Graham, A. McGill, and L. Epp.

On August 30 a preliminary Royal Navy inquiry into the dispute was conducted by Lt T. Corner, RNVR. He reported his findings to his superiors resulting in a formal hearing being held aboard the ship on September 3, under the direction of LtCmdr McClintlock, RNVR. When individually interviewed all members of the deck crew stated that they could not work under the present chief mate, but would accept a replacement.

To prevent any further delay in the ship's departure Captain Wallwork decided to replace Mr. Ridley, and temporarily promoted Second Mate Gordon Fraser to that position. Mr. Fraser had just received his Second Mate's Certificate and was making his first voyage in that capacity when he joined the ship on July 1 at Port Alberni. As a result of this change the deck crew, after six days of idleness, returned to work.

On September 6, *Westbank Park* was ready to shift from the pier to a buoy, where she would await final sailing orders. Tugs were available, and a pilot was aboard. The deck crew noted that Chief Mate Ridley was at his normal position for leaving harbour, and, when ordered to lift the accommodation ladder and stand by the lines, they refused. The captain informed the ship's agents of the problem and requested that they notify the local police, and also to engage local shore-side riggers to handle the ship's lines.

The following morning eight riggers boarded the ship and when ordered to let go the lines the deck crew climbed on to the ship's railings and threatened to jump overboard. It was their consensus that as long as the ship was tied to the pier the dispute was of a local nature, but once they were at sea it would be mutiny. The hired riggers, in sympathy with the crew, refused to comply with the order to cast off and disembarked.

On the morning of September 8, Chief Mate Ridley was discharged, without prejudice, and left the ship. He was replaced by Geoffrey Fenton, a Port of Halifax pilot, who had been on leave in the United Kingdom.

With the arrival of Mr. Fenton the ship left Newport in ballast. In this state a ship's draught and trim are controlled by the amount of bunker fuel and water contained in various tanks throughout the ship. At the time of departure the draught of the ship was eight feet forward and seventeen feet aft, meaning that approximately eight feet of the ship's bow would be submerged when the ship was in a steady state. Five of the six double-bottom tanks were filled with either bunker fuel or water, the fore and after peak tanks were full of fresh water and the 750-ton Deep Tank straddling the after end of the engineroom and No. 4 hold was filled with sea water. The only empty bottom tank was No. 1, located at the forward portion of the ship. Except for the Deep Tank the contents of all remaining tanks would be accessible for use during the voyage, resulting in a continuous lightening of the vessel between refuelling ports.

During wartime the British Admiralty had regulations requiring "in ballast" merchant ships to carry some solid ballast. This was necessary during convoy passages in order to keep a ship's propeller submerged, thus better enabling it to maintain its appointed station in the convoy. Under normal weather conditions the procedure for a Canadian Victory-type vessel, during peacetime, was for no solid ballast to be carried, and it was left to the master's discretion whether the ship was seaworthy enough for the weather conditions that might be encountered during a voyage.

The hurricane season was still in effect in the Caribbean and the cyclone occurrences of the North Pacific were most common during the months of September and October. As *Westbank Park* proceeded south from the United Kingdom a chain of tropical storms (seedlings) was forming just north of the Equator off the African coast. On September 11 the wind velocity in one of these "seedlings" accelerated to hurricane force (in excess of seventy mph) and moved northwestward into the eastern Caribbean. This storm was identified as Hurricane #9 (1945) by the Hurricane Forecast Office, at Miami, Florida.

As the ship was entering the Caribbean area on September 18, the hurricane had passed over most of the southeastern seaboard of the United States, but was still causing rough seas in the area.

These weather conditions continued as the ship arrived at Aruba to refuel on the twenty-third. A sister ship, *Tipperary Park* (J. Parsons, Master), chartered to Anglo-Canadian Shipping, was already alongside refuelling, requiring *Westbank Park* to stand off while awaiting the former's departure. Both ships were subjected to very heavy seas and buffeting winds during that day.

The weather during the westward voyage from Aruba to Panama Canal was pleasant. The ship arrived at Colon, at the Caribbean approach to the Canal, on September 27 and after passing through received clearance from the US Navy Tenth Fleet to depart Balboa and proceed into the Pacific Ocean.

Steaming northward from September 27 to October 5, the ship encountered normal weather conditions for that time of year, namely, intermittent rain squalls, fair to gusty winds, and a sea with heavy swells.

During the morning watch (0400 to 0800 hours) of Saturday, October 6, Chief Radio

The view from near sea level. The moderate sea that was running still created boiling surf close inshore among the rocks.

Operator Vern Christenson received a weather report warning of a tropical storm moving northwesterly off the Gulf of Tehuantapec. This storm was the dissipation stage of Hurricane #10, which had formed in the Caribbean off the coast of Nicaragua, and had accelerated into full hurricane strength on October 2. This disturbance quickly lost strength after crossing the Gulf of Honduras and Guatemala, and on October 5 was down-graded to a tropical storm. Mr. Fenton plotted the storm as being 400 miles astern and moving in a direction approximating *Westbank Park's* course.

During that morning the ship was closing Cabo San Lucas, at the southern tip of Baja California, Mexico. Mr. Fenton had the ship secured against possible rough weather should the reported storm overtake them. The timing of this action was prompted more by the fact that the deck crew on day work would finish at noon (Saturday) and would be off duty until the following Monday.

Still very much an intact ship. Oil stains from escaped bunker oil leave their telltale marks amidships.

Spreading oil stains can be seen on the starboard side of the hull in this aerial shot of the wreck, which looks like a toy boat thrown up on the rocks.

At noon, October 6, a good position fix was made on the lighthouse at Cabo Falso, located five miles due west of Cabo San Lucas. At this time the weather was overcast with a moderate sea. Captain Wallwork set a course of 310° to allow the ship to stay in visual contact when coming up on a lighthouse at Playa Punta Lobos, some forty miles to the north, and a fourteen-mile light at Punta Redonda, at the entrance to Magdalena Bay, 155 miles ahead. Approximately eight miles north of the Punta Redonda light was Punta Magdalena, which, when viewed from the 310° course, was the extreme wester-

ly point of land before the shoreline fell sharply eastward. The course change to 310° placed the wind and sea on the ship's beam, resulting in a moderate roll.

The weather started to deteriorate soon after leaving Cabo San Lucas. The wind increased to Force 6 (25 to 30 mph) and the barometric pressure dropped to 29.52. No sighting of the Playa Punta Lobos lighthouse was possible because of reduced visibility, however an approximate longitudinal fix was made when the sun momentarily broke through. No further sightings were possible the remainder of the day.

By 1600 hours the southwesterly had increased to moderate gale force and the ship was rolling excessively. When crew members of the afternoon watch came off duty they appeared reluctant to go below and many gathered on No. 3 hatch (located between the bridge structure and the engineroom) to discuss how much further the ship would have to roll before the ship's funnel gave way. Also, as the ship came to the extremity of a roll it started hesitating for what seemed like an eternity to the crew, before righting herself. A sigh of relief could be heard when this occurred.

The barometer reading continued to drop until 1800 hours at which time it had reached 29.35. An increase was noted on the next hourly reading, and at 2000 hours it was up to 29.40. The wind did not abate, however, instead it increased to 50 knots, but because of the rise in the barometric pressure the master felt that the worst was over.

Any thought of sleep by the off-duty crewmen was dispelled by the severe rolling of the ship, especially for those with the misfortune of having athwartship bunks. At 2200 hours the chief mate called out the off-duty deck crew, the carpenter, and the bosun to check for loose hatch tarpaulins and any other ship's equipment that was not properly secured. Some repairs were also attempted on one of the lifeboats that had been damaged. This work was very difficult and dangerous because of the heavy rolling.

The wind continued to increase in velocity, finally reaching hurricane strength at 2300 hours, with the barometric pressure falling to 29.17. Captain Wallwork had ordered a course change at 2245 hours to 285°, and again fifteen minutes later to 275°, hoping to keep well clear of Punta Redonda. The ship was still moving at maximum speed, approximately twelve knots, assisted by a one-knot current.

Hurricanes originating along the Pacific coast of Central America and Mexico were infrequently reported owing to the lack of weather ships patrolling this area, and storms often struck without warning. The Weather Bureau in San Francisco was unaware of this particular hurricane until notified of *Westbank Park's* distress signal.

Able Seaman Gerry Davis and seventeen-year-old Ordinary Seaman Lloyd Tyerman alternated at the wheel on this watch. When the course changes to port were given, steering became very difficult with the ship fighting her way to the desired course, only to fall away again. By 2300 hours the wheel was being held hard a-port in an attempt to maintain the desired course of 275°, but this was counter-productive. The telemotors used for the steering of this class of ship tended to leak pressure when held hard over, causing the rudder to ease back to a midships position. At the end of his watch at midnight Davis had to remain at the wheel as the relieving watch was still required on the open deck.

At approximately 2330 hours the master had Second Radio Operator Victor Decloux transmit a weather and position report. This position would be an estimation only, based on the noon position off Cabo San Lucas, the 310° course, and with adjustments for the wind and current. Decloux received an acknowledgement from *Tipperary Park*, which was left astern of *Westbank Park* during the evening of the 5th.

When the midnight to 0400 watch came on duty the wheel was still hard a-port, the barometer reading was 29.18 and the ship was battered by 65- to 75-mph winds. There were heavy rain squalls and the vessel was shipping spray from the wave tops that at times reached the height of the bridge, cutting visibility to nil. For a brief moment around 0100 hours a navigation light was observed off the starboard beam by Captain Wallwork, Second Mate Fraser, and the seamen carrying out the deck work. This light was identified as Punta Redonda and was estimated to be five miles distant.

At 0125 hours, October 7, the master and second mate saw what appeared to be land ahead. Fraser was ordered to place the engineroom telegraph on "standby." He also checked the depth sounder but found no reading, then alerted the on-duty radio operator, Lewis Brewer. Immediately after, Captain Wallwork called into the wheelhouse that there were breakers in sight and ordered "full astern" on the telegraph, and to activate the lifeboat alarm bells. Fraser carried out these orders then prepared a position fix for the radio operator. It was then the ship hit the first reef.

Brewer turned on and tested the low frequency transmitter and then was relieved by Chief Radio Operator Christenson. He descended the inside stairway (located at the after end of the chartroom) to get a lifejacket from his cabin. When he reached the Captain's Deck the vessel hit the second reef throwing Brewer forcefully against the bulkhead. His first thought was that he could be trapped inside, and he hurried to his cabin to get his lifejacket.

Meanwhile, in the engineroom, when Third Engineer Robert Larsen received the "standby" order on the telegraph he had steam put on the reversing engine. He was able to immediately execute the order when the bridge asked for "full astern." When the ship hit the second reef, water could be heard rushing into the engineroom bilges.

Christenson received the ship's position from the second mate and transmitted the first of many distress signals (SOS), however, because of the heavy radio static in the hurricane area, no acknowledgement was received. The distress signal had been picked up by *Tipperary Park* steaming approximately fifty miles astern, and by United States Naval Receiving Station, NPG, at San Francisco.

Westbank Park grounded heavily at 0130 hours and immediately took on a twenty-degree list to port. Captain Wallwork gave orders to place the engines on "slow ahead", and to let both anchors go. Because of the heavy pounding the vessel was taking he decided it would be necessary to abandon ship. He ordered the engineroom personnel to evacuate and proceed to the forecastle and directed the chief and second mate to set up the searchlight to assist the crew in leaving the ship. The searchlight was located on the monkey island, a small, open navigation bridge above the wheelhouse. It provided some illumination of the forecastle and the rocks immediately off the bow.

After getting his lifejacket Brewer went to the lifeboat station on the top of the engineroom housing to assist Decloux in setting up the portable emergency lifeboat transmitter. This equipment would normally go into a lifeboat, but because of the heavy windward list it was decided that it would not be safe to lower a boat, and the set was activated while on the deck.

Most of the crew were at their lifeboat stations and were very calm and quiet. The ship was still being pounded heavily by the waves, and the deck was awash with rain and sea spray. One of the deck crew was detailed to alert the seamen at the lifeboat stations and

other locations that the "abandon ship" order had been given and everyone was to proceed to the forecastle.

Engineers Jim Cruickshank and Ray Harling, who shared the same stateroom, had started dressing after the alarm bell rang. They were alerted to proceed forward immediately, and had to finished dressing while forcing their way along the open deck.

Chief Engineer Bell was in charge of the evacuation of the crew. Able Seaman Stan Haigh, who had previously survived four merchant ship sinkings by torpedoes, was selected from the many volunteers to swim ashore with a line. Unfortunately, on his attempt he found that his line was too short and continued swimming to the rocky shore. A second attempt was made, this one by Wilkinson, assisted by Ordinary Seaman Irwin Palmer, who was making his first voyage to sea. These two were able to reach shore with their line and, with the assistance of Haigh, secured it around a large boulder.

When the vessel struck the reefs and was holed in the double-bottom tanks, bunker fuel immediately spilled into the sea. The oil soon covered the nearby shoreline and was also washed over the ship's deck by the waves and spray. This condition, as well as the continuous lurching, made any movement on deck extremely hazardous. The three crew members who swam ashore with the lines had to fight huge waves coated with oil, fuel-covered rocks, and even encounters with sea lions. No words can describe their bravery.

Approximately one hour after the grounding the water in the engineroom had risen to the level of the boilers. Steam to the dynamotor was cut off resulting in the loss of electrical power throughout the ship. Christenson switched over to the battery operated auto-alarm transmitter. This unit was designed to send out a series of "dashes" used to activate the emergency receivers on any ships carrying only one radio operator. He then vacated the radio shack and proceeded to the forecastle. The shutting down of the dynamotor also meant the loss of lighting for the remainder of the abandonment.

A gantline and bosun's chair were rigged from the forecastle and the crew were able to leave *Westbank Park*. Only minimal injuries and some minor panic occurred during this operation, specifically when the

Some of the crew standing on shore directly above the wreck site. As can be seen some were heavily stained with oil as the result of events described in the narrative.

bosun's chair reached the water and the survivors found they had to swim, or go hand-over-hand on the rope, for the remaining distance to the shore. After leaving the water everyone suffered from exposure to the oil and the cold wind. By tearing the kapok from their lifejackets they were able to remove some of the oil, and used some of it inside their shirts to act as an insulator. One individual had the foresight to bring a bottle of spirits from the ship and this was passed to each of the crew as they arrived ashore, enabling them to wash the oil from their mouths.

Some of the crew chose to remain aboard rather than attempt disembarking in the dark. They felt that with the anchors down there was little likelihood of the vessel slipping astern, but ignored the possibility the ship might break up as a result of the constant pounding she was getting. There were a few crew members who could not swim, including seventeen-year-old Jim Ewanchook, the galley boy. The reason Christenson and Chief Steward Charlie Hunter remained aboard was they felt they had a better chance in daylight to salvage their prized possessions, Hunter's new Panama hat, and Christenson's wellington boots. Unfortunately, neither item survived the passage ashore.

Westbank Park had grounded in one of the few coves in the immediate area. This cove is located about one mile north of the four-and-a-half-mile-wide entrance to Magdalena Bay and is approximately 800 feet long, 350 feet wide, ending with a rocky shelf. The position of the grounded ship, and the high cliff on the cove's south side, provided some shelter against the southwesterly wind, permitting the crew to escape with only minor injuries and discomfort. Except for West Canon, located approximately one mile further north, anywhere else the vessel would had been driven ashore against a cliff with no easy means for the crew to make their way ashore.

At first light the remaining crew members left the ship and Captain Wallwork decided that everyone was ashore. Radio Operator Brewer and Palmer volunteered to climb the cliff to see whether there was habitation nearby. After a short, steep climb they found they were on a fairly level, cactus covered plateau. They could not determine which way to go, and decided to keep the ship at their backs. After walking approximately a mile they found they were on a bluff overlooking a large bay, in which were ten tuna fishing boats. They were looking down at Magdalena Bay, where the tuna boats had taken shelter to escape the hurricane.

A skiff had just departed the beach, but immediately returned when the two oil-covered seamen made their way down to the shore. They were taken to one of the tuna boats where they showered and were fed, and then were returned to the beach. They retraced their earlier journey and arrived back at the wreck approximately two hours later to report their discovery.

By 0800 hours the wind had abated considerably, but the swells were still very heavy. Captain Wallwork formed a party to swim back to the ship for blankets, food, and clothing for the scantily clad seamen. This party consisted of himself, the chief and second mates, Christenson, Cadet Campbell, Able Seamen Tom Ciebien, Jerry Davis, and Jim Wallace, and Ordinary Seaman Steve Michaud. They were able to lower the accommodation ladder and one of the motor launches. Supplies were removed from the ship throughout the morning using an aerial line and the gantline employed in the abandonment. The launch's crew, under the direction of Second Mate Fraser, were unable to start the motor and found themselves adrift, finally grounding under one of the towering cliffs approximately one mile from the wreck.

Tipperary Park, which had received the distress signal earlier, arrived off Punta Redonda at about 1000 hours and after communicating by Aldis lamp with *Westbank Park's* third mate, Jim Surrey, proceeded into Magdalena Bay. Surrey was positioned above the wreck on the plateau for that purpose, and gave Captain Parsons information on the condition of the wreck and survivors.

The US tuna boat *Liberty Bell* had anchored in the bay the previous day to escape the storm. Her crew were not aware of *Westbank Park's* grounding as they kept no radio watch while at anchor. When *Tipperary Park* informed them of the other ship's predicament they were most helpful in providing assistance to the survivors.

Tipperary Park anchored and made an attempt to send her two motor launches to the wreck but the currents were too strong, and the boats had to be towed back to their ship by *Liberty Bell's* launch. At 1730 hours a second attempt was made, but on this occasion the crew were unable to start the motor.

The crew of *Westbank Park's* abandoned motor launch had climbed a very steep cliff onto the plateau, arriving there at 1630 hours, and joined the last of their ship's survivors as they were transported to *Liberty Bell* for showers and meals. They were

then taken to *Tipperary Park*, the last arriving on board by 2100 hours. Captain Wallwork remained on *Liberty Bell*, accompanied by Chief Engineer Bell and Second Mate Fraser. A radio message was sent to Seaboard Shipping Co., the ship's operator in Vancouver, requesting instructions.

Next morning, October 8, a medical officer attached to the US Navy ship *K107* arrived aboard *Tipperary Park* to provide any assistance needed. Three of the survivors, Cadet Mike Hornak, Messboy Edward Bowcott, and Second Cook Charles Bentley, as well as one of *Tipperary Park's* crewmen were examined for minor injuries and oil irritation. *Liberty Bell* proceeded to Man-of-War Cove, located approximately twelve miles inside the bay, where Captain Wallwork reported to the Mexican customs officer at the small village of Puerto Magdalena.

At noon the chief mates of both Park ships, William Goldie and Mr. Fenton, formed parties in order to obtain more provisions from the wreck. They returned that evening and *Tipperary Park* prepared to sail next morning at first light. The master of *Westbank Park* and the other two officers remained aboard *Liberty Bell* and would eventually be transferred to the American vessel *Nevadum* for passage to the United States and Canada.

Next morning when *Tipperary Park* rounded Punta Entrada, at the northern entrance to Magdalena Bay, the ship's starboard railing was lined with crew members from both ships, silently waiting for a glimpse of the grounded *Westbank Park*. For the majority, this would be the last view of the wreck. A few who passed by later as crew aboard other ships, may have had a distant glimpse.

One *Westbank Park* crew member, Radio Operator Brewer, returned to Magdalena Bay in 1948 and 1949, while serving in the cruiser HMCS *Ontario*. A fleet of Canadian ships had left Esquimalt, British Columbia, in January of those years and spent ten days in the bay prior to sailing into the Caribbean. During those stays Brewer hiked the twelve miles from Man-of-War Cove to the cliffs overlooking the wreck. He noted that the stern portion of the ship (from the after-engineroom bulkhead) had broken away and sunk, also that the remaining after portion was closer to the shore.

Having recovered most of their personal belongings, crew pose for a photo on their way back to Vancouver. Some were to serve time in jail for mutinous conduct while the ship was in the UK. (Lewis R. Brewer)

Brewer felt that it was probably at the after engine-room location that the vessel originally came to rest on the third reef.

Crew members of *Tipperary Park* were very hospitable to the survivors, sharing their accommodations with their *Westbank Park* counterparts for a total of five days. Accommodations on this type of ship were not spacious, and to receive double the people, provide them with sleeping space and feed them was a logistical nightmare.

Westbank Park's survivors left the rescue ship at San Pedro, California, on October 12, 1945, and then proceeded to Vancouver, British Columbia, by train.

Prior to October 12 Park Steamship Co. of Montreal, managers of the ship, had arranged to have a team of marine surveyors from San Diego,

California, sent to the wreck site. They declared *Westbank Park* a total loss.

On October 24 the Supervising Examiner of Masters and Mates, Department of Transport, held a preliminary hearing at Vancouver, British Columbia, into the loss of *Westbank Park*. A total of eighteen crew members were interviewed, after which a preliminary report was forwarded to Ottawa for review and action. On February 14, 1946, the Department of Transport closed its file on the loss of the ship, pending any forthcoming information that might indicate that the grounding was caused by anything other than the hurricane.

Nine crew members of *Westbank Park* were arrested in Vancouver on October 26 and charged, under the Canada Shipping Act, with unlawful and

Lew Brewer, the writer of this account, served in HMS *Uganda* and was able to revisit the wreck site in 1946. There he found that the stern section of the vessel from the aft engine room bulkhead had broken off and had sunk in deep water although the top of the mainmast was still visible.

(Lewis R. Brewer)

willful neglect of duty for their actions during August 28 through September 4, 1945, in Newport, Monmouthshire. They appeared in Vancouver City Police Court and were convicted as charged. Three of the crewmen were given twelve weeks of imprisonment, two received six weeks, and the remainder were given suspended sentences because of their age. Four of the seamen appealed their sentences and were heard in the County Court in Vancouver on February 8, 1946. Their appeals were dismissed but their sentences were reduced to time served.

The action of *Westbank Park*'s deck crew, in refusing to take the ship to sea, was not the only such incident experienced by operators of Park ships. In court at the same time were seamen off *Cromwell Park* who faced the same charge as the men of *Westbank Park*.

The subject of the large number of arrested sailors from Park ships was discussed in the House of Commons on November 6, 1945, and prompted the Department of Transport to hold an investigation. On December 14, the Minister of Transport reported to the House that those seamen charged were from *Westbank Park*, *Bridgeland Park* and *Cromwell Park* and that as the seamen's actions fell under the jurisdiction of local police courts rather than the Department of Transport, no action by the Department would be taken.

The *Westbank Park* story did not end there. International implications started arising as early as January, 1946. The Canadian Ambassador to Mexico received a copy of a communication from the Mexican Marine Department to the Foreign Minister of Mexico disclosing that under Mexican law, "any vessel remaining for thirty days outside a Mexican port, unattended, and without a permit to remain so, will become the property of the Mexican Government." The communication also indicated that because the *Westbank Park* was deemed by the Marine Department to be "in danger," all removable gear had been taken off to prevent it from being stolen, and stored in a Naval warehouse at Puerto Cortes, on Isla Margarita.

Park Steamship Co. was informed of the Mexican communication and reported that they had been approached by a Mexican salvage expert who lived at Puerto Cortes. The salvor felt that there was still salvageable material aboard, but that he would have to act as Park Steamship's agent to enable him to deal effectively with the Mexican courts. Park Steamship also requested of the Canadian Embassy in Mexico City, that the Mexican government be informed that *Westbank Park* had not been abandoned, and under international law was still the property of His Majesty the King, in right of Canada.

After a period of time no reply was received from the authorities in Mexico City, in addition the Mexican salvage expert lost interest in the project. Therefore, on May 2, 1947, the last voyage of S.S. *Westbank Park*, was finally "terminated" when the Canadian Government abandoned all claim to the ship.

CHAPTER TEN

Maintenance and Supply Ships for the Pacific War: Task Force 57 and the East Indies Fleet

From the moment it started, the Pacific naval war was to shake up many preconceived notions in a most revolutionary way. While not exclusively a naval war, the geographical and distance factors, plus the fact that the enemy had a large first-class navy and merchant fleet with great fighting capability, ensured that it would be the largest amphibious war ever fought.

It also introduced a new enemy whose philosophy of war was utterly different from our own; whose ideas of chivalry often perpetrated the worst kinds of cruelty on those who were vanquished or became its captives; whose highest goal was to sacrifice one's life in the pursuit of glory, to be reborn in a heaven reserved for the heroes of a regime which held its Emperor as a god. New words entered the English language: Kamikaze! Zero! and Banzai! took on their own significance.

Pearl Harbor not only repeated the lesson of Taranto, when British carrier planes sank or damaged major units of the Italian fleet, but also the relative helplessness of a battleship against air attack by a resolute enemy. Soon after came the loss of the British battleship *Prince of Wales* and the battle cruiser *Repulse* to air attack in the Japanese advance on Singapore, which once again confirmed that without adequate air cover the battleship was doomed. If there was any lingering thought about the battleship, little changed

since HMS *Dreadnought* and *Jutland*, being the primary fighting vessel and the aircraft carrier only secondary, this concept was to be transformed forever by events that took place in the Pacific.

In one fell swoop the Japanese navy took the United States sufficiently by surprise that it was able to knock out almost the entire US Pacific battle fleet. The remaining major ships, the American carriers which happened to be away from Pearl Harbor on exercises, were saved from the same fate.

During the Battle of Midway, neither side saw the other's ships from the surface. The battle was conducted entirely in the air and became a matter of superior tactics in the deployment of the carriers and the utilization of air power. With the devastation of Pearl Harbor and the loss of major fixed land bases at Manila, Hong Kong and Singapore, the Allied navies fell back on Sydney, Australia; Trincomalee, Ceylon and Pearl Harbor itself. The latter was brought back to full operational efficiency in record time, as were the salvable battleships, raised and removed to the mainland United States for rebuilding.

More quickly than anyone, the Americans, with huge distances to traverse in the Pacific, realized that new forms of naval support facilities would be needed if a highly mobile long-distance war was to be successfully fought. The challenge was to operate huge fleets without fixed full-facility shore bases such as Pearl Harbor and Singapore. Fortunately for the United States they had initiated a merchant marine replacement program in 1936. This program ostensibly was to replace the large fleet of First World War merchant tonnage, much of which was obsolescent and had been almost from the time it was originally built. The United States Maritime Commission initiated four basic standard design freighters and a tanker. Known as the C1, C2, C3 and C4 cargo ships and the T2 tanker, they appeared in a number of variations designed to suit the needs of individual owners on given trade routes.

Great attention was given to speed, turbine and turbo-electric propulsion systems, and cargo-handling facilities. They tended to run counter to European ideas of efficiency and economy, but even before the US entered the war, some

Launch OF HMS *Berry Head.* A special day at Burrard Dry Dock, North Vancouver, complete with launching party, Scottish pipe band and a huge crowd in early 1945. Hull 224, the third of the maintenance ships for the Royal Navy, is ready to go. Among the crowd are to be seen several hard hats which were then becoming standard on construction sites. The significance of the sign ahead of 224 is not recorded, but it reads "994, Vancouver, BC".

(North Vancouver Museum & Archives #27-02303)

of these ships had been converted to auxiliary use with the US Navy as attack transports, ammunition carriers and a variety of other uses. After Pearl Harbor the shipbuilding programs continued, so that many of the ships coming off the launching ways were finished as auxiliary aircraft carriers and components of what the British called the "Fleet Train".

After the surrender of Singapore, British influence and naval activity was mostly confined to Southeast Asia and Australia, where the priority was to stem the Japanese advance through Burma and into India, or southward beyond New Guinea to Australia. Britain at that time had relatively little in the way of a fleet of auxiliaries suitable for combat in this theatre of war. This was in large measure a con-

sequence of a different, more traditional form of naval war in Europe. Distances were far shorter in the principal theatres, the Mediterranean, the North Atlantic and the North Sea. Large well-equipped bases were near at hand for all the navies of Western Europe when war broke out in 1939.

The consequences of the blockade of German naval and merchant shipping, the fall of France and the entry of Italy into the war altered many circumstances, but the need for auxiliaries on the scale required for naval warfare in the Pacific was not there. All these navies had small fleets of such vessels as submarine depot ships, repair and salvage vessels and oilers, but with the exception of the Royal Navy they were largely inconsequential.

HMS *Beachy Head*. This was the first of the RN maintenance ships, later to become HMCS *Cape Scott*. As standard equipment, the class all came with two wooden landing craft, handy to the heavy-lift derricks, about 42 feet long, mounted on top of No. 2 and 4 holds which accommodated underdeck installation. The landing craft functioned as yard and crew workboats wherever the maintenance ships were based.
(Burrard Dry Dock Co.)

HMS *Hartland Point*. After disposing of uncompleted ships and those which became surplus to the Royal Navy peacetime establishment, a core fleet was kept which included this vessel. *Hartland Point* underwent major modifications so that her ancestry was barely recognizable.
(Vancouver Maritime Museum)

HMCS *Cape Scott*. After service in the Far East, *Beachy Head* was transferred to the Dutch Navy as *Vulkaan*. In 1953 she became *Cape Scott*, in the RCN.
(Dept. of National Defence Photo # 59747)

With the plans for invasion unfolding, first in North Africa, then Sicily, Italy and finally France, British and American developments of auxiliary ships and craft for amphibious warfare proceeded apace, with many improvements in designs and techniques being developed. The first invasion where the early British tank-landing craft was successfully used was the taking of Iceland. This was done in order to frustrate suspected German plans to take the island. Here these ships were able to demonstrate their oceangoing capacity by ferrying vehicles and tanks from Scotland to Iceland, across one of the bleakest sections of the North Atlantic.

As the war in Europe progressed in favour of the Allies, combined operations vessels were transferred in large numbers from the Mediterranean and

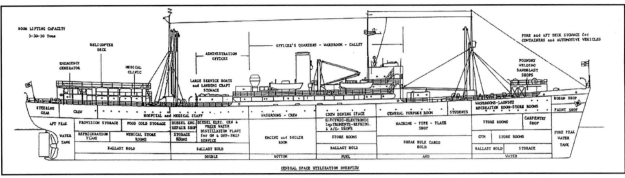

HMCS *Cape Breton*. This side elevation plan of *Cape Breton* probably differs little from when the ship was built. In the accompanying photo of *Cape Scott*, the large landing craft carried on deck and a good deal of deck gear and armament have gone. Today *Cape Breton* is the only survivor of any of the North Sands and its variants in North America. She is soon to become an artificial reef off the West Coast, fifty-five years after her completion. (Hill Wilson)

SPACE USE	Number of Rooms or Spaces	Areas of Dedicated Space (sq. ft.)	(cu. ft.)
Accomodation (Ship operation - 24, Students - 20 / Medical/Mission Staff - 32)	44	4,942	
Hospital and Medical Clinic	47 (30 beds)	10,541	
Offices	6	520	
Food Services	6	2,044	
Washrooms (private & public)	18	3,185	
Mechanical	10	6,680	
Lounge/Recreation	7	3,761	
Storage	29	11,248	101,004
General Purpose Area (evacuation berths - 250, exhibitions, meetings - 300 seats)		3,761	
Break Bulk Cargo Hold	1	4,086	57,232
Refrigeration Stores	6		10,126
Repair Shops	10	7,702	
Ship's Services	24	2,615	
Open Deck Storage Areas	5 - (14 containers or vehicles)		

Note: Passage ways, Ballast Holds and Tank Spaces are not included

SHIP'S SPECIFICATIONS

Length - 441'-6"
Beam - 57'-0"
Draft - 28'-0"
D.W.T. - 11,270
Speed - 11 Knots
Range - 7,000 N.M.

Northern Europe to India and Ceylon in readiness for the retaking of Burma, Malaya and the Dutch East Indies. The ability to service this armada grew proportionately, but it was mostly land-based.

It has been suggested that the Americans would have been quite satisfied if British efforts were confined to Southeast Asia as they already had a British East Indies fleet and, constituted separately, an Eastern Fleet. The latter was made up mostly of older units not appropriate to the Pacific Fleet, which had all the most modern and biggest British aircraft carriers and battleships. The East Indies and Eastern fleets were based in Indian ports and Trincomalee in what was then Ceylon. As the British and Indian Army advanced into Southeast Asia, the East Indies fleet would be the spearhead.

In building the Pacific Fleet, it was Churchill who laid down the edict that the British would fight alongside their American allies right through to the final overthrow of Japan, a proposal that was not always welcome to Admiral Ernest J. King, Chief of Naval Operations. Admirals Chester Nimitz, William "Bull" Halsey, Raymond Spruance and others of the US fighting admirals saw it differently and welcomed the British. The British in turn agreed to harmonize their Pacific Fleet operations with the Americans and place themselves under the command of Admiral Nimitz, the growing British Pacific Fleet being designated as Task Force 57.

However, the British were not well equipped for the Pacific war which had thus far largely been an American effort. Their capital ships tended to be slower than the Americans' and lacked the anti-aircraft fire-power needed against the massive aerial attacks of the Japanese. These deficiencies, except for speed, were remedied over time. The Swordfish torpedo bomber so successful at Taranto, but woefully inadequate against the German battleships *Gneisenau* and *Scharnhorst* in their successful dash through the English Channel, was hopelessly outclassed in the Pacific war and so far as the author is able to confirm was never used east of Singapore. The short-range Seafire and Firefly which were adequate for European waters were wholly inadequate for service in the Far East and were largely replaced by American types, including the Corsair, Dauntless, Hellcat and Avenger.

It was not always a case of American superiority however. The six big British carriers, *Indefatigable*, *Illustrious*, *Implacable*, *Indomitable*, *Formidable* and *Victorious*, with their armour-plated flight decks, soon proved their superiority over their American counter-

Fort Wrangell and part of Task Force 57. In the foreground, *Fort Wrangell,* a naval stores issuing ship, puts on speed to overtake the escort carrier *Ruler* on a safe converging course. In the background the tanker *Carelia* moves along at a more leisurely pace. The escort carriers provided air cover against attacking enemy planes for the fleet train ships. There were six large fleet carriers, four light fleet carriers and eight escort carriers in Task Force 57. The escort carriers were available as replenishment ships to the larger carriers in providing replacement planes. (North Vancouver Museum)

Fort Kilmar. As a typical stores issuing ship, some of her 'tween-deck space was turned into extra accommodation and offices. Not only did the ships carry a regular ship's crew with a gun crew, but a substantial additional staff had to be accommodated to dispense stores.

(Burrard Dry Dock Co.)

parts when hit by Kamikaze suicide planes. They were usually back in service in a matter of hours, being fully capable of making emergency repairs to holed flight decks, quickly dousing fires and clearing up other damage. The American carriers with their wooden flight decks fared much worse. In theory a wooden flight deck was more easily replaced than one of steel, but in fact they practically guaranteed the ship's becoming blazing infernos, and more than one American carrier was lost or suffered major damage.

In order to develop their fleet train of auxiliaries the British pressed a variety of vessels into service. Some were clearly unsuitable but it was a matter of making do with what was available. However, in preparation for the longer war that was anticipated plans had already been initiated to build a substan-

tial fleet of maintenance and supply or victualling ships in Canada. With the exception of three victualling ships all were built in West Coast yards. The maintenance ships were commissioned as regular naval vessels while the victualling ships were placed in service as merchant ships under the management of well-known liner companies.

In all, twenty-one maintenance ships based on the Canadian Victory ship design were ordered, of which 16 were completed by West Coast yards. The uncompleted hulls were finished as merchant ships and, being built to a high specification, found a ready market as cargo liners. The sixteen victualling ships were completed mainly in 1944 only the very last one being delivered about a month after the end of the war. The maintenance ships were all owned by

HMS *Tarbet Ness* as *Lautoka*. W.R. Carpenter of Sydney, NSW purchased three of the uncompleted maintenance ships for their transpacific services. This vessel and one other were quickly disposed of leaving one ship to maintain the service for quite a few years. This was one of the last oceangoing ships to leave the False Creek yard of West Coast Builders in 1947. Since then traffic has been purely local.

(Vancouver Maritime Museum)

HMS *Selsey Bill* as *Waitemata*. Canadian Union Line, a subsidiary of Union Steamship Company of New Zealand purchased this vessel to run alongside four ex-Park Victory ships in the Canadian-Australasian Transpacific service.

(Vancouver Maritime Museum)

HMCS *Cape Wrath* as *Ditmar Koel*. The only ship built in Canada under the wartime programs to become a unit of the German merchant marine. After she had been sold out of the RN and had two other owners, Hanseatic Line of Hamburg employed the ship in their regular service to her birthplace at Vancouver.

(S.C. Heal)

the Royal Navy, and after the war two of them were transferred to the RCN, but the victualling ships were owned in the name of the Dominion of Canada and placed on bareboat charter to the British government. All were returned to Canada following the war except five which were permanently transferred to the Admiralty.

At a speed of 11¹/₂ knots they could not match the equivalent American ships for speed, but typi-cally once stationed at a base they remained until shifted to another base or until returning to an Allied port for reprovisioning. After the defeat of Japan the ships moved from forward bases, such as Manus in the Bismarck Archipelago, to the original bases such as Hong Kong and Singapore, both of which rapidly reverted to their role as centres of British power and commercial interests in the Asian region.

The Needs Served by a Fleet Train

The following table illustrates the range of services provided by the fleet train, showing the make-up of the British Pacific Fleet/Task Force 57 in May 1945 when the war in Europe ended and, by comparison, the state of the fleet train on V-J day in August 1945. Among other aspects it illustrates the massive buildup in the fleet train being achieved by the British. This great momentum actually carried on after the war as some ships were already on their way to take up station in the Pacific, where their services were needed in the process of reconstruction.

Fleet Train	May, 1945	Aug. 1945
Air Maintenance Ships	-	3
Aircraft Stores Ships	-	2
Armament and Stores Issuing Ships	11	31
Boom Carriers	-	2
Command Ship, Logistics Supply Group	-	1
Danlayers	-	2
Distilling Ships	1	2
Escort Carriers (Replenishment)	4	6
Escort Carriers (Ferry Duties)	2	3
Escort vessels	7	30
Fleet Accommodation Ships	-	2
Hospital Ships	1	6
Landing Ships Infantry (LSIs)	5	2
Light Fleet Carrier (Repair/Maintenance)	1	-
Minesweepers	-	18
Netlayer	1	1
Oilers	9	23
Repair Ships	2	10
Salvage vessels	-	3
Store Ships	3	31

The buildup in the East Indies fleet was an entirely different mix and to assist in detailing the disposition of the Canadian-built vessels only the position at VJ day is set out:

Anti U-boat Netlayer	1
Base and Depot Ships	24
Boom Carriers	2
Danlayers	1
Escort Carriers (Front line, Replenishment or Ferry not specified)	16
Landing Ships Infantry (LSIs)	24
Merchant Transports and Auxiliary	7
Oilers	3
Repair Ships	11
Salvage Vessels	2
Surveying Vessels	7

Plus, a large fleet of landing craft and LSTs

The Canadian Contribution

Individual ship histories are set out in the Fleet List. The following list outlines the role allotted to each ship and shows how each would fit into the Royal Navy fleet train:

Armament Maintenance Ship
  Portland Bill
Coastal Craft Maintenance Ship
  Cape Wrath.
Escort Maintenance Ships
  Beachy Head, Berry Head, Duncansby Head, Flamborough Head, Mull of Galloway, Rame Head.
Experimental Base HQ Ship for target trials
  Mull of Kintyre
Landing Craft Maintenance Ships
  Buchan Ness, Dodman Point, Dungeness, Hartland Point, Girdle Ness, Fife Ness, Spurn Point

Not completed and disposed of as merchant ships:
  Mull of Oa, Rattray Head, Orfordness, Selsey Bill, Tarbat Ness.

The Supply or Stores Issuing Ships were as follows:
Ammunition Carriers
  Fort Rosalie, Fort Sandusky, Fort Wayne.
Air Stores Ships
  Fort Colville, Fort Langley
Stores Issuing (Naval)
  Fort Providence, Fort Wrangell
Stores Issuing (Victualling)
  Fort Alabama, Fort Beauharnois, Fort Charlotte, Fort Constantine, Fort Dunvegan, Fort Duquesne, Fort Edmonton, Fort Kilmar, Fort McDonnell.

Request for a Photo: HMS *Beachy Head*

Crewmembers wishing for a photo of their ship usually relied on a snapshot taken by a fellow crewman with an amateur's box camera, with all the limitations of an amateur's technique and wartime film, if one could find it. Often the last time that a studio quality photo was taken was when the ship was new and on trials. Consequently the yards often received requests for photos from crew looking for something special to hang in their mess or wardroom. This letter, written with the traditional service salutations, also testifies to the important role of the maintenance ships.

```
C/MX 647075
E.R.A, Longstaff, L.
HMS "Beachy Head"
c/o G.P.O. London
Oct. 21, 1945

Clarence Wallace Esq.
Burrard Dry Dock Company Ltd.
North Vancouver, BC
```

Dear Mr. Wallace,

Would you please excuse my writing to you in this way, but having steamed her so many thousands of miles, along with the other E.R.A.'s of the Mess, who originally commissioned her in Vancouver, I take the liberty of asking you if you could send me an official photograph of "Beachy Head" - 222.

We feel so proud of her and I can tell you that as a part of "Escort Force" East Indies Fleet, we have done some really vital work. From the day we joined the fleet in Colombo, Ceylon, we have never but had three or four sweepers and escort vessels alongside. The crews of other ships come on board us to have a look around, and believe me they are surprised to find what a great ship she is. From Colombo we were to join the invasion fleet which was preparing to land in Malaya. However, when the Japs "stacked their hand", we proceeded, as I surmise we would have normally, and joined the Occupation Forces at Port Swettenham, Malaya. No sooner were we there than the inevitable repairs were alongside. After only a few days we sailed to Singapore and since the day we dropped anchor, we have never been clear of ships alongside for repair.

We have had many signals of congratulation from various units of the fleet for the work we have carried out on them. I suppose the work will go on like this until all the mines are cleared up and the "Escort Force" is disbanded. I along with many others would then like to be bringing "Beachy Head" back to Vancouver where we had such a great time standing by the ship.

Hoping my request for a photograph meets with your approval and wishing "Burrards" all the best of luck.

```
          I am, Sir,
          Your obedient Servant
          Leonard Longstaff
```

A Slick Switch of Engines: HMS *Buchan Ness*

S.C.Heal

All twenty-one of the maintenance ships which were ordered by the Royal Navy were built by one or other of the three Vancouver shipbuilding companies, Burrard Dry Dock Company Limited, West Coast Shipbuilders Limited, or North Van Ship Repairs Limited. The latter company was a smaller concern previously named Pacific Dry Dock Company, which became a subsidiary of Burrard and changed its name upon acquisition. The two yards were only separated by the foot of Lonsdale Avenue, the main north-south thoroughfare of North Vancouver.

Buchan Ness was the second of five such ships built by West Coast Shipbuilders. Her assigned role was to provide service to all types of landing craft from the smallest up to LCT and LCI sizes. She and her sister *Beachy Head* were at anchor in a bay on the Singapore side of Johore Strait servicing the different types of ships or craft to which they had been allotted when I had my first experience of the Canadian-built maintenance ships.

I had recently been posted as extra watchkeeping officer to HMLCT *913*, a Mk IV, British-built vessel, powered by twin Paxman-Ricardo diesel engines. We were under orders to sail to Hong Kong in company with three sister craft.

Our port engine had been giving a lot of trouble, so we placed ourselves alongside *Buchan Ness* to await inspection of the diesel. Very soon an engineer officer and two E.R.A.s came off the maintenance ship and clambered into our engineroom. They soon diagnosed the problem and came back up to tell us to our surprise that they were going to "whip" the engine out and replace it. The job would be done as quickly as they could get to it, meanwhile we were to lay alongside and bide our time.

Our skipper and No. 1 were ashore when word came that they wanted our LCT to turn about and place herself portside to, using just our one good starboard side engine for the manoeuvre. This was necessary so that *Buchan Ness's* cargo boom serving No. 4 hold could have sufficient outreach to lift the old engine out and place the replacement. These LCTs being shallow draft, flat bottomed and very beamy, handled easily enough on both engines, but were pretty hard to handle on one engine. Worse still as *Buchan Ness* was swinging around her anchor and our assigned position was on her port side we had to go upstream and coast down with the strong ebb tide behind us. I had had no experience of handling an LCT under these circumstances, but the people on board *Buchan Ness* were not prepared to wait until our two experienced officers came back, so one of the skippers off another LCT was asked to lend a hand. This he did most willingly and we cast off doing a wide sweep in Johore Strait until we had lined our vessel up to make as easy a landing as possible, as he had to depend on reversing the starboard engine to stop the vessel.

I stood by at the stern with two hands to secure our stern line in a timely fashion as once that was done the current would do the rest and bring our bow in. Almost simultaneously, the temporary skipper threw the starboard engine into full reverse which had the effect of kicking our stern away to the wrong side. The stern line being secured on the adjoining vessel held her and for a moment or two it seemed like the vibrating engine would shake us to pieces. As soon as the way was off her we fully secured the vessel and in a matter of minutes the workcrew off *Buchan Ness* swarmed aboard, the boom swung out and the damaged engine was airborne. Probably within a half hour the new engine was sitting on the bedplates and the maintenance crew were busy hooking everything up. That evening when our skipper returned we were ready for a trial trip up Johore Strait and the following day we sailed with our sister craft for Hong Kong. It was the slickest switch I had ever seen and said much for the built-in efficiency of the maintenance ships and their crews.

"Let's Not Forget the Foremen": HMS *Berry Head*

Burrard Dry Dock had already had lots of experience in dealing with Royal Navy crews as they already had processed 17 such crews standing by to man the ex-American escort aircraft carriers which they converted to British standards. Two additional vessels were taken into the RCN and were manned by Canadian crews. Sociability was a hallmark of the Royal Navy ships and golf was often an abiding passion of many of the officers as the second of two letters tends to confirm.

```
H.M.S "Berry Head"    9th June, 1945

Mr. Wardle,
Burrard Dry Dock Company
North Vancouver, BC

Dear Mr. Wardle,
   Having assumed command of "Berry Head" I feel I must write to say how
very much I appreciate all that has been done by Burrards to make "Berry
Head" the fine ship she is.
   Although it is usually possible to personally thank the heads (of
departments), it is not always easy to do the same as far as the many
foremen and the important workers of such a large concern as the Burrard
Dry Dock Company undoubtedly is.
   Under the circumstances, I should be very grateful if you would convey
to all concerned my appreciation of the good work and workmanship which
has gone into the production of OUR ship.
                     Yours very sincerely
                     K.M. Drake
                     Commander, R.N.R. in-Command
```

The second letter came from overseas:

```
Dear Mr. Wardle,
   Just a brief note to let you know how we are progressing — so far
favourably. The Chief seems to be very satisfied with the mechanics and the
ship's company with the comfort — which reduces my worries considerably
although I feel that (the) Admiralty have shown a considerable lack of
common sense navigationally speaking.
   Have not played any more golf (??) since the big day at Capilano. Have been
tempted to try, but my courage has so far failed me. But that evening was a lot
of fun and No.1, the Chief Pay and myself frequently foregather over a glass of
rye and play it all over again stroke by stroke.
   Please remember us all to our very good friends, "The Burrards"
particularly the "Golfing Burrards" and especially yourself as the one who
saved me from complete ignominy.
Constructionally you have every good reason to be proud of "Berry Head". It
is now up to us to see that you may be proud of her operationally too.
                     Sincerely yours,
                     Kenneth M. Drake,
                     Commander-in-Command
```

Commander Drake, being RNR obviously came from a merchant ship background. RNR officers, probably with justification, felt they could criticize the Admiralty as they usually had a more versatile background than their RN contemporaries, hence his remarks about the navigation equipment. Also the fact that the ship had been "stored" in Vancouver meant that there would be plenty of rye whiskey on board, but likely a shortage of good scotch. Rye was virtually unknown in Britain at that time, but has now become available in most bars. The war changed many tastes.

A Letter of Commendation: HMS *Dungeness*

This ship followed immediately after Buchan Ness at West Coast Shipbuilders, but her completion date came after the termination of the war in the Pacific. Completed also as a Landing Craft Maintenance ship, Dungeness sailed straight for Britain following completion, whereas Buchan Ness might well have been the last to arrive in the Far East. Nothing disappeared as fast as most of the structure of Combined Operations with its huge fleet of landing ships and craft of all sorts. Vessels were paid off, many going to an early date with the scrappers while some were sold to local owners, crews were dispersed to any posting that could be found for them, to await demobilization and their return to civilian life. It is thought that the beautifully fitted-out Dungeness went into reserve almost as soon as she arrived in Britain, for she, along with others of the class, were quickly disposed of for merchant ship conversion, in her case in 1947. The two following letters came from her captain and chief engineer:

> Both my officers and myself would like to express to you and all personnel of West Coast Shipbuilders Ltd., our appreciation and thanks for the very fine ship which you are handing to us. In spite of delays caused by late delivery of material and the general upset following the cessation of hostilities, we feel that we have the best maintenance ship so far to be commissioned in Vancouver.
>
> James Allen
> Commander, RN
> Commanding Officer
> HMS Dungeness

> We are now on the eve of our departure to the Old Country which, with luck, we should reach in time for Christmas leave.
> I may say for all on board that we are happy and proud to take "Dungeness" home, as she is a great credit to you, the builders, and is a fitting addition to His Majesty's Navy. We have finished our working up program. Everything has gone splendidly which no doubt, will contribute to making her a comfortable and happy ship. We wish to thank you, and all others in the yard for their good workmanship; also for many other things done for our comfort, convenience and ease of working the ship.
>
> W. Irwin
> Lt-Commander, RNR
> Esquimalt, BC
> 8 November, 1945

"No. 5 and 6 Main Bearings Ran Hot": *Fort Providence*

Just because some of the letters or reports from the Burrard collection quoted deal with engineering matters, rather than the general state of the ship, it should not be concluded that Burrard ships were in a special class of their own for engineering problems. Running in of a new ship can always be relied upon to require adjustments and possible failures of gear. These ships were built and after a short quick trial went right on to the loading berth. Wartime was a different world when time was short, compared to peacetime. In peacetime a great many adjustments and corrections are made following a more leisurely and exacting period for trials and acceptance. *Fort Providence* was a Victory-type stores issuing ship built for the Fleet Train.

Mr. James Robertson   July 23, 1944
Burrard Dry Dock Company Ltd.
North Vancouver, BC

Dear Mr. Robertson,
   Just a few lines as promised to let you know how this ship behaved on the passage down here. Well, I am pleased to say that everything worked well, with one exception and that is that for no reason at all Nos. 5 and 6 main bearings ran a bit warm, but we had them under control in no time. I have written to Mr. Davies and Mr. McDonald telling them that I have received the refrigeration spares from Carriers and also told them that the main refrig plant is doing OK.
   I daresay you were informed about the spot of trouble we had with the winch stop valve at No. 5 before we left Vancouver and I was led to believe that we were to get a couple of spare stop valves before we left, but none forthcame.*
   There is just one more item that gave us trouble before we left and that was the refrigerator in the P.O.'s mess. The thermostat conked out and it will require a new one if I can get one here. I have suggested that one or two spares should be supplied in future. Anyhow the above bits of trouble are a mere detail and if no worse happens, there will be no room for complaint.
   I don't think there is much more that I can say except to wish your firm and yourself every success in the future.

                    Yours etc.
                    A.H. Davison
                    Chief Engineer
                    S.S. Fort Providence

   *(A note on the letter said that the stop valves arrived after the ship had sailed.)

CHAPTER ELEVEN

From State Ownership to Private Ownership

After the First World War there were strong political calls for the nationalization of British Shipping, with all the ideological reasons offered as to why this would provide a perfect panacea for an industry which had traditionally been impossible to shield from the vicissitudes of world trade cycles. No government had been faced before with the large-scale task of absorbing such a huge fleet back into the peacetime economy. The British answer was to call in Lord Inchcape, the head of the giant P&O group. Inchcape's response was to arrange to buy most of the fleet and then to resell to individual owners. The method worked well and, no doubt, the process brought its own financial rewards for Inchcape.

The October Revolution had already taken place in the Russia of 1917, and calls for sweeping changes in everything from the abolition of monarchies to the dictatorship of the proletariat had been issued from ideologues who saw a cure for everything in the newly founded politics of communism.

Communism developed a strong core of support in most of the Western democracies during the early 1920s. Dedicated to undermining established government, the Communists very nearly succeeded in taking Germany in the same direction as Russia. They also developed a major presence in France and Spain. There was widespread infiltration into the trade unions of the western countries and official communist parties quickly sprang up in Canada, Britain, throughout Western Europe and a great many other countries including the United States and Australia. In Canada the large-scale forced amal-gamation and nationalization of the Grand Trunk, Intercolonial, Canadian Government and Canadian Northern Railways provided a socialist answer to the predicament of over development of the country's railway system. When the country found itself the owner of a sizeable fleet of war emergency type ships, the attractive idea of forming a government-owned shipping enterprise and running it in close conjunction with the Canadian National Railways System appeared to make sense.

It was as if envious eyes, cast in the direction of the successful Canadian Pacific Railway with its comprehensive transportation network of railways, ships and hotels, saw this as a pattern to be copied. It was perhaps seen as the opportunity to prove that government-owned business could successfully compete with private enterprise. The experiment did not succeed and in 1936 the shipping enterprise, Canadian Government Merchant Marine (CGMM), was finally wound up at great cost. The Canadian National Railways lumbered on for many years and accumulated massive losses, but new thinking saw it rationalized and privatized in the 1990s and now it is a profitable modern enterprise which has dropped the cloying role of being an instrument of government policy.

The Canadian Communist party took an active role in forming the Canadian Seamen's Union in 1935, and this well-remembered affiliation had much to do with the labour problems which beset the Canadian merchant navy and its unsuccessful continuation after the war.

Whiteshell Park. Near the end of the war, this coalburning North Sands was at anchor in Annapolis Basin awaiting orders. It is one of seven finally disposed of by Park Steamship through transfer to Britain for charter with option to buy.   (Murray Somerville)

Whiteshell Park. Placed under management of Canadian Pacific, London, a concern which could hardly have been termed a trampship company, this ship was evidently chartered to a tramp operator whose colours she is wearing. Later she was purchased by Counties Ship Management, the British associate of Rethymnis & Kulukundis, and was brought up to that concern's high standards, as illustrated elsewhere in this book.

(National Maritime Museum, Greenwich)

Fort Tremblant as Beatus. Casualties among the 90 ships purchased by the US Maritime Commission were heavy. Of the survivors a majority remained in lay-up until sent for scrapping. A few were sold by the US to foreign operators, this ship going to Cardiff owners.

(Ian Stewart Collection)

Shakespeare Park as *Sunprince.*
The 4,700-ton Gray/Scandinavian type were very handy ships for more localized operations. The type was popular in the lumber trades from the St. Lawrence, North Russia and the Baltic, but Saguenay Terminals and Canadian National Steamships among Canadian companies found them useful on services to and from the Caribbean area.

(Ian Smith Collection)

In the second photo, *Sunprince* is shown loading Canadian produce and groceries for the West Indies. Astern can be seen one of the postwar Canadian National ships

(see photo of Canadian Constructor).

The solutions previously devised in Britain and Canada following the First World War were not applied following the Second. There was no large-scale negative reaction from unions or management in Britain, but in Canada there are resentments to this day. Promises made by Government ministers during the war that there would be a continuation of the Canadian Merchant Marine proved hollow in practice. They were promises made somewhat irresponsibly, without an understanding of the factors that governed international shipping commerce. When an in-depth analysis was made immediately after the war it killed the idea of the Government of Canada remaining in the shipping business and repeating the mistake of the CGMM. As a result there was widespread dissatisfaction among seagoing personnel who felt that they had been let down. Since then there have been complaints about "giving

the ships away" at bargain basement prices and repeated demands for maintaining a merchant service regardless of economics and international market conditions. The battle cry was always jobs, job security and working conditions. We shall see in retrospect how valid these expectations might have been and if they have validity today.

THE DISPOSAL PROGRAM IN CANADA AND BRITAIN

At the end of the Second World War, Britain and Canada were faced with the disposal of war-built standard type shipping, perhaps made a little more complex by some sizeable adjustments in the fleets operated during the war. A total of 182 "Sam" Liberty ships had been turned over to Britain and 14 became war losses. Very soon after the war the United States started calling in the surviving 168 ships, plus the 67 North Sands vessels sold to the United States Maritime Commission (USMC) which had survived the war from the original 90. Collectively the withdrawal of these ships represented a tremendous reduction in available British tonnage in the immediate postwar period. However this was alleviated through the USMC making available for purchase over 900 Liberty ships, which were distributed among American domestic owners, the Allied powers and Italy. British owners alone purchased 125 Liberties and a small number of the Fort North Sands ships which had been redelivered to the American owner, the US War Shipping Administration.

In a similar way the 28 survivors of 32 Canadian Victory type ships bareboat chartered to Britain were also returned and while names were not changed from a Fort to a Park designation, the port of registry changed from London to Montreal and all were disposed of to nominal Canadian owners.

A nominal owner, for example, would be a Greek firm setting up a Canadian corporation in Montreal to act as its owner of record of ships on the Canadian registry. The beneficial owners are all the shareholders in the Canadian corporation who might be entirely foreign nationals.

On January 26, 1946 a first invitation to tender on British government ships was published. Appendix A of the publication contained the names of 72 higher class vessels described as cargo liners, refrigerator ships and tankers. Appendix B (I) contained 160 British-built tramps including coasters, the remaining 38 Ocean type ships, and the first two Fort North Sands ships. Appendix B (II) contained sixty Fort North Sands ships owned by the then Dominion of Canada and available for time charter. At that time the Canadian interest as owners was registered as Dominion of Canada in shipping documents, such as bareboat charters, and in *Lloyd's Register*.

The second Invitation to Tender came out May 2, 1946. A great many ships had been disposed of in the three months between the tenders. The available Forts had been reduced from 60 to 21, and 7 Park North Sands vessels where turned over to the British Ministry of War Transport, again without change of name, but with a change of registry from Montreal to London. These ships were:

Belwoods Park, Dentonia Park, Hillcrest Park, Mount Orford Park, Stanley Park, Whiteshell Park, Yamaska Park.

These 7 Park Ships were the remnants of the 28 exchanged with the British for their 28 surviving Victory ships in 1945. The first 18 had been sold by the Canadian government with flag convenant mostly to London Greek owners

None of the vessels carried a basic price in the British Invitation to Tender, unlike all the British Government owned ships which included the Ocean class, but all were available for three-year charters at a monthly charter rate of £1,025. The two MOWT-owned ships, *Fort Ville Marie* and *Fort St. James*, were offered at £110,000 and £110,500 respectively, The first ship was not fitted with superheaters which might have reflected the small difference in price, but it was an indication of the price at which the balance of the ships were available through Canadian Crown Assets Disposal Corporation. Taking into account the prevailing exchange rate this would have worked out to about $400-440,000 Cdn.

In summary the transfers went like this:

Type	Original number transferred to UK	Number lost while controlled by UK	Returned to Canada/USA/UK for disposal
North Sands			
Fort	66*	6	60 Canada
Fort (USMC purchased)	90	26	64 USA
Park, ex-Canadian	28	1	27 UK
Victory			
Forts	32	4	28 Canada
Gray/Scandinavian			
bareboat charter	1	0	1 Canada
Short term loan	14	2	12 Canada

---

*The total of 66 included *Fort Highfield* (1), *Fort Miami* (1) and *Fort Spokane* which had seen service as Park ships prior to transfer.

The above figures pay no regard to the sizeable number of Park Steamship vessels which had been

Victoria Park was the only 4,700-ton ship to be acquired by a West Coast owner, Johnson Walton Steamships Ltd. As *Tatuk,* the owners used her for lumber shipments to Central America.

(David Martin-Smith Collection)

Canadian Constructor. Representative of a limited class of ships built for Canadian National Steamships at the end of the war, the type was designed by US architects Gibbs & Cox, and bears a resemblance to the US C1 type. Although Davie, Canadian Vickers and Burrard built a variety of vessels for foreign owners, this design appears to have been the only effort made to design a specialist Canadian-built dry cargo deep-sea operation by Canadian owners, until Saguenay had *Sunrip,* built in 1964.

(Burrard Dry Dock Co.)

under the management of the Crown Corporation from the beginning.

Also noteworthy was the high proportion of losses at 29 per cent among the USMC owned Fort vessels and 27 per cent among the Ministry's 60 Ocean Class vessels. This compares with 8 per cent among the USMC Sam Liberties. The probable reason for this is that the bulk of the higher losses came from the earlier deliveries of North Sands and Ocean ships when the chances of loss by enemy action were greater in 1942-43 than in the two following years. Another factor is that the North Sands and Ocean ships generally were worked very hard and were present at every invasion from North Africa to the final operation, the re-taking of Malaya. However, why

the Forts owned by the Dominion of Canada should have had a better loss experience than the USMC at just 9 per cent, is not readily apparent as there is no indication that this latter group were dealt with any differently than the USMC vessels. A reason for this might be that the majority of the group were delivered after the USMC deliveries were made, when exposure to potential loss was reduced.

In reality, a majority of the 60 Forts shown as "returned to Canada" were sold off to mostly London Greek buyers who took advantage of favourable sales terms to Canadian corporations, by incorporating nominal Canadian subsidiaries, even when the beneficial owners were foreign nationals. For the most part the ships were offered through

Crown Assets Disposal Corporation along with the balance of Park ships.

Crown Assets offered each vessel at a price of about $500,000 for the Victory ships and about $400,000 for the coal-burning North Sands ships. The actual price realized was a figure broken down to the last cent. Thus the Victory type, *Bridgeland Park* realized $525,764.30, whereas her sister, *Kitsilano Park*, sold for $443,137.21. Both ships were built at North Van Ship Repairs, but the *Kitsilano Park* was nine months older. The difference in price could have reflected a number of factors including depreciation, general condition, improvements in the latter ship that were not available in the older vessel, the time expired since last drydocking (and therefore the closer proximity of the first four-year classification survey), inventory of spares and stores on board, etc.

Accompanying the disposal of the fleet was a variety of arguments at the economic, political and labour levels. The ships had been built with wartime emergency needs as the principle consideration in their design and construction. In every sense they were sound, well-found vessels, but peacetime operating considerations became more of a factor as the war's end drew nearer. The British, who had built a substantial number of unadorned tramps, equivalents of the North Sands and Liberties, realised that these vessels had only a limited usefulness on cargo liner services in postwar conditions, although a somewhat longer life in tramp service, particularly as most would pass to flags of convenience. The British Ministry of War Transport, with an eye to more competitive peacetime conditions, had built 12 of a new design termed simply the Standard Fast Cargo Liner with a deadweight of 12,000 tons and a speed of 15 knots, some being powered by steam turbines, others by diesels. Additional private owners' prototype designs including refrigerator ships were also allowed. This permitted established lines to obtain a quick start with rebuilding their fleets as the war came to an end. Overall the specifications were superior to any of the standard tramps. The Ministry vessels of the 15-knot fast cargo liner class all went to the management of first-class liner companies. It also licensed private owners to order additional ships off this design, and Canadian Pacific Steamships

ordered four vessels and purchased two of the same design from the MOWT to replace their pre-war Beaver ships, all of which had been lost. Other first-class British liner owners took the opportunity to make adjustments in the basic design to incorporate features of value to them in their trades.

In the United States, the Liberty ship was supplemented by the US Victory type. Designated as an attack transport, it had excellent potential as a fast cargo liner which could double as a tramp, on a fuel consumption only a little more than that of the Liberty ship. Some 600 of these ships were built so that when peace came many American owners were able to acquire these ships along with C1, C2, C3 and C4 types. This put them in an excellent position to serve vital trade routes, as the US defined them, and gave them a reserve fleet of fast quality tonnage when first the Korean and later the Vietnam war broke out. These ships in the right hands were efficient and economical and a number were acquired by British and other foreign owners. The Americans, however, required operating subsidies, as the high cost of American crews would permit no alternative other than operating under flags of convenience, which had been the case with some of their tankers going back to the depression years of the 30s.

The British and American standard vessels planning showed foresight. In Canada the improvements made to the original North Sands design resulted in the Canadian and Victory types, where emphasis was placed on fuel economy, improved boiler arrangements and improvements in the accommodation, but none of these ensured a vastly superior vessel. What did result amounted to housekeeping improvements in a tramp design which would be quickly outpaced by a variety of technical improvements in postwar ship design–greater deadweight tonnage, cubic capacity, and speed; more economical propulsion machinery and cargo handling arrangements.

In spite of pronouncements from politicians and others about maintaining a peacetime merchant navy, it might be assumed that these were simply sops to appease our maritime trade unions and the seagoing personnel who hoped for a peacetime career at sea. Very limited plans were made for a superior new Canadian design to supplant the North Sands ships, although three new vessels of a uniquely Canadian

Weston Park. When Western Canada purchased the largest West Coast fleet, many of the ships were painted in their smart new colours without renaming, as was the practice of charterers. As the company had to raise about ten million dollars of purchase money to complete the transaction, the ships were operated in the meantime on an interim charter arrangement.

(Wm. Hutcherson)

Dunlop Park as Lake Chilco. Once purchase arrangements were completed, Western Canada went ahead with renaming the newly acquired ships and proudly painted its corporate name on the sides, displaying a new shipping entity to the world.

(David Martin-Smith Collection)

type, designed by Cox & Stevens of New York, were constructed for Canadian National Steamships, as well as others for France and Brazil.

This type was an interesting step forward. Similar in size, dimensions and layout to the American C1 type, a highly versatile type built in fairly large numbers in the late 30s and through the war, the three ships of the class were built to the order of Wartime Merchant Shipping, at Davie and Canadian Vickers in the Montreal area, and at Burrard Dry Dock Company at North Vancouver. Powered by diesels, with a speed of 16 knots, they were employed for about 12 years under the Canadian National banner before being sold to Cuba. The move to build these ships in the immediate postwar era seems to have been an attempt by one government agency to pro-

vide ships to another government agency, in what might have been perceived initially as a government postwar shipbuilding policy. However, no government in Canada has yet developed a fully comprehensive merchant shipping development program.

Canada has not been alone in this regard, and while conditions in Britain and the US have been different, all three countries have let their shipping industries decline to the point where the balance of shipping power is now in the Orient and even Greece, the archetypal "cheap flag" of the interwar years, has gone into decline.

Rapid improvements in foreign designs as the world's shipbuilding industries returned to peacetime conditions ensured that the Forts and Parks were already obsolescent as they returned to peacetime service. This in turn meant that the euphoria of having a merchant marine for management, politicians and labour to argue over was, in retrospect, a somewhat specious argument, although in fairness few saw it that way at the time. Canadian shipowners, shipbuilding and labour interests could all see the need for moving ahead with the times and replacing the war-built tonnage as quickly as possible, and considerable lobbying along these lines was undertaken to develop an official plan for peacetime replacement with modern competitive designs.

The Canadian yards had demonstrated their versatility through the war and in some cases had successfully designed, built and sold to a variety of foreign owners in the early postwar period. The legacy of a bad record in the aftermath of union problems in the Canadian merchant marine after the war however meant that investors did not find further investment in Canadian ships attractive.

One good move initiated by the Canadian government was the adoption of the Canadian Vessels Construction Assistance Act of 1949. This provided a direct subsidy to the shipyards of 40 per cent of the building cost of a new vessel, guaranteed to remain on the Canadian register for five years.

Additionally the write-off provisions for tax purposes were extended to allow an owner, who could also be an outside investor, to claim depreciation at the rate of 100 per cent over three years against all his sources of income. This proved to be a very attractive tax shelter and ensured an inflow of fresh capital into a great many new shipping enterprises. By this means many doctors and similar professional men became shipowners without necessarily understanding the first thing about the shipping industry.

Finally, the other major assistance to shipping generally was the allowance by the Canadian Maritime Commission of the transfer, at a discount of escrowed funds from the sale of ex-Fort and Park ships. By this time, in the early fifties, it became apparent that few funds of this nature would be reinvested in foreign-going shipping, and allowing transfer into coastal shipping and the fishing industry was a good way to free these funds to benefit a rapidly expanding Canadian coastal shipping industry, and provide work for the shipyards.

Owners or investors could have the benefit of purchased escrowed funds, and depreciation, or the lowered price provided by the shipbuilding subsidy and depreciation, but not all three. The effect, of course, was that coastal shipping and the fishing industry, shielded as they were from foreign competition, were the main beneficiaries of this largesse and in pursuing the available processes largely renewed themselves and greatly expanded over a 20-30 year period. The generous provisions of the Canadian Vessels Construction Assistance Act and the special tax write-off provisions could not be expected to last forever and in fact they were gradually phased out so that there is now no construction assistance and the tax shelter loophole has been largely closed.

Helpful though these provisions were they did not amount to a Canadian National Shipping policy which would do anything for the sustenance of a Canadian deep sea merchant marine.

Only two of the postwar ship owning interests were able to accomplish change in an effort to develop with the times. Western Canada Steamships Ltd. of Vancouver started the process of replacing its wartime fleet with three secondhand modern British diesel ships and then decided to retire as it did not find market conditions attractive enough to stay in business. The other company, FedNav or as it used to be known, Federal Commerce & Navigation Co. of Montreal took a different tack and went in for foreign joint ventures and readily embraced the concept of the flag of convenience. Today it is the sole survivor, as an owner, of the early postwar companies and owns a large fleet operating in international trade, fully utilizing all the devices available to an alert shipowner. This was a distinctly different position to that of Canadian Transport Co., Seaboard, or Saguenay Terminals, none of whom are now owners, although they function as such through their chartering activities.

Of the prewar owners, Canadian Pacific, through its subsidiary Canada Maritime, retains a dominant position in its traditional North Atlantic trades as a container operator. Canada Steamship Lines has developed more versatility with a variety of Great Lakes and Ocean services using specialized bulk-carriers, but in both cases the tonnage involved is registered in Bermuda or another tax-shelter country.

Few could visualize the vast changes which gathered speed once the war was over. These included the container, bulk carrier and large tanker revolutions which not only rendered all conventional breakbulk and other shipping obsolete, but would also completely reshape the world's shipping industries. Passenger ships were built in significant numbers, but once again the airliner was to ensure that for some there would be a short life and for others the only employment left was to be found in a cruise industry which grew at a fantastic pace. Shipping lines which had been household names and had sometimes employed three and even four generations in a family simply disappeared unless they moved with the times, and in the western world taxation policies and a lack of government foresight often finished them off.

DISPOSAL AND LABOUR FACTORS

In considering the aspects of disposal of the Forts and Parks, John Stanton in his paper dealing with the *Green Hill Park* disaster published in *The Northern Mariner* and *The Beaver* magazine in 1991, portrays the leftwing point of view:

> The fleet was sold off after the war to private shipping companies at a fraction of the cost by the King and St. Laurent governments. After 1949 even the use of the Canadian flag was no longer required, and owners were free to sell to foreign companies or use "flag-of-convenience" registries. Thus Canada, bounded by three oceans, having more than five hundred ports and the longest coastline of any country, and being dependent on foreign trade, placed herself at the mercy of foreign—mostly American—shipping lines. For the third time in history the Canadian Government had done away with a national fleet.

> A ship is governed by the laws of the country whose flag she flies. That fact permits shipowners in more developed countries to take advantage of the low wages, low safety standards and the low maintenance costs prevailing in third world countries. The owners make more money than if their ships were subject to the laws of the home coun-

try with its higher standards. For example, Canadian Pacific has a fleet of some 20 ships using the flag of Bermuda and depriving Canadian seamen of jobs and Canadian shipyards of work.

The points which should be set out in rebuttal of the foregoing are:

1) A ship once built and sent to sea is only worth her freight-earning capacity in terms of the market, the degree of annual depreciation applied, her physical condition and performance factors and her overall capability in terms of obsolescence. Generally speaking the older the vessel the more these factors weigh against her value. There never was a question that the Canadian government could expect to sell its ships at replacement cost in terms of what they cost in Canadian yards. The ships when released had to compete with a whole host of Empire, Liberty and a variety of other tramp type ships. If they were to be carried on the books at what the Canadian taxpayer paid for them they could never have been viable trading propositions.

2) It was incorrect to state that most of Canada's trade was carried in American ships. US liner companies and some tramps called at Canadian ports, but after the 60s the American merchant marine, like the British, went into severe decline. However, once peacetime conditions returned ships of many foreign flags engaged in Canada's offshore shipping trades. Very prominent in the early postwar period were those from many Western European countries, to be followed later by those from Oriental countries.

3) There is no guarantee that repair business will come to Canadian yards whenever Canadian ships are in international trade. Had a Canadian ship been stranded in a foreign location, ordinary ship and marine insurance economics would ensure that she be towed to the nearest, most economical foreign yard for repairs. It is incorrect to

FROM STATE TO PRIVATE OWNERSHIP

Alexandra Park as *Mont Sandra*. Montship Lines had their own ideas for improvements to the Canadian Victory ships. In this photo new ventilator king posts serve No. 2 and 4 holds along with two more derricks each. The king posts at No. 3 have been heightened to above the funnel and No. 1 and 3 lifeboats have been moved onto the captain's bridge deck.

(Ian Stewart Collection)

Fort Enterprise as *Mahsud*. Like her sister, *Fort Ville Marie*, this ship was adapted for the Brocklebank service to India. Galley stovepipes can be seen aft plus substantial on-deck houses abreast of the mainmast to accommodate the large Lascar crews that manned these ships. No. 1 and 3 lifeboats have also been moved aft and have become No. 2 and 4.

(John Clarkson)

claim that Canadian shipyards are deprived of work. They would obtain the work as they do with foreign vessels if they are properly placed to handle the work competitively and it should never be forgotten that geography is a major factor.

4) Shipping is an international industry more and more governed by the concept of the global village, which is one reason why the bigger bulk of major world shipbuilding is now undertaken by countries in the Orient–they do it more competitively and turn out first-class ships. The engagement of crews is equally international and the concept of highly rigid national flag covenants has been steadily eroding away ever since the Second World War. This is why shipping capital gravitates towards the cheapest available safe haven. Canadian Pacific, for example, could not compete globally without subsidy if under the Canadian flag. It has until recent times always operated its deep sea ships, almost entirely under the British flag, but now that Britain has become a high-cost economy, it uses one of the flags of convenience set up by Britain itself in one of its several dependencies, such as Bermuda and the Isle of Man.

A brief reference was made at the commencement of this chapter to political influence in combining railways to form the Canadian National system, then the creation of the Canadian Government Merchant Marine, then bringing the rail interests together with the national steamship line in a state-owned combine competitive with the Canadian Pacific Railway. Forced on the nation by circumstances, this new combination met the ideological criteria of socialist thinking of the time and perhaps enshrines the self-perceived right of labour to hold employment when everything in economic terms indicates the opposite.

The founding of the Canadian Seaman's Union in 1936 and a long description and history of this union and the incursion of the Seamen's International Union into Canadian maritime affairs is beyond the scope of this book, but for those interested there is fairly extensive literature available which is included in the bibliography. Stanton, Green, and Kaplan have all commented at length on the issues involved.

For a summation of the labour point of view the following, quoted from *A History of Shipbuilding in British Columbia* as related by the shipyard workers is of value. Commenting in 1977 on the difficult times faced by the West coast shipbuilding industry Jeff Power, President, Marine Workers & Boilermakers Industrial Union, Local No. 1, offered the following:

> An improvement could result if the government of Canada builds some escort and other vessels to enforce and protect our new 200-mile fishing limit. The pressure of US multi-nationals on Canada for the right to exploit our rich oil and gas reserves in the Arctic for their own purposes may result in some shipbuilding, such as ice-breakers and oil tankers, but whether BC coast shipyards would get any contracts to build such vessels is not at all certain.
>
> The two big steps that need to be taken by Ottawa to restore shipbuilding to a viable industry and to enhance Canada's shipping and trade position are: 1) building a new drydock in Vancouver capable of repairing ships up to 100,000 or more tons, and 2) build a Canadian merchant marine, built, owned and registered in Canada and manned by Canadian crews.
>
> These projects are as much in the interests of Canada as they are in the interests of our Union members.
>
> That is why we ask not only all trade unionists, but all Canadians and all political parties and people's organizations to assist us in realizing these objectives.

> We have fought for a Canadian merchant marine for over 30 years and we will not give up now. We are convinced that it is long overdue.

In the events that followed the war, fisheries patrol vessels were built, and a large floating drydock was provided for Vancouver. But the constant pushing for a new merchant marine was eventually taken up in the mid-70s, by the first New Democratic Party premier of British Columbia, the Hon. David Barrett, who like a true Messiah finding the promised land, acted as though he had discovered that the "peoples" railway, the profitable functional and successful Pacific Great Eastern (now BC Rail), could raise its sights and build bulk carriers so that BC exports of sulphur, potash, coal, fertilizers, wheat and lumber could be carried offshore in furtherance of the union aim for an all-Canadian built, owned and operated shipping line. It is suspected that shipping interests once consulted soon laid out the realities of the day and after a weekend flurry in the local newspapers the idea was allowed to die.

Reverting to the disposal of the Canadian war-built ships and regardless of how organized labour saw the situation it was hard to argue against the logic of John Valentine Clyne, at that time a leading establishment marine lawyer in Vancouver who was invited to come forward with recommendations for the disposal of the Canadian wartime ships. Clyne's recommendations took into account the militancy of the Canadian unions and the sad financial history of the Canadian Government Merchant Marine in the interwar years. But, drawing on many sources including the US experience, and after consultation with Admiral Emory S. Land, chief of the US Maritime Commission, Clyne recognized the fact that a post-World War II Canadian merchant marine would require a significant long-term commitment of taxpayers' funds by way of subsidy. A one-time shipbuilding subsidy, as provided by the Canadian Vessels Construction Assistance Act, is a beginning, but an operating subsidy would amount to a permanent bloodletting of the national exchequer, as the Americans found out.

Some Postwar Conversions

Many of the wartime standard designs evolved into subcategories almost amounting to an entirely new design. This was particularly so with some of the British and American designs which were adapted as aircraft carriers, infantry landing ships and a variety of auxiliaries.

We have seen in Chapter 4, how the original North Sands came out in two almost identical versions, the American built Ocean and the Canadian version of the North Sands, which was a closer copy of the British original. Then followed improved variants, the oil burning Victory and the oil/coal version which was designated as the Canadian. There were further adaptations in the North Sands tanker, a proposed North Sands troopship conversion and Victory tankers. The Victory also proved to be an ideal platform for a range of Maintenance ships built for the Royal Navy, as described in Chapter 10.

As the vessels were sold changes were made which reflected the ideas and needs of the new owners. The most frequent changes were improvements in the accommodations. Some at least of the Canadian Victory ships transferred to the British had extra accommodation added to what was the equivalent of the boat deck in the bridge accommodation. The same accommodation was added to each of the Victory ships acquired by Canadian-Australasian Lines, and presumably was meant to serve a limited complement of passengers.

The two North Sands ships, *Fort Ville Marie* and *Fort Enterprise*, acquired by T&J Brocklebank of Liverpool, England had an innovative addition in the form of additional crew accommodation added on either side of the mainmast upon which extra lifeboats were added. The Brocklebank ships had traditionally been one of the main lines in UK-India trade and utilized large Lascar deck and engineroom crews along with British officers. Special attention was given to their accommodation and galley requirements since religious scruples also had to be observed.

Possibly none of the postwar Canadian owners saw more need for greater derrick capacity than Montship Lines of Montreal. Their actual need is hard to gauge but unquestionably, there were owners who by some standards tended to over-equip their vessels in this regard. Alfred Holt's Blue Funnel line believed in a generous provision of cargo handling gear. Although Holt took none of the Canadian-built ships, upon acquisition of ex-American Victory and Liberty ships, they promptly added additional derrick posts and derricks to ships which were already fully equipped.

Montship possibly took its lead from its British and French parent companies, for both Buries Markes of London and Louis Dreyfus of Paris owned exceptionally well equipped and handsome vessels. The picture of *Mont Sandra, ex-Alexandra Park*, with extra tall derrick posts serving No. 2 and 4 hatches, each with ventilator caps, illustrates how substantially the appearance of the vessel was altered. Another alteration to the standard Victory ship configuration was to shift the leading two lifeboats on the boat deck forward to the captain's deck to form a small boat deck in the bridge accommodation, a reversion to the original North Sands arrangement.

Most of the ships retained their original flying bridges throughout their lives. One that did not was *Fort St. James*, the first West Coast ship. This vessel, renamed *Temple Bar*, was purchased by a tramp operator, Lambert Brothers of London, who removed the flying bridge and made sundry other cosmetic improvements to the bridge structure. This gave the more comfortable appearance of Lambert's other peacetime-built ships, instead of the somewhat more starkly utilitarian structure which many of the earlier Forts presented. This ship was one of the few built without the distinctive lid-like structure surmounting the funnels of most of the Canadian war-built ships of both the 10,000-ton classes and the 4,700-tonners. The "lid" was in fact a sheet metal capping to the main exhaust pipe in the funnel.

The only instance that can be found when a Canadian type was altered to look like a Victory concerned *Cromwell Park*. At some point after her purchase and renaming to *Harmac Vancouver*, this ship's boat deck was extended forward and the lifeboat mounted on the small boat deck in the bridge structure was transferred to the customary position in the Victory ship. The never-used coal bunker space was used on

Cromwell Park as *Harmac Vancouver*. Canadian Transport had their own requirements for servicing the needs of parent MacMillan, Bloedel. Extra-length derricks were installed at all hatches. Built as a Canadian type ship, her new owners went to some trouble to extend the boatdeck forward, creating extra accommodation, and then removing No. 1 and 3 boats off the short boat or captain's deck in the bridge accommodation to their new position which made the ship look like a Victory type.
(Pacific Cameras, Port Alberni)

Spurn Point as *Lakemba*. Purchased as an incomplete maintenance ship, this vessel underwent a greater degree of customisation than any other Canadian-built Fort or Park when turned over to peacetime service. A raised forecastle, remodelled bridge and motorship style funnel made for a distinctive and attractive appearance. She was able to accommodate some 90 passengers. The funnel came off a tanker which was in shipyard hands at the time of conversion.   (Ian Stewart Collection)

Ocean Virtue as *Andrea C*. This ship represents one of the most remarkable ship conversion jobs in maritime history. A sister of *Ocean Liberty* and *Ocean Courage* illustrated earlier, the ship was damaged by enemy action. Acquired by Costa Line immediately after the war she was rebuilt as a passenger ship for the South American service. Her original steam propulsion was removed and replaced with a more powerful diesel.
(Paoli Piccione Collection, Genoa)

Ocean Virtue as *Andrea C*. In 1958 she underwent a second reconstruction, which increased her length and depth. Italian designers are masters of conversions by which an ancient vessel is turned into a handsome modern vessel. It is almost impossible to envisage the beautiful result of this conversion job as once having come off the drawing board which gave rise to thousands of Liberty, Ocean, Fort and Park ships. She was given yet another diesel engine of even greater power, lengthened with a redesigned bow of finer entry and classic handsome lines. Through her several versions she lasted a total of 40 years. (Paoli Piccione Collection)

occasion as additional ballast capacity. The primary purpose of the change was to create additional accommodation, mostly for the benefit of those who otherwise occupied the bridge section ahead of No. 3 hatch. *Cromwell Park* and *Albert Park* were the two Canadian type ships in the six-vessel Canadian Transport fleet. So far as can be determined these changes in the accommodation were not made in *Albert Park* before or after she was renamed *Harmac Victoria*. However, most of the Harmac ships eventually sported a varnished wood bridge front, Scandinavian style, as befitted a major carrier of wood products.

Some of the best looking conversions concerned the uncompleted Maintenance ships sold to W.R. Carpenter & Co. of Sydney, NSW.

The one which had the most startling changes was *Lakemba, ex-HMS Spurn Point*. Converted to a passenger cargo liner with accommodation for over 100 passengers, this ship had a high forecastle installed and her entire bridge front closed in as favoured by many of the Scandinavians. With the provision of a large motorship type funnel it was hard to visualize her actual origins from the North Sands design. This funnel evidently came off another ship while *Lakemba* was in shipyard hands for conversion purposes.

The Victory tankers and one North Sands tanker were all converted back to dry cargo ships by 1956. There were two exceptions which remained tankers for their operating lives. One was *Quetico Park* which evidently remained a tanker until scrapped in 1962 and the other was *Silver Star Park*, which following her serious accident in 1945 became a Brazilian navy tanker. She was wrecked in 1962.

Italy is the country with the greatest talent for taking a ship and then by a process of clever redesign and skilful building, turning it into a superior vessel, often with handsome features which most others would not have thought possible or even worthwhile. Some of the earlier generation of cruise ships were conversions from refrigerator ships or passenger ships which had seen their best days, but in the hands of Italian designers and engineers some remarkable makeovers took place.

A good example was Italnavi Soc. di Nav. per Azioni of Genoa, who took four Liberty ships and two Fort North Sands, re-engined them with Fiat diesels, built special erections on the fore and after flush decks especially to accommodate Italian-built motor cars for export, and sent them to sea capable of a speed of 14 knots. Reputedly, in spite of the bluff lines of these ships they operated with considerable fuel savings and with the overall reduced operating cost which one would expect with a modern diesel ship. *Fort La Traite* and *Fort Hudson's Hope*, the North Sands ships selected for this interesting conversion, became *Italsole* and *Italvega*, respectively.

An even better example of turning a "sow's ear into a silk purse," was *Ocean Virtue*, No. 26 of the thirty Oceans built by Permanente at Richmond, California. In July 1943, almost exactly a year after her completion, this ship was severely damaged by aircraft bombs at Augusta, Sicily, where she lay in damaged condition until salvaged by the Italians. Major conversion work which included overall lengthening to 466 feet 9 inches, from the original 441 feet 6 inches, with a new bow structure, gave her a finer entrance. A reconditioned Fiat diesel with a designed 7,000bhp and long accommodation decks fitted her as the immigrant carrier, *Andrea C.* of the Costa Line, on the Italy-Argentina route, Argentina being the popular objective for a large postwar Italian migrant population.

This good-looking ship underwent a further major conversion when a new, more powerful diesel and greatly improved accommodation was added to give her a further lease on life in the general passenger trade. To have had such an enormous amount of money and effort spent on an ordinary coal-burning tramp twice in her lifetime must have been a record, but it says a great deal about the basic soundness of the original design.

There was only modest upgrading among any of the Gray/Scandinavian type ships. Sundry small improvements were made in the housing by Canadian National Steamships Ltd., in the five of the Dominion sub-type and two of the 3,600-ton tankers ended up as barges. Irving Oil purchased *Nipiwan Park*, renamed her *Irvingdale* and cut her down to a barge in 1962. Branch Lines of Toronto purchased another of the Lakes tankers, *Springbank Park,* which they renamed *Poplarbranch*. In 1953 this ship stranded near Barranquilla, Colombia and following refloating was judged to be a constructive total loss. Straits Towing Ltd. of Vancouver purchased the vessel and following arrival at Vancouver in 1956, she was cut down to the barge *Straits Conveyor*, functioning as an early log carrier. She was eventually lost in the North Pacific.

CHAPTER TWELVE

World Trading under the Canadian and Foreign Flags

Chartering operations in the shipping industry deal with one of the most interesting aspects of international shipping and demonstrate how every phase is so totally interlocked with many others. A knowledge of how they work and what they achieve is one of the main factors to be taken into account when considering the Fort and Park ships and why in general they saw such a short life in Canadian ownership. There are many factors at play when considering ocean shipping and no claim is made that the following brief description is exhaustive and all encompassing for the subject is far too vast and includes so many economic and legal issues. Everything from the cost of fuel and a ship's fuel consumption, her deadweight capacity and speed, to her registry and therefore manning costs are taken into account. The objective in all commercial shipping operations is to determine by formula the lowest economic cost in carrying the maximum deadweight for delivery in the shortest possible time.

It is a finely tuned formula by which so many details can fall out of line and create a disruption or an uncompetitive situation to arise. The responsibility of the owner to himself is to secure the best possible employment cover for his vessel and to do this he has a theoretical range of options providing he is competitive and understands that he has obligations to his charterer all of which create restraints on the profitability of his venture. The responsibility of the charterer is to cover his needs with adequate tonnage at the right time and in the right place so that his cargo can be moved economically and in a timely fashion. To achieve these ends both have options as to the type of charter they enter into and how that charter best serves their respective ends.

As the years have progressed increasingly sophisticated charter instruments have been created by highly innovative shipowners, charterers and the go-betweens, the chartering brokers. The latter is a highly skilled totally informed professional who has his finger on all aspects of the shipping markets in which he functions or might tend to specialize, but before taking a more detailed look at modernday chartering let us take a look back to a century or more ago.

In the nineteenth century when sailing ships provided the bulk of the carrying capacity and when most of the prime cargoes, other than coal and nitrates, tended to be harvested on a seasonal basis the patterns of trade were easily defined. The world's leading freight exchange, the Baltic Exchange in London, was an extremely busy place as ships were matched with cargoes. If a world wide chart could have been presented it would have shown that in the Southern hemisphere grain carriers would crowd into the River Plate and Australian ports in the first and second quarters of the year and do exactly the same in the Northern hemisphere when the third and fourth quarter crops were coming in. Typically, for what was then the world's largest sailing ship fleet, a British barque would load coal in South Wales for

Fort St. James as *Temple Bar*. British Columbia's first ship in the Fort and Park program looked smart in her peacetime guise with a rebuilt bridge. This ship was one of two purchased by the British Government. She was sold postwar to Lambert Brothers Ltd. a shipping, insurance and financial firm in London.

(Ian Stewart Collection)

Crystal Park as *Chandler*. Elder Dempster (Canada) Ltd., the Montreal-based management subsidiary, purchased four of the Victory ships to replace chartered North Sands ships employed on the company's service to West and South Africa.

(Wm. Hutcherson Collection)

Wellington Park as *Sunwhit*. Saguenay Terminals Ltd., the shipping arm of the aluminum giant, Alcan, purchased a mixed fleet of Victory, Canadian and Gray/Scandinavian ships for its varied services in the Caribbean, Europe and South America. This ship looking very clean in her owner's livery was a Canadian type ship. Saguenay is now out of deep-sea shipowning but still charters.

(S.G. Docker, Liverpool)

Connaught Park as *Seaboard Ranger*. Like all other West Coast owners Seaboard had a marked preference for the Victory type for its fleet of six vessels. Always well looked after, Seaboard chartered ships follow the same tradition to this day.

(Ian Stewart Collection)

San Francisco. From there or other N. Pacific ports, including Vancouver, she might load lumber for Australia. At Melbourne or South Australian ports, if in season she might load grain back to the UK and return by the long leg across the South Pacific via Cape Horn. Thus in three giant passages the ship would have done a global voyage and presented herself back on berth in South Wales for another coal cargo.

Most of these moves were predictable and the first two legs were probably done by single voyage charters. The third could have been a little different, in that a grain broker might have engaged the ship "to Falmouth for orders," (Falmouth being the first port of call for a vessel entering the English Channel), rather than to a specified port for discharge as would have certainly happened in the first two stages of the voyage. By the time the ship was due at Falmouth it was likely the grain cargo had been sold, "subject to delivery" and the ship would be given orders to proceed to Liverpool, Hamburg or Antwerp, or some other port in the Northern range of European ports for discharge to a consignee.

As the world's commerce speeded up with the advent of steamers and later, as communications improved with the adoption of wireless and the telegraph, many of these slow moving stages were eliminated. Sail was very unpredictable. So much depended on the sailing qualities of a given ship and the ability of a master, which is one of the reasons why for many years the master's name was always entered with a given ship in *Lloyd's Register*. Master's records were kept at Lloyd's and actually

Louisbourg Park as *Harmac Chemainus*. An interesting photo of a Victory ship in the Esquimalt graving dock. She was obviously in for bottom painting and might have been there for purchaser's inspection pending sale of the ship.   (John Hetherington)

still are, even though the records are now handled in a different way. A summary of a captain's career from the time of becoming a mate could be presented at the time of negotiating a fixture for a ship and some had a tremendous reputation for safety and reliability, which in turn might shave the rate on marine insurance and conceivably improve the freight rate by a small margin. The author has in his possession the complete record of his great grandfather, Captain John Callow Heal, late of Bridgewater, Somerset, and Liverpool, England. It gives a summary of his complete career taken from the Lloyd's collection in the Guildhall Library in London from the time that he shipped as second mate in 1865 to his retirement as master in 1899. During this time he worked continuously for well-known Liverpool shipowners and was regarded as a

Tecumseh Park and *Bowness Park*. Both these ships were under management by Canadian Transport and are shown here loading lumber at New Westminster BC. However, neither was allocated for purchase to Canadian Transport and both went to other owners.

(John Hetherington)

reliable master who would finish a voyage in a timely fashion. He lost one ship, the barque *Corona,* which was driven ashore while making for the Straits of Sunda, in an Indian Ocean cyclone and became a total loss with loss of life. Happily he survived and was immediately given another command which suggests that he was held blameless. *Corona,* owned by McVicar, Marshall & Company, of Liverpool was carrying a full cargo of South Wales coal for Singapore and was driving into Sunda Strait when she was caught on a lee shore and the stranding occurred.

Powered ships by comparison were more reliable and predictable and with them the chartering process started to become more sophisticated. Time charters, meaning the engagement of a ship for a specified period or for a series of consecutive voyages became more common and provided a ship owner with a less speculative period of employment than placing his ship in the voyage market where it was subject to the vicissitudes of the market place with strong profitable rates at a given time, whereas three months later events in trade, war, politics, overtonnaging in a certain trade, etc. might have depressed rates badly. Some owners used to build new ships with an eye to the

time charter market as the availability of a good ship suited to the liner trades often resulted in offers of time charters from first class liner companies. Such a time charter while not necessarily guaranteeing a fortune in profits for the shipowner, would have to be profitable to be entered into in the first place and like a strong lease on real estate was often highly bankable when the owner was financing through a financial institution.

The use of long term time charters from oil companies was one of the reasons why Norwegian tanker owners were able to build high class, fast diesel tankers through the 1930s when many others simply watched from the sidelines. The Norwegians went to major international oil companies who took the ships and provided a period charter sufficient to amortize the underlying ship's mortgage. After World War II, the Greeks adopted and expanded the same method and owners like Livanos, Onassis, Niarchos and Goulandris, became some of the world's most powerful shipowners. They used their Liberty and other warbuilt tonnage, including former Fort and Park ships, to work the voyage market and in effect built and collateralized a second fleet which was more likely to be used in the time charter market.

Captian John Hetherington. When the editor of the H.R. MacMillan organization's house journal claimed that John Hetherington was the youngest captain at the time of his appointment to command of *Harmac Victoria*, he was employing some journalistic license as there were others who were even younger. The captain of *Mount Douglas Park* gave his age as 26 when his ship left Vancouver on her final voyage. (Harmac News, April 1947)

Effectively the first provided periodic cash bonanzas when the voyage market was high, such as resulted from the Suez crisis, but also exposure to loss when the market was low, which usually involved putting vessels into layup and therefore reducing downward pressure on rates. The newer vessels provided the underpinnings by way of time charters, for secure long term growth in much the same way as a shopping centre developer secures his key long term leases from major tenants. In reality bareboat charters are not too frequently developed in the peacetime market. Far more frequently the standard time charter is preferred. It involves a specific named vessel in the charter party, taken for say two years or for a specific number of voyages, which when added together, meets the test of being a time charter. Such charters usually state the port at which delivery and redelivery are to be effected, and even though it may be for a specific vessel, there may be provision for substitution of an equivalent vessel in specified circumstances. Under a bareboat charter, the charterer, not the owner, takes responsibility for manning and all other functions of managing the vessel as if it was his own property. He will probably rename the vessel with a name of his choice and paint the funnel and probably the rest of the vessel in his colours. Under a time charter which could easily run for a similar period as a bareboat, the charterer may do all the same things such as renaming and using his own colour scheme and funnel colours, but there is unlikely to be any change of registry or national flag. The owner under a time charter will provide many services to his vessel including her manning, maintenance and insurance. Utilizing a bareboat charter is more than likely to arise when a vessel is leased from a leasing company, where the terminology would be different but the practical result the same. The terminology would describe the parties as lessor and lessee rather than as owner or charterer. Leasing companies are not normally set up to take on ship management duties so would want to place that responsibility on the shoulders of the lessee.

A more sophisticated form of charter party is a Contract of Affreightment. This has particular appeal to large scale shippers of bulk cargoes such as coal, iron ore, potash and sulphur. Under this versatile type of contract the shipper undertakes to deliver a certain volume of cargo over a specified period of time and the shipowner or operator undertakes to load and deliver it usually in evenly spaced voyages. An owner with a sufficiently large fleet can nominate any vessel he chooses which happens to be in the right position always assuming the vessel meets the shipper's contract specifications. This leaves the owner in the position of being able to work his vessels as he sees fit once the vessel has completed its voyage under the Contract of Affeightment. An example might be that the shipper requires 15-knot, 15,000-ton d.w. vessels to load potash. Vessel A on the berth is consigned to importers in Australia, while vessel B in the same fleet delivers to Chile. The Australian vessel might then carry grain to Turkey, then proceed to North Africa to load iron ore for Britain. From there she perhaps loads Belgian steel for Eastern Canada, then phosphate rock

Albert Park as *Harmac Victoria*. Captain Hetherington's first command is shown ready to sail. The deck load was carried too far forward by the loading superintendent so that in heavy seas lashings broke and caused the lumber to peel back on itself. Hetherington did the wood panelling on the bridge while he was mate in the ship.

(John Hetherington)

Bowness Park. The carriage of such oversize cargo was frequently undertaken by specialist heavylift vessels. The Victory type demonstrated its versatility when it carried four large locomotives and their tenders from the US to France in winter conditions. The total weight of this on deck cargo was 688 tons, well within the ship's capacity, but very much an awkward outsize cargo.

(Hetherington)

from Florida for Puget Sound and from there presents herself back on the potash berth at Vancouver. Meanwhile ship B has discharged her potash in Chile, so loads copper concentrates for France. There being no bulk cargo from France, she ballasts across to Florida and then loads phosphate rock for California and then presents herself at the potash berth in Vancouver. Being on a shorter series of international voyages, vessel B might arrive back on berth at Vancouver before

vessel A. If the shipowner or contractor cannot place a vessel of his own fleet on the berth at a specified time, the contract of affreightment would likely permit him to take a suitable vessel owned by another owner under another flag, on a simple voyage charter to meet his committment to the shipper. And so the cycles go on and might well involve several vessels all working to pick up potash from the charterer under the contract of affreightment. An important feature is that the

The Last of the 4,700-Tonners. The West Indies Service of Canadian National Steamships had five of the Dominion subtype, which were simply the original design fitted with 'tween-decks to make them more suitable for mixed general cargo. In 1957 they were laid up and sold to Cuba, but delivery was never completed. *Sutherland Park* as *Canadian Conqueror*, *Cartier Park* as *Canadian Victor*, and *Lorne Park* as *Canadian Leader* are seen here. They never sailed again in commercial service and went for scrap in Spain in 1964.

(Maritime Museum of the Atlantic)

owner works the vessel in the crosstrades, whereas companies like Seaboard and McMillan, Bloedel, through their shipping affiliates, did for many years take their vessels on time charters and look after the crosstrades themselves. To all intents and purposes as charterers, they acted entirely like owners, but left the manning and the other day to day matters of being a shipowner to the owner himself. In this way they often made a good return on the intermediate cross trade voyage charters without capital investment in the ship.

In reverting to the Park ships which passed into the hands of owners on the Canadian register we should now look for reasons as to why the Canadian Merchant Marine so quickly folded into virtual oblivion after the war. The most obvious in the mind of many was the labour situation including union rivalries and high manning costs when compared to foreign flags and secondly the already obsolescent state of the ships in peacetime trade, both of which have been covered elsewhere in this book.

There were additional reasons which are not quite so well known. Having described the different types of charters, the first reason is that Canadian ships generally never got beyond simple time or consecutive voyage time charters and then fairly uncommonly. It afforded little opportunity to develop the bankable contracts of affreight-

ment or other long term charters that enabled European owners to build modern tonnage. British and Continental tramp companies had a substantial selection of strong liner operators who commonly took up national-flag, in the case of the British, former Fort ships on time charter which as noted gave a tramp fleet stability of a sort they would not necessarily gain through reliance on the voyage market. Canadian tramp companies did not have a ready market with Canadian liner companies as with the exception of Canadian Pacific and Canadian National Steamships there were no liner companies in regular trade. Elder Dempster (Canada) Ltd. had a regular liner service from the East Coast to West and South Africa and the Canadian Australasian Line operated a berth service from Vancouver to Fiji, New Zealand and Australia, but they were seldom known to take tonnage on charter. One other company with liner services was the British Furness Withy Group, but its Canadian subsidiary like Elder Dempster and Canadian Australasian, functioned as a unit of a far larger international group, which gave them versatility not usually available to purely Canadian owners.

In 1957, one company, Western Canada Steamships, did develop a contract of affreightment, whereby it used its vessels for delivering alumina from Japan into the Columbia River, but

Lake Atlin. Built in 1954, this diesel ship was the second of three Welsh-owned ships acquired by Western Canada in what appeared to be an effort to take advantage of escrowed funds and break away from dependence on the war-built Park ships. *Lake Pennask* was the first and *Lake Atlin* was to be the last ship owned by Western Canada.

(S.C. Heal)

Lake Burnaby was the third acquisition of postwar tonnage and also the biggest ship in the Western Canada fleet. She is also a good example of the split profile, traditional since coal burner days when No. 3 hold was sometimes used for additional bunker space. In a diesel ship such as this there was really no justification for such a design by tradition. *Lake Burnaby* was to be the only total loss suffered by the company.

(A. Duncan)

the charterer frustrated the contract, after the first delivery, on the grounds that the vessels nominated were unsuitable. Western Canada took steps to sue in the California courts, but elected to accept an out of court settlement as liquidated damages, rather than fight a lengthy and expensive court battle, even though right appeared to be on Western Canada's side, but this is the only one that can be now identified largely because the author possesses several annual reports of the company from that period which traces the decline in the fortunes of a Canadian tramp company in world trading conditions. Reference will

be made again to the fortunes of Western Canada Steamships Ltd.

Considering the amount of information that has to be provided, usually including ship plans, in the negotiation of a long term charter contract of any sort, the reason of unsuitability seems to ring quite hollow. Usually charterers of ex-war-built tonnage of the North Sands type would not have gone beyond relatively short term time charters, because charterers already knew they would become increasingly out of date and therefore less competitive before a long term time charter was completed. Western Canada was the only West

Coast owner to have some success in breaking away from the limitations of the North Sands Victory type vessels and its negotiation of long term employment by way of a contract of affreightment for its new postwar vessels seemed to be part of its strategy to assist its aquisition of superior postwar tonnage.

One only has to consider the affiliations of individual Canadian owners to understand why the Canadian Merchant Navy dissolved so quickly after the war. There were seven West Coast operators who actually acquired tonnage and became owners. Three, Canadian Transport, Seaboard Shipping and Johnson Walton Steamships were subsidiaries or affiliates of companies with major interests in forest products. The last named was actually a subsidiary of the Danish East Asiatic Company of Copenhagen, a powerful shipping and trading company, which had developed a corporate policy of investment in foreign natural product producers as a means of controlling some of their trade and filling their ships with paying cargo.

The first two were the shipping divisions of the H.R. MacMillan lumber interests and Seaboard Lumber Sales both of which competed with each other and the rest of the world's forest product producers in what, at times, could be a savage world of cutthroat competition. They quickly found that once the lustre of high rates and the thirst of a market for ready ships had been satisfied, falling rates and high labour costs took away a lot, if not all, of the profit potential and the attraction of being shipowners quickly diminished. Foreign owners were gradually coming back into the market place, offering new postwar ships not built with wartime conditions in mind. Rapid advances were made in cargo handling equipment, all steel roller hatches, improved cargo stowage designs such as the open hatch type vessel, increased deadweight and speed with new higher powered, but more economical diesel engines all of which made the Canadian vessels less attractive to charterers and less profitable to owners.

Indeed the East Asiatic Company's own Danish flag vessels of both prewar and postwar vintage were of a superior specification and while they were not built with the lumber trade specifically in mind they were highly competitive in terms of speed, economy and capacity and serviced East Asiatic's interests in tropical hardwoods as well as handling Canadian forest products.

One cannot help thinking that the attraction to all three of these Canadian owners was short term and highly speculative. For one thing the philosophy of competitive lumber trading in international markets where low cost transportation was always a factor, was at variance with the aims of another section of the same group. Canadian Transport and Seaboard Shipping from being charterers on behalf of their principals with the aim of being an auxiliary in maximising lumber profits, stepped into the opposing camp in becoming shipowners charged with the need to maximize their profits as shipowners and effectively reduce lumber profits depending on their success in upholding freight rates. It may be open to argument, but one role contradicted the other and needless to say it took very little time for senior management in all three companies to deduce that lumber, not shipowning, was their core interest.

This was a lesson not always remembered. In *Pick up Sticks: A History of the Intercoastal Lumber Trade,* the author, the late Richard M. Hallock who was also a retired lumber shipping executive, tells much of the shipping history of both Canadian Transport and the Seaboard group and their competitors and how they were projected to be profitable enterprises benefitting from the relationship with strong parent companies. Both companies became major factors in international shipping as they worked their chartered vessels in the cross trades in order to effect a redelivery to British Columbia ports. So long as they could work the voyage and short term time charter market to advantage they made good profits on their shipping enterprises, but as the parent companies' demands for larger and more complex vessels developed so also did the requirements of owners in order to finance these vastly larger and more expensive ships, not to mention the infrastucture to support them, such as larger lumber terminals and assembly areas.

Success in shipping can be a heady wine and shipping history is full of bright stars which quickly fell into oblivion and such was almost the case with Canadian Transport. In *HR: A Biography of H.R. MacMillan,* Drushka tells how, due to too many long term chartering committments at high rates, and a collapsing voyage charter market which was essential to working time chartered ships back to BC, Canadian Transport piled up massive losses which if it had not been for prompt action on the part of MacMillan Bloedel's board of directors, might have seen Canadian Transport sinking into bankruptcy with all the potential for dragging the parent company down with it. The pivotal problem became four, so-called "Flensburg", 50,500 tdw, German-built geared bulkcarriers, which were the largest of this type ever built. Built in or around 1974, they were according to Hallock, too big for important trades serviced by the parent company. This was particularly so with Eastern USA. lumber importing ports which often were quite small and shallow and could not fully benefit from fully laden carriers of this size.

Canadian Transport from its founding, in 1924, had served the needs of the parent H.R. MacMillan interests through slump and war with excellent results and, after having taken a fling at owning and operating ex-Park Steamship vessels, it quickly retired from shipowning partly because it was no longer financially attractive and also because of the different philosophies that governed shipowning and lumber sales, but chartering when overdone was just as hazardous and the excursion into big scale chartering, in 1974, just described, saw the then Chairman and President of MacMillan Bloedel, fired in 1975, along with a number of others.

Seaboard Lumber Sales was owned by a consortium of some 20 BC lumber producers and with its subsidiary, Seaboard Shipping Ltd. provided a comprehensive sales and shipping service to its owners. The shipping arm developed a small fleet of ex-Park vessels which it ran quite successfully so long as they remained viable. However like other Canadian owners the need to develop higher class tonnage from the 50s on, was apparent and as it disposed of its Park ships it developed time charters, mostly with Norwegian and Danish owners. Always innovative it assisted the develop-

ment of the open hatch vessel and roll-on, roll-off type carriers, but with so many masters behind Seaboard Lumber many changes followed after certain key members dropped out to develop their own lumber shipping interests. The lumber sales company is no more, but Seaboard International Shipping Ltd. is still an active and viable carrier of lumber products using chartered tonnage.

The Canadian-Australasian Line was a subsidiary of the Union Steamship Company of New Zealand, and Canadian Pacific. Union Steamship was controlled by the giant P&O Group of London, and in that it ran a berth liner service from Vancouver to the Antipodes it was well sheltered from most of the vicissitudes of the international tramp trades. It operated with regularity and a fair degree of success but was finally put out of business when the route was containerized. Some of the former Park ships on this route lasted even longer than those of Western Canada.

Kerr-Silver was one of the two remaining Vancouver-based owners of wartime tonnage. It was a joint venture of a US liner and shipping agency company, Kerr Steamship Company of New York and Silver Line Ltd. of London. It was obviously, like most of the Canadian companies a straight speculation to take advantage of early postwar conditions. Silver Line was a liner concern operating a round-the-world service in which Kerr had a substantial interest. Kerr was a chartering agent and as such was in the tramp chartering business, but it was Silver that contributed the running expertise.

The other was Vancouver-Oriental Line, a convenience arrangement, nominally run from Vancouver presumably to give its principals, London tramp managers, Counties Ship Management, a foothold in the West Coast shipping market with its high access to major lumber producers in British Columbia and the Northwest states. Counties was a London-Greek concern controlled by the Rethymnis and Kulukundis families of Piraeus and its two ships were the only North Sands coalburners to be registered postwar at Vancouver. The Counties group was the largest international buyer of ex-Fort ships, mostly North Sands coalburners.

A breakdown of the real benefical owners of Canadian shipowners on both coasts is set out in sufficient detail in the author's book *Conceived in War, Born in Peace*. From that, it will be seen that the majority of East Coast beneficial owners of Canadian shipping companies were Greeks. One company, I.H. Mathers & Son Ltd. should be mentioned again as they were instrumental in negotiating the purchase of 84 ex-Park and Fort ships from the Canadian Maritime Commission. These were parcelled out to a number of Canadian subsidiaries of Greek concerns and represented the biggest block of warbuilt ships in the disposal program. At the time press reports identified Mathers as the owner and while Mathers might have had a beneficial ownership interest in some of the ships, the truth was that the firm was the intermediary for its Greek principals. When transfers off the Canadian register were permitted most of the ships found their way into flag of convenience subsidiaries of the same principals.

That book also contains a detailed history of the Western Canada Steamship Company Limited. This was a most interesting company as, if companies reflect the personality of their owners, this one carried its founders' stripes for far longer than most. Its four founding owners were four of the leading Vancouver shipping agencies each with experience in the tramp trades, namely Anglo-Canadian, Canada Shipping, Empire Shipping and North Pacific Shipping. They had all functioned as managers of Park Steamship vessels during the war and, at the end of the war, joint ventured to form Western Canada which became the most genuinely shipowner-oriented and longest lived of all the Vancouver companies and this description is used to differentiate it from the short term speculations described above.

In its efforts to progress into the later generations of shipping, Western Canada Steamship's annual reports make some intriguing comments on the affairs of a Canadian trampship company. They comprise a little bit of history not recorded elsewhere and now unlikely to ever be repeated as all the records of the company, in one colossal senseless act were consigned to the incinerator some years after the company finally closed down its shipowning activities.

The six reports in the author's possession for the years 1956 to 1961, cover the period when Western Canada was divesting itself of its last Park ships and was re-equipping with almost new diesel ships. The first report, that for the ninth fiscal year ending June 30, 1956 showed that three ex-Park ships remained out of the original 21 that had been owned. They were *Lake Kootenay (Fort Colville)*, *Table Bay (ex-Lake Shawinigan, ex-Tipperary Park)* and *Walvis Bay (ex-Lake Tatla, ex-Winona Park)*. The Bay ships were two of four Western Canada ships that had been previously transferred to British registry and management under special license from the Canadian Government in an effort to alleviate the deteriorating position of Canadian owners with ships bound by covenant to the Canadian register. The other two ships had already been disposed of. This report also announced the acquisition of *Lake Pennask*, formerly the Welsh owned *Jersey Spray*, on March 25, 1956 and her sister *Jersey Mist*, which was renamed *Lake Atlin* on July 5th. Both were modern postwar diesel ships which gave Western Canada a fresh competitive edge. Delivery was taken at British ports and both ships were immediately fixed, the first to load Potash at Hamburg for Japan and the second sailed in ballast to Norfolk, Virginia to load coal for Japan.

The 1957 report details the sale of the three remaining ex-Park ships at an average price of US$1,381,000 each which reflected the high ship values pertaining through the Suez crisis. Once this was settled, ship values slumped and the same ships would have only fetched a possible US$650,000 each. That is the nature of ship values and how the market affects them once built. That is also something that many Canadian critics of government action in disposing of the Park fleet never understood in complaining that the ships were originally given away at roughly a half million dollars apiece and not sold at original cost to operators like Western Canada. The company did what any smart operator would have done in the knowledge that it wished to dispose of its older more obsolescent units and was fortunately able to take advantage of a market upswing.

The proceeds of sale were placed in escrow with the Canadian Maritime Commission under the flag covenant which meant that Western Canada had three alternatives for their disposition. It could either sell the funds at a discount to another Canadian owner building a new vessel for Canadian flag operation, or secondly, build a new ship for its own account in Canada, or finally buy a foreign flag vessel and take it on to the Canadian register. This all had to be done within one year to avoid certain tax consequences. Western Canada chose the latter and purchased the modern Welsh-owned motor ship *Llantrisant* and renamed her, *Lake Burnaby*. Built in 1952 she became the largest ship in the fleet and also the fastest at 13$\frac{1}{2}$ knots, both of which confirmed the trend that was now underway by 1952, for faster larger trampships. Unfortunately at a cost of $4,001,000 which was $232,000 in excess of the sum received for the last three ex-Park ships in its fleet. The price realized on the three ships was an excellent sale for Western Canada, but conversely they probably paid more than they would have done months later for *Lake Burnaby* as the market declined with the settlement of the Suez crisis.

Lake Burnaby was transferred to British management under the transfer scheme negotiated between the Canadian and British governments but unfortunately this new ship was not to last long for she was wrecked November 3, 1958 on passage from the Philippines for Hamburg/Rotterdam with a full cargo of copra. The amount realized from insurance provided a surplus over the original purchase cost, so there was a silver lining to the loss after all. This seemed to be a watershed for Western Canada. Market conditions, labour costs and the difficulties of dealing back and forth with government agencies seemed to occupy the company from then on as it went into a slow decline. It was still able to make money in spite of all the hurdles and by 1961 the two remaining ships constituted its fleet, but their time was running out under Canadian ownership/British management. British labour costs

were mounting and the trend to bulkcarriers and the serious start of the container age was now well established. The first to be sold was *Lake Pennask* as she was not subject to Canadian flag covenant having been purchased originally out of free surplus funds. *Lake Atlin* was the last to go in 1965. The sale of *Lake Kootenay* in 1957 effectively ended the saga of the war-built ships on the West coast and the disposal of *Lake Atlin* ended deepsea shipowning on the West coast.

As previously noted, the one survivor of the companies which grew out of the Second World War, FedNav of Montreal, continues to flourish to this day, owning a modern fleet of bulkcarriers and specialist ships almost entirely under foreign flags. It has been controlled by younger vigorous men who have been less likely to be inhibited by government restrictions and fears of flags of convenience. Their achievements in skirting the obstacles are seldom trumpetted by them, partly it seems reasonable to suppose, because there is no profit in being criticized by labour and politicians alike who simply do not understand the realities of shipowning.

One wonders why Western Canada did not fully make the transition following its first three acquisitions, in spite of the obstacles that have been related. The reasons seem obvious as it eventually gets down to the human element. The late Captain J.S. "Jack" Clarke, president and general Manager, was a great shipping man who would be enshrined in a Hall of Shipping Fame, if such ever existed. He was not only the leader of the company and probably the mortar holding much of it together, but he was also growing older and facing retirement. There was no obvious successor and the directors, likely all men in their senior years were less motivated by cutting a dash in financial circles and more concerned about protecting their investments. A new leader with fresh ideas was probably needed, but timidity about being led into the unknown would have probably proved to be a major obstacle. FedNav, by way of contrast, was and remains a private company controlled by the Pathy family who could make decisions without becoming publicly accountable, whereas Western Canada was a public company, and although not widely held, it attracted the attention of the public through media treatment, a factor which would cause an older board of directors to exercise caution bordering on timidity. Age combined with caution and shrewdness in recognising the right time to bail out were probably contributing factors in bringing about the demise of the always interesting, Western Canada Steamship Company Ltd. It was the end of an era.

FOREIGN FLAG OPERATIONS

From the first moment of disposing of the Fort and Park ships a percentage found their way to flags other than Canadian or British. Greek owners, particularly those based in London and New York, viewed them collectively along with the Liberties, Oceans, Sams and Empires, as did the international freight markets, as being "Liberty Ship Equivalents". In fact this term became a matter of common usage in shipping circles which was to persist until the ship types involved were reduced through the attrition of increased marine losses and ship breaking activities. In general the first sales following the war went to good class owners, many of whom, like Livanos and Goulandris, were respected names with good reputations. This class of owner usually only regarded the warbuilt ships as a stepping stone to bigger and better postwar freighters and tankers, so that often the ships were resold to small, obscure owners, some of whom were clients of the big well-established companies who continued to work the ships on behalf of their clients. Others, however, ran the ships often with only the one objective -- maximized profit and minimized expense. For them the flags of convenience like Panama, Liberia and Costa Rica, held immediate appeal with their licence to effect crew economies, reduced running costs and maintenance that would not be tolerated under the flags of established maritime countries with proper classification societies like Lloyd's, the American Bureau of Shipping and Bureau Veritas.

In the vernacular, they were "run into the ground", usually at the considerable expense of marine insurance underwriters. Periodic classification surveys would have revealed with increasing frequency the fact that many of the ships could barely maintain class. This was not because of poor original construction which was certainly not the case with the Canadian built ships, but because of wanton neglect including unrepaired damage, accelerating obsolescence and the attitude that a worn out ship could just as easily be "sold to the underwriters," by stranding, at a possibly greater profit than a sale to the shipbreakers. However, any idea that in some way underwriters could be misled in such matters as accepting the risk of insuring such doubtful tonnage was dispelled when Lloyd's acting in concert with the company market through the Institute of London Underwriters, in concert with other insurance bodies elsewhere, particularly New York, laid out new rules in 1966. These governed warbuilt tonnage and were designed to clear such vessels from the seas. The rates for marine cargo insurance were surcharged for over-age vessels and rates on Hull & Machinery increased in such a way as to add to the burdens of owners and make it a more attractive proposition to hasten their sale to the shipbreakers.

There is little more to be said about the Forts and Parks. Any remaining vessels after the end of the 60s were those that had passed into the hands of the Chinese Peoples government in Beijing, who were a power unto themselves in that period. Old ships could survive for an incredible period, as those on the Chinese Register were mostly engaged in domestic trade and did not have any bearing on the commerce of the capitalist world. When they needed more modern tonnage and required to finance such vessels using the processes and instruments of the capitalist world they placed them under the ownership of one of their front companies in Hong Kong, such as Yick Fung Industrial & Enterprises Company Ltd. After the mortgage, most probably with a Hong Kong bank, had been retired the vessel could then be transferred to the Chinese flag. The last entries found in *Lloyd's Register* for Fort, Park or Ocean class ships transferred to the Chinese flag were for the register year 1991-92 where:

Zhan Dou 27 ex-Fort St. James
Zhan Dou 30 ex-Yamaska Park
Zhan Dou 50 ex-Fort St. Paul

This was also the registry of the last Ocean class ship:

Zhan Dou 26 ex-Ocean Merchant

The 1992-93 register contained none of the above ships, but whether they actually lasted until 1991-92 is not known with any certainty.

At an age of 50 years, and presumably still in commercial service, the last of the Fort and Park ship fleet constructed in Canada had a very extended life span for tramps of any type. The Canadian Forts and Parks were indeed a great fleet of ships.

Albert Park as Harmac Victoria. After ploughing into a headsea, lashings and chains on the ship were broken back to the foremast by the force of the water. Captain Hetherington had complained about loading the deck cargo over No. 1 hold too far forward, which increased the exposure to heavy weather damage. The second picture shows lumber hanging over the side which was restowed at Panama. The broken chain lashings are visible in the photo.

The World Voyage of *Harmac Victoria ex-Albert Park*

Contributed by the late John Hetherington, M.M. of Vancouver, BC

A photo on the back of *Harmac News,* April 1947, shows the vessel on her last day of loading - finishing at the after deck. (See picture on p. 186) The Blue Peter was already flying aloft. Captain Hetherington was not too pleased with the overhang forward on the deck cargo stow. The photos above show what happened in the Caribbean as a result of this stow. Varnished wood overlay of the flying bridge was done by Hetherington when he was chief officer of the vessel in 1945.

The Log of the Voyage

-The subject voyage commenced with a full lumber cargo for South African and Portugese East African ports. The ship loaded 5,550,000 fbm including 875,000 fbm on deck.

-Voyage commenced Vancouver to Balboa, Canal Zone - 3,997 miles - 14 days - 11.9 knots, consumed 27 tons per day, or 384 tons clean bunker "C" fuel.

-Second morning out of Cristobal to Port of Spain for bunkers we experienced brisk N.E. trade winds and took a heavy sea over the bow. Tons of water over the flush forward deck lifted the deck cargo and snapped the for'ard heavy chain lashings like shoe strings. Although on deck at "shippers risk", I was not about to risk any hands by attempting to jettison deck cargo, so put back to the Canal for restow. As it turned out we only lost about 3,000 fbm. The agent, crusty old George Harper of Wilford McKay was not at all pleased to see us back and the stevedores promptly took the day off having declared a picnic!

-Cristobal to Trinidad - 1,150 miles average only 8.4 knots against N.E. trade headwinds.

-Trinidad to Capetown - 5,400 miles - 21 days - 10.75 knots, fair weather.

-Ports of discharge around South African coast - Capetown, Port Elizabeth, East London, Durban and then to Portugese East Africa at ports of Laurenco Marques (now Maputo) and Beira. There were port delays with rail-car congestion and no discharging to barges. At Beira for 26 days.

-In Beira, received cable from Furness Withy, London, ordering us to Aden for a full cargo of salt for Japan.

-Beira to Aden - 2,683 miles at 11.5 knots. Experienced sandstorm off Cape Guardafui.

-Aden to Singapore - 9,500 tons of sea salt - 16 1/2 days - 9.3 knots. Had to anchor off North tip of Sumatra with thrust block problems (see photo with explanation).

-Made Singapore. Due to heavy lift derrick at No. 4, we were able to drag the thrust shaft along the boat deck, then float it free as the derrick was topped and put it over the side onto the stern of a tug to be taken ashore for the collar to be machined.

-One week at anchor without propulsion and with no room at any berth alongside.

Albert Park as Harmac Victoria. While carrying a cargo of salt from Aden for Japan the lubrication for the thrust shaft broke down and caused severe scoring. The picture shows the thrust shaft being lifted out with the aid of a stiffleg to go ashore for repairs at Singapore.

-Singapore to Miike-ko, Kyushu, Japan - 2450 miles - 11 days - 9.4 knots. August weather in Kyushu felt tropical, Pilot boat not on station at mouth of Shimabara Gulf, had to proceed right up to area of Miike to pick up pilot who proceeded to put us bow first into the mud just above the entrance to the blunderbuss-shaped entrance. The tide was flooding and he misjudged his starboard turn approach.

Once I could see we were going to by-pass the breakwater entrance, I put her full astern and dropped both anchors, but still took the mud stem on and saw the fo'c'sle head raise slightly against the background area. She pulled herself off immediately without damage, but no one relished the idea of going aground. The pilot "doffed" his straw boater and made himself scarce as soon as we came alongside. The town was still in very rough shape as a result of firebombing raids by US B-29's. American occupying forces remained up north in Fukuoka.

I had to travel there by train to report our arrival. Port master there was Captain Sakae, ex-master of *Hikawa Maru* which used to trade into Vancouver pre-war. She was one of the few Japanese merchant ships to survive the war. Sakae's routine was to visit us nightly to share a 40-ounce bottle of Seagram's VO rye with Chief Engineer Colin Munro and I. He seemed highly amused by the tender years of us both and could not figure out how such a thing was allowable in Canada!

The voyage home to Vancouver was a fortunate one weatherwise, because with only 750 tons of ballast water in the deep tanks abaft the engine room bulkhead, plus fuel in the double bottom, our propeller was barely submerged and we were surfing for'ard. A rhumb line course and quite rainy overcast weather all the way home was most welcome. We did 4,900 miles in 18½ days at an average 10.9 knots.

Total distance of sea passages for entire voyage was 26,282 miles, average 10½ knots, 104 days. Total elapsed time was 5 months, 3 weeks.

One of our cadets for this voyage, Colin Donaldson from Trail, BC was an excellent piper, so he always piped us in and out of port from his station on the monkey island. Gliding into her berth at Ballantyne Pier on a quiet autumn morning (Sept 15th) was a most gratifying feeling. (Amen!)

My only skirmish with the medicine chest on this lengthy trip was when I had to stitch up the forehead of a tough little Newfoundlander A.B. after he had gone 'arse over tit' down the slimy Jardine Matheson steps in Singapore after an evening ashore. After paying off in Vancouver I bumped into him on Hastings Street and was enthusiastically thanked for "that neat job of hemstitching you done on me, Cap." In fact it was puckered up and looked terrible!

The late Captain John Hetherington was a well-known figure in the BC lumber industry until his death in 1997. When he was appointed to command he was one of the youngest masters in the Canadian merchant service in command of deep-sea ships. His chief engineer, Colin Munro, was equally young at the time of appointment. After leaving *Bowness Park,* evidently Hetherington's plan had been to join the BC pilotage service for which purpose he had joined the Frank Waterhouse Company to gain coastal experience. Soon after, he took up the offer of command of *Harmac Victoria.*

Captain Hetherington was born in 1918 whereas Captain S. Fisher, master of *Tatuk ex-Victoria Park,* was born in 1920, which might have established Fisher as the youngest Canadian master in charge of a former Park ship.

At the End of a Towline: *Tuxedo Park* and *Lake Sicamous ex-Weston Park*

Contributed by Bill Hutcherson, Wireless Operator, Richmond, BC

The reliability of the war-built Park ships appears to have been of a fairly high standard although they did cause some concern due to being severely underpowered, a fact which showed up during heavy seas and strong storms. Generally speaking they were able to provide good service with a minimum of fuss and bother and incidences of them breaking down at sea seem to have been a rare event. The fact that I sailed on two of the ships which suffered such indignities seems to contradict the above statements but, then again, it may indicate that I was somewhat of a Jonah and should have been prevented from joining either of them!

The first occurrence took place in the fall of 1945 during the third voyage of *Tuxedo Park* while she was proceeding homeward along the coast of Guatemala. Two days out of Panama the ship slowed to a virtual stop when it was reported by the Chief Engineer that a series of boiler tubes had packed it up. This happy event deprived us not only of locomotion, but also of electricity and running water. The Captain, Frank Stewart, was a heavy drinker and the event unfortunately, found him in his cups which resulted in him panicking and handing me an order to transmit an SOS which far

Rupert Park lends a hand. Following a major boiler failure, *Rupert Park* answers the call of *Tuxedo Park* to tow the distressed ship into Panama for repairs.　(Wm. Hutcherson)

exceeded the requirements of the moment. After explaining that an SOS would lay the ship open to salvage claims and other unfavourable results he abdicated any action to my own judgement. Opening up on the emergency battery-operated transmitter I contacted

Rupert Park which was on her way down the coast and only a couple of hours from us. Her first signal from her Aldis lamp was a request to talk salvage which invoked a reply from our Captain which was unrepeatable.

The rigging of the towline was no simple matter as without steam for the winches, the four-inch insurance cable had to be hauled into place by manpower, but after much cussing and such, the two ships were finally linked and we began the trip back to Panama. The officers' saloon saw much lively conversation as the mates took the credit for saving the ship. The engineers, of course contributed their two cents worth, but were not able to take much credit as most of us felt it was their fault that we found ourselves in such a predicament. The two radio officers (our third had been left in England and the chief and I were standing six on-six off radio watches) kept very quiet as even though we knew that it was my contact with *Rupert Park* that brought our rescuer, radio types are always too gentlemanly to toot their own horns!

Tuxedo Park at the end of a towline. Conditions on board became very uncomfortable, with no power for auxiliaries. Water had to be sent over on a line by the bucketful.   (Wm. Hutcherson)

The trip to Panama was not without its hardships as the heat of the tropics raised havoc with the stores in the freezers and all of us on board became rather high due to the lack of any water to shower or wash in. We were passing through an area of squalls and as we approached one which appeared darker and thicker than others, we grabbed soap and towels and stood naked on the hatches of three, four and five holds. Down came torrents of warm rain and we soaped ourselves thoroughly as we enjoyed the escape from sweat and stink, but just as suddenly as it arrived, the rain stopped as if a faucet had been turned off. There we stood, covered in soapy lather with no way to be rid of it. Believe me, as one who knows, that dry soap became mighty itchy. Drinking water was provided by hauling a bucket from *Rupert Park* to *Tuxedo Park* along the tow line. The *Rupert's* mate was nearly lost at Balboa when he was pulled overboard while recovering the insurance cable. Luckily, he had a mop of red hair which was picked up in the beam of her searchlight and he was recovered.

Weston Park as *Lake Sicamous*. Bill Hutcherson thought he was a jonah when for the second time in his seagoing career he was aboard a broken-down ship dependent on a long tow. *Lake Sicamous* dropped her propeller and the first stage of her tow to Los Angeles was handled by the little fishpacker *Kanak*. Here the fishpacker is shown drawing alongside.

(Wm. Hutcherson)

Weston Park as Lake Sicamous. At Los Angeles the tow was handed over to the Victoria-based tug *Snohomish*, a powerful deep-sea tug which made good time to Vancouver with her tow despite severe headwinds.

(Wm. Hutcherson)

Replacing the boiler tubes became a four-week effort which gave the members of the crew the opportunity to have more than the usual look at the sights and delights that the Canal Zone had to offer. This was the only event of its sort to affect the *Tuxedo Park* that I know of.

My second experience with the infallibility of man's creations took place during a voyage in *Lake Sicamous*, (ex-*Weston Park*). Passing through the Gulf of Tehuantepec off the coast of southern Mexico and almost abeam of the small town of Puerto Arista, *Sicamous* gave a sudden lurch as her propeller went spinning off into the deep. It was a beautiful winter's evening with a mirror calm sea and a buttermilk sky.

After dipping our mate overside to probe around the stern and confirm that we were propless, Captain Charlie Alltree instructed me to contact our owners, Western Canada Steam Ships in Vancouver, to let them know of our current plight.

At this point I should mention that I was much pleased by the fact that every Park ship I served in was equipped with McKay radio which I swear was the finest made at the time. The shortwave transmitter and receiver were capable of raising stations anywhere in the world. At the time of losing our propeller, I sent the message shortwave to CKN, the naval radio station located in Aldergrove, BC and then it was a matter of waiting for a reply from our owners. This did not come through until the next morning, a time when the atmospherics were rapidly reaching the point of causing any and all signals to fade away. Nevertheless, the faithful McKay equipment picked up the faint message to the effect that *Lake Minnewanka (ex-Princeton Park)* would stand by us until a tow arrived.

As *Minnewanka* approached us on her way down the coast, her sparks and I carried on a regular correspondence regarding our position and certain provisions we would require. Waiting for help to arrive was not uncomfortable as the weather remained fine with a nice prevailing breeze to keep things cool. We still had steam so electricity, running water, fans etc. were all functional. The one thing lacking was the means to move the ship. The only concern was that Captain Alltree's supply of rye whiskey was at a low ebb and would require replenishment well before we saw the port of Vancouver again. Luckily, *Minnewanka* was able to relieve our concerns in this department and the motor lifeboat was used as a transporter of the necessary medication. After a week of hobnobbing with our standby sister ship, a fish packer came sniffing over the horizon with the intention of investigating why two freighters were parked out in the middle of nowhere, but on closer inspection, we realized that this little thing, the packer *Kanak*, was our tug and after securing a line, she huffed and puffed and began the long tow to Los Angeles.

Lake Minnewanka disappeared over the horizon within two hours but we seemed to be lingering not far from where we had started. No communication existed between us and our tow boat although I could listen in to his voice transmissions. He could not read Morse so even the Aldis lamp was useless for expressing any needs to him.

Two days after leaving Tehuantepec, one of its regular bi-weekly storms came along and even though we had reached its fringe, the little *Kanak* was almost abeam of us as she strove to keep moving ahead. Christmas came and went as did New Year's and still we plodded along. On January 4, 1947 we arrived at the Port of Los Angeles and the next day we were picked up by the Victoria-based tug *Snohomish* owned by Island Tug & Barge of that city, to continue the long tow home.

The skipper of the tug was a spry little old fellow who gave me the frequencies he would be using for voice communication and for us to reply using Morse code on the Aldis. Leaving Los Angeles at a brisk pace, for the *Snohomish* was a real deep-sea tug with lots of power, we headed out to sea and into a developing full gale. We passed up the California, Oregon and Washington coasts, but were slowed as we battled continuous headwinds. It was not until January 15, 1947 that we dropped anchor in English Bay to await daylight before being towed into harbour. Unknown to me, my parents had obtained the frequencies of the *Snohomish's* radio and had tuned their DeForest Crossley radio to listen in as the skipper of the tug talked to the Sparks of the freighter.

Our cargo of powdered cement in the 'tween-decks had managed to spill on to the cargo of salt in the lower holds with the result that we had a five- or six-inch cement pavement over the bulk of the cargo in the lower holds. The longshoremen arrived with jackhammers to break up the solid crust covering several thousand tons of salt. Whatever became of the stuff is unknown to me as it had been contracted to provide salt for the Christmas trade, the Windsor salt mines in Ontario having been on strike. By the time we arrived, Christmas was past and the salt strike had been settled.

Lake Sicamous was an excellent ship and one I will always recall with fond memories. I was very sorry to learn that she had changed owners two more times and that while sailing as *Silver Valley* in 1963, she had run aground on the River Douro bar off Oporto, Portugal, had broken in two and was declared a total loss.

INSURANCE CONSIDERATIONS

These incidents provide interesting examples of the manner in which marine insurance works. *Tuxedo Park*, in ballast at the time and carrying no freight-earning cargo, was an example where the extraordinary costs of the tow would have been recovered from the vessel's Protection and Indemnity Insurance. *Rupert Park* could not claim salvage as the two ships were sisters with a common owner. To have debited one and compensated the other would have been like transferring money from one pocket to the other. The costs of repair for the damaged boiler tubes would have been recovered under Hull and Machinery policies had Park Steamship carried insurance. Mr. Bill Ingram, who was galley boy aboard *Rupert Park* at the time of the incident, remembers receiving a $25 bonus which was likely given as an "ex-gratia" payment for services rendered by his ship's crew in lieu of salvage.

Lake Sicamous would have declared a general average. Almost the first act of the ship's captain would have been to produce the ship's logs, both bridge and engine room, to support the circumstances of the event and to register his protest declaring a general average. The test for a general average is to determine if the sacrifice was made for the benefit of "all parties to the adventure". The hiring of tugs was such a sacrifice incurred by the shipowner for the benefit of all, as if the ship was left at sea a virtual derelict, she would sooner or later have foundered or drifted ashore without freight being earned and with cargo lost.

Under a general average, the ship's expenses including the towing bills for both tugs would have been pooled among the ship's owner, the owners of cargo and the owners of the freight money, all of whom would have recovered their rateable proportion. This would usually have been expressed as a common percentage of the gross loss under their respective insurance policies as general average is always an insured risk. Only certain owners insured their freight money and, of course, freight can be earned by a charterer as well as an owner. In this instance it appears that Western Canada Steamship Co. was the owner of the freight money.

For the purpose of drawing up a general average statement, an average adjuster would have determined the insured value of the ship, the cargo and the freight paid or payable. The cost of repairing and replacing the lost propeller would have been settled as a particular average (partial loss of hull) born entirely by the Western Canada fleet policy covering Hull and Machinery which would also have paid out for the ship's proportion of the general average. Whatever loss occurred in the cement would have been dealt with as a particular average (partial loss of cargo) the loss falling entirely on to the insurers of the cement cargo, unless it could be shown that the loss was a result of the incident giving rise to the general average.

The Last Voyage of *Bowness Park*: Voyage No. 6

Contributed by John Hetherington, M.M. of Vancouver, BC

After discharging lumber in the UK, *Bowness Park* was sub-chartered to a New York company, Polaris Steamship. We lifted a cargo of heavy machinery for the French Supply Council including four railway locomotives with tenders for discharge at Le Havre. Prior to commencement of loading the 'tween decks were shored up from the tank tops with 12 x 12' timbers, likewise 'tween decks to weather decks. Something like 120 eye pads were welded to the deck for chain lashings and bottle screws to attach. The locomotives ran 127 tons each and were stowed two abreast at No 2 hatch and two at No 4. The four tenders were 45 tons each stowed two at No. 1 and two at No. 5 hatches. The locomotives were lowered by floating crane onto 6 x 12' timbers into which the flanges of the driving wheels sank.

The vessel was very stiff due to a high metacentric height and the weather was not all that great. Being a late November passage, it was quite a sight to see those locies over the bridge dodger arching through the night as we rolled along before a strong south-easter. However all our lashings remained bar tight. They were checked regularly and all was well. After completion of discharge at Le Havre we proceeded to London where the vessel was sold to Kerr-Silver Line and became *Manx Marine*. I then proceeded home to Vancouver as a passenger on the *Pacific Exporter* (Furness Line) under the command of Captain Roy Holland who later became Vancouver Harbour Master. Christmas and New Year was celebrated aboard, during a rough and stormy westerly passage from which we eventually limped into Sydney, NS with a flooded forepeak. From Sydney, I took the CPR train to Vancouver with snow over the entire distance.

A Cadet's Memories of Voyages in *Cromwell Park*, later *Harmac Vancouver*

This memoir is condensed from two privately published accounts prepared by Peter Tull, a former cadet in the ship and now a retired tugboat master residing in Richmond, BC.

I was born in Duncan, BC. My mother was a single parent and brought up my sister and myself aided by a job as a bread truck driver. When war broke out we moved to Victoria where Mother got a job as a guard at the gate of Yarrow's Shipyard. Because she knew Mr. Yarrow, he was able to direct her as to how best she could get me hired as a cadet with Park Steamship Company. One day my mother asked me if I would like to go to sea. "Yes, what boy wouldn't," I replied.

Before I was accepted as a cadet I had to travel to Vancouver for an interview with a gentleman from Park Steamship Company, who did just about everything to discourage me from joining my first ship. I don't know why, but maybe he had someone else in mind for the job or maybe it was on account of my extreme youth.

Certainly at 15, I was about as young as anyone who started a sea career during the war. More than that the four-year indentures of my fellow cadet, Ken Clapp of Powell River, and myself were served out in the same ship from beginning to end, which may have been something of a record, although I don't doubt that there may have been others. Ken Clapp was a 17-year-old graduate of St. Mary's School at Hubbards, Nova Scotia so had a distinct advantage over me as I was completely green and without any previous sea experience to talk of.

We were assigned to the brand-new *Cromwell Park*, a "Canadian" type variation of the North Sands ships designed to use oil or coal fuel. In the four years that I spent in the ship, coal was never used as a bunker fuel.

I reported on board and eventually found the chief officer, who called out to Ken to come and meet "the new cadet." Seemingly from nowhere, Ken landed from a great height alongside me. We got on well from the beginning and in four years only had one serious disagreement. Somewhere on

our voyages Ken had bought a monkey and I a parrot which we kept in our cabin. Neither of the animals were very clean and we soon realized we had made a mistake. We gave both animals away before the rift between us ruined our friendship.

We shared an 8ft by 10ft cabin. There were double-decker bunks on one side with a settee on the other, a drawers-desk combination between them under the porthole and a hanging locker on each side. We soon discovered that our cabin was actually the one allocated to the two cooks who had surreptitiously exchanged the brass plates above the door before we took possession. The cabin meant for us was better so, at the end of the first leg of the voyage when the cooks left us in Melbourne, we did a quick switch again and regained our rightful cabin.

By the time Ken had shown me around the ship on our first day it was time for supper. Somewhat gingerly, we got into our new uniforms and entered the officer's saloon for the first time. There was a distinct pecking order which everyone respected, in accord with the time-honoured routine followed on most deep-sea ships. The Captain had the head of the table with the Chief Engineer on one side and the Chief Officer opposite to him and so on in order of seniority. Down at the far end we two cadets sat, content to be as far away as possible from the centre of activities at the other end of the table. We had to be dressed cleanly at all times when entering the saloon which presented problems on many occasions. We were often covered in paint and grease and did not have the time to get cleaned up for meals, so just as often had the cooks pass out our meals where we sat on No. 3 hatch. Here we could eat in peace and take our time doing it.

There were many shipboard routines to get used to, but as time passed we cottoned on to everything expected of us. We were fortunate in having two chief officers in succession who were conscientious teachers. The first was Leslie Thompson who took

The following four photos depict life aboard *Cromwell Park* for a young cadet. They are from the collection of Peter Tull.

Painting the Foremast. Painting was an ongoing chore aboard any well-run ocean ship. Here Tull is the highest figure working on the topmast. Fellow cadet Ken Clapp is at work on the crosstree, while one of the deckhands is hard at it below him.

Deck Crew Clean-up on Foredeck. As the anchor chain is drawn in a deck hand plays a high-pressure hose over the chain to clean off caked mud.

When There's Nothing Else To Do. Ken Clapp (right) and Peter Tull have lots of opportunity to hone up their splicing skills.

Shooting the Sun. A daily ritual attended by, from left, the Captain, Cadet Clapp, Cadet Tull and the Second Mate.

his task to heart and drilled us in everything we had to know in the way of Rules of the Road, navigation and seamanship until they became second nature to us. Sundays were the favoured day for our weekly examination by Mr. Thompson who left us after completion of the first voyage and was succeeded by Egon Christensen, a man every bit as capable who, like me, became a tugboat skipper in the same company following the war. I have sometimes wondered how cadets made out when the chief officer, whose role was to act as teacher and mentor to the cadets, was less than good at his duties or simply shirked them as must have happened in some cases.

One small incident which always amused me came along many years later. My wife and I boarded the BC ferry from Mill Bay to Brentwood Bay north of Victoria. I was surprised to find Charlie Scoles, our first second mate aboard *Cromwell Park* when we joined her. It was Second Officer Scoles who insisted that the bridge was all "spic and span" before he came on watch each morning. Ken and I took it to heart and were up at 0500 each morning to get the windows clean, brass polished and deck scrubbed in good time before the second mate appeared to take his watch. We even kept this routine up in port until the captain shouted "No, not when we're in port. No one uses the wheelhouse then."

I asked Charlie if he knew anything of the whereabouts of Ken Clapp. "Oh, yes," he replied. "He's the skipper of this very ferry." I enjoyed the irony and wondered if Ken had Charlie clean up the wheelhouse every morning! Ken and I had a nice reunion and swapped yarns about our buddies.

On the ship's maiden voyage we finally set sail from New Westminster bound for India. We carried a full cargo made up of grain, lumber and a large consignment of canned herrings in tomato sauce, which according to my friend the author of this book, was so frequently on the menu for troops and sailors stationed in India, that it took many years for him to look another one in the face. We also carried six landing craft as deck cargo.

We called at San Pedro, California, for oil bunkers and then headed for Melbourne, taking a somewhat circuitous route to the South as the Japanese war was still on. On arrival we enjoyed our shore leaves. On the first day ashore we visited a store at the end of our dock and were asked by the storekeeper how old our ship was. When we told him that she was 3 months old, he wouldn't believe us. *Cromwell's* hull was a mass of rust from stem to stern. This was the only complaint I ever heard of BC-built ships. The trouble was that there was then no such thing as a covered building berth and in the damp winter climate, paint just would not stick for any length of time. Our ship was laid down in October of 1944 and she was completed in February of 1945. The time frame tells it all.

Ken and I greatly enjoyed a visit to an amusement park and felt very liberated being there without the ever-present shipboard supervision. There was one exception. When we first joined the ship in Vancouver, the mate had taken us aside and warned us that if he ever caught us drinking or misbehaving, he would kick us so hard we would have to untie our shoelaces to breath. The mate had been a professional wrestler at one time and was a heavyset man. Ken and I would sometimes horse around with him trying to wrestle him to the ground. He would just get his arms around each of our heads and roll his arms on our ears which was very painful. We were never able to subdue him. As these bouts usually occurred in the wheelhouse the only defence was to make a lot of noise with our feet. The mate would soon stop as he didn't want to disturb the captain whose quarters were below.

We stayed at Melbourne for a couple of days and when we were ready to leave a lot of the crew had not returned to the ship. The mate was very angry at this and when he heard that this defiant group were drinking at a local pub, he and the bosun commandeered a Navy truck and drove off to bring them back. The story goes that the mate and bosun marched into the pub where those who were slow to leave were picked up like cordwood and thrown into the truck. I bet there were a lot of sore ears the next day. The crew had a lot of respect for the bosun and mate after that.

Refuelling at Melbourne, we then passed along the southern Australian coast and made our way from there on a northwesterly course for Cochin, India. The war in the Far East was still underway and Japanese submarine activity in the Indian Ocean could not be ruled out. There was even an outside chance of a surface warship doing a sortie against Allied shipping in the Indian Ocean.

Cochin was my first introduction to the so-called exotic East. Perfumes mixed with outright stinks, burning cowdung used as fuel gave off a sweetish odour like that of burning grass and the smell of strange new foods added to the overall impression of a whole new world unlike anything I had ever experienced before.

We discharged cargo at Cochin and then sailed for Calcutta. We passed up the Hooghly River, the western arm of the Ganges and the direct access to the largest port and city in India. I was at the wheel with Third Mate Charlie Ickringill and the pilot on the monkey island, the top steering station above the wheelhouse. Supposedly by now an experienced helmsman of all of two months and into my sixteenth year, I suddenly got confused when the pilot gave me an order to steer a little to port. I put the wheel a little to starboard. He told me to go to port some more so I went more to starboard. Finally he said hard-a-port and I realized that I had been going the wrong way. I quickly turned the wheel hard to port when the pilot whirled round and asked me if I had the wheel hard to port. I was able to answer "yes, Sir" as by then I had. He shook his head and marked something on the chart. I think he thought he had found a new sandbar. The third mate was watching me and couldn't believe that I was so stupid. He sure gave me a heavy talking-to later.

While at Calcutta, the mate, fourth engineer and myself were put into hospital suspected of having cholera. Meanwhile the ship had sailed for Bombay and it turned out that none of us had the disease, although we had certainly suffered a severe stomach upset. The three of us travelled across India by train to await the arrival of *Cromwell Park*. In a matter of a few days she arrived, discharged cargo and then we left for Beira, Mozambique.

We ballasted in the usual way by flooding No. 4 and 5 holds to the top of the shaft tunnel as well as No. 1 and 2 holds, to hold her bow down as otherwise these ships could become unmanageable in a heavy seaway. At Beira we loaded iron castings and copper ingots for New York. We called at Durban and then rounded the Cape of Good Hope to run into very large westerly swells from the roaring for-

ties. Pounding into heavy seas can be rough for the engineers as when the propeller comes near to the surface the reduced resistance can cause the engine to speed up and the propeller to race. The engineer has to pull a damping lever which reduces steam to the engine to prevent excessive revolutions. As it takes a little time for the engine to actually slow it calls for some pretty fine judgement on the part of the engineer who in effect has to anticipate the next movement of the ship. Because the crew quarters are directly above the racing propeller and the steam steering engine also creates noise, the two combined can be pretty excruciating on sleep.

We arrived in New York in time for VJ Day, discharged our Beira cargo and then made for Houston and Galveston, Texas, to load sulphur for Vancouver. We passed through the Panama Canal and enjoyed a swim in Gatun Lake while awaiting the passage of Eastbound traffic. After an uneventful trip we arrived at Vancouver. It was the end of a world-girdling maiden voyage for Ken and I, as well as *Cromwell Park*.

Now that the war was over, Canadian Transport quickly reverted to peacetime patterns of trade. There were two more voyages for *Cromwell Park*, Ken and myself, and then she along with five other Park ships were purchased and became the owned fleet of the H.R. MacMillan organization. All six ships took names beginning with the word Harmac followed by the name of a town or city in BC where MacMillan had interests. Our ship became *Harmac Vancouver* and in her, Ken and I were to do another six voyages to complete our contracts as cadets.

On the final voyage I was promoted to unlicensed third mate for the final trip to England. Ken would have got the appointment, I am sure, but he was on leave in Powell River when this happened. The owners knew that a sale was pending and they didn't want the extra expense of hiring a new third mate only to have to repatriate him upon completion of the sale. *Harmac Vancouver* became *Amaryllis* and her end is described elsewhere in this book.

After repatriation to Vancouver I briefly tried selling vacuum cleaners for my stepfather, but when an opportunity occurred to join a fine old family company, Gulf of Georgia Towing Company in Vancouver, I took it. I quickly obtained my towboat master's certificate of competency and spent a good part of my remaining working life towing barges up and down the coast.

The remaining voyages of *Cromwell Park/Harmac Vancouver* until the ship's sale to the Greek Embirocos interests are noted below.

Voyage No. 2 — Lumber from Vancouver and BC ports, refuelling at San Pedro, Cal., for Manila, Philippines, Calcutta, Madras and Bombay, India. In ballast to Persian Gulf. Loaded aviation gas and kerosene in drums for Woosung, China. In ballast back to Vancouver, BC.

Voyage No. 3 — Railway ties from Vancouver and BC ports for Port Sudan. In ballast to Bahrein. Loaded aviation gas and kerosene in drums for Taku Bar, N. China. At Taku Bar loaded last consignment of rugs from China to Vancouver prior to closing of trade by Mao Tse-Tung's forces. Otherwise in ballast to Vancouver, BC with two passengers. Renamed *Harmac Vancouver*.

Voyages No. 4/5 — Lumber from Vancouver and BC ports, refuelling at San Pedro, for London, England. Return voyage in ballast.

Voyage No. 6 — Lumber from Vancouver and BC ports. Refuelling stops at San Pedro and Pulao Bukam, Singapore for Port Sudan. In ballast to Aden, loading salt for Sasebo, Japan. Return to Vancouver in ballast.

Voyage No. 7 — Lumber from Vancouver and BC ports for London, England, returning in ballast.

Voyage No. 8 — Lumber from Vancouver and BC ports for Plymouth and Falmouth, England. In ballast to Matthewtown, Inagua Island, Bahamas loading salt for Vancouver, BC.

Voyage No. 9 — Lumber from Vancouver and BC ports for London, England. Delivered there to the ship's new Greek owners.

AUTHOR'S NOTE: There was good reason for concern about desperate Japanese naval action against shipping during 1945. The Japanese were already in full retreat in Burma and the softening-up process by the British East Indies Fleet against Japanese military airfields and oil installations in the East Indies had been under way with attacks by carrier aircraft since June of 1944. These had included successful attacks on the Andaman and Nicobar groups as well as Sumatra and Java. They continued into 1945 when the long-awaited retaking of Malaya was accomplished just as the war was drawing to a close.

On May 14, 1945, the Japanese heavy cruiser *Haguro* was caught in an evening action near the Andamans when she was probably on her way, without air cover, to do damage to Allied shipping in the Bay of Bengal. The Japanese repeated the mistake of the British in 1941 when the major capital ships, *Prince of Wales* and *Repulse* were destroyed by air attacks during the Japanese assault on Malaya. *Haguro* was damaged in an evening attack by carrier planes from the British carrier *Shah*. The cruiser retreated towards Penang, but was caught the following day by HM destroyers, *Saumarez, Vigilant, Virago, Verulam* and *Venus* which together sank the damaged Japanese cruiser. It was the last surface action between warships in the Indian Ocean area.

The Last Voyage of *Cromwell Park*. Shown here as *Amaryllis*, owned by London Greeks. Here she is hard aground on the Florida Coast following a hurricane. This was her last resting place, almost in the forecourt and swimming pool of a motel. She was here for so long that the coastline underwent long-term change.

(Peter Tull)

The Loss of *Amaryllis*, ex *Harmac Vancouver*, ex *Cromwell Park*.

Contributed by Peter Tull, retired tugboat master and a cadet aboard *Cromwell Park*, excerpted from a privately published memoir.

During the night of September 7, 1965, the steamship *Amaryllis*, a Greek-owned ship registered in Panama, was steaming off the Florida Coast. On this ill-fated night *Amaryllis* was on a ballast voyage bound from Manchester, England, to Baton Rouge, Louisiana where she was to load a cargo for Brazil.

It was common practice for this type of ship to ballast with sea water by flooding the two after holds to the top of the shaft tunnel. The tunnel is a structure about seven feet high with two sides and a rounded top, built to protect the propeller shaft from cargo. As well as protecting the propeller shaft the design allows the engine room crew to walk alongside the shaft from the engine room to the stern gland, to grease the bearings and inspect the shaft. It is a scary place to be during rough weather.

Despite the ballasting which was mainly to get her screw down to an acceptable depth, she would still be riding very high and in severe weather could be almost unmanageable.

September 7 was early in the hurricane season, but Hurricane Betsy, the second hurricane of the season, was gathering strength.

Betsy's winds steadily increased to 140 miles per hour. These winds and the heavy seas they created, soon overcame the *Amaryllis* and drove her ashore on Singer Island, just off the Routledge Motel, a popular waterfront resort. It is possible that the ship's captain, realizing that he was being driven ashore on a hurricane tide, chose the sandy beach at Singer Island in an attempt to save the 28-man crew and possibly the ship. The captain reported that the vessel had pounded severely while grounding, but that none of the crew were injured.

Several years later, after much legal wrangling and efforts to tow her off *Amaryllis* and a salvage barge, which was impaled while trying to salve the freighter, are dismantled on the spot. The stern end was towed off eventually and rests offshore, used as an artificial reef.

(Peter Tull)

During the height of the storm Mr. Routledge Crouse, the owner of the motel had his own emergencies to look after and then was confronted with 28 uninvited guests with no reservations sitting on the beach in front of his inn.

The guests continued to live on *Amaryllis* for four months, while vain attempts were made to dislodge the vessel. Because the ship had come ashore perfectly upright, the crew were able to live aboard and keep steam up for their living needs. However, like all uninvited guests, the ship soon wore out her welcome even though she had become a great tourist attraction. Her steam boilers often gave off black smoke which drifted ashore raising havoc with the local residents' laundry and clean paint. Also the ship's sewage together with some bunker oil found its way onto the pristine beach.

Hurricane Betsy had caused immense damage along the Florida coast and it was several days after the grounding before marine surveyors and salvage experts could examine the stranded ship. Merritt Towing Company's salvage tug *Cable* was dispatched to see if she could pull the *Amaryllis* off the beach. Before the *Cable* could reach Singer Island she was diverted by the Coast Guard and sent to New Orleans where she was to help clean up the devastation in the harbour caused by the hurricane.

On September 10, the powerful Dutch tug *Ierse Zee* was standing by, ready to attempt a salvage oper-

ation on a "no cure, no pay" basis. I do not know if the Dutch tug ever tried to pull *Amaryllis* off the beach, but Captain George Koehn of Florida's Coastal Towing did make an attempt, but the ship would not move.

On September 16, it was determined that because part of the vessel was resting on a rocky shelf, the ship could not be pulled free without sustaining further serious damage. One suggestion made by Vulcan Iron Works was to erect a steel cofferdam around the ship extending into deep water some 200 feet astern of the ship. The plan was to fill the cofferdam with water to float the ship and move her to the end of the cofferdam where she would remain afloat when the water was pumped out. This proposal, although an excellent idea, was expected to be very expensive, probably costing more than the ship was worth. Consequently it was never acted upon.

After four more months of failed salvage attempts, the Greek crew were sent back to Greece, the owners tendered notice of abandonment to the underwriters at Lloyd's of London who paid out the insured value of the ship in the amount of $325,000 as a constructive total loss and assumed ownership of the wreck as became their right through subrogation. The ship lay on the beach for almost a year before she was sold to Florida resident Samuel McIntosh's Panamanian shipping company for $25,000. This money became a salvage recovery which would have been apportioned out to the original underwriters.

Despite Mr. McIntosh's hopes for an early reward, the ship by now was becoming increasingly unpopular as it was altering the shape of the beach and building up a new sand bar at the stern. On the other hand local surfers liked it and it became something of a swinging discotheque, very popular with the boys and girls who eagerly climbed aboard to party.

After many complaints Mr. McIntosh hired a local personality called "Pop" as a watchman to keep an eye on things. Unfortunately Pop was an enthusiastic entrepreneur in his own right and was soon conducting tours of the ship. He also allowed some of the cabins to be used by runaway teenagers for which he was eventually sentenced to 60 days in jail for contributing to delinquency in minors. Some of the young people became very upset at being deprived of this unorthodox lodging place. One night the ship was set on fire and what was quickly becoming an eyesore was made even worse and soon there were lawsuits against Mr. McIntosh to remove his property from the beach.

Mr. McIntosh was unfortunately killed in an accident and the ship became part of his estate. The ship was sold by the estate in 1975 after being in the family for ten years.

Efforts were started to cut her up as she lay and an ex-wartime landing craft, the *Irwin No. 1*, an LST by designation, was secured to take off scrap, but in a later hurricane this vessel sank alongside. Finally the Federal government got involved through the US Army Corps of Engineers. Federal Court Judge Emmott Coates finally authorized funds for the purpose, and OMC Corporation of Buffalo, NY, was hired to remove the ship with a bid of $67,000 with a time limit which would cost $100 per day once the limit was exceeded.

James Herring of Riviera Beach, who is still active in the paving business today, built a gravel road out to the ship so that the cut-up steel could be trucked to Tampa, some 200 miles away. The work was started in December 1967 and went on for almost a year. What was left of *Amaryllis* was finally floated off and sunk off West Palm Beach as an underwater fish reef.

It is interesting to note that the original *Cromwell Park* took four months to build. By comparison the old girl took a year to be finally broken up and her remains removed.

CHAPTER THIRTEEN

WHAT'S IN A NAME?

For many of us it is as important for a ship to have a meaningful name as it is to name one's child. Names often tell something of personality, if not that of the person so named then certainly that of the person who confers the name. Names confer hope–the hopes of the person doing the naming. Names convey love, compassion, humanity, strength, boldness, chivalry, bravery and a great many more things which we associate with good qualities. We give names for boys which convey strongly masculine qualities, and likewise for girls those names which convey equally strong feminine qualities. Or at least we used to.

The naming of ships has many parallels with the naming processes used by the human race. Aside from the need to have a registerable, classifiable, easily identifiable system, man has always seemed to find that a ship has a special quality that calls for a name. A mere number alone will not do even though from a legal standpoint the registered number of a ship is probably more important than its name. The official number is like a birth certificate. Unlike the name, it does not change during the life of a ship so long as it remains under the same flag, being tied directly to the matter of legal title and registered ownership. Numbers when used as names are usually reserved for barges, lighters or small utility craft, but more often than not even they are dressed up with the owner's name, initials or trade mark. Thus in Vancouver, as a typical example, *Seaspan 412* identifies this utilitarian woodchip carrying barge as one of her owner's 400 series.

However, in Canada, as in most countries once a hull has a means of propulsion, sail or mechanical it invariably is given a distinctive name. The exceptions, on the few occasions when they arise, are more commonly to be found in the Orient. For example

Japanese owners have been known to add a number after the name of quite large ships. Thus *Nichiyu Maru No. 3* implies that there are at least three *Nichiyu Marus* which seems to take away considerably from the individual personality of any of them.

Sometimes the system of nomenclature told something of the nature of each country and its history. Britain, still with many ties to its Imperial past, chose the prefix "Empire" with a host of varied names from many sources, geographical, historical or denoting human qualities. These names were conferred on new British vessels for government account, the acquired fleet of elderly US vessels from the First World War taken over prior to Lease-Lend and Axis war prizes. Typical examples included, *Empire Strength, Empire Liberty* and *Empire Malta*.

The US chose the names of significant Americans who had played a role in the country's history in naming its vast fleet of Liberty ships. These ranged all the way from heroes like Jeremiah O'Brien, an early US Navy hero, to Hollywood actress Carole Lombard who died in a plane crash while selling war bonds. The later, much improved American Victory ships sounded a martial call with names which signified that a given city, university and in some cases an Allied nation was behind the push for victory. Thus *Quinault Victory, Harvard Victory* and *USSR Victory*, became typical examples.

The big T2 tanker building program was the only one where some duplication of names as between one Allied program and another occurred. The T2s were named for historic parks, monuments, battlefields, forts and geographical features of historic significance. Thus we find *Forts Clatsop, Cumberland, Dearborn, Duquesne, Erie, George, Niagara* and *Pitt* appearing as US tankers in addition to the Canadian-built ships of the same name. Obviously this was an indicator that both originating names figured in the history of both countries, even if the common names applied to different forts in each country, as was the case in some instances.

The names of the American-built Ocean group of ships were chosen by the British who evidently wished to treat them as a distinctive group and thus did not give them Empire names. Most of the names added to the Ocean prefix had a distinctly British ring to them. No explanation of the names chosen is offered as all appear to be self-explanatory.

What did the Naming Committee in Ottawa have in mind in bestowing names on the war-built ships? Unfortunately no record appears to exist in the form of minutes which might have indicated some degree of debate in choosing names, even though occasional small collections are to be found in shipyard records or museums in the form of embellished parchments which gave the name of the ship and an explanation of its significance. The idea was that these parchments could be framed and displayed on board, but whether this happened in all cases is not known. Fortunately a complete collection of the chosen Fort names is held by the Vancouver Maritime Museum which made the task of identification a great deal easier, but so far no equivalent lists of the chosen Park names have been found.

The Park names were reserved for the Canadian-flag ships and unlike the naming routine for the Forts, it appears that Park Steamship Company chose the names for its own ships, but with only a few exceptions after the war, they were immediately renamed with a Fort name if transferred to British control. The exception to this rule occurred near the end of the war or shortly thereafter, when a number of North Sands Parks were transferred to Britain without renaming, but this appears to have been part of the disposal process dealt with more fully in Chapter Eleven.

In a similar way many of the ships went down the launching ways bearing a Fort name and were intended for British bareboat charter, but evidently a decision was made to retain them under the Canadian flag for Park Steamship management. In these cases the Fort name was dropped and a new Park name selected.

There was, as a consequence, much renaming particularly when a ship was launched as a Fort and then left the yard and went to sea with a Park name. Typically both *Beaton Park* and *Dominion Park* were launched as *Fort Mackinac*. This Fort name and that of *Fort St. Ignace* were used more than once, but never went to sea and could almost be described solely as convenient launching names. There were other Fort names selected and used as launching names which likewise never went to sea as they were given Park names prior to, or at, completion. They are listed in the introduction to the Fleet List. Parchments were not issued for any of these names which has left us with the same research challenge as has occurred with the entire range of selected Park names. In other words, Mr. Conway-Brown and the author, had to go to whatever sources we could find to establish the origins of a name and as we have found there is often some uncertainty. A typical conundrum occurred with some frequency when locating as an example, Victoria Park. In this instance there are perhaps some 20 Victoria Parks spread across the land and a number of others that recur with frequency.

Canada did something a little different again from our Allies, the US and Britain. The Forts reflect the history of the country from the earliest times of colonization, both British and French. The wars between the two nations for domination in the settlement and trade of the country were mostly through the 17th and 18th centuries. The American names among the Forts were not an attempt to please our big cousin and wartime ally, but simply reflected the fact that the boundaries between British and French colonial expansion staked out a map entirely different from the map of today.

New France comprised today's Southern Quebec and thrust through Upper Canada and the Great Lakes and into the central area of a vast country from present day Michigan south to link up with French settlement in the Louisiana territory. This was strategic as much as anything and was designed to contain the British in New England and provide a springboard for French settlement further west. The intrepid French voyageurs and others including priests and missionaries, did in fact press as far west as Alberta and British Columbia, as is suggested by names such as Vermillion and Quesnel, but by then the future of the land had been more or less settled and the French colonial fact based in Quebec largely eliminated.

In many ways this was the most romantic and yet the hardest period of settlement, with fortunes on both sides waxing and waning. After the War of Independence the newly established United States added a new dimension to the tug-of-war between British and French interests. With independence the Americans' insatiable aim to spread republicanism and their own settlement of the country to the west, proved to be a determined enemy only stopped by an equally determined defence by the British and Canadians. The War of 1812 was seen by the Americans as being a pushover in their favour, but they were to reap a number of painful surprises. Canada was not to be the ripe plum they anticipated.

Once French interests in North America were eliminated the stage was set for British advancement west. Even though there had been determined efforts by French fur traders to dominate the Canadian plains and reach across the future Dominion, the two British rivals, the Hudson's Bay Company and the North West Company were already in possession of much of the territory. The Hudson's Bay Company following merger with the North West Company in 1821 reached the west coast and was the biggest colonizer from the Yukon down to the Columbia River giving rise to a host of new Fort names including *Fort Vancouver, Fort Astoria, Fort Spokane, Fort Clatsop and Fort Boise*, all of which are now an integral part of the American scene. Some of these names, of course, were originated by American sources opposed to the Hudson's Bay Company.

Tracing the chosen names of the ships proved to be an exercise in previously unexplored history and geography and many were the gems which showed up. Famous parks and little-known ones outside and within city limits, the latter being hard to locate, exercised one's detection skills. Up until the time of locating the official list of chosen Fort names, this was only equalled by the names of forts long gone and forgotten outside of their immediate areas as well as a relatively limited list of well-known easily identified forts. Fort Louisbourg, Fort Langley, Fort McLeod and Fort Lennox, to name a few, are pre-

served as museums and examples of how these forts looked in their heyday. But for every one easily identified many others required harder work. Many were police or trading posts and some disappeared hundreds of years ago, leaving only ancient records and mounds of old earthworks as evidence. Some have been obliterated. An example of an historic fort is Fort Rouge whose earthworks and timbers are buried deep under Main St. and Portage Avenue in modern day Winnipeg. Another which time has obliterated is Fort Jemseg, destroyed some 300 years ago and never rebuilt.

A few of the old forts have been remembered in the ship names more than once. Fort La Tour appears also as Fort Howe for example. Some names apply to more than one fort. Fort George was used eight times in history although the original name of Prince George, BC turned out to be the one selected. Several others like Fort McLoughlin and Fort McLeod at least twice each, so that which one actually represented the ship was sometimes an educated guess settled only by the aforesaid collection of official parchments. There were some teasers also; for example, none of the history books that were referred to listed Fort Nakasley as the original name of Fort St. James and it was only when we found the original list that this one was settled.

There were some surprising omissions among the chosen names. The name Beacon Hill Park, a famed park in Victoria, BC was not used and yet many of the ships were built in Victoria. Wells Grey, Waterton Lakes and Wood Buffalo Parks seem like important omissions. Fort Vancouver was not remembered even though this was an important HBC post in modern Washington on the Columbia River and not the modern West Coast metropolis. Nanaimo, BC with its fortified bastion had just as much right to be designated as a fort when one compares this piece of local history with that of many of the chosen others. In fact it was left to Canadian Pacific to name some of its more modern bulk carriers so that Nanaimo, Vancouver and Victoria where commemorated with the "Fort" prefix. Some names were related to a special story which whenever possible has been enlarged upon in anecdotes, or in the list of geographical names. These include the story of the heroism of Madeleine de Verchères, who turned back a band of marauding Indians at "Castle Dangerous," and the epic voyage of the immigrant ship *Hector* with its cargo of Scottish immigrants destined for Nova Scotia (found later in this chapter).

In truth, when the shipbuilding program first started no one knew for how long the war would go on, or just how pressing the need for new ships would remain. No record appears to exist of potential names of ships which under other circumstances might have been built for an extended war after 1945. When one looks at the maps and historical records there seems little likelihood that we would have run out of suitable names. According to the reports in each of the four volumes of Fort names, the names were selected by, or on the recommendation of E.L. Harrison who was later joined by P.K. Page, both of Wartime Merchant Shipping Ltd. One can be excused for speculating on how the names chosen were actually arrived at. Were they influenced by local or parliamentary politics? Were invitations put out asking for ideas? Did they rely entirely on historians or the Geographical Records division of the Canadian government? Did the shipyards in some instances influence names? Most of the 4,700-ton ships were built in the Maritimes, so that it may not be surprising that the majority of names chosen by Park Steamship came from that area for this smaller class of ship.

As earlier noted, an official list of chosen names does not ever appear to have been published for the selected "Park" names and one immediately wonders why?

The parchments which were prepared for the Forts were issued with instructions to place one in the master's cabin and a second in the crew quarters. Questioning of men who served in the Park ships confirmed that they never saw a parchment mounted on the bulkhead to explain the origin and significance of the chosen name. Nor do the Vancouver Maritime Museum or the North Vancouver Archives and Museum have examples in their collections. In fact North Vancouver holds the vast Burrard collection which includes memorabilia, photos and plans of many of the ships built at their two yards.

The most probable conclusion is that when Wartime Merchant Shipping Ltd. as managers of the building program turned a ship over to Park Steamship Company, they simply expunged the Fort name originally allocated, did not issue a parchment for it, and seem to have left Park to make their own choice of name. As the Park names were all current at the time this was relatively easy, whereas Harrison and Page probably had to do some historical research to support their choice of Fort names.

One wonders also, why the Fort names and not the Parks in terms of an official explanation? It is suggested that this might have been because all the Fort names were used on ships bareboat chartered or transferred to the British and some importance was seen in the idea of explaining names. British crews from the Clydeside, Mersey, Tyne and Thameside areas could perhaps be relied upon to murder some of the names usually out of irreverent humour. Two that come to mind are *Fort Crevecoeur* and *Fort Ville Marie*. A man associated with the former vessel once stated that its adapted name became "Creepy Whore" or, maybe it was "Creepy Sewer". In the case of *Fort Ville Marie*, she was affectionately known at T & J Brocklebank, her managers or owners during her entire career (which was itself a record), as "Vile Mary". Most of the Park names were easier to deal with in their pronunciation, but imagine signalling the name *Winnipegosis Park* in plain language. She quickly reverted to a more affectionate "Winnie" among crews and others.

Where is Bell Park for certain? How many Mohawk Parks are there? Victoria Park, Coronation Park and Centennial Parks recur with remarkable frequency as towns across the land sought to honour a queen or pay homage to a major event. Not all chosen names, particularly among the Fort names, agree with the official record on matters of spelling. Where names could not be matched to the officially chosen name alternatives have been set out, but in some cases it has not proved easy to read the minds of those who chose names, over half a century after the event. However, every effort has been made to provide a reliable answer.

This list might well prove to be the only one ever published and, it represents a worthwhile historical and geographical record which relates each name to the ship, the park or the fort, and the name it inspired.

The Story of Madeleine de Verchères

Fort Verchères as *Maple Hill*. Here the ship named in honour of the fort defended by the young Madeleine makes its sedate way through English Channel waters, looking every bit the lady in her Counties Ship Management livery. (Ian Stewart Collection)

Of all the stories of battle, conflict, intrigue and colonial politics none quite equals that of this 14-year-old girl, Madeleine de Verchères, who defended her home against marauding Iroquois and successfully held it until help arrived.

In the New France of the day country houses of some substance were often fortified with stockades against attack. They were referred to as seigneuries, being similar in their status to the English Manor. The seigneur was the equivalent of the Lord of the Manor, and when war was anticipated the seigneurs along with their able-bodied retainers left the seigneuries in the hands of old unfit retainers, womenfolk, and whoever else might be available, for the call to arms was important above all else. It was a holdover from the feudal system in which the king always had a reserve army to rely on.

This was the scene in 1692 when the Iroquois, traditionally allies of the English, went on the rampage and attacked French settlements through New France, slaughtering many of the inhabitants and laying waste to the land. These attacks were particularly strong in the region of the Richelieu River to the southeast of Montreal.

Fort Verchères or Castle Dangerous, as the stockaded house was also known, was in a badly deteriorated condition with holes in the stockade through which a man could crawl. Things had been a lot quieter during the summer and many people who had

fled their homes returned. There was also a pressing need to get their crops harvested for the coming winter. Madeleine's father was away in Quebec and Mme. de Verchères was in Montreal.

The people from Fort Verchères were working in the field when a band of Iroquois came out of the trees and with murderous musket fire killed many of the people on the spot. Madeleine ran for the gate to the stockade while the Indians fired at her. Musket balls whistled past her, but fortunately she was not hit. One Indian faster than the rest caught up with her and grabbed her by the shoulder, but she broke free, passed through the gate and with the strength of desperation managed to close it in their faces.

Everybody in the fort was in a state of panic. One of the two soldiers left to defend the place had actually lit a fuse, intending to blow up the powder magazine and take everyone with him. Fortunately Madeleine intervened just in time and shook both soldiers out of their state of cowardice.

Her two younger brothers aged 10 and 12 were not lacking in courage either. She stationed them on the rampart at two of the four corners of the stockade. They maintained musket fire against the Indians while periodically she would have the cannon fired at their attacker. If nothing else, it kept the Indians at bay. During the night one of the defenders would periodically call out, "All's well" and between this, the musket and cannon fire, the Indians were misled into thinking that the fort was held by a far larger body of defenders than the handful actually engaged.

On one occasion a family by the name of Fontaine came downriver in a canoe, not knowing anything of the state of affairs at Castle Dangerous. Madeleine with a show of great courage rushed down to the river and shepherded the Fontaines back to the shelter of the fort before the Indians could react. Today, descendants of that Fontaine family live in Powell River, BC, and for them the siege of Fort Verchères is very much a part of well-remembered family annals.

They held the fort for eight days until a relief party of forty soldiers under Lieutenant Monerie arrived on the scene. In a gesture of submission Madeleine handed her sword to the lieutenant who gracefully returned it.

Madeleine's heroic leadership earned her a place in history. The Comtesse de Beauharnois, wife of the governor, was requested to gather the details of the young girl's life and forward them to the Royal Court in Paris ensuring her immortality–and a possible pension.

Many years later a bronze statue was erected to honour the young heroine "Who adorned the age in which she lived and whose memory is dear to posterity." This was placed at Verchères Point, the site of the old fort and the place she had so brilliantly defended.

The Origins of *Hector Park*
Contributed by George Conway-Brown of Blind Bay, BC

While many of the Canadian Fort and Park ships carried names that appear to have been chosen for obscure reasons, the ship named *Hector Park* carried a name of great historical significance for Canada. *Hector* was the name of a sailing vessel that brought the first Scottish settlers to New Scotland, now Nova Scotia, much as the *Mayflower* carried the original English settlers to New England in the present day United States. In the year 1773, *Hector* sailed from Loch Broom in Scotland, carrying some 200 Scottish settlers, who would never return to their original homes in the counties of Inverness and Sutherland.

These immigrants were to establish new homes for themselves in a new land. They experienced hardships from the start. Sickness broke out aboard the ship. Some of them died and were buried at sea. *Hector* was not the most seaworthy of vessels; rotten hunks of wood could be picked from her stringers. In a trip that normally took two months at that time, *Hector* reached her destination on Northumberland Strait, in what is now central Nova Scotia, in September 1773. The settlement that was established where *Hector* landed became the Village of Pictou.

As the village grew and became a town, a park was established by the settlers which they chose to name Hector Park for the ship that brought them to this new land. Hector Park is still a prominent part of Pictou and it seemed most appropriate that when Canadian merchant ships were constructed during World War II and named for Canadian parks, one of these ships should carry the name of Hector Park. It is a distinguished and proud name for all Canadians.

The people of Pictou have memorialized the pioneering spirit of their Scottish ancestors by erecting a bronze statue within Hector Park. This figure is of a highlander, depicted as he would have appeared, stepping ashore from the vessel *Hector*, prepared to build a new settlement in the forest. He is a kilted pioneer, mounted on a pedestal, carrying a gun in one hand, the other holding an axe across his shoulder. The kilt was obviously unsuitable and inadequate dress for the harsh Canadian winter weather conditions and this fact has given rise to a local legend. It is said that during the coldest days of the year, the bronze figure will drop his gun and axe and place his hands into the sporran of his kilt, to keep them warm.

The ship *Hector Park* was one of the forty-five 4,700 dwt ships that were constructed in east coast shipyards during the war. They were usually identified as the Gray or Scandinavian type. *Hector Park* was one of eighteen vessels of this type built by the Foundation Maritime shipyard in Pictou, NS.

Several of the 4,700 dwt ships were planned for the Ministry of War Transport in Britain, and to set them apart from the others, a decision was taken to start a new name series. These ships were to be named for military camps using the prefix "Camp", followed by the individual ship name. The first ship of the group happened to be *Hector Park* and this name had to be changed to *Camp Debert*, for the large central Nova Scotia military camp. This was the place of embarkation for army personnel proceeding overseas by ship from nearby Halifax. There was a subsequent change in the program and *Hector Park* ended up being the only ship of this class to have her name changed during the war.

During the invasion of Continental Europe, planning staffs attempted to select and assemble the most suitable fleet of merchant ships for participation in the invasion operations. The amphibious assault on the beaches of Normandy would be named Operation Neptune and it would require some 5,300 warships, landing craft and merchant ships of all types.

The 4,700 dwt vessels with their maximum draft of 21 feet, were more suitable for many tasks than the bigger 10,000 dwt ships with their greater draft of 27 feet. For one thing, with their shorter length they could be allowed to take the ground between tides with greater safety and while beached, unloading could go on overside to vehicles driven alongside. Fully one third of the Canadian ships of this class were selected for the invasion and they included *Camp Debert*. These fourteen Canadian ships continued to provide support to military operations in the European theatre until the war ended. While employed in this role, two of these ships were lost to enemy actions.

POINT PLEASANT PARK: THE STORY OF THE SHIP, HER LOSS AND HER NAMESAKE PARK

Contributed by George Conway-Brown of Blind Bay, BC

Sorrento is a small village located on the Trans-Canada Highway. It is situated on a hillside, overlooking the huge Shuswap Lake of central British Columbia. The village was settled by immigrants from England some generations ago, and curiously, one of them chose "Sorrento" because the location reminded him of that place in Italy. The village and its first inhabitants were definitely of British origin.

The only church in the village is St. Mary's Anglican and it is generally regarded as the most charming and attractive building in Sorrento and is irresistible to pen and ink artists. The church is constructed in the Tudor style, with exposed dark-stained wood beams separating wall sections of white stucco. It is very easy to imagine this church as a part of some quaint English village, far across the Atlantic Ocean.

St. Mary's Church has both an adjoining graveyard and a small concrete cenotaph to remember local young men who gave their lives for Canada and freedom in two world wars. They were lost or buried far from home. The names of the twenty dead of World War I are inscribed on the cenotaph, and for World War II a bronze plaque was added listing the names of another three young men. In addition, there is a brass plaque mounted on the wall inside the church that bears the following inscription:

IN MEMORY OF
JOSEPH STANLEY BAYLISS
AGE 18 YEARS
KILLED AT SEA BY ENEMY ACTION
Feb. 23rd 1945

Joseph Bayliss (spellings elsewhere show the name as "Bayless") did not serve in the Army, Navy or Air Force. He served as a merchant seaman and the name of his ship was that of a Canadian Park, far removed from Sorrento and the little church that honours his memory. This is the story of the park and the ship named *Point Pleasant Park*. It is also the brief story of young Joseph Bayliss which typifies that of many other people who gave their lives and have a place in our Canadian history.

Of the Canadian merchant ships named for geographical parks during the Second World War, perhaps the closest correlation between ship and park exists in the name of *Point Pleasant Park*. The park stands at the entrance to Halifax Harbour and Bedford Basin, places of great historical significance, where wartime convoys assembled and many a Park ship sailed past in procession to join a convoy. The park has witnessed many great events, all related to its strategic position, guarding the entrance to a harbour that at one time was termed "The most important seaport in the world." Certainly it could have been named as the most important convoy assembly port in the world.

Point Pleasant Park was a North Sands type ship, constructed by Davie Shipbuilding Company of Sorel, Quebec. On February 23, 1945, German submarine *U 510* intercepted this ship in the South Atlantic Ocean and attacked her with a torpedo, killing several crew members. After the surviving crew had abandoned ship, the submarine shelled and sank the freighter.

The place named Point Pleasant was recognized even before there was a town named Halifax, in what was then a colony of British North America. In the year 1749, Britain sent about 3,000 soldiers and colonists who were embarked in about twenty ships, to establish a new colony. This was to be located in an area of Nova Scotia then known as Chebucto. The newly appointed governor and captain-general of this great expedition was an experienced military commander, Edward Cornwallis. A military camp was quickly established at Chebucto, and a favourable location for a town was sought.

The naval authorities preferred the shores of what later became known as Bedford Basin, named for the Duke of Bedford, First Lord of the Admiralty. They saw this tremendous sheltered harbour as a place that would be easy to defend against attack from the sea. Governor Cornwallis, with his considerable expertise as an army commander, favoured a more seaward location at Point Pleasant. He felt that this peninsula site could be defended easily against attack from the land side.

In the end, both the Bedford Basin and Point Pleasant sites were rejected. Bedford Basin was viewed as too far inland for practical fishing purposes and Point Pleasant was rejected by the navy because the rocky shoreline was considered too shallow as a harbour and exposed to southeast gales. A compromise site was chosen for the town, two miles farther up the harbour from Point Pleasant, on the west side and inside George's Island, named for the reigning monarch. The new town was given the name of Halifax, for the Earl of Halifax.

In July of 1757, a group of British seamen, often called "jack-tars," went strolling on the outskirts of the new town and into the woods of Point Pleasant. There they were attacked by lurking Micmac Indians, who took two sailors captive and killed and scalped another two. Apparently the tarred pigtails of sailors were considered by the Indians to be prized scalps. Following this incident, military patrols were increased at Point Pleasant. The subsequent disappearance of Cope, the ferocious and feared Micmac chief, leads historians to conclude that he was killed and buried in an unmarked grave in Point Pleasant Park.

The wealthy merchants and officials of early Halifax were much like the influential classes of all ages. They chose to escape from the rough and tough elements of their seaport town by constructing country residences and estates beyond the town limits. Lieutenant Governor Fanning chose the site for his country estate on Point Pleasant, opposite Purcell's Cove. He surrounded his house with elaborate gardens and the estate became a popular attraction for Halifax residents as they proceeded on country walks. This area proved a natural selection later when it was chosen to become a public park.

Point Pleasant is now a 75-hectare wooded sanctuary and municipal park operated by the City of Halifax. The park property is still considered to be British colonial soil, but it is placed on a 999-year lease to Canada at the rental rate of ten cents per year. It lives up to its name of "Pleasant," being a place for peaceful recreational activities. It contains walking trails, picnic sites, a restaurant, Black Rock Beach and various other recreational facilities to attract strollers, joggers, sun-bathers and perhaps occasionally soldiers and sailors who are no longer threatened there by Micmac Indians.

Point Pleasant Park also contains some remains and reminders of war. For two centuries, the strategic location of the park has served as the site for defence fortifications to guard the entrance to Halifax Harbour and Bedford Basin. The fortifications and gun positions have included the Point Pleasant Battery, Fort Cambridge, Fort Ogilvie and the Prince of Wales Tower. The remains of these historic sites still stand as silent sentries and park attractions. The park also contains relics and reminders of the more recent conflicts of two world wars, indicating the strategic role of Halifax as the place of origin and destination for Allied shipping convoys. The Atlantic bridge formed by Canadian and Allied merchant ships, to sustain the people and military operations of Britain and her Allies was crucial to the successful but costly outcome of both world wars.

Point Pleasant was witness to the very high price that Halifax paid for being a convoy port during World War I, when in 1917 a great tragedy occurred, forever known as "The Halifax Explosion." On December 6, 1917, the French steamship *Mont Blanc* met with disaster as she proceeded into the harbour to enter Bedford Basin to join other ships in the formation of a convoy. *Mont Blanc* was loaded with 2,766 tonnes of explosives and combustibles including picric acid, TNT, guncotton and benzol. While passing Richmond pier in Halifax, *Mont Blanc* was struck by the Norwegian steamer *Imo*.

Little damage was done on impact, but the 35 tonnes of benzol in steel drums, loaded as deck cargo aboard *Mont Blanc*, caught fire. When *Mont Blanc* exploded, the entire ship vanished into a huge mushroom-shaped pillar of white smoke with a core of splintered steel fragments that rose to a height of one mile. *Imo* was stripped of her superstructure and the remaining hull was flung ashore at Dartmouth. Much of Halifax was destroyed and the final death count was 2,000 people. It was the most devastating man-made explosion in the history of mankind, until surpassed by the atomic blast at Hiroshima on August 6, 1945. One of the few recognizable parts of *Mont Blanc* recovered after the blast was a half-ton anchor shank, which was found in woods two miles from the blast site. That part of *Mont Blanc's* anchor is today displayed in Point Pleasant Park, as a reminder of this tragic event.

The Point Pleasant Park monument connected to World War II is a cairn, erected within the park in 1967, in memory of the nine seamen who were killed when their merchant ship of the same name was struck with a German torpedo. The names of the war victims as listed on the mounted plaque are:

Joseph Bayless, Fred Breen, George Edwards, Patrick Guthrie, Robert Hallahan, Alfred Malmberg, Robert Munro, Leslie Toth and Louis Wilkinson.

Their bodies remain with their ship. The sea is their resting place, the cairn is their monument.

The ship *Point Pleasant Park*, commanded by Captain Owen, became a war casualty through her chance encounter with a German submarine. *Point Pleasant Park* had departed from St. John, NB in a southbound convoy for Trinidad in January, 1945. The ship then proceeded independently, bound for Cape Town, South Africa, on February 11th.

Submarine *U 510*, commanded by Kapitänleutnant Alfred Eick was a large Type IXC U-boat, heading home for Germany with a cargo of tungsten from the Far East. Tungsten was a strategic material that Germany lacked during the war. It was then a critical element for the manufacture of filaments in electronic vacuum tubes and when combined with iron it produced a special steel for high speed tools, armour plate and armour-piercing military projectiles including bullets.

On February 23, 1945, under mild and pleasant weather conditions, *U 510* sighted *Point Pleasant Park* at position 2942S and 098E and attacked the ship by firing two torpedoes. One of them found its target, hitting the ship near the stern, killing eight men in the crew's quarters, blowing away the propeller and flooding the aft end of the ship. One of the seamen killed was Joseph Stanley Bayliss of Sorrento, BC. The time was 1355 hours and the position was about 500 nautical miles northwest of Cape Town. The ship started to settle slowly by the stern and the crew prepared to abandon ship. Some crew members had sufficient time to retrieve their lifejackets, some clothing, cigarettes, sextants and binoculars.

The crew then made for the boat deck to abandon ship. During the launching of the lifeboats, the falls at one end of a boat accidentally slipped away too rapidly. The boat entered the water on end, swamped and was lost. The crew then divided themselves between the remaining three boats resulting in some overcrowding. When the survivors and their lifeboats had cleared the ship, the surfaced submarine shelled the vessel in the midships section. *Point Pleasant Park* flooded slowly and sank at approximately 1615 hours, over two hours after the torpedo attack. The final death cry of the ship was heard as muffled explosions, when the boilers burst deep under the sea. Kapitänleutnant Eick did not interfere with the survivors, but he did question them before submerging and leaving the area. Both Eick and his submarine survived the war.

The survivors spent ten days and nine nights in their lifeboats. They attempted to sail to the coast of Africa, some 375 nautical miles to the east. They roasted under the hot subtropical sun during the day, but it became so chilly at night that they thought they might freeze. One severely injured crew member died the first night out. Their main activity was bailing water out of the boats using small cans. Fishing was another pastime, and a few fish were caught, dried in the hot sun and used for food. The limited supply of fresh water in the boats was restricted to one or two ounces per man per day.

On the eighth day, the boats became separated in a storm. On the ninth day, the seventeen survivors in the second officer's boat were successful in using a heliograph mirror to attract the attention of the fishing vessel *Boy Russel* off the Kalahari coast. The fishing vessel took them to the Southwest Africa port of Luderitz.

On the tenth day the other two boats with thirty-three survivors were found by the South African Navy trawler *Africana*. The lifeboats were towed to Walvis Bay. All of the survivors suffered from exposure and needed medical attention. When they were moved to Cape Town, many of them found a temporary residence in a Seamen's Club in that city. Later, some of them returned to Montreal, along with their rescued lifeboat aboard *Prince Albert Park*. Five of the *Point Pleasant Park's* crew were subsequently recommended for awards for their conduct during the loss of the ship.

The cairn erected in Point Pleasant Park was established largely through the efforts of the late Captain Paul Tooke of the Canadian Coastguard. Captain Tooke had been third officer on the ship at the time of her sinking. At a Remembrance Day service and dedication ceremony in 1967, one of the wreaths placed on the cairn indicated that it expressed the sorrow of the crew of *U 510*. Both the war and the *Point Pleasant Park* story had ended and young Bayliss and his shipmates are remembered in their great sacrifice. They rest far from Sorrento and Point Pleasant park, but occupy an important place in our history.

There's a Lot in a Name

Systems of nomenclature, or naming, were frequent and rigidly adhered to by many owners, particularly those of British or American origin or those who adopted British shipping traditions. Anyone who knew anything about the Odysseus of Greek mythology, the Scottish Clans, the Barons, Kings or Cities would quickly associate a given ship's name with Blue Funnel, the Clan Line, "Hungry" Hogarth and the Baron Line, the King Line or Ellerman and there were many other examples. There was a certain sense to what was often regarded as patriotic sentiment, in that it helped build

immediate recognition to the point that many lines became household names, known and understood by everyone. It had a value largely forgotten by today's generations of shipowners.

Then there were the "Hills", a group of mostly former Fort or Park ships which for a while were so common around the ports of the world and in the daily list of tramp fleet fixtures that as the original Fort and Park names disappeared with renamings, the Hills seemed to take over.

In 1936, the well known Greek firm of Rethymnis & Kulukundis (R & K) established a

Fort Brunswick as Mulberry Hill. The last Canadian-built North Sands coal burner.   (Ian Stewart collection)

Fort Connolly as Marina Hill, wearing the colours of her time charterer, British India Steam Navigation Co.   (Ian Stewart collection)

Fort Coulonge as Andover Hill. Under the management of associated London Greek concern, Coulouthros Ltd.   (Ian Stewart collection)

Fort Nottingham as Alendi Hill, looking neat and clean in the colours of her time charterer, T & J. Harrison of Liverpool. Note the extended stovepipe ahead of the funnel, which must have been heavily braced.   (Ian Stewart collection)

Rondeau Park as Sycamore Hill. Of the 31 North Sands ships comprising the "Hill" fleet, seven were ex-Park ships and the remainder Forts. (Ian Stewart collection)

London management company named Counties Ship Management Ltd. This was in keeping with the trend for Greek owners to establish offices in London, initially as branch offices, but very quickly after that as bonafide British domiciled companies which often overtook, in size and importance, the Greek owner's other shipping businesses under flag of convenience or the Greek flag itself. The last half of the 30s was also a period when shipping markets were reviving from the depression and the British government was giving major financial assistance to owners and shipbuilders in an effort to encourage this revival.

One of the key figures in the London Greek community was Basil Mavroleon who with his Kulukundis relatives ran Counties and had connections with other Greek owners through family or business ties. Mavroleon is central to this short account, but before dealing further with him be it noted that it was a close knit community which maintained much of its own privacy, but always in the manner of its traditions, outgoing, internationally minded, and highly motivated in an opportunistic way to seize any chance without regard to flag, nationality and sometimes the laws of a given country. In many ways the war and the huge pool of warbuilt shipping that came up for disposal following the war was tailor made for them. What the Greeks did not acquire initially they purchased later in the second hand market, so that by the end of the conventional tramp period in the 60s and 70s they collectively owned or controlled the largest fleet of warbuilt shipping, plus new ships which they had been building in large numbers. These were often financed by the country in which the ship was being built. With the coming of the container, bulk carrier and large crude oil carriers, the Greeks ignored the first and concentrated on the two latter categories.

Basil Mavroleon is recognized as having been one of the great shipping personalities of the third quarter of the twentieth century. He initiated or was very much a part of some key moves which altered the face of Canadian and British shipping as soon as the shipping markets got back to a peace time footing. In conjunction with the Halifax firm of I.H. Mathers & Son, Ltd., a deal was struck to purchase 84 warbuilt, mostly North Sands ships for Canadian flag operation by the London Greek owners. The Canadian press of the day identified the purchaser as Mathers, which the Halifax firm neither affirmed or disputed. The reality was that Mathers was acting for his London Greek clients who in addition to R & K included Coulouthros, Fafalios, Hadjilias, Frinton Shipbrokers, C.M. Lemos and P.D. Marchessini. Most if not all of these appeared to have connections at least as clients, in varying degree with Counties or R & K. A more complete explanation of ownership entanglements is to be found in the author's book, *Conceived in War, Born in Peace*, but information on the connections between these companies can sometimes only be inferred from interagency sources, one of which was Mathers. Mavroleon was a key figure in this huge transaction. Thirty of the ships came under the direct management or ownership of Counties plus additional vessels held by Coulouthros and some of the others, to a probable total of some fifty vessels. The Counties fleet of North Sands ships was to be the biggest of all made up of this type.

With a huge trampship fleet under control Mavrolean and his Kulukundis uncles started London & Overseas Freighters in 1948 which was to become their publicly financed vehicle for building up a substantial fleet of tankers. This in turn led to the acquisition of Austin & Pickersgill and the development of the SD14, SD15 Liberty ship replacements and SD26 bulkcarriers. Of all the post-war designs developed to succeed the warbuilt standards the SD14 was the most successful in competition with Japanese and German standard designs.

The Hills became prominent and the accompanying pictures show them to advantage. Kept as clean and shipshape as any tramp vessel they were frequently taken on time charter by liner operators to take advantage of heavy demand on their liner routes.

Fort Wellington as Muswell Hill. Another Harrison time charter. T & J Harrison, originally wine importers from the Charente district of France grew into the largest privately owned British cargo-liner fleet with services to India, South Africa and the West Indies.

(Ian Stewart collection)

Fleet List and Ship Histories: Historical and Geographical Namesakes

INTRODUCTION

ABBREVIATIONS

SHIP	TYPE
Cana	Canadian
Lakes/T	Lakes tanker
NS	North Sands
NS/T	North Sands tanker
Scan	Scandinavian-Gray
Scan/D	Scandinavian-Gray/Dominion
Scan/R	Scandinavian-Gray/Revised
Vic	Victory
Vic/T	Victory tanker

SHIPBUILDER

BDD	Burrard Dry Dock Co. Ltd. North Vancouver, BC
BDD/VDD	Burrard Dry Dock Co. Ltd. (Vancouver Dry Dock Co., South Yard, Vancouver, BC)
CSY	Collingwood Shipyards Ltd. Collingwood, ON
CVL	Canadian Vickers Ltd. Montreal, QC
DSBR	Davie Shipbuilding & Repair Co. Ltd. Lauzon, QC
FM	Foundation Maritime Ltd. Pictou, NS
MI	Marine Industries Ltd. Sorel, QC
ME&D	Morton Engineering & Drydock Co. Ltd. , Quebec City, QC

NVSR	North Van Ship Repairs Ltd. North Vancouver, BC
PDD	Pacific Drydock Co. Ltd. North Vancouver, BC
PRDS	Prince Rupert Drydock & Shipyard, Prince Rupert, BC
SJDD	Saint John Drydock Co. Ltd. St. John, NB
USY	United Shipyards Ltd. Montreal, QC
VMD	Victoria Machinery Depot Ltd. Victoria, BC
WCSB	West Coast Shipbuilders Ltd. Vancouver, BC
YAR	Yarrows Ltd. Esquimalt, BC

GENERAL

dt	Displacement tonnage, applicable to Navy maintenance ships
gt	Gross tonnage, applicable to merchant ships
HBC	The Hudson's Bay Company
MOWT/	British Ministry of War Transport, which became
MOT	Ministry of Transport by 1946.
NWC	North West Fur Trading Co. of Montreal/ Nor'Westers
NWMP	North West Mounted Police
TL/CTL	Total Loss or Constructive Total Loss

Nominated Manager

This refers to the shipping firm which provided specific management services to the Park Steamship Company Ltd. or the Ministry of War Transport.

Managing owner

Every ship bearing a Park name had the Park Steamship Company as its Managing Owner. This was the Crown corporation representing the Dominion of Canada. There was an exception however, when 28 North Sands Park ships and 15 Scandinavian/Gray ships were transferred to Britain without change of name. In these instances Park dropped off the registered ownership documentation and the bareboat charter was drawn between the Government of the Dominion of Canada, as owner, and the Ministry of Transport (or War Transport) as Bareboat Charterer.

With Fort ships bareboat chartered to Britain, if the vessel was owned by Canada, the initials

(DOC) appear before the nominated manager's name; if owned by the United States War Shipping Administration or the United States Maritime Commission the initials (WSA) appear before the manager's name. In two instances only among the general trade Fort ships, *Fort Ville Marie* and *Fort St. James* were owned outright by the British government. In these cases the initials MOWT appear before the manager's name. Two of the Stores Issuing ships, *Fort Beauharnois* and *Fort Duquesne* were also owned by the MOWT/MOT and three, *Fort Rosalie, Fort Sandusky* and *Fort Wayne,* were not found in *Lloyd's Register,* but appear to have been taken on to Navy strength from point of transfer to Britain, probably as auxiliaries through the Royal Fleet Auxiliary.

The Selection of Park Names

Many of the names used for Park ships exist in multiple examples across the country. In these cases the most likely parks have been given, but it cannot be assumed that the specific park suggested is the one originally selected. It is better to assume that commonly recurring names such as Buffalo, Confederation, Connaught, Coronation, Victoria and many others apply to all parks so named.

Other names are site specific, but may be small insignificant parks named after an unknown individual or simply bear the name of the township or village in which they are located. When only a town can be identified with a name, it is not certain that a park exists within the town. In a few instances a name cannot be identified from any available reference source. To add to the complication some park names, usually minor ones, have had their names changed since the Second World War to conform to revised social or political attitudes.

Transfers to Britain and Returned Vessels

The Park and Fort ships were not two distinct types as is sometimes assumed. They were in every way interchangeable. A substantial number were launched with Fort names, but completed with Park names. A few served as Parks for a period of time but in ship exchanges were transferred to the MOWT and renamed as Forts. They were confined to the three types, the North Sands and its derivative Victory type as well as some of the 4700-ton ships. None of the Canadian type or any of the Victory tankers were transferred to Britain.

Aside from the regular transfers of ships there were two 'en bloc' transfers that demand a specific note. A total of 15 of the Scandinavian-Gray ships were transferred to Britain and, so far as can be determined, were probably handed over from the builder's yard to a British crew sent over by a nominated manager. These ships were:

Ainslie Park	Avondale Park
Camp Debert	Cataraqui Park
Chignecto Park	Confederation Park
Crescent Park	Dartmouth Park
Kensington Park	Lansdowne Park
Manitou Park	Montmorency Park
Taber Park	Willow Park
Woodland Park	

An earlier plan was to give these vessels "Camp" names, but only seven were selected and only *one*, *Camp Debert, ex-Hector Park*, was carried through.

Unlike the Forts they were all shown in *Lloyd's Register*, until the 1946-47 issue, as being owned by "the Dominion of Canada, Park Steamship Company, manager". By that time 11 had been disposed of, mostly to France without the nominated manager being recorded in annual issues of *Lloyd's Register*, although they might have been noted in supplements. The four remaining, *Camp Debert, Cataraqui Park, Chignecto Park* and *Woodland Park* had been placed in charge of managers named in *Lloyd's Register* pending disposal. Details are included in the fleet list.

The second 'en bloc' transfer involved 28 coal-burning North Sands Parks sent to Britain and the return of 28 Victory oil-burners to Canada. The ships involved were:

Parks to Britain, port of registry becoming London, England.

Algonquin Park	Banff Park
Belwoods Park	Dentonia Park
Gatineau Park	High Park
Hillcrest Park	Kawartha Park
Lafontaine Park	Laurentide Park
Mount Douglas Park	Mount Orford Park
Mt. Revelstoke Park	Nemiskam Park
Port Royal Park	Prince Albert Park
Rideau Park	Rocky Mountain Park
Rondeau Park	Rosedale Park
Runnymede Park	Sibley Park
Stanley Park	Tweedsmuir Park
Westmount Park	Whiteshell Park
Withrow Park	Yamaska Park

Forts Returned to Canada, port of registry becoming Montreal, QC.

Fort St. Antoine	Fort Aspin
Fort Astoria	Fort Biloxi
Fort Boise	Fort Brisebois
Fort Clatsop	Fort Columbia
Fort Crevecoeur	Fort St. Croix
Fort Dearborn	Fort Hall
Fort Island	Fort Kaskaskia
Fort Kullyspell	Fort La Baye
Fort La Have	Fort Machault
Fort Marin	Fort Orleans
Fort Panmure	Fort Perrot
Fort Prudhomme	Fort Sakisdac

Fort Saleesh	*Fort Venango*
Fort Wallace	*Fort Yukon*

The Selection of Fort Names

These were chosen on a far more methodical and logical basis than the Park names. Every ship that went to sea with a Fort name did so with a recorded explanation of the name on board ship. In the cases where a ship was launched with a given Fort name and had this changed to a Park prior to commissioning, the recorded explanation of the name was not provided. The following names were selected but never went to sea as a commissioned ship. The explanation of the name is therefore the result of separate research and is often far shorter.

Fort Beaver Lake	*Fort Berens*
Fort Chimo	*Fort Conti*
Fort Crown Point	*Fort Daer*
Fort Frontenac	*Fort Grand Rapids*
Fort Green Lake	*Fort Harrison*
Fort Mackinac	*Fort Niagara*
Fort Norway	*Fort Rouge*
Fort Simcoe	*Fort Toulouse*

There is one other 'en bloc' transfer which should be mentioned. This concerns the 69 Forts returned to the United States Maritime Commission. Of these 18 were disposed of in what appears to have been a government-to-government transaction between the USMC and Italy. Allocated among Italian owners, all but one appear to have remained on the Italian register for the balance of their active careers until going to the scrapyard, again mostly in Italy. Italian owners thought enough of the ships to re-engine two with turbines and several more with diesels. Such longevity and repowering was almost unknown under any other flag, but the Italians with their flair for design and marine engineering proved many times over that they could do wonders with a basic steamer and turn it into a combination of utility and great beauty.

Ownership Histories

In the ship biographies that follow, the careers of individual ships were wide and varied, ranging from the staid, dignified and trouble-free 22 years of *Fort Ville Marie* and her unbroken record of service with one owner, to her West Coast sister *Fort St. James*, with her 18 years of British ownership which was followed by a further 31 on the Chinese register with very little known of her subsequent career and if, in fact, she actually lasted until 1991, when she made her last appearance in shipping registers.

An interesting feature of these ships was the degree to which the London Greek owners played a role in their careers from the time of their disposal by the Canadian Government. If a Greek was not the first owner, and many were, he frequently was the second and often through several following stages. When Canadian flag operation became uneconomical, during the 1950s, permission was granted to transfer many vessels to British articles and effective domicile, under the "Canadian Maritime Scheme", without diminishing the other covenants to do with the escrowing of proceeds of sale.

Major owners, such as Goulandris and Counties/Rethymnis & Kulukundis, had a ready-made channel whereby the ship, despite transfer, remained under their control. When it became covenant free, that is, free of guarantees attached to the original purchase from Canada, they moved their vessel to a flag of convenience still within their same managing organization. For that reason the underlying ownership has usually been identified under the legal registered ownership and from it will be seen how these owners kept their ships through flag changes. With each change often came deteriorated standards and an increasing tendency towards loss and resultant insurance penalties, which tended to make the ships increasingly uneconomical, even if they were saving money in other directions including low manning standards.

In the notes that follow there may have been later ownerships between the one last noted and the ship's final ending. After the early 60s international marine insurance underwriters took steps, through the imposition of heavy premium penalties, to clear the seas of old and warbuilt ships over 20 years of age. Any ships that continued, frequently under Far Eastern ownerships, usually remained with obscure owners under flags of convenience and tracing the balances of their careers beyond 1960 had little purpose in terms of this book. For that reason there may be gaps between the last noted ownership and date of scrapping or final fate, where this is known or noted, and in some instances an owner has not been matched with a name.

AINSLIE PARK 2875gt 12.43 Scan FM Pictou, NS

Transferred to MOWT. No record of nominated manager.

1946	*Henri Mouhot*	Centre d'Approvisionment d'Indochine/Chargeurs Reunis, Marseilles, France
1950	*Tran Ninh*	Denis Freres d'Indochine, S.A. Saigon
1955	*Woodlock*	Trans. Mar. Atlantida, SA. Panama/Wheelock Marden & Co. Ltd. Hong Kong
1964	*Loong An*	
1972		Scrapped

AINSLIE PARK - It is believed that this name refers to a park in the vicinity of Ainslie Lake, Cape Breton Island, NS, about 7km SE of Inverness.

ALBERT PARK 7130gt 4.45 Cana BDD North Van, BC

Nominated manager, Canadian Transport Co. Ltd. Vancouver.

1946	*Harmac Victoria*	Canadian Transport Co. Vancouver
1948	*Beacon Grange*	Furness Withy (Canada) Ltd.
1949	*Constantinos*	Conquistador Cia. Nav S.A. Panama/A.Lusi
1967		Scrapped at Shanghai

ALBERT PARK - Albert, town 18km NW of Napanee, ON, Bay of Quinte region.

ALDER PARK 7130gt 4.44 NS USY Montreal, QC

Launched as *Fort Crown Point*

Nominated manager, Canadian Pacific Steamships Ltd. Montreal

1946	*Arthur Cross*	Dominion Shipping Co. Montreal
1946		Transferred to Liberian flag
1970		Scrapped at Hong Kong

ALDER PARK - Alder, 8km East of South end of Lake Simcoe.

ALEXANDRA PARK 7130gt 4.44 Can USY Montreal, QC

Nominated manager, Montreal Shipping Co. Ltd. Montreal.

1946	*Mont Sandra*	Montship Lines Ltd. Montreal
1953	*Violando*	Insular Trading Corp. Monrovia, Liberia.
1958	*Aegean Sun*	Seas Trading Corp. Monrovia
1963	*Mindenao Logger*	Republic Log Carriers S.A. Monrovia
1965	*Ocean Logger*	Pacific Coast Shipping Co. Monrovia
1968		Scrapped at Kaohsiung, Taiwan

ALEXANDRA PARK -

1. Located, Hillsborough Bay. 10km SE of Charlottetown, PEI.

2. City park bordering English Bay Park and Sunset Beach in Vancouver, BC.

All three parks are extensions of Stanley Park.

3. City park located near the heart of downtown Toronto, ON.

4. City park located in St. Lambert across river from Montreal QC.

Algonquin Park as *Johnstar* (Foto-Flite)

ALGONQUIN PARK 7130 gt 10.42 NS MI Sorel, QC

Nominated manager, McLean Kennedy Ltd. Montreal

1946		Transferred to MOWT without name change
1946		Nominated manager, (DOC) Aviation & Shipping Co. Ltd. London
1950	*Johnstar*	Fairview Overseas Freighters Ltd. Halifax/C.M. Lemos & Co. Ltd.
1957	*Santhy*	Record Shipping Co. S.A., Panama

1960 *Glafkos*	Record Shipping Co. S.A., Panama (both under Lemos management			
2.1.62	Aground 2 miles East of Amphitrite Point, West coast of Vancouver Island.			
3.1.62	Refloated, C.T.L. Stripped Capital City Iron & Metals, Victoria, BC. Hull towed to Seattle for final dismantling.			

ALGONQUIN PARK - Oldest provincial park in Ontario, located approximately 210km North of Toronto, ON.

ARGYLE PARK 2895gt 6.43 Scan/R SJDD St. John, NB

Nominated manager, Interprovincial Steamship Co. Ltd.

1946 *Liverpool Packet*	Mersey Paper Co. Ltd. Liverpool NS			
1963 *Westport*	Westport Cia. Nav. S.A. Piraeus			
1965 *Athos*	Athos Shipping Co. Special S.A Piraeus. Greece			
1976	Scrapped at Split, Yugoslavia.			

ARGYLE PARK -

1. Abbreviated from Argyle Shore Park on coast of Northumberland Strait, near Charlottetown, PEI.

2. Name repeated five times in NB, NS, ON, and MN.

ARLINGTON BEACH PARK 7130 gt 2.44 V/T WCSB Vancouver, BC

Nominated manager, Imperial Oil Ltd. Toronto

1946 *Ageroen*	A/S Saguna/H E Hansen-Tangen Kristiansand, Norway.			
1954 *Mar Corrusco*	Converted to dry cargo - Franco Maresco, Genoa, Italy			
1959 *Subicevac*	Slobodna Plovidba, Sinenik, Yugoslavia.			
1965 *Millstrader*	Aries Shipping Co. Hong Kong			
1968	Scrapped at Kaohsiung, Taiwan			

ARLINGTON BEACH PARK - Located East Shore, Lost Mountain Lake, 100km NNW of Regina, SK.

ASHBY PARK 2895 gt 12.44 Scan/Rev. FM, Pictou, NS

Nominated manager; no record available.

1945 *Siderurgica Tres*	Cia Siderurgica Nacional, Rio de Janeiro, Brazil			
1971	Scrapped at Rio de Janeiro,			

ASHBY PARK - Located S end of Belmont Lake, about 50km ENE of Peterborough, ON.

ASPEN PARK 7130 gt 4.44 Victory BDD/VDD Vancouver, BC

Nominated manager, Anglo-Canadian Shipping Co. Ltd. Vancouver

1946 *Lake Athabasca*	Western Canada Steamships Ltd. Vancouver. BC			
1949 *Agathi*	Comp de Transportes Del Mar, S.A. Panama			
1959 *Nissi*	Same owner as preceding			
1967	Scrapped at Yokohama, Japan.			

ASPEN PARK -

1. Alberta provincial park.

2. Community very close to, but W of Gimli, MN on highway leading N from Stonewall, MN.

ATWATER PARK 7130 gt. 6.44 Victory WCSB Vancouver, BC

Nominated manager, Anglo-Canadian Shipping Co. Ltd. Vancouver.

1946 *Lake Atlin*	Western Canada Steamships Ltd. Vancouver, BC			
1953 *Halcyon*	Santa Rita Comp. Nav. SA Monrovia			
1969	Scrapped in Japan			

ATWATER PARK - Located 50 miles ESE of Melville, SK.

AVONDALE PARK 2875 gt 5.44 Scan. FM Pictou, NS

Transferred to MOWT, no name change, no nominated manager available.

7.5.45	Sunk by submarine torpedo, 1 mile SE of May, Firth of Forth. Scotland. This was the last British ship sunk by enemy action prior to the end of WWII.			
	(See account in Chapter Seven)			

AVONDALE PARK -

1. Four locations of the same name in NB, NS and PEI. A popular name often associated with a river of the same name.

2. Municipal park in Burnaby, BC.

BALDWIN PARK 2895 gt 11.44 Scan/R DSBR Lauzon, QC

Nominated manager, Pickford and Black Ltd.

1946 *Chi Chung*	China Merchants S.N. Co. Ltd. Taipei, Taiwan			
1961 *Kai Lung*				
1964	Scrapped Kaohsiung. Taiwan			

BALDWIN PARK -
1. Provincial park located on Gaspé Peninsula of Quebec.
2. A location 3km south of Sutton, Lake Simcoe area, ON.
3. City park in Montreal.

Banff Park as *Oakhurst* (Foto-Flite)

BANFF PARK   7130 gt   9.42   NS   DSBR Lauzon, QC
    Nominated Manager, McLean Kennedy Ltd. Montreal
    1946   Transferred to MOWT
    1947   (DOC) Mgd. Ohlsson S.S. Co. Ltd. Hull, UK
    1949   (DOC) Mgd. Constantine S.S. Lines Ltd. Middleborough, UK
    1950 *Oakhurst*   Rex Shipping Co. Ltd. Halifax, NS/Hadjilias & Co. London, clients of
                    I.H. Mathers & Son, Halifax.
    1957 *Catalunia*   Asturias Shipping Co. Panama/Hadjilias & Co. Ltd. London
    1961 *Zenophon*
    26.10.62   Wrecked on rocks off Ushant, France.
    BANFF PARK - National park located at Banff, Alberta. It shares boundaries with Kootenay and Yoho Parks.

BEACHY HEAD, see Cape Scott

BEATON PARK   7150 gt   10.43   Vic   BDD North Van, BC
    Launched as *Fort Mackinac* (I), completed as *Beaton Park*.
    Nominated manager, North Pacific Shipping Co. Ltd. Vancouver
    1946 *Lake Babine*   Western Canada Steamships Ltd. Vancouver, BC
    1951 *Mountainside*   Andros Shipping Co. Ltd. Montreal/Goulandris Bros. London.
    1953 *Santa Marina*   Araucana Cia. Armadora, SA Panama/Orion Shipping & Trading Co. Inc. New York
                    Goulandris Bros. London
    1960 *Assimina P.*
    1961 *Assimina Piangos*
    1967   Scrapped at Kaohsiung, Taiwan
    BEATON PARK - Town located on NE arm of Upper Arrow Lake, BC, about 70km N of Nakusp, BC. The community plan
    was devised by Thomas Beaton for whom the town was named.
    FORT MACKINAC - see under separate entry.

BELL PARK   2960 gt   6.45   Scan/D   DSBR Lauzon, QC
    Nominated manager, Canadian National Steamships Ltd. Montreal
    1947 *Federal Pioneer*   Federal Commerce & Navigation Co. Montreal, QC.
    1950 *Sant Helena*   Transmaritima Commercio SA. Rio de Janeiro, Brazil.
    1992   Uncertain. Deleted from register in 1992
    BELL PARK -
    1. From the preserved historical site known as the Bell Homestead, 10km S of Brantford, ON.
    2. City park located at Sudbury, ON.
    3. City park located at Vancouver, BC.

Belwoods Park as *Brookhurst* (Foto-Flite)

BELWOODS PARK 7130 gt 12.43 NS MI Sorel, QC

Launched as *Fort Chimo* (II)
Nominated manager, Furness Withy & Co. Ltd. Montreal
Transferred. to MOWT, London
Nominated manager, Manchester Liners Ltd. Manchester UK
Then to South American Saint Line Ltd. Cardiff, UK
Then to G. Heyn & Sons Ltd. Belfast

1950 *Brookhurst* Rex Shipping Co. Ltd. Halifax NS/I.H. Mather & Son, Ltd. Halifax/Hadjilias & Co. Ltd.
1957 *Galicia* Asturias Shipping Co. SA, Panama/Hadjilias & Co. Ltd. London
1967 Scrapped at Mihara, Japan.

BELLWOODS PARK - About 10km north of Fergus ON, on the Grand River. About 20km NNE of Guelph, ON. Now known as Belwood Lake Conservation Area.

FORT CHIMO - see separate entry under this name.

BERESFORD PARK 2875 gt 4.44 Scan FM Pictou, NS

Nominated manager, Montreal Shipping Co. Ltd. Montreal.

1947 *Federal Ambassador* Federal Commerce & Navigation Co. Montreal, QC
1948 *Gerda Toft* D/S Jutlandia A/S/Jens Toft, A/S, Copenhagen, Denmark.
23.12.54 Foundered in heavy seas, 54.20N, 6,25E, N of Frisian Islands.

BERESFORD PARK -
1. New Brunswick town, 9km N of Bathurst. Now a residential community named for William Carr Beresford, one of Wellington's generals at the Battle of Waterloo, 1815.
2. Village in Manitoba.

BERRY HEAD 8580 dt 5.45 Vic BDD North Van, BC

Royal Navy, UK.
Built as an Escort Maintenance ship for Far Eastern service in the Royal Navy Fleet train.

1945/46 In service SE Asia and Far East
1960/62 Refitted and modernized at Chatham, Kent
1963 Placed in Operational Reserve at Portsmouth, UK

BERRY HEAD - High prominent headland overlooking Brixham, Devon, with commanding view of about 800 sq. miles of sea. Smallest lighthouse, 15 feet high on highest point of any in England at 200 ft. above sea level.

BLOOMFIELD PARK 2875 gt 9.44 Scan FM Pictou, NS

Nominated manager, Saguenay Terminals Ltd. Montreal, QC

1948 *Sundale* Saguenay Terminals Ltd. Montreal QC
1958 *Amigo* Caribbean Federation Lines. Ltd. Liberia/Kervin Shipping Corp. New York
1960 *Christian S.*
4.3.63 On fire while undergoing refit at Barranquilla, Colombia, declared CTL. Sold Colombian ship breakers July 1963.

BLOOMFIELD PARK -
1. Provincial Park near Alberton, PEI.
2. Village in Ontario.

BOWNESS PARK 7130 gt 6.44 Vic BDD/VDD Vancouver, BC

Nominated manager, Canadian Transport Company Ltd. Vancouver

1947 *Manx Marine* Kerr-Silver Lines Ltd., Vancouver BC
1948 *Jean* Orinoco Cia. Nav. SA Panama/Global Shipping Co. Ltd/A. Moschakis, Ltd./London
1957 *Seamew* Dia. de Nav. Almirante/Salvatores & Racah SRL. Genoa, Italy.

1963	Scrapped at Yokohama, Japan.			

BOWNESS PARK - City Park located on the Bow River at Bowness, a suburb on West side of Calgary, AB.

BRENTWOOD BAY PARK   7130 gt   11.43   Vic   VMD Victoria, BC

Nominated manager, Imperial Oil Ltd.

1946 *Norse King*	Odd Godager & Co. Oslo, Norway
1951 *Dodger*	Rio Verde Cia. Nav. Panama/Mgr. Capeside S.S. Co. Ltd./Goulandris Bros. London.
1953	Converted to dry cargo
1953 *Arosa*	Panamerica Transhipping Co. SA, Panama
1956 *Antonios D.S*	Eastern Seafaring & Trading Company, Panama.
1959 *Apj Ambar*	Surrendra Overseas Private, Bombay.
1962	Scrapped in India

BRENTWOOD BAY PARK - Located on the Saanich Peninsula, near Sidney, BC. It is believed that the name was chosen on account of the community's park-like appearance and proximity to famed Butchart Gardens.

BRIDGELAND PARK   7130 gt   9.44   Vic   NVSR North Van, BC

Launched as *Fort Green Lake (II)*

Nominated manager, Canada Shipping Co. Ltd. Vancouver..

1946 *Cambray*	Elder Dempster Lines (Canada) Ltd. Montreal, QC
1960 *Simeto*	
1971	Scrapped at Bilbao, Spain.

BRIDGELAND PARK - Believed to refer to area around Fort Erie where several important road and rail bridges converge. Modern Fort Erie was the result of amalgamating the village near the British fort, with nearby Bridgeburg.

FORT GREEN LAKE (II) - see separate entry under this name.

BUCHAN NESS   8580dt   7.45   Vic   WCSB Vancouver, BC

Royal Navy, UK

Built as a Landing Craft Maintenance ship.

1945/46	Service in Far East.
1947	Placed in reserve.
1959	Scrapped in UK.

BUCHAN NESS - Prominent headland on East coast of Scotland. Southern point of Peterhead Bay and about 2km S of the town and harbour.

BUFFALO PARK   7130 gt   4.44   Vic   NVSR North Van, BC

Nominated manager; may not have been allocated as the ship went into conversion soon after completion for Park S.S. Co.

1945 *Fort Charlotte*	Transferred to MOWT for service as a stores issuing ship.
1968	Scrapped at Singapore

BUFFALO PARK - It is believed that this name is an abbreviation for Wood Buffalo Park, the huge national park in Northern Alberta which extend into the NW Territories. There are ten other locations in Canada bearing the name Buffalo, the largest being Buffalo Narrows, SK, plus many additional local parks.

FORT CHARLOTTE - See separate entry under this name.

CAMP DEBERT (II)   2875 gt   1.44   Scan   FM Pictou, NS

On bareboat charter to MOWT, London, England

Nominated manager; (DOC) Wm. Dickinson & Co. Ltd. Newcastle- on-Tyne.

Launched as *Hector Park* completed as *Camp Debert (II)*

1946 *Capitaine Do Hu VI*	
1950 *Kontum*	Cie. Cotiere de l'Annam/Denis Freres d'Indochina, Saigon, Vietnam
1955 *Lynghein*	Wallem & Co. Hong Kong
1956 *South Hope*	Uwajima Unyou KK, Uwajima, Japan
1957 *Takashima Maru*	As above
1958	Converted to diesel propulsion

CAMP DEBERT - This was an important military camp in Central Nova Scotia during WWII. It was the assembly and embarkation point for troops proceeding overseas from Halifax. Also a hunting and archeological site in the general area.

HECTOR PARK - see separate story.

CAPE BRETON   8580 dt   4.45   Vic   BDD/VDD Vancouver, BC

Royal Navy, UK

Built as an Escort Maintenance ship *Flamborough Head*

1951	Transferred to Royal Canadian Navy. Renamed *Cape Breton*
1953	Training ship for Artificers

Vessel Name:	Tonnage:	Completion date:	Type:	Builder & Yard location

1958	Converted to Escort Maintenance ship			
1959	Commissioned as second Mobile Repair ship			
1999	For disposal at Esquimalt FB, Victoria, BC. This is the last known survivor of all the warbuilt ships of this type built in Canada.			
17.5.99	Sold to Artificial Reef Society for $20,000. Stern and main engine to be preserved for incorporation into the new North Vancouver Museum and Archives location in the old Burrard Dry Dock yard where she was built. Hull to be scuttled in the Canadian Gulf Islands as a dive site.			

FLAMBOROUGH HEAD - Prominent headland on the Yorkshire Coast. Marks northern flank of Bridlington Bay and overlooks town and harbour of Bridlington.

CAPE BRETON - Separated from mainland by the Straits of Canso. The name refers to Cape Breton Island. There is no geographical point that forms a cape of this name on the island which is located at the north end of the Nova Scotian land mass.

CAPE SCOTT	8580 dt	3.45	Vic	BDD Vancouver, BC
Royal Navy, UK				
Built as Escort Maintenance Ship *Beachy Head*				
1947	Transferred to Royal Netherlands Navy as *Vulkaan*			
1950	Returned to RN as *Beachy Head*			
1952	Acquired by RCN			
1953	Renamed *Cape Scott*			
1959	Commissioned as first mobile repair ship. Broken up in 1978.			

BEACHY HEAD - Prominent headland about 5km SW of the City of Eastbourne, East Sussex, UK

CAPE SCOTT - Located at the N end of Vancouver Island. Created as a provincial park after the Second World War.

CAPE WRATH	8580 dt	3.46	Vic	WCSB Vancouver, BC
Royal Navy, UK				
Built as a Coastal Craft Maintenance ship				
1951	Sold for conversion to a merchant ship at Bremerhaven and renamed.			
1951 *Marine Fortune*	Marine Enterprises Ltd. London/Lyras Bros. Ltd., London.			
1954 *Saint Marcos*	Hanseatische Reederei/Emil Offen & Co. Hamburg, Germany.			
1955 *Ditmar Koel*	As above.			
1963	Scrapped at Hong Hong			

CAPE WRATH - Located at NW tip of the Scottish mainland. To the immediate south are to be found the highest sea cliffs in Britain at 850 ft above sea level.

CARTIER PARK	2960 gt	8.45	Scan/D	DSBR Lauzon, QC
Nominated manager, Canadian National Steamships Ltd. Montreal.				
1947 *Canadian Victor*	Canadian Victor Ltd. Montreal QC/Canadian National Steamships Ltd.			
1957	Laid up at Halifax, NS			
1958	Sold to Cuba, transfer not completed.			
1965	Scrapped at Bilbao, Spain.			

CARTIER PARK

1. Provincial park at southern end of Laurentide region of Quebec. Full name is Jacques Cartier Provincial Park.

2. Provincial park located near Alberton, PEI. Full name is Jacques Cartier Provincial Park.

3. Village in Ontario.

CATARAQUI PARK	2875 gt	6.44	Scan	FM Pictou, NS
Transferred to MOWT. Nominated manager; (DOC) Wm. Robertson Shipowners Ltd. Glasgow, Scotland.				
1946 *Pigneau de Baheine*	Central Supply Co. of Indo-China, Saigon			
1955 *Ambouli*	Comp. Asiatique de Nav. Djibouti.			
1958 *Mukali*	Same as above			
1963 *Waywind*				
1969	Scrapped at Hong Kong			

CATARAQUI PARK - Located outside city limits of Kingston, ON.

CHAMPLAIN PARK	7130 gt	12.44	Can	MI Sorel, QC
Nominated manager; Furness, Withy & Co. Ltd. Montreal				
1946 *Vinland*	Mersey Paper Co. Ltd. Liverpool NS			
1960 *Vinkon*				
1.9.62	Wrecked in Tolo Harbour, Hong Kong during typhoon			
1963	Scrapped in Hong Kong			

CHAMPLAIN PARK -
1. Ontario provincial park located at position 46.18N, 78.52W, in the region of North Bay. Full name Samuel de Champlain Provincial park.
2. Quebec town on St. Lawrence 15km NE of Cap-de-la- Madeleine.

CHIGNECTO PARK   2,875 gt   3.44   Scan   FM Pictou, NS
Transferred to MOWT, London
Nominated manager, (DOC) E.R. Newbigin Ltd. Newcastle-on -Tyne, England.
1946   Alexandre de Rhodes, Government of France
                    Comp de Nav. Asiatique, Haiphong, Vietnam
1956 *Tadjouri*   Comp, Asiatique de Nav. Djibouti, French Somaliland
1965   Scrapped at Hong Kong

CHIGNECTO PARK - Name of Nova Scotia wildlife park, established in 1937 and now designated as a game sanctuary. Located west of Springhill NS.

CHIPPEWA PARK   7,130 gt   8.43   NS   DSBR Lauzon, QC
Nominated manager, McLean Kennedy Ltd. Montreal
1946 *Argobec*   Argonaut Navigation Co. Ltd. Montreal, QC/John C. Yemelos/A.Lusi Ltd. London
1959 *Rahiotis*   Strovile Cia Nav. Piraeus, Greece
1965   Scrapped at Shanghai, China.

CHIPPEWA PARK -
1. May be inspired by site of the Battle of Chippawa just south of Niagara Falls, ON, where General Winfield Scott defeated an inferior Canadian force under General Phineas Riall in 1814.
2. Municipal park located at south end of Fort William, ON.

CLEARWATER PARK   7,130 gt   1.44   Vic/T   VMD Victoria, BC
Nominated manager, Shell Canadian Tankers Ltd. Toronto
1946 *Norse Mountain*   Odd Godager & Co. A/S, Oslo, Norway
1951 *Tioga Star*   Tioga Star Corp. Liberia/Sieling & Jarvis Corp. New York
1955 *Marinegra*   Mariblanca Nav SA. Liberia
1955   Converted to dry cargo
1965   Scrapped at Shanghai

CLEARWATER PARK - '
1. Parkland surrounding Clearwater Lake, Clearwater River and town of Clearwater in Central BC
2. An abbreviation of the name for Clearwater River Wilderness Park in Northern Saskatchewan, SK.

CONFEDERATION PARK   2.876 gt   6.44   Scan   FM Pictou, NS
Transferred to MOWT. Nominated manager not confirmed.
1946 *Gialong*   Cie. de Transportes Oceaniques, Paris
1956 *Obokil*   Cie. de Trans. Mar. de l'Ouest Africain, Konakri, French Guinea/Chargeurs Reunis, Paris
1961 *Tawau Bay*
1966 *Shin Chong*
1971   Scrapped in Taiwan

CONFEDERATION PARK -
1. At Charlottetown, PEI.
2. Park in Burnaby, BC, one of many across the country.

Connaught Park as *Ranger* (Phil Chandler)

CONNAUGHT PARK   7130 gt   6.44   Vic   NVSR North Van, BC

Nominated manager, Seaboard Shipping Ltd., Vancouver, BC

1946 *Seaboard Ranger*   Seaboard Shipping Ltd. Vancouver.
1950 *Ranger*   Cia Mar. del Este/Goulandris Bros.(Hellas) Ltd. Greece
1968   Scrapped at Tsuneishi, Japan.

CONNAUGHT PARK - Name inspired by the Duke of Connaught and Strathearn, while Governor-General of Canada 1911-16. Probably there are a number of local parks of this name across the country.
1. City park in Regina, SK.
2. City park in Vancouver where local cricket teams play on a regular basis in season.

CORNISH PARK   7130 gt   10.44   Vic   WCSB Vancouver, BC

Launched as *Fort Grand Rapids*
Nominated manager; believed not allocated as the ship went straight into conversion as below:

1945 *Fort Beauharnois*   To MOWT for use as Stores Victualling ship.
1948   Transferred to Royal Navy.
1963   Scrapped at Spezia, Italy.

CORNISH PARK - No satisfactory explanation of the name found, but it is thought to possibly be earlier name of a small City park on Cornish Street, Vancouver, BC
FORT GRAND RAPIDS - see separate entry
FORT BEAUHARNOIS - see separate entry

Coronation Park (Burrard D.D.)

CORONATION PARK   7130 gt   11.44   Vic   BDD Vancouver, BC

Nominated manager; Seaboard Shipping Co. Ltd. Vancouver

1946 *Seaboard Star*   Seaboard Shipping Ltd.
1954 *Classic*   Belmar Cia. Nav. SA, Panama/Ormos Shipping Co. Ltd. London.

CORONATION PARK - Since parks were created in Canada there have been at least four royal coronations. Each one brought a fresh crop of the popular name in cities and smaller communities across the country.
1. City park in Edmonton, AB
2. Gardens of this name in Toronto, ON.

CRESCENT PARK   2875 gt   6.43   Scan   FM Pictou, NS

Launched as *Camp Debert (I)*
Transferred to MOWT. Nominated manager not confirmed.

1945 *Julia*   Red A/B A.T. Jonasson, Raa, Sweden
1951 *Lona*   Ese Bancks Red. A/S/Percy Banck, Helsingborg, Sweden.
9.9.56   On fire at Hull. Scuttled 11.9.56. Refloated, CTL. Towed Germany converted to diesel,
1956 *Senator Hagelstein*   Red. Kapitan Heinrich Krohn, Gmbh. Lubeck-Travemunde, Germany
1962 *Agia Sophia*
1969   Scrapped at Izmir, Turkey.

CRESCENT PARK - Another frequently found name. Most likely in terms of the ship's name are:
1. Crystal Crescent Beach park, located at Cape Sambro immediately S of Halifax, NS.
2. City parks at Calgary, Fort Garry, MB and Surrey, BC.

Vessel Name:	Tonnage:	Completion date:	Type:	Builder & Yard location
CROMWELL PARK	7130 gt	2.45	Can	BDD North Van, BC

Nominated manager, Canadian Transport Company Ltd. Vancouver.
1946 *Harmac Vancouver*   Canadian Transport Company. Vancouver.
1948 *Amaryllis*   Amaryllis S.S. Co. Ltd. Panama/S.G. Embiricos, Piraeus
11.9.65.   Aground in hurricane 1½ miles N. of Palm Beach Inlet, Florida.
Abandoned as a CTL (see separate story)

CROMWELL PARK - Despite extensive research no indication can be found that the name Cromwell has any geographical or historical significance within Canada. However, a street, heavily overgrown, has been located in SE Vancouver which might have been an unofficial park, as no park with that name is listed. Given the notional way in which Park S.S. Co. seems to have chosen some of its names, this is probably the origin of the name for a Vancouver-built ship.

CRYSTAL PARK	7130 gt	5.44	Vic	NVSR North Van, BC

Nominated Manager, Canadian Pacific Steamships, Montreal
1946 *Chandler*   Elder Dempster Lines (Canada) Ltd.
1960 *Natale*
1969   Scrapped at Spezia. Italy

CRYSTAL PARK -
1. Crystal Lake, 25m N. of Bobcaygeon, ON.
2. Possibly an abbreviation for Crystal Crescent Beach Provincial Park located at Cape Sambro
(see entry above under Crescent Park).

CYPRESS HILLS PARK	7130 gt	2.44	Vic/T	VMD Victoria, BC

Nominated manager; Imperial Oil Ltd.
1946 *Gundine*   Jorgen P. Jensen, Hisoy, near Arendal, Norway
1954 *Sterling Venture*   Sterling Shipping Co. Ltd. London
1955   Converted to dry cargo
1956 *Alcyone Angel*   Nolido Cia de Nav, SA, Panama/Marcou & Sons (Shipbrokers) Ltd. London.
1971   Scrapped at Bombay, India

CYPRESS HILLS PARK - Saskatchewan provincial park, established in 1931 and located in S.W. part of the province adjacent to the Alberta border. Park of the same name in Alberta was not established until 1951. The two were joined in 1989 to become Canada's first interprovincial park.

DARTMOUTH PARK	2875 gt	4.43	Scan	SJDD St. John, NB

Launched as *Camp Sussex*.
Transferred to MOWT. Nominated manager not confirmed
1946 *Captain Polemis*   Northern Star S.S. Co. of Canada, Montreal
1949 *Lumberman*
1952 *Chepo*
1952 *S.N.A. 6*   Soc. Nat. d'Affretements, Paris
1964 *Tourliani*
1976   Scrapped following fire

DARTMOUTH PARK - Municipal Park in Dartmouth, NS.

DENTONIA PARK	7130 gt	8.44	NS	USY Montreal, QC

Nominated manager; Canadian Pacific Steamships Ltd.
Transferred to MOWT. (DOC) Nominated manager, Watts, Watts & Co. London
1950 *Cedar Hill*   Halifax Overseas Freighters Ltd./Counties Ship Management Ltd. London
Clients of I.H. Mathers & Son Ltd. Halifax
1966   Scrapped at Hirao, Japan.

DENTONIA PARK -A city park in Toronto, ON.

DODMAN POINT	8580 dt	10.45	Vic	BDD Vancouver, BC

Royal Navy, UK
Built as Landing Ship Maintenance ship
1956   Became a depot ship
17.4.63   Arrived Spezia, Italy for scrapping

DODMAN POINT - Southernmost prominent headland among many between Falmouth to the west and St. Austell to the east, in the County of Cornwall, England.

Dominion Park as *Waitomo* (IG Stewart collection)

DOMINION PARK   7130 gt   8.44   Vic   WCSB Vancouver, BC

Launched as *Fort Mackinac (II)* which see under *Beaton Park*
Nominated manager; Canadian-Australasian Line Ltd. Vancouver

| 1946 *Waihemo* | Canadian Union Line Ltd./Canadian-Australasian Line, mngr, Vancouver |
| 1972 | Scrapped at Kaohsiung, Taiwan |

DOMINION PARK -
1. May commemorate the Dominion Parks Branch formed in Canada in 1911 to develop National parks.
2. Dominion City, Manitoba.
In view of the fact that the word "Dominion" is now outdated in the political evolution of Canada, it is thought that there might have been other Dominion Parks whose names have since been changed.

DORVAL PARK   7130 gt   5.44   Vic   NVSR Vancouver, BC

Nominated manager; North Pacific Shipping Co. Ltd. Vancouver.

1946 *Lake Canim*	Western Canada Steamships Ltd. Vancouver, BC
1950 *Durban Bay*	Western Canada Steamships Ltd./Mgr, Lyle Shipping Co. Ltd. Glasgow
1954 Sea Rover	Soc. de Transportes Maritimos, SA, Panama/S.G. Embiricos Ltd. London
1960 *Niobe*	
1967	Scrapped at Onomichi, Japan

DORVAL PARK - Municipal park at Dorval. Also site of Montreal's International airport.

DUFFERIN PARK   2875 gt   8.43   Scan   DSBR Lauzon, QC

Launched as *Camp Farnham* for bareboat charter to MOWT
Completed as *Dufferin Park*
Nominated manager; Pickford & Black Ltd. Halifax, NS

| 1946 *Dufferin Bell* | Picbell Ltd., Halifax NS |
| 13.5.51 | On passage from New Orleans for Dalhousie and Montreal with cargo of sulphur, ashore in fog at Framboise Cove, Cape Breton Island. TL. |

DUFFERIN PARK -
1. Community 15km west of Pictou, NS.
2. Community 5km SE of Chipman, NB.
3. Fort Dufferin, MB, the original name of Emerson, MB on border with Minnesota.

DUNCANSBY HEAD   8580 dt   8.45   Vic   BDD North Van, BC

Royal Navy, UK
Built as an Escort Maintenance Ship.

| 1960 | HQ ship for reserve fleet at Rosyth, Scotland |
| 1962 | Recommissioned at Rosyth with *Girdle Ness*, the two ships being designated as HMS *Cochrane*, the base at Rosyth. |

DUNCANSBY HEAD - Prominent headland at NE tip of Scotland. Marks eastern entrance to Pentland Firth separating Mainland Scotland from the Orkney Islands.

DUNDURN PARK   7130 gt   11.43   Vic   NVSR North Van, BC

Nominated manager; Canada Shipping Co. Ltd.

| 1946 *Marchdale* | Canadian Shipowners Ltd. Montreal |
| 1948 *Shahin* | Mohamed Nemazee/Wallem & Co. Hong Kong. |

Vessel Name:	Tonnage:	Completion date:	Type:	Builder & Yard location
1953 *Stella*	Cia de Nav. Giuseppe Mazzini, Genoa			
9.65	Scrapped at Spezia, Italy.			

DUNDURN PARK - Town and military camp, 40km S of Saskatoon, SK.

DUNGENESS	8580 dt	10.45	Vic	WCSB Vancouver, BC

Royal Navy, UK
Built as a Landing Craft Maintenance ship

| 1947 *Levuka* | W.R. Carpenter & Co. Ltd. Sydney NSW | | | |
| 1948 *Triadic* | British Phosphate Commissioners, London, UK | | | |

DUNGENESS - A prominent windswept headland with a lighthouse on South coast of Kent, England. Located between Rye and New Romney.

DUNLOP PARK	7130 gt	8.44	Vic	BDD/VDD Vancouver, BC

Nominated manager; Canada Shipping Co. Ltd. Vancouver.

1946 *Lake Chilco*	Western Canada Steamships Ltd. Vancouver, BC			
1949 *Annitsa L.*	Cia de Nav. Annitsa, SA, Panama/Seres Shipping Inc. New York.			
1964 *Oriana*				
1965	Scrapped at Kaohsiung, Taiwan.			

DUNLOP PARK - Location 4km N of Goderich, ON, inland from Sunset Beach. Other locations with same name in New Brunswick and Manitoba.

EARLSCOURT PARK	7130 gt	4.44	Vic	PRDS Prince Rupert, BC

Launched as *Fort Conti*, completed as *Earlscourt Park*
Nominated manager, Empire Shipping Co. Ltd. Vancouver.

1946 *Lake Chilliwack*	Western Canada Steamships Ltd. Vancouver, BC			
1950 *Mossel Bay*	Western Canada Steamships Ltd./Mgd. Sir R. Ropner & Co. (Management) Ltd. Darlington UK			
1954 *Noutsi*				
28.3.65	Aground 2m from Constantza, total loss.			

EARLSCOURT PARK - The land surrounding Earlscourt Library in Toronto..
FORT CONTI - see entry under this name.

EASTWOOD PARK	7130 gt	10.44	Can	USY Montreal, QC

Nominated manager; Cunard White Star Ltd., Montreal

1948 *Sunavis*	Saguenay Terminals Ltd. London, UK			
1953 *Sunkirk*	Saguenay Terminals Ltd. London, UK			
1960 *Ameise*				
1971	Scrapped at Kaohsiung, Taiwan.			

EASTWOOD PARK - Location 3km ENE of Woodstock, ON.

EGLINTON PARK	2400 gt	6.44	Lakes/T	MI Sorel, QC

Managing owner, Park Steamhsip Company, Ottawa
Nominated manager; Imperial Oil Ltd. Toronto

1945 *John Irwin*	Canadian Oil Companies Ltd. Toronto			
1956 *White Rose II*	Same owner			
1956 *White Rose*	Same owner			
1989	Scrapped in Ontario.			

EGLINTON PARK -
1. District of Toronto and important street, Eglinton Avenue.
2. At easterly end of P.E.I. on Haile Bay, inside Howe Point.

ELGIN PARK	7130 gt	2.45	Can	PRDS Prince Rupert, BC

Launched as *Fort Simcoe (II)*, completed as *Elgin Park*.
Nominated manager; Seaboard Shipping Co. Ltd. Vancouver.

1946 *Royal Prince*	Furness Withy (Canada) Ltd. Montreal			
1949 *Atlantic Star*	Nav. Maritima Panama SA, Panama/S. Livanos & Co. Inc. New York.			
1961 *Nadir*				
1971	Scrapped in Turkey			

ELGIN PARK -
1. On Lac Elgin, 13km NE of Weedon Centre, Eastern Townships of Quebec.
2. Communities bearing the name Elgin are in Ontario, New Brunswick and Manitoba.
3. Old community on the Nikomakl River in Surrey, BC, the name has now disappeared.

Vessel Name:	Tonnage:	Completion date:	Type:	Builder & Yard location
ELK ISLAND PARK	7130 gt	6.43	NS	USY Montreal, QC

Nominated manager; Constantine Line (Canada) Ltd. Montreal.

1946 *Louisburg*	Dominion Shipping Co. Ltd. Sydney NS
	Dominion Steel & Coal Corp. Ltd. Montreal QC
1964	Transferred to Liberian flag.
1976	Scrapped in Pakistan, after sustaining damage in 1972

ELK ISLAND PARK - National park located about 30km east of Edmonton, AB.

Vessel Name:	Tonnage:	Completion date:	Type:	Builder & Yard location
ELM PARK	7130 gt	3.43	NS	MI Sorel, QC

Nominated manager; Cunard White Star Ltd. Montreal

1946 *Tricape*	Triton S.S. Co. Ltd. Montreal QC/March Shipping Agency Ltd. Montreal
1957 *Palma*	Nueva Sevilla Cia. Nav. SA, Panama/N.J. Goulandris Ltd. London
1962 *Pella*	
31.7.64	Aground in fog. Amrum Is. German (Schleswig-Holstein) North Sea coast.
	Broke in two. Total Loss

ELM PARK - Location on main C.N. Line near Brandon, Ontario. Otherwise it could be the name of many city or municiapl parks across Canada.

Vessel Name:	Tonnage:	Completion date:	Type:	Builder & Yard location
EVANGELINE PARK	2895 gt	4.45	Scan/R	FM Pictou, BC

Nominated manager; Interprovincial Steamship Co. Ltd.

1947 *Federal Marine*	Federal Commerce & Navigation Co. Montreal.
1950 *Santa Monica*	Commercio de Petrolio, Rio de Janeiro.
1954 *Navem Monica*	Navegacao Mercantil, SA. Rio de Janeiro.
1991	Last register entry. Presumed scrapped.

EVANGELINE PARK -
1. There were no National parks in New Brunswick during the war years. It is believed that this name was chosen with the intention of creating a park there, in keeping with the popular expression "Land of Evangeline". When a National park was created in this area in 1949, the name chosen was Fundy National Park.
2. 12km SE of Shippigon, NB.
3. 15km W of Shediac, NB and 15 km NNE of Moncton, NB.

Vessel Name:	Tonnage:	Completion date:	Type:	Builder & Yard location
FAIRMOUNT PARK	7130 gt	1.45	Can	BDD/VDD Vancouver, BC

Nominated manager; Montreal, Australia, New Zealand Line, (MANZ) Montreal.

1946 *Montreal City*	Bristol City Line (Canada) Ltd. Montreal, QC
1959 *Huta Baildon*	Polish S.S. Co. Szczecin, Poland
1969	Dismantled, cut down to a barge.

FAIRMOUNT PARK - Four locations of this name in Nova Scotia, Ontario and Saskatchewan.

Vessel Name:	Tonnage:	Completion date:	Type:	Builder & Yard location
FAWKNER PARK	2875 gt	1.44	Scan	SJDD St. John, NB

Loaned to the Commonwealth Government of Australia. Nominated manager not recorded.

1947 *Kooralya*	McIlwraith, McEacharn, Ltd. Melbourne, Australia
1960 *Mandarin Star*	
1968	Scrapped in Japan

FAWKNER PARK - One of two of this class of ship loaned to the Australian government at completion (the other was "Taronga Park". The name chosen is that of a park in Melbourne.

Vessel Name:	Tonnage:	Completion date:	Type:	Builder & Yard location
FIFE NESS	8580 dt	11.45	Vic	BDD/VDD Vancouver, BC

Royal Navy, UK
Built as a Landing Craft Maintenance ship.

1947 *Adastral*	Royal Air Force depot ship
1953 *Granhill*	Goulandris Bros. Ltd. London
1954 *Merlin*	San Pedro Cia. Armadora, SA, Panama Goulandris Bros. Ltd., London

FIFENESS - Headland at tip of Fife Peninsula. About 16km SE of world famous golf centre of St. Andrews, Scotland.

FLAMBOROUGH HEAD - see CAPE BRETON above

Fort á la Corne (Burrard D. D.)

FORT Á LA CORNE   7130gt   8.42   NS   NVSR North Van, BC

Nominated manager, (WSA) MacGowan & Gross Ltd. London, UK
30.3.43   Sunk by submarine torpedo, 36.52N, O1.47E (NW of Algiers, Algeria.)
FORT Á LA CORNE - Built in 1848 by the famous French trader and explorer, de la Verendrye, on the Saskatchewan River, about 20 miles below the junction of the North and South Saskatchewan Rivers. The NWC rebuilt the fort in 1797 but abandoned it in 1805. The HBC built a new structure at the site in 1846, but moved it three miles upstream to its present site.

FORT ABITIBI   7130gt   5.42   NS   CVL Montreal, QC

Nominated manager, (WSA) Smith Hogg & Co. Ltd. West Hartlepool MOWT later transferred management to
Sir R. Ropner & Co. Ltd. West Hartlepool, UK
1947   Returned to USMC, in reserve lay-up
1958   Scrapped at Baltimore, Maryland, USA
FORT ABITIBI - Built by the Chevalier de Troyes in 1686 on a long flat point projecting into Lake Abitibi. It was on the direct route taken by de Troyes and Sieur d'Iberville on their expedition from Montreal against the HBC forts on James Bay. Fort Abitibi passed to the British with the Treaty of Utrecht in 1713, which gave Hudson's Bay and the James Bay areas back to the British. It became an outpost of HBC Moose Factory in 1783 and was maintained until 1914.

FORT ACTON   7130 gt   2.43   NS   PRDS Prince Rupert, BC

Nominated manager, (WSA) Court Line Ltd. (Haldin & Phillips Ltd. London, UK
1947   Returned to USMC
1948 *Bacinin*   Giuseppe Bozzo, Genoa, Italy
FORT ACTON - A post of the HBC on the North Saskatchewan River near the mouth of the Clearwater River. It was built in 1810 to compete with the NWC's nearby Rocky Mountain House. Following the merger of the HBC and the NWC, Fort Acton fell into disuse.

FORT AKLAVIK   7130 gt   3.43   NS   BDD/VDD Vancouver, BC

Nominated manager, (DOC) Dodd, Thomson & Co. Ltd. London, UK
1950 *Irene Dal*   Dalhousie Steam & Motorship Co. London/Nomikos (London) Ltd.
1952 *Volcan*   Transoceanic S.S. Co. Karachi,
1953 *Ocean Envoy*   Same owner as above
FORT AKLAVIK - A HBC trading post in the Delta of the Mackenzie River established in 1912 on the Middle Peel Channel. In 1925 it was moved to its present site 50 miles from the Arctic coast and was an important RCMP post when the ship was built in 1943.

FORT ALABAMA   7130 gt   8.44   Vic   BDD/VDD Vancouver, BC

Nominated manager, (DOC) T & J Brocklebank Ltd. Liverpool
1947 *Gulfside*   Andros Shipping Co. Montreal/Goulandris Bros., London
1951 *Anthony*   Cia Nav. Panamena Antares, SA, Pan/Coulouthros Ltd. London
1964 *Blue Marlin*
FORT ALABAMA - Erected in 1717 at the juncture of the Toosa and Tallapoosa Rivers in French Louisiana. Recommended by Bienville three years earlier, but Governor Cadillac distrusted Bienville's advice for fear it would precipitate war with the local tribes. La Tour headed a party which built the fort to secure the French position. It was named both Fort Alabama and Fort Toulouse. (See also Fort Toulouse.)

Vessel Name:	Tonnage:	Completion date:	Type:	Builder & Yard location
FORT ALBANY	7130 gt	5.43	NS	DSBR Lauzon, QC

Nominated manager, (DOC) Frank S. Dawson, Newcastle-on-Tyne
1948 *La Fleche*   Papachristidis Company Ltd. Montreal
1961   Scrapped at Mihara, Japan

FORT ALBANY - A HBC post on the south shore of Albany Island at the mouth of the Albany River on James Bay. It changed hands from English to French five times before finally remaining a post of the HBC. At the time the ship was built in 1943 it was an important trading post for the HBC.

FORT ALEXANDRIA	7130 gt	5.42	NS	NVSR North Van, BC

Nominated manager, (WSA) Headlam & Son, Whitby, Yorkshire, UK
1948   Returned to USMC, sold
1948 *Vettor Pisani*   "Sidarma", Genoa. Italy
1952 *Ardea*   Mar. Napolitana, Soc de Nav, Naples
1954   Converted to diesel
1963 *Tornado*
1964 *Victoria Venture*

FORT ALEXANDRIA - The last post west of the Rocky Mountains established by the NWC in 1821, just before the HBC and NWC merged in the same year. It was the receiving point for furs shipped down the Stuart, Nechako and Fraser Rivers from where furs were shipped down the Columbia to Fort Vancouver. (The name was also carried at one time by Fort Tremblant. Also see Fort Chilcotin.)

FORT ANNE	7130 gt	12.42	NS	BDD/VDD Vancouver, BC

Nominated manager, (WSA) Hain Steamship Co. Ltd. London, UK
1947   Returned to USMC, in reserve lay-up.
1948   Scrapped at Baltimore, Maryland.

FORT ANNE - Located on the SW tip of Nova Scotia, this fort was originally known as Port Royal. Changing hands many times it was finally surrendered by the French in 1710. It was renamed Fort Anne and later became Annapolis Royal in honour of the reigning monarch, Queen Anne, the last of the Stuart line. (See also Port Royal Park)

FORT ASH	7130 gt	4.43	NS	BDD North Van, BC

Nominated manager, (DOC) Dene Shipping Co. Ltd. London, UK
1950 *Royston Grange*   Houlder Line Ltd. London
1952 *Giuan*   "Insa" Soc de Nav. Genoa, Italy
1960 *Cinqueterre*
1961 *Tilemahos*
1965 *Elicos*   Gibraltar flag

FORT ASH - Also known as Ash House, it was a post of the NWC on the Souris River in what is now SW Manitoba, Rivalry with the HBC at Fort Souris caused the NWC to establish Assiniboine House near Brandon with Fort Ash as an outpost. It was abandoned in 1796 on account of its vulnerable position.

FORT ASPIN (II)	7130 gt	1.44	Vic	PRDS Prince Rupert, BC

Nominated manager, (DOC) Thomas Dunlop & Sons, Glasgow, UK
1946 *Triport*   Triton SS. Co. Ltd. Montreal/Goulandris Bros., London
1950 *Heron*   Cia Mar del Este SA, Panama/Goulandris Bros (Hellas) Ltd. Piraeus.
1960 *Tinos*
1963 *Evergreen*

FORT ASPIN - Built by Cuthbert Grant in 1793 for the NWC. Located on the Assiniboine River on the Saskatchewan side of the border with Manitoba. It was also known as Grant's House and Aspin House and did a large trade in furs for a number of years.

Fort Assiniboine as Olympos (Phil Chandler)

Vessel Name:	Tonnage:	Completion date:	Type:	Builder & Yard location
FORT ASSINIBOINE	7130 gt	4.43	NS	BDD North Van, BC

Nominated manager, (DOC) H. Hogarth & Sons, Glasgow, UK
1948 *Laurentian Lake*   Laurentian Overseas Shipping Ltd. Montreal./Coulouthros Ltd. London
1954 *Olympos*   Monovar Cia. Nav. Liberia/Coulouthros Ltd. London
1960 *Pentelli II*
1963 *Gialia*
1963 *Paxoi*

FORT ASSINIBOINE - Also known as Assiniboine House, this was a NWC post on the Assiniboine River two miles above the mouth of the Souris, Western Manitoba. Built to compete with HBC's Brandon House or Fort Brandon, it was moved by John McDonnell to the south side of the Assiniboine in 1795 at the mouth of the Souris River. It was a busy post for ten years but with the decline in the fur trade and the merger of the two trading companies in 1821 it was discontinued.

FORT ASTORIA	7130 gt	7.43	Vic	WCSB Vancouver, BC

Nominated manager, (DOC) Counties Ship Management Co. London/Rethymnis & Kulukundis Ltd.
1946 *Yarmouth County*   Acadian Overseas Freighters Ltd. Halifax/I.H. Mathers & Son Ltd.
        Connected with Counties S.M. London
1948 *Santa Despo*   Cia. de Nav. San George, Panama/Rethymnis & Kulukundis Ltd. London
1955 *Mount Ithome*   Paranalto Cia Nav, SA Panama/Mar-Trade Corp., New York, associated with R & K above

FORT ASTORIA - Founded by John Jacob Astor of the Pacific Fur Company in 1811. With the threat of capture by the British in the War of 1812, the Astorians were glad to sell out to the NWC who renamed the fort Fort George. The Treaty of Ghent concluded the war but Astoria's position was uncertain until in 1846 the 49th parallel was agreed upon which left Fort Astoria and the town around it on the south bank of the Columbia, at its mouth, in American territory.

FORT ATHABASKA	7130 gt	5.43	NS	BDD North Van, BC

Nominated manager, (DOC) J & C Harrison Ltd., London, UK
1.12.43   Blew up and sank after explosion in nearby munitions ship at Bari, Italy following air
        attack. (See separate story)

FORT ATHABASKA - Built by fur trader Peter Pond in 1778 on the west bank of the Athabaska River about thirty miles above the river of the same name. Later Pond joined the NWC. In 1788 the NWC built Fort Chipewyan on the shore of Lake Athabaska and the original site was then abandoned.

FORT AUGUSTUS	7130 gt	6.42	NS	NVSR North Van, BC

Nominated manager, (WSA) Watts, Watts & Co. Ltd. London, UK
1948   Returned to USMC, in reserve lay-up.
1959   Scrapped at Beaumont, Texas

FORT AUGUSTUS - Built in 1794 by Shaw and McGillivray for the NWC of Montreal, it was first situated on the north bank of the Saskatchewan River just above the mouth of Sturgeon Creek, but in 1801 it was moved 20 miles upstream to the site of the present City of Edmonton. With the merger of the NWC into the HBC, Fort Augustus was then abandoned in favour of HBC's Fort Edmonton.

FORT BABINE	7130 gt	6.42	NS	NVSR North Van, BC

Nominated manager, (WSA) Wm. Thomson & Co. (Ben Line), Edinburgh, UK
13.9.43   Bombed and sunk, 41.31N, 14.39 W/SW of Cape Finisterre, Spain

FORT BABINE - Chief trader William Brown established this post for the HBC about 25 miles from the North end of Babine Lake, BC Some years after it was moved to the north end of the lake where it was still in operation at the time of launching the ship in 1942.

FORT BATTLE RIVER	7130 gt	7.42	NS	NVSR North Van, BC

Nominated manager, (WSA) John Cory & Sons Ltd. Cardiff, UK
6.3.43   Sunk by submarine torpedo, 36.33N, 10.22W, (W of Gibraltar)

FORT BATTLE RIVER - Shortly after the HBC-NWC merger in 1821, the HBC built this fort at the junction of the North Saskatchewan and Battle Rivers. A considerable trade was conducted through this post until the North West Rebellion of 1885. Troops arrived on the newly-built Canadian Pacific Railway but were too late to prevent an attack and plundering. The City of Battleford, SK, stands on the site of the old fort.

FORT BEAUHARNOIS	7130 gt	10.44	Vic	WCSB Vancouver, BC

Launched as *Fort Grande Rapids*
Nominated manager, (MOT) Alfred Holt & Co. Ltd. Liverpool
1945   Stores Issuing Ship in Fleet Train
1948   Transferred to Royal Navy as Fleet Stores Ship
1963   Scrapped at Spezia, Italy

FORT BEAUHARNOIS - Following explorations and recommendations of Jesuit Father Charlevoix, who saw a line of fur trading and missionary posts from Illinois, via the Mississippi Valley to Louisiana, the French built Fort Beauharnois in 1727 at Point de Sable on Lake Pepin the present State of Minnesota. Named for Charles de la Boische, Marquis de Beauharnois, Governor of New France. By 1766 the fort was in ruins. (See also Buffalo Park.)

FORT BEAUSEJOUR	7130 gt	11.43	NS	MI Sorel, QC

Nominated manager, (DOC) Sir R. Ropner & Co. Ltd., Darlington, Yorks.

1949 *Theogennitor*   Soc. Armadora del Norte, Panama/Goulandris Bros. (Hellas) Ltd. Piraeus.
1962 *Lillian K*
1964 *Golden Lily*

FORT BEAUSEJOUR - Completed by the French in 1755, the fort stood on a ridge overlooking Cumberland Basin on the New Brunswick side of the Missaguash River. Erected under orders from de la Jonquière, Governor of New France, as a defence against the British Fort Lawrence, built on a parallel ridge a little over a mile distant. Captured by a British army from Massachusetts under Moncton it was renamed Fort Cumberland after the Duke of Cumberland who massacred the Scots at the Battle of Culloden. It played a role in the American Revolution and the War of 1812, but later fell into ruins. In 1928 the site became Fort Beausejour National Park. (See also Fort Cumberland)

FORT BEAVER LAKE- Completed as WESTVIEW PARK.

FORT BEAVER LAKE -
1. Located about 3km east of the town of Lac la Biche, Alberta, on lake of the same name.
2. An outpost near Fort Concord.

FORT BEDFORD	7130 gt	3.43	NS	BDD North Van, BC

Nominated manager, (DOC) J. Morrison & Son, Newcastle-on-Tyne, UK

1951 *Othrys*   Othrys Shipping Co. Ltd. Montreal/Marcou & Sons Ltd. London
1952 *Mount Othrys* San Felicia Cia. Nav. Panama/Marcou & Sons Ltd. London
1961 *Alba Feliz*
1963   Scrapped at Hong Kong

FORT BEDFORD - Built for the HBC in 1796 on the NW shore of Reindeer Lake in Northern Saskatchewan. The post was built by David Thompson and was also known as Deer Lake House, Carlton House and Bedford House. In 1797 Thompson left the service of the HBC and joined the NWC in whose employ he later gained fame as a geographer and explorer of the Prairies and the Columbia Basin. (See also Fort Caribou and Fort Fairford.)

FORT BELL	7130 gt	6.43	NS	BDD North Van, BC

Nominated manager, (DOC) Dene Shipping Co. Ltd. London

1950 *North Cambria* North Shipping Co. Ltd./Hugh Roberts & Son, Newcastle-on-Tyne
1951 *Canada Maru*   Nihonkai Kisen K.K. Tokyo, Japan
1965 *Tenyo Maru*
1965 *Asahi Maru*

FORT BELL - Often used as a substitute name for the HBC post, Fort McPherson. It was built in 1840 on the right bank of the Peel River which is the lowest tributary of the Mackenzie River, about 150 miles from the Arctic Ocean. It was established by Trader John Bell whose explorations in the area and across the Yukon into Alaska were of considerable importance.

FORT BELLINGHAM	7130 gt	8.43	Vic	BDD Vancouver, BC

Nominated manager, (DOC) Hain Steamship Co. Ltd. London

25.1.44   Sunk by submarine torpedo, 73.23N, 25.10E (Off North Cape, Norway)

FORT BELLINGHAM - Bellingham Bay on the Puget Sound coast of Washington State was surveyed by Captain George Vancouver in 1792 and named by him for Sir William Bellingham who had checked Vancouver's supplies before he left England. The discovery of coal in 1852 and plentiful local timber led to the establishment of a village. Captain George Pickett and a company of infantry were sent to erect a permanent post in the district. Nothing remains of the fort today, but it played an important part in establishing the City of Bellingham, Wash.

FORT BERENS - Completed as *Mission Park* (see entry).

FORT BERENS - The settlement of Berens River was evidently a HBC post located on the river of the same name where it empties into Lake Manitoba opposite Berens Island and near Cape Berens. The name originates with Governor Berens of the HBC.

FORT BILOXI	7130 gt	10.44	Vic	BDD North Van, BC

Nominated manager, (DOC) J & J. Denholm Ltd. Glasgow, UK

1946 *Maria G*   Andros Shipping Co. Ltd. Montreal
1947 *Riverside*   Same as above./Goulandris Bros. London
1952 *Doxa*   Alvorada Cia. Armadora, S.A. Panama/National Shipping & Trading, Corp.
                    New York. Probably related to Goulandris

1954 *Makron*   Western Transport Corp. Liberia
1960 *Fray Martin*
1963 *Aghios Demitris*

FORT BILOXI - Established by the French under Sieur d'Iberville as Fort Maurepas or Fort Biloxi in 1698, in what is present day Mississippi. The first site was unhealthy so it was moved in 1702 to a new site on the Mobile River, in present day Louisiana. To avoid flooding yet a third move was made in 1710 to its final place in what became modern day Biloxi.
(See also Fort Maurepas)

FORT BOISE   7130 gt   9.43   Vic   WCSB Vancouver, BC
Nominated manager, (DOC) Hain Steamship Co. Ltd. London
23.8.46   Aground, broke back. Grand Shoal, E. of St Pierre & Miquelon. TL. (See separate story)

FORT BOISE - In 1834 N.J. Wyeth of the Columbia River Fishing and Trading Company, an American concern, established Fort Hall on the Snake River. Feeling threatened, the HBC erected Fort Boise on the east bank of the Snake. In 1837 Wyeth was forced to acknowledge defeat and sold out to the HBC. After that Fort Boise diminished in importance. In 1853 the fort was inundated and partly destroyed by the flooding Snake. The following year an Indian massacre at the site caused the HBC to abandon the fort. (See also Fort Hall.)

FORT BOURBON   7130 gt   7.42   NS   NVSR North Van, BC
Nominated manager, (WSA) Headlam & Son, Whitby, Yorkshire, UK
1948   Returned to USMC. In Reserve lay-up
1960   Scrapped at Beaumont, Texas

FORT BOURBON - Built in 1741 by Pierre Gaultier de Varennes, one of the sons of the famous French Canadian explorer and fur trader, Sieur de la Verendrye. Fort Bourbon, named for the French royal family, was situated on the west side of Cedar Lake near the mouth of the Saskatchewan River, in present day Manitoba. It diverted the fur trade away from the HBC on Hudson's Bay which cause the HBC to build Fort Cedar Lake to counter the French. Fort Bourbon was destroyed sometime after 1775. (See also Fort Cedar Lake.)

Fort Brandon as *Laurentian Hill* (Foto-Flite)

FORT BRANDON   7130 gt   6.43   NS   BDD North Van, BC
Nominated manager, (DOC) W.H. Seager & Co. Ltd. Cardiff
1948 *Laurentian Hill*   Laurentian Shipping Co. Ltd. Montreal/Coulouthros Ltd. London
1955 *Taygetos*   Monovar Comp de Nav. Liberia/Coulouthros Ltd. London
1960 *Aegean Sea*

FORT BRANDON - In order to cut off the trade of the NWC, the HBC built Fort Souris on the Souris River in 1793 and Fort Brandon or Brandon House, near the junction of the Assiniboine and Souris rivers in 1794. These moves were countered by the NWC with the result that by 1995 there were no less than five such trading posts in the vicinity, a classic case of oversupply of facilities. For 20 years Brandon was the chief post of the HBC in this vicinity. It closed in 1860.

FORT BRISEBOIS   7130 gt   3.44   Vic   BDD North Van, BC
Nominated manager, (DOC) J & J Denholm Ltd. Glasgow, UK
1946 *Pictou County*   Acadia Overseas Freighters Ltd./I.H. Mathers & Son, Halifax
        Counties S.M. Co. London
1950 *Archimede*   Comp. de Nav. Bayano, SA, Monrovia, Liberia/Constantine Hadjipateras &
        Sons. Athens, Greece.
1963 *Primavera*

FORT BRISEBOIS - Named for Ephrem A. Brisebois of the NWMP. He was sent with a troop to establish a fortified post at the confluence of the Elbow and Bow Rivers. His superiors insisted that it was to be known as Fort Calgary, but Brisebois persisted in calling it after himself. His action lost him his job, but he went on to greater things elsewhere. Today Fort Brisebois has grown into the modern city of Calgary.

Vessel Name:	Tonnage:	Completion date:	Type:	Builder & Yard location
FORT BRULÉ	7130 gt	11.42	NS	**WCSB Vancouver, BC**

Nominated manager, (WSA) Sir R. Ropner & Co. Ltd. Darlington, Yorks., UK
1947   Returned to USMC Reserve fleet, but sold
1948 *Jalamoti*   Scindia Steam Navigation Co. Bombay
1961 *Adawind*
1964 *Island Venture*

FORT BRULÉ - Also known as Island House, was a HBC post on the North Saskatchewan River, a few miles below their important post at Manchester House near the mouth of the Englishman River. It was built in 1790, but in 1793 the Fall Indians attacked many of the HBC posts on the North Saskatchewan. Manchester House was plundered and Fort Brulé burnt.

FORT BRUNSWICK	7130 gt	12.43	NS	**DSBR Lauzon, QC**

Nominated manager, (DOC) Allan, Black & Co. Sunderland, UK
1950 *Mulberry Hill*   Halifax Overseas Freighters Ltd./I.H. Mathers & Son Ltd. Halifax/Counties S.M Co. Ltd. London
1966   Scrapped in Yugoslavia

FORT BRUNSWICK - The first trading post, built in 1744, by the HBC on the Missanabie River in Northern Ontario was Fort Brunswick or Brunswick House. It was abandoned in 1790 in favour of New Brunswick House, 100 miles upstream which lasted until 1895. HBC consolidated its activities in the region at Fort Missanabie which operated into the 1930s and was frequently referred to by the Brunswick name which originated with the German Duchy of Brunswick-Lunenbery which had connections with the British Hanoverian Royal family. (See also Fort Missanabie)

FORT BUCKINGHAM	7130 gt	2.43	NS	**BDD North Van, BC**

Nominated manager, (WSA) Joseph Constantine & Sons, Middlesborough, Yorks, UK
20.1.44   Sunk by submarine torpedo, 08.50N, 66.25E. (off Maldive Islands, Indian Ocean)

FORT BUCKINGHAM - The first Fort Buckingham or Buckingham House was built by Mitchell Oman for the HBC in 1780. Situated on the North Saskatchewan River, 175 miles above the Saskatchewan River forks, it was then the most westerly HBC post. It was abandoned soon after completion, perhaps because of a terrible smallpox epidemic which swept the area. It was rebuilt a further 200 miles upriver over what is the present day Alberta-Saskatchewan border. It was finally abandoned in 1801 in favour of Island Fort. (See also Fort Turtle)

FORT BUFFALO	7130 gt	3.43	NS	**NVSR North Van, BC**

Nominated manager, (DOC) Turner Brightman & Co. London.
1949 *Radnor*   North River Freighters Ltd. Montreal/Ships Finance & Management Co. Ltd. George Nicolau Ltd. London, UK

FORT BUFFALO - Situated at the south end of the point between Buffalo Lake and Churchill lake in what is now NE Saskatchewan, a few miles to the SW of the Methye Portage discovered by Peter Pond in 1778. This portage passed over the height of land between the Mackenzie and Churchill Rivers and became an important route for NWC and HBC traders, Built in 1791 Fort Buffalo was still operating as Buffalo River Post, 150 years later.

FORT CADOTTE	7130 gt	3.43	NS	**BDD/VDD Vancouver, BC**

Nominated manager, (DOC) Sir R. Ropner & Co. Ltd. Darlington, Yorks, UK
1950 *Fry Hill*   Nova Scotia Marine Enterprises Co. Ltd./Nordic Ship Management Co. Ltd., Montreal. Counties S.M. Co. Ltd. London
1957 *Akti*   Portofino Comp. Nav. SA. Liberia/Rethymnis & Kulukundis Ltd. London
1961 *Gloria*
1964 *Helen*

FORT CADOTTE - Built in 1797 for NWC by J.B. Cadotte this post was situated on the south bank of Red Lake River at the mouth of the Clearwater River close to the present site of Red Lake Falls, Minnesota. Intensive trapping in the area resulted in overkill so most posts were of short duration. Cadotte apparently abandoned the post in 1799 and it then fell into ruin.

FORT CAMOSUN	7130 gt	6.42	NS	**VMD Victoria, BC**

Nominated manager, (WSA) T & J Brocklebank Ltd. Liverpool
This vessel had the rare distinction of being torpedoed on two separate occasions and surviving both.
20.6.42   Damaged by submarine torpedo 47.22N, 125.30W, (Off the Washington Coast).
3.12.43   Damaged by submarine torpedo 11.23N, 46.03E, (Off the East African Coast).
1947   Returned to USMC, Placed in Reserve Fleet.
1960   Scrapped in USA.

FORT CAMOSUN - Located on the present site of the city of Victoria, BC this fort was built in 1843 by James Douglas for the HBC. Shortly after the name was changed to Fort Victoria. In 1846 the Oregon Treaty was signed between Great Britain and the United States which left Britain with all of Vancouver Island. With the loss of Fort Vancouver on the Columbia River, the HBC transferred its western seat of operations to Fort Victoria.

Fort Capot River as *Notting Hill* (Phil Chandler)

FORT CAPOT RIVER   7130 gt   5.43   NS   NVSR North Van, BC

Nominated manager, (DOC) Larrinaga Steamship Co. Ltd. Liverpool, UK

1948 *Haligonian Duke*   Acadia Overseas Freighter (Halifax) Ltd./I.H. Mathers & Son. Halifax
Counties S.M. Co. Ltd. London.

1950 *Notting Hill*   Same owner, but managed by Counties/Rethymnis & Kulukundis Ltd. London.

1957 *Cepheus*   Transoceanic Finance & Trading Corp. Monrovia, Liberia
Rethymnis & Kulukundis Ltd. London

1960 *Brisa Feliz*

1964 *Zakia*

22.11.64   In collision off Cape St. Vincent. Sank, 36.48N 8.48W TL.

This is a good example of the flexibility of Greek owners. The first ownerships under the Canadian, British and Liberian flags all took place with the Rethymnis & Kulukundis group.

FORT CAPOT RIVER - Built a little after 1800, Fort Capot River was located on the SE shore of Nut Lake near the source of the Red Deer River which flows into Lake Winnipegosis. Later it was moved to a small stream between Nut Lake and Little Nut Lake. The HBC maintained an advantage over the NWC as it could bring its trade goods into the area from Hudson's Bay whereas NWC had at least a month's longer journeying overland from Montreal.

FORT CARIBOU   7130 gt   5.43   NS   BDD/VDD Vancouver, BC

Nominated manager, (DPC) Haldin & Phillips Ltd. (Court Line) London

1950 *Falcon*   Soc. Armadora del Norte, Panama/Goulandris Bros.(Hellas) Ltd. Piraeus, Greece.

1964 *Guna*

1964 *Progress*

FORT CARIBOU - This was a NWC post built in 1790 on Reindeer Island in what is now NE Saskatchewan. The competing HBC post was Bedford House built by David Thompson in 1796, but destroyed by the NWC in 1796. Shortly after 1800 the HBC built another fort at the south end of the lake which was also commonly referred to as Fort Caribou and was still in business as South Reindeer Lake House as at the launching date of the ship in 1943. (See also Fort Bedford.)

FORT CARILLON   7130 gt   5.43   NS   DSBR Lauzon, QC

Nominated manager, (DOC) Dodd. Thomson & Co. Ltd. London

1950 *Mount Royal*   Fort Carillon Shipping Co. Ltd./J.P. Hadoulis Ltd. London

1956 *Monte Rico*   Callao Cia. Nav. SA, Panama (Giannis A. Kairis), Rethymnis & Kulukundis Ltd.
London, managers

1960 *Lamyris*

1963 *Bararino*

FORT CARILLON - This was a French fort on the north bank of the Ottawa River, 15 miles above the Lake of Two Mountains. It was built for trade with the Algonquins, Nipissings and the Iroquois. Fort Carillon was probably abandoned during the Seven Years War which ended with the Treaty of Paris in 1763. There was another Fort Carillon later renamed Fort Ticonderoga.

FORT CARLTON   7130 gt   6.43   NS   NVSR North Van, BC

Nominated manager, (DOC) Sir Wm. Reardon Smith & Co. Ltd. Cardiff.

1950 *Sorel*   Laurier Freighters Ltd. Montreal

1952 *Surfside*   Oakmount S.S. Co. Ltd.
(The above two were transfers within the Goulandris group.)

1953   TheomitorMontezuma Cia. Armadora, SA. Panama
Spiros Polemis & Sons, Athens, Greece

1963   Scrapped at Onomichi, Japan

FORT CARLTON - Established in 1795 by the HBC on the Saskatchewan River, just below the forks. In 1805 Fort Carlton was moved to the South Saskatchewan River and again to a place on the North Saskatchewan River known as La Montée a few miles west of the present city of Prince Albert, SK. In 1876, it was the place where an historic treaty was signed with the Plains Indians by which a huge acreage between the branches of the Saskatchewan River was surrendered to the Crown. In 1884 it was leased to the NWMP as a headquarters from which to put down the halfbreed rebellion. (See entry under Fort La Montée.)

FORT CATARAQUI	7130 gt10.42	NS	DSBR Lauzon, QC

Nominated manager, (WSA) Raeburn & Verel Ltd. Glasgow, UK

1947   Returned to USMC. Placed in Reserve Fleet.

1960   Scrapped at Mobile, Alabama.

FORT CATARAQUI - This was a French military fort on the site of the present city of Kingston, ON. Built by the Compte de Frontenac in 1673 as a defence against the Iroquois and to prevent the Iroquois trading with the British at Albany, it fell into disrepair when Frontenac returned to France. In 1694 Frontenac returned and built a new stone fort which was generally known as Fort Frontenac. It was destroyed when captured by the British under General Bradstreet in 1758. (See entry under Fort Frontenac.)

FORT CEDAR LAKE	7130 gt	12.42	NS	NVSR North Van, BC

Nominated manager, (WSA) Hain Steamship Co. Ltd. London

17.3.43   Sunk by submarine torpedo, 52.14N 32.15W (SE of Cape Farewell).

FORT CEDAR LAKE - Following the destruction of Fort Bourbon in 1775, the HBC established itself in the vicinity. In 1856 the HBC built Fort Cedar Lake about half a mile down river from Cedar Lake on the Saskatchewan River. As at the time of launching the ship in 1942, the HBC still operated a fur trade post at Cedar Lake, 200 years after the original establishment in 1741 of the old French fort of Fort Bourbon. (See also Fort Bourbon.)

FORT CHAMBLY	7130 gt	4.42	NS	DSBR Lauzon, QC

Nominated manager, (WSA) Port Line Ltd. London

1947   Returned to USMC. Placed in Reserve Fleet

1959   Scrapped at Mobile, Alabama

FORT CHAMBLY - A French military fort 21 miles SE of Montreal on a promontory overlooking the River Richelieu. Built in 1665 by Jacques Chambly, an officer of the Carignan regiment, it was designed as a defence against the Iroquois. Burned by the Indians in 1702, it was rebuilt of stone in 1709-11 and surrendered to the British in 1760. It fell to the Americans in 1775 but was recaptured by the British in 1776. It is now restored as a museum.

FORT CHARLOTTE	7130 gt	4.44	Vic	NVSR North Van, BC

Completed as *Buffalo Park*.

Nominated manager, (DOC) Eastern & Australian S.S. Co. Ltd.London.

1945   Converted to Stores Issuing Ship

1947   Acquired by Royal Navy, as a Fleet Stores Ship

FORT CHARLOTTE - The NWC built the Grand Portage Fort in 1778 at the easterly end of the Grand Portage, the easiest route between Lake Superior and the West. A few years later, approximately 1781, they established Fort Charlotte at its western end on the south bank of the Pigeon River in present day Minnesota, named for Queen Charlotte, wife of King George III. The newly defined boundary between Canada and the United States forced the NWC to withdraw to Canadian territory in 1800-01. Fort Charlotte was abandoned and quickly fell into ruin.

FORT CHARNISAY	7130 gt	2.43	NS	BDD/VDD Vancouver, BC

Nominated manager, (WSA) Anning Bros. Ltd. Cardiff, UK

1947   Returned to USMC

1948 *Matilde Corrado*   Soc. di Nav. Corrado. Genoa, Italy

1963   Scrapped at Tsuneishi, Japan

FORT CHARNISAY - This fort had a more checkered history than most. Charles de la Tour had already been granted the rank of Lieutenant Colonel to the King of France and had built a fort in Saint John, when D'Aulnay de Charnisay was appointed to the same rank with the same mandate as de la Tour, whose fort Charnisay destroyed and then built his own new fort, Fort Charnisay, on the opposite side of the harbour. When Sieur Martignon came on the scene in 1672 he renamed the fort, Fort Martignon. It later bore the names Fort St. Jean and Fort Menagoueche and finally Fort Frederick. (See also Fort La Tour and Fort Frederick.)

FORT CHESTERFIELD	7130 gt	3.43	NS	BDD/VDD Vancouver, BC

Nominated manager, (DOC) Hain Steamship Co. Ltd. London.

1949 *Hawk*   Soc. Armadora del Norte, SA, Panama/Goulandris Bros. (Hellas) Ltd. Piraeus.

1965 *Cabahawk*

FORT CHESTERFIELD - Built in 1791 for the NWC, Fort Chesterfield or Chesterfield House was situated on the South branch of the Saskatchewan River at the mouth of the Red Deer River. The post was abandoned in 1804 and then rebuilt as New Chesterfield House. It was finally abandoned in 1860 due to difficulties with the Indians.

FORT CHILCOTIN — 7130 gt — 6.41 — NS — WCSB Vancouver, BC

Nominated manager, (WSA) H. Hogarth & Son, Glasgow, UK

24.7.43 — Sunk by submarine torpedo, 15.03S, 32.35W (off Bahia, Brazil).

FORT CHILCOTIN - Built in 1830 for the HBC in the valley of the Chilco River about 100 miles NW of Fort Alexandria. There was much hostility from the Indians, but perseverance paid off and it became the means of developing the fur trade with the Chilcotin Indians. Fort Chilcotin served as a trading post until 1850.

FORT CHIMO see under POINT PELEE PARK (I) and BELWOODS PARK (II)

FORT CHIMO - An early HBC post on Ungava Bay on the Quebec side of Hudson Bay. The name was previously used by the Hudson's Bay Company as Baychimo on one of its Arctic trading vessels which was abandoned in the ice and then floated around the Arctic for a good many years, being referred to as "a ghost ship" until she finally disappeared at a location and time unknown.

FORT CHIPEWYAN — 7130 gt — 7.42 — NS — WCSB Vancouver, BC

Nominated manager, (WSA) Idwal Williams & Co. Ltd. Cardiff, UK

1947 — Returned to USMC, sold out of Reserve Fleet to

1949 *Bharatraja* — Bharat Line Ltd. Bombay, India. Clients of J & C Harrison, London

1962 — Scrapped at Bombay

FORT CHIPEWYAN - Built in 1788 by Roderick Mackenzie of the NWC on the south shore of Lake Athabaska in what is now NE Alberta. It was from Fort Chipewyan that Alexander Mackenzie set out on his famous journeys to discover the Mackenzie River in 1789 and overland to the Pacific at Bella Coola in 1792. In 1802 the fort had been moved to the NE corner of the Lake. Following the merger of the NWC and the HBC, the latter abandoned their Fort Wedderburne in favour of Fort Chipewyan which was still in operation after 154 years when the ship was launched in 1942.

FORT CHURCHILL — 7130gt — 2.42 — NS — BDD North Van, BC

Nominated manager, (WSA) T & J Brocklebank Ltd. Liverpool

1947 — Returned to USMC

1948 — Transferred or chartered to Iranian Government

1949 — Returned to USMC placed in Reserve Fleet

1958 — Scrapped at Baltimore, Maryland.

FORT CHURCHILL - The name came from Winston Churchill's great ancestor, John Churchill, first Duke of Marlborough and Governor of the HBC from 1685 to 1692. Built in 1688. The French captured and burned the fort the following year. By the Treaty of Utrecht the Hudson's Bay territory, including this site, was returned to Britain. A fort with walls of stone was built in 1734. It fell to the French in 1782, but reverted to the British once again when the French finally left Canada.

FORT CLATSOP — 7130 gt — 8.43 — Vic — DSBR Lauzon, QC

Nominated manager, (DOC) J & J Denholm Ltd., Glasgow, UK

1946 *Mont Clair* — Montship Lines Ltd. Montreal. Assoc. with Buries Markes Ltd. London and Louis Dreyfus et Cie, Paris.

1948 *Husaini* — Muhammadi S.S. Co. Ltd., Karachi, Pakistan.

1948 *Al Huseini* — Same as above

FORT CLATSOP -The Oregon territory was a source of dispute between the United States and Britain. The HBC had established its territory down to the Columbia River, but the Lewis and Clark expedition of 1804 which successfully traversed the North West territory did much to settle the issue in favour of the US when the International Boundary Commission determined the frontier to be the 49th parallel. For a wintering place the two intrepid explorers built Fort Clatsop on the Lewis and Clark River which flowed into Youngs Bay, Oregon.

FORT COLUMBIA — 7130 gt — 7.43 — Vic — BDD North Van, BC

Nominated manager, (DOC) Charlton, McCallum & Co. Ltd. Newcastle-on-Tyne, UK

1948 *Sunrell* — Saguenay Terminals Ltd. Montreal

1959 *Sula* — Pacific Trading & Navigation Co. Ltd. Liberia

FORT COLUMBIA - On the amalgamation of the NWC and HBC, John McLoughlin was sent to the Oregon country as factor and virtual governor. Finding Fort George, formerly Fort Astoria unsuitable as a headquarters he founded Fort Vancouver in 1824-25. Often known as Fort Columbia this fort was on the North bank of the Columbia in present day Washington. With settlement of the boundary treaty of 1846, it became American territory, but the HBC hung on until 1860 when American military authorities stepped in. The HBC under Peter Skene Ogden removed itself to Fort Victoria which had been prepared for such an eventuality.

Fort Colville as *Lake Kootenay* II (Phil Chandler)

FORT COLVILLE   7130 gt   9.43   Vic   NVSR North Van, BC

Nominated manager, (DOC) Alfred Holt & Co. Liverpool/The Blue Funnel Line

1945	Air Stores Issuing ship
1950 *Lake Kootenay*	Western Canada Steamships Ltd. Van.
1957 *Andros Cygnet*	Orion Shipping & Trading Co. New York, Ass'td. with Goulandris Bros. London.
1957 *Theoskepasti*	Cia. Mar. Las Perlas SA, Panama/B.J. Mavros, client of Goulandris Bros. London.
1965 *Marietta T*	

FORT COLVILLE - This was a HBC post built in 1825 near the junction of the Colville and Columbia Rivers at Kettle Falls in present day Washington State. It was built on orders of Governor Simpson to replace old Spokane House or Fort Spokane a NWC post. It was abandoned following the boundary treaty of 1846. Named for the Colvilles who occupied key posts at the HBC, they spelled their name with one "l". (See also Fort Spokane.)

FORT CONCORD   7130 gt   11.42   NS   DSBR Lauzon, QC

Nominated manager, (WSA) Larrinaga Steamship Co. Ltd. Liverpool

12.5.43   Sunk by submarine torpedo 46.05N, 25.20W, (North of the Azores)

FORT CONCORD - Built about 1830 for the HBC on Lake Wapikopa in Northern Ontario. This lake is near the headwaters of the Winisk River flowing North into Hudson's Bay. This was good fur country where the HBC established many posts. In 1850 they built Beaver Lake post as an outpost of Fort Concord. Concord closed in 1870, but Beaver Lake was still being operated in 1942 when the ship was launched (see also Fort Beaver Lake).

FORT CONFIDENCE   7130 gt   7.42   NS   WCSB Vancouver, BC

Nominated manager, (WSA) Maclay & McIntyre Ltd. Glasgow, UK

7.16.43   On fire at Algiers while loading petroleum in drums, beached, TL. See separate account.

FORT CONFIDENCE - Built on Dease Lake in 1837 by the famous Arctic explorers Thomas Simpson and Peter Dease. Under instructions from the HBC to explore the Arctic Coast, they made their way from Fort Chipewyan, passed down the Mackenzie River and travelled west to Point Barrow in Alaska. They returned to Fort Confidence to overwinter and then went east in 1838 reaching King William Land and the mouth of the Coppermine River. Rebuilt in 1848 Fort Confidence was still standing in 1898.

FORT CONNOLLY   7130 gt   4.43   NS   BDD North Van, BC

Nominated manager, (DOC) Gibbs & Company, Newport, Mon. UK

1950 *Marine Hill*	Nova Scotia Marine Enterprises Co./Nordic Ship Mgmt. Co. Montreal
	Counties S.M. Co. Ltd. London.
1957 *Fotoulia*	Portofino Cia. Nav. SA, Panama/Rethymnis & Kulukundis Ltd. London.
1961 *Alison*	

FORT CONNOLLY - Built in 1826 by James Douglas for the HBC, It was situated at the North end of Bear Lake, a headwater of the Skeena River in North West British Columbia. This was the second post established in BC for the HBC, all the earlier forts being NWC developments which were taken over by the HBC following the merger of 1821. It was named after William Connolly, super-intendent of the territory then known as New Caledonia.

FORT CONSTANTINE

	7130 gt	4.44	Vic	BDD/VDD Vancouver, BC

Nominated manager, (DOC), Ellerman & Bucknall SS Co. Ltd. London
1949   Fleet train stores ship. Transferred to permanent strength of the Royal Navy.

FORT CONSTANTINE - In 1894 Inspector Charles Constantine travelled through the gold mining camps of the Yukon and Alaska to assess the needs for policing services. In 1895 his recommendations led to the dispatch of a troop of 20 policemen, under Constantine's command, for the Upper Yukon to establish a fort at a spot where Forty Mile Creek entered the river. This place already known as Fort Cudahy was a shanty town of miners searching for gold. Here Fort Constantine was built to bring law and order to the territory. With the discovery of gold on Bonanza Creek, a tributary of the Klondike River, the police abandoned Fort Constantine and moved their headquarters to Dawson City.

FORT CONTI completed as EARLSCOURT PARK.

FORT CONTI - Established by the French under Henri de Tonty on the Niagara River in 1678. At Fort Conti he built a warship, the Griffon in 1679 to back up French power on Lake Erie. (See also Fort Crevecoeur.)

FORT COULONGE

	7130 gt	5.43	NS	USY Montreal, QC

Nominated manager, (DOC) Sir R. Ropner & Co. Ltd. West Hartlepool, Yorks.
1950 *Andover Hill*   Ottawa S.S. Co. Ltd./I.H. Mathers & Son Ltd. Halifax/Coulouthros Ltd. London
1961 *Louria*
1964 *Surabaja Steer*
1965 *Beryl*

FORT COULONGE - This French stockaded trading post was located on the left bank of the Ottawa River at the mouth of the Coulonge River, between Grand Calumet and Allumettes Islands. It was built in 1680 by the family of Louis d'Ailleboust, Sieur de Coulonges. During the Seven Years War which ended in the cession of Canada by the French, Fort Coulonge was abandoned. It was later restored by the NWC. Following the 1821 merger the HBC operated the post until 1865.

Fort Covington as *Bedford Earl* (Foto-Flite)

FORT COVINGTON

	7130 gt	10.43	NS	USY Montreal, QC

Nominated manager, (DOC) Counties Ship Management Ltd. London
1950 *Bedford Earl*   Bedford Overseas Freighters Ltd./I.H. Mathers & Son, Halifax
                      P.D. Marchessini & Co. Ltd. London and New York.
26.9.56   Aground on reef off Ie Shima, Ryuku Islands, during typhoon, CTL, sold.

FORT COVINGTON - Built by the Royal Canadian Volunteers as Fort Malden between 1797 and 1799, it was a rallying point for British forces engaged in the taking of Detroit in the War of 1812. It was later occupied by the Americans who renamed it Fort Covington.

It was re-garrisoned by the British in the rebellion of 1827 but fell into disrepair afterwards. Called into use once again some ten years later, it was an important defence against raiders from the South.

Vessel Name:	Tonnage:	Completion date:	Type:	Builder & Yard location
FORT CREVECOEUR	7130 gt	8.43	Vic	WCSB Vancouver, BC

Nominated manager, (DOC) H.M. Thompson & Co. Ltd. Edinburgh, UK
1946 *Trimont* Triton S.S. Co. Ltd. Montreal/March Shipping Agency Ltd. Ass'td.
with Goulandris Bros. London.
1949 *Eagle* Soc. Armadora del Norte, Panama/Goulandris Bros. (Hellas) Ltd. Piraeus, Greece
1957 *Seacrow* Cia de Nav. Almirante SA, Panama/Salvatores & Racah SRL, Genoa Italy

FORT CREVECOEUR - The famous explorer Sieur de la Salle built this fort in 1680. The site was on the left bank of the Illinois River sixty miles from its junction with the Mississippi at what is now Peoria, Illinois. La Salle began to build a ship to travel down the Mississippi but the equipment for the new ship went down in the "Griffon" on the Great Lakes. Leaving Henri de Tonty in charge at Crevecoeur he arrived at Fort Frontenac (Kingston) to hear that his men had revolted and destroyed the fort and his trusted Tonty had disappeared. Crevecoeur means "heart break" which might have been a reference to the "Griffon", but more probably was named to honour a French victory at Crevecoeur in the Netherlands. (See also Fort Conti)

FORT CREVIER	7130 gt	10.43	NS	USY Montreal, QC

Nominated manager, (DOC) Joseph Robinson & Sons, North Shields, Yorks. UK
14.4.44 Badly damaged in the Fort Stikine explosion at Bombay, CTL.
Later used as hulk for grain storage.
1948 Scrapped at Bombay

FORT CREVIER - Jean Crevier was given a piece of land south of Lake Saint- Pierre which was later known as the Saint-François Village. To protect the village he built a fort at Notre dame de Pierreville in 1687. This fort became known as Fort Crevier or Fort Saint-François and was subject to continuous attacks by the Iroquois which continued until 1693 when Jean Crevier was taken captive. In 1700 Crevier's widow gave Saint-François to the Abenakis Indians which they still retain. The last time Fort Crevier appeared on a map was in 1714. Other than a memorial cairn nothing remains to indicate the site of the fort.

FORT CROWN POINT completed as ALDER PARK.

FORT CROWN POINT - A historic site at Crown Point on Lake Champlain. This British fort replaced Fort Frederic, a French fort, which the French had destroyed while retreating from the area in 1779 after evacuating Fort Ticonderoga.

FORT CUMBERLAND	7130 gt	5.43	NS	BDD/VDD Vancouver, BC

Nominated manager, (DOC) Lyle Shipping Co. Ltd. Glasgow, UK
1950 *Cape Franklin* Lyle Shipping Co. Ltd. Glasgow
1956 *African Sky* General Navigation Ltd. Monrovia, Liberia/Salvatores & Racah SRL, Genoa, Italy

FORT CUMBERLAND - Built by Samuel Hearne in 1774 for the HBC, Fort Cumberland or Cumberland House was situated on Pine Island at the south east end of Cumberland Lake four miles north of the Saskatchewan River. Cumberland House was named after Prince Rupert, Duke of Cumberland and first Governor of the HBC, At the time of launching the ship the post was still in operation, 169 years after its establishment. (See also Fort Beausejour.)

FORT DAER completed as WHITEROCK PARK.

FORT DAER - This fort was built by Captain Miles McDonnell leading a group of the Selkirk Scottish settlers near present day Pembina, North Dakota.

FORT DAUPHIN	7130 gt	6.43	NS	BDD/VDD Vancouver, BC

Nominated manager, (DOC) Joseph Constantine Lines Ltd. Middlesborough, Yorks
1950 *Warkworth* Watergate S.S. Co. Ltd./R.S. Dalgliesh, Newcastle-on-Tyne
1957 *Bodoro* Cia. Mar. Amaconte SA, Panama/Joaquin Punta Naya, mgr. Corunna, Spain

FORT DAUPHIN

1. The first Fort Dauphin was a French post built by Pierre de la Verendrye on the NW shore of Lake Manitoba, at the mouth of the Mossy River in 1741. It was destroyed by the Indians, but rebuilt in 1743 and occupied until the cession of Canada in 1763.
2. Peter Pond built another Fort Dauphin on Dauphin Lake in 1775. The NWC later moved this fort to Ochre River a few miles south of the lake. When NWC was merged into the HBC the latter abandoned its small post at Mossy River and took over the NWC fort calling it Dauphin Lake House. It operated until about 1870.

FORT DEARBORN	7150 gt	1.44	Vic	BDD North Van, BC

Nominated manager, (DOC) Haldin & Phillips Ltd. (The Court Line) London.
30.7.44 Damaged by E-boat torpedo in English Channel, repaired.
1947 *Manx Navigator* Kerr-Silver Lines Ltd. Vancouver.
1949 *Aloe* Union Gov't of South Africa, Johannesburg.
1955 President SteynSouthern S.S. (Pty) Ltd. Johannesburg/E.P. Nomikos, Athens, Greece.
1962 *Demirel*
23.9.64 Ashore at Ahirkapi, Istanbul Roads. Refloated with severe bottom damage, CTL
6.65 Scrapped in Turkey

FORT DEARBORN - The first white men known to have visited the site were two French Canadians, Pere Marquette and Joliet, in 1673. A fur trading post was established here called Chicagou. The French regime ended in 1763 with the termination of the Seven Years War. The British occupation followed and lasted until 1783 when the United States took possession of the territory. Fort Dearborn was established by the Americans at the mouth of the Chicago River in 1803-04 and 33 years later it received a city charter and became the modern city of Chicago. Chief Tecumseh burned the post in 1812 and murdered the garrison, but it was rebuilt four years later. Named after General Henry Dearborn, US Secretary of War during the period.

Fort Dease Lake as *Ivor Jenny* (W.S.S., NZ Branch)

FORT DEASE LAKE   7130gt   4.43   NS   BDD/CDD Vancouver, BC

Nominated manager, (DOC) Buries Markes Ltd., London

1948 *Ivor Jenny*	Ivor Shipping Co. Ltd. (Quebec Steamship Lines Ltd. Montreal) Ass'td. with Chandris (England) Ltd. London.	
1955 *Novor Jenny*	Novor Shipping Co. Ltd. London/Chandris (England) Ltd.	
1958 *Jenny*	Marifortuna Nav. S.A. Panama/AJ & DJ Chandris, Piraeus, Greece	

FORT DEASE LAKE - Built for the HBC in 1837 by Robert Campbell. In 1836, at the age of 28, he was in temporary charge at Fort Simpson, the HBC depot for the Mackenzie River district at the junction of the Mackenzie and Liard Rivers. He set out with a party to reach Dease Lake, over 500 miles distant. The party wintered at Fort Halkett, situated where the Smith River meets the Liard, and then pushed on to Dease Lake, building Fort Dease Lake about five miles from its outlet. Here Campbell met Indians who were trading with the Russians at Fort Highfield at the mouth of the Stikine. Campbell was rated as one of the finest officers in the service of the HBC and was noted for his explorations of Northern BC and the Yukon. Abandoned for a while Dease Lake was an active trading post at the time of the launching of the ship in 1943. (See also Fort Highfield.)

FORT DOUGLAS   7130 gt   8.42   NS   VMD Victoria, BC

Nominated manager. (WSA) Haldin & Phillips Ltd. (Court Line) London

1946	Returned to USMC. Placed in Reserve fleet
1958	Scrapped at Baltimore.

FORT DOUGLAS - This fort was built by Miles McDonnell in 1813, on the Red River where the City of Winnipeg now stands. (This was not the only Fort encompassed by Winnipeg - see Fort Rouge). It was named after Lord Selkirk whose family name was Douglas and was the administrative centre for the Selkirk settlers. In 1816 Fort Douglas was captured by Cuthbert Grant of the NWC in a battle with its rival the HBC at nearby Seven Oaks. Remembered as the Battle of Seven Oaks, where there were a number of deaths. The following year a band of soldiers led by Lord Selkirk recaptured the fort. After the NWC-HBC merger, the new HBC abandoned the fort in 1822 in favour of a new fort nearby.

FORT DREW   7130 gt   12.42   NS   NVSR North Van, BC

Nominated manager, (WSA) Maclay, McIntyre Ltd.   Glasgow, UK

6.9.43	Damaged by mine, 35.52N 14.47E
1948	Returned to USMC. Placed in Reserve Fleet
1961	Scrapped at Mobile, Alabama

FORT DREW - A HBC post on Dease Lake at the mouth of Carribeau River in NW British Columbia. Instructions were given by the governor and council in 1836 to intercept the valuable fur trade which was finding its way via the Stikine to the Russians on the coast. Chief trader McPherson tried to establish the post on the Stikine River but had to abandon the project because of sustained hostility from the Indians. In 1841 the HBC leased the Russian forts on the coast which removed the necessity for the projected fort on the Stikine. Fort Drew was established a few years later, west of Fort Halkett and northeast from Fort Dease Lake, but it was abandoned by 1850. (See also Fort Dease Lake, Fort Halkett, Fort Stikine, Fort Highfield and Fort Wrangell).

Vessel Name:	Tonnage:	Completion date:	Type:	Builder & Yard location
FORT DUNVEGAN	7150 gt	4.44	Vic	BDD North Van, BC

Nominated manager, (DOC) Ellerman & Bucknall Line Ltd. London
Completed as a Stores Issuing Ship for Service with the Pacific Fleet Train.

| 1949 | | Transferred to the Royal Navy. |

FORT DUNVEGAN - This was a NWC fort built in 1805-6 by Archibald Norman McLeod on the south bank of the Peace River, 57 miles above Smoky Forks in present day Alberta, It was established on land given by the Beaver Indians to the NWC. Named by its founder after the ancestral home of the Clan McLeod at Castle Dunvegan on the Isle of Skye, Fort Dunvegan was noted for its land cultivation and the excellence of the produce that it produced. Except for a brief three year period following Indian disturbances it reopened in 1828. It operated continuously until the beginning of the 20th century. Although the fort was then abandoned a settlement has since grown up around the site.

| FORT DUQUESNE | 7150 gt | 11.44 | Vic | WCSB Vancouver, BC |

Completed as *Queensborough Park*
Nominated manager, (MOT) Alfred Holt & Co. Ltd., Liverpool

| 1945 | | Renamed *Fort Duquesne*, converted to a Stores Issuing ship for Fleet Train service. |
| 1947 | | Acquired by Royal Navy as a store ship. |

FORT DUQUESNE - To secure their position preceding the Seven Years War the French built a line of forts along the Ohio Valley to assure its possession by the French. Hearing of this Governor Dinwiddie of Virginia sent young George Washington to ask them to retire from British soil. The French refused claiming prior discovery through La Salle. Dinwiddie then ordered Washington to build a fort at the confluence of the Allegheny and Monongahela Rivers on the site of what is now the City of Pittsburgh. Before Washington arrived some of his men had already started construction only to have it captured by the French. On Washington's arrival he found the fleur-de-lis flying and the name Fort Duquesne on the fort. General Forbes with Washington, captured the fort for the British after the French had set it afire and retired to Fort Machault. Washington renamed the post Fort Pitt for William Pitt, British Prime Minister at the time. (See also Fort Pitt and Queensborough Park.)

| FORT EDMONTON | 7130 gt | 9.44 | Vic | BDD/VDD Vancouver, BC |

Nominated manager, (DOC) Ellerman, Bucknall S.S. Co. London.
Completed as a Stores Issuing ship for the Fleet Train

| 1947 *Federal Voyager* | | Federal Commerce & Navigation Co. Ltd. Montreal. Used by the owner as a supply ship for servicing outposts, mining and oil exploration ventures. As such she was engaged in coastal service and thus remained on the Canadian register. |
| 1961 | | Scrapped at Chiba, Japan. |

FORT EDMONTON - Built by George Sutherland for the HBC in 1795 it was situated very close to the NWC establishment at Fort Augustus. Both forts were taken by the Blood Indians in 1807 and demolished. In 1808 the rival companies built new forts higher up the Saskatchewan River on the site of the present day City of Edmonton. Upon the merger of the HBC and NWC Fort Augustus was abandoned and Fort Edmonton began to grow in importance. Between 1823 and 1825 it was greatly rebuilt by Chief Factor James Rowand and became the most important trading centre on the Saskatchewan River. It had bastions and great studded gates sufficient to discourage the Indians from making trouble. Inside it contained workshops, warehouses, kennels, stables and stores, and York boats were built there. The arrival of the Canadian Pacific Railway started to take away from its role, but it was not until 1913 that the old fort was demolished to make way for the new Alberta Parliament buildings.

| FORT ELLICE | 7130 gt | 6.42 | NS | BDD/VDD Vancouver, BC |

Nominated manager, (WSA) Lambert Bros. Ltd. London

1946		Returned to USMC. Placed in Reserve Fleet
1948 *Jag Vijay*		Bharat Line. Ltd. Bombay
1960		Scrapped at Bombay.

FORT ELLICE - The HBC built this fort in 1832 at the junction of Beaver Creek and the Assiniboine River near the present interprovincial border between Manitoba and Saskatchewan. It was named after the Hon. Edward Ellice, a British member of Parliament who had been interested in the NWC and had a hand in bringing the two companies together in merger. It was still in use in 1889 as it was on the route of the Red River cart brigades from Fort Garry to Fort Edmonton, but was abandoned shortly after that date.

| FORT ENTERPRISE | 7130 gt | 4.43 | NS | WCSB Vancouver, BC |

Nominated manager, (DOC) Hall Brothers, Newcastle-on-Tyne.

1951 *Tavistock*		Tavistock Shipping Co. (Noel Purvis) London
1952 *Southwick*		Island Shipping Co. Ltd. Nassau, Bahamas/Ivanovic & Co. Ltd. London
1956 *Mahsud*		T & J Brocklebank Ltd. Liverpool UK
1961 *Marine Traveller*		
1962 *Bandahara*		
1964 *Otone*		
1966		Scrapped Hirao, Japan.

FORT ENTERPRISE - This was an explorer's fort or depot built in 1820 for Sir John Franklin, the intrepid British explorer. It was situated at Winter Lake near the source of the Coppermine River. Franklin mounted three expeditions to the Arctic coast covering the entire distance from Herschel Island in the West to the mouth of the Coppermine River in the East. Franklin's last ill-fated expedition left England in 1845 in two ships, the Erebus and Terror, from which none were to return. In 1859 a stone cairn was found on Point Victory which contained Franklin's log and proved that they were on the verge of breaking through the North West Passage when they became fast in the ice off King William Island. Since then other artifacts have been found, including frozen bodies in a high state of preservation, who were members of Franklin's crew. (See also Fort Franklin.)

FORT ERIE	7130 gt	5.43	NS	USY Montreal, QC

Nominated manager, (DOC) Frank S. Dawson Ltd. Cardiff, Wales

1951 *Maidenhead* Fort Erie S.S. Co. Ltd./J.P. Hadoulis Ltd. London

1957 *Aristefs* Aguaruta Cia. Nav. SA, Panama/Rethymnis & Kulukundis Ltd., London

FORT ERIE - This was a defensive fort raised on the Canadian side following the American revolution. It was situated a mile west of the point where Lake Erie flows into the Niagara River. In the war of 1812 it became of some importance as part of the strategy of General Brock in the capture of Detroit. In July, 1814 it was captured by the Americans. In August of that year the British counter attacked, but just as they gained a foothold on a bastion an ammunition magazine exploded killing a thousand men. The Americans blew up the fort in November 1814 and retired to their own side of the border.

FORT ESPERANCE (II)	7130 gt	11.43	NS	USY Montreal, QC

Nominated manager, (DOC) Allan, Black & Co., Sunderland, UK

1950 *Nimaris* Morland Navigation, Ltd. Montreal/J.P. Hadoulis Ltd. London

1956 *Captain Nicos* Cortes Cia. Nav. SA, Panama/J.P. Hadoulis Ltd. London

1963 *Luzon Logger*

1965 *Judy*

FORT ESPERANCE - The NWC established this fort as an important post on the south bank of the Qu'Appelle River about 15 miles above its junction with the Assiniboine in what is now eastern Saskatchewan. Built by Robert Grant it was a large, strong and easily defended position situated on a small tableland half way up the Qu'Appelle Valley. For some years it was the company's most important western outpost in the Prairie region. It was rebuilt in 1806 by McDonald and became the chief provision depot for the company where large numbers of buffalo were slaughtered.

FORT FAIRFORD	7130 gt	1.43	NS	NVSR North Van, BC

Nominated manager, (WSA) Morel Ltd., London.

1947 Returned to USMC

1948 *General Rivera* Oceanic Transport Corporation, Monrova, Liberia/Aristotles S. Onassis, Buenos Aires, Argentina and Paris, France

FORT FAIRFORD - This was a HBC fort built in 1795 and also known as Fairford House. It was situated on the Churchill River below the mouth of Reindeer River in what is now NE Saskatchewan. The NWC was already trading on Reindeer Lake through Fort Caribou thereby cutting off much of the trade before it reached Fort Fairford. To counter this David Thompson went to the north end of the lake where he set up Fort Bedford or Bedford House in 1796, wherupon Fort Fairford was abandoned. (See also Fort Bedford.)

FORT FIDLER	7130 gt	5.43	NS	NVSR North Van, BC

Nominated manager, (DOC) Smith Hogg & Co. West Hartlepool. Management later transferred to Sir R. Ropner & Co. Ltd.

14.5.44 Damaged by submarine torpedo, 36.45N, 00.55E

1.3.45 Arrived at Lisbon in damaged condition, repaired,

1946 *Alcoutim* Soc. Geral de Commercio I & T., Lisbon, Portugal

FORT FIDLER - Another fort which occupied part of the present day area of Winnipeg was Fort Fidler. Its origins were founded upon the importance of the Red and Assiniboine Rivers as a cross roads of commerce from the time of Verendrye's early establishment of Fort Rouge in 1737 and other forts in the immediate neighbourhood through the building of the famous Fort Garry a hundred years later. Fort Fidler was one of the later establishments having been erected by Peter Fidler in 1818. It was a palisaded structure at the present junction of McDermot Avenue and Notre Dame Street. Until the company rebuilt the first Fort Gibraltar as Fort Garry this was their establishment at the Forks as distinct from Fort Douglas, about a mile away. (See also Fort Douglas and Fort Gibraltar.)

FORT FINLAY	7130 gt	1.43	NS	WCSB Vancouver, BC

Nominated manager, (WSA) Sir R. Ropner & Co. Ltd. West Hartlepool.

1948 Returned to USMC. Place in Reserve Fleet

1959 Scrapped at Baltimore, Maryland.

FORT FINLAY -

1. The first Fort Finlay or Finlay's House was built on the Saskatchewan River at Nipawin Rapids, 35 miles east of Fort a-la Corne in what is now central Saskatchewan. It was built in 1767 by James Finlay, Senior, who was one of the first English-speaking free traders to enter the West after the cession of Canada by the French.

2. The second Fort Finlay was built by James Finlay, Junior, in 1792 for the NWC. This was situated on the Peace River. The younger Finlay was the discoverer of the Finlay River a tributary of the Peace River.

FORT FITZGERALD 7130 gt 3.43 NS WCSB Vancouver, BC

Nominated manager, (WSA) E & R Management Co. Ltd., Cardiff.

4.10.43 Sunk by aircraft torpedo, 36.42N, 01.17 E (West of Algiers, Algeria.

FORT FITZGERALD - This latter day fort was built in 1870 by the HBC at the head of the rapids on the Slave River near the northern border of Alberta. These rapids were the only impediment to navigation between Fort McMurray at the confluence of the Clearwater and Athabaska Rivers and the Mackenzie River Delta. The York boats and scows of the fur traders often shot the rapids, but when steam navigation came in 1886 cargo from Fort McMurray was unloaded at Fort Fitzgerald and taken over the portage to Fort Smith for onward navigation down river.

FORT FORK 7130gt 9.42 NS BDD North Van, BC

Nominated manager, (WSA) Sir Wm. Reardon Smith & Co. Ltd. Cardiff.

1947 Returned to USMC. Placed in Reserve Fleet

1948 *Punta Amica* Unione, S.p.a./Piero Ravano, Genoa

1962 Scrapped in Italy.

FORT FORK - Built in 1792 for the NWC by Alexander Mackenzie, this fort was situated on the north side of the Peace River five miles above the mouth or "forks" of the Smoky River in what is now the NW part of Alberta. Fort Fork was a stop on the way for many famous travellers, including David Thompson in 1802 and John Stuart in 1803. Fort Fork remained a fur trading post for the HBC for some years after the merger with the NWC. In 1875, the HBC rebuilt on the site of Fort Fork and renamed it Fort McMurray (See also Fort McMurray.)

FORT FRANKLIN 7130 gt 12.42 NS WCSB Vancouver, BC

Nominated manager, (WSA) Dodd, Thomson & Co. Ltd. (The King Line), London, UK

16.7.43 Sunk by submarine torpedo, 22.36S. 51.22E (Off Reunion Island, Indian Ocean)

FORT FRANKLIN - Except for the location of this fort the details of Franklin's expeditions are the same as in the entry dealing with Fort Enterprise. Fort Franklin was built by Sir John Franklin on the western end of Great Bear Lake, NWT, as a base for his Arctic explorations.

FORT FRASER 7130 gt 4.42 NS BDD North Van, BC

Nominated manager, (WSA) Mungo Campbell & Co. Ltd. Newcastle-on-Tyne, UK

1948 Returned to USMC. Placed in Reserve Fleet.

1959 Scrapped at Beaumont, Texas

FORT FRASER - Located on the east end of Fraser lake in Central British Columbia, this was the third fort built for the NWC in the territory which Simon Fraser called New Caledonia. It was built by John Stuart in 1806 and named after his leader, Simon Fraser. In 1817 the fort was burned but later rebuilt. Following the merger of the HBC with the NWC, the new HBC operated Fort Fraser until 1912.

FORT FREDERICK 7130 gt 11.42 NS NVSR North Van, BC

Nominated manager, (WSA) J & A Gardner & Co. Ltd. Glasgow, UK

1947 Returned to USMC

1948 *Dodin Marsano* Cia. Ligure de Nav./Andrea Marsano, Genoa, Italy

1957 *Golfo di Augusta* Same owner as above

FORT FREDERICK - The origins of Fort Frederick are the same as those described above for Fort Charnisay. In 1758 Colonel Monckton arrived with a force of Massachussetts militia. They rebuilt and garrisoned the fort, renaming it Fort Frederick. It was finally destroyed when a raiding party of Americans burned the fort in 1775. (See also Fort Charnisay and Fort la Tour.)

FORT FROBISHER 7130 gt 2.43 NS NVSR North Van, BC

Nominated manager, (WSA) Maclay & McIntyre Ltd. Glasgow, UK

1948 Returned to USMC. Placed in Reserve Fleet

1962 Scrapped in USA

FORT FROBISHER - This fort was built by Joseph Frobisher in 1772 on the Red River near the present site of Selkirk, Manitoba. Frobisher was one the famous Frobisher brothers who as free traders penetrated the rich fur regions of the Saskatchewan and Churchill Rivers cutting off much of the lucrative trade that had been going to the Hudson's Bay Company. The success of these free traders led to the establishment of the North West Fur Trading Company of Montreal (NWC) in 1783 in which the Frobisher brothers were partners. Although Frobisher's fort was the first English fort on the Red River, it was a very temporary structure which did not last long.

FORT FRONTENAC (II) 7130 gt 9.43 NS MI Sorel, QC

Nominated manager, (DOC) J & C Harrison Ltd. London

1950 *Laurentian Valley* Laurentian Marine Co. Ltd./Coulouthros Ltd. London

1957 *Aegean Sea* Sea Trading Corp.n. Panama/Coulouthros Ltd., London

1958 *Achille*   Uzeda Cia. di Nav/Matteo Scuderi, Catania, Sicily

FORT FRONTENAC - The account of Fort Frontenac has been told in the entry under Fort Cataraqui. This was also the site of what became Kingston, capital of Upper Canada and today, a cultural and administrative centre. It is also home to a major Canadian forces base and the Kingston Penitentiary.

FORT GASPEREAU   7130 gt   1.43   NS   BDD North Van, BC

Nominated manager, (WSA) Watts, Watts & Col Ltd. London
1947   Returned to USMC
1948 *Orfeo*   Soc. Ligure di Armamento, Genoa, Italy.
1963 *President Quirino*

FORT GASPEREAU - Built in 1751 by order of de la Jonquière, Governor of Canada at the head of Baie Vert not far from the Gaspereau River, a short distance from the modern village of Port Elgin, NB. A crude wagon road was built from Fort Gaspereau to Fort Beausejour. The following year the New England colonial army under Colonel Monkton, using nearby Fort Lawrence as their base, captured Fort Beausejour and Fort Gaspereau. Due to attacks on the small English garrison, the governor and council in Halifax ordered Fort Gaspereau to be abandoned and burned in 1756.

FORT GEORGE   7130 gt   4.42   NS   BDD/VDD Vancouver, BC

Nominated manager, (WSA) Sir R. Ropner & Co. Ltd. West Hartlepool.
1948   Returned to USMC. Placed in Reserve Fleet.
1962   Scrapped at Baltimore, Maryland.

FORT GEORGE - The site of this fort was near the confluence of the Fraser and Nechako Rivers in Central British Columbia. The first white man to set foot on the site was Sir Alexander Mackenzie on June 19, 1793, when on his famous overland journey to the Pacific at Bella Coola. The fort was built for the NWC in 1807 and from 1821 on it was held by the newly merged HBC. It played an important part in the fur trade of the North until the arrival of the Grand Trunk Pacific Railway in 1914. Today's City of Prince George, an industrial and university centre has grown up on the original site of the old fort.
It is also noteworthy that a "Fort" George appears at least seven times in Canadian/US history. which is something of a record reflecting the fact there were four English kings of this name in continuous succession during the period.

FORT GIBRALTAR   7130 gt   9.42   NS   NVSR North Van, BC

Nominated manager, (WSA) C.T. Bowring & Co. Ltd. London.
1947   Returned to USMC
1948 *Alcione*   Marittima Capadorso S.p.a./Fratelli D'Amico, Rome, Italy.
1963   Scrapped at Trieste, Italy

FORT GIBRALTAR - Built in 1805 for the NWC by John McDonald of Garth, it was situated at the confluence of the Assiniboine and Red Rivers where now stands the City of Winnipeg. During the conflict between the NWC and the HBC, Fort Gibraltar, with Duncan Cameron in charge, was captured by Governor Semple of the HBC in April, 1816, by whom it was completely demolished. Semple used the material salvaged from Fort Gibraltar to strengthen his company's Fort Douglas. The infuriated Nor'westers later killed Governor Semple and several of his retainers in a battle near the fort. After the merger of 1821 the new company built a new fort, the first Fort Garry on the site of Fort Gibraltar.

Fort Glenlyon as Glenlyon (Phil Chandler)

FORT GLENLYON   7130 gt   4.43   NS   WCSB Vancouver, BC

Nominated manager, (DOC) Henry M. Thomson, Edinburgh, Scotland
1950 *Glenlyon*   H.M. Thomson, Edinburgh
1959 *Soker*   Ithami Soker, Istanbul, Turkey
1964 *M. Eregli*

FORT GLENLYON - This was a HBC fort at the south end of Frances Lake near the source of the Frances River which flowed into the Dease River in what is now the Yukon territory. Built in 1841 by Robert Campbell it was first called Glenlyon House or Fort Glenlyon, then Frances Lake House and later Fort Frances. It was abandoned in 1851 but reopened about 1880. At the time of the launch of the ship it was still in operation as a HBC post. Robert Campbell was very highly thought of and explored much of Northern British Columbia.

FORT GLENORA   7130 gt   5.43   NS   WCSB Vancouver, BC

Nominated manager, (DOC) Trader Navigation Co. Ltd/Bunge & Co., London

1950 *George K*   N.G. Kyriakides Shipping Co. London

1956 *African Marquis*   General Navigation Ltd., Monrovia, Liberia/Salvatores & Racah SRL, Genoa, Italy.

25.2.58   Aground on Kassos Island, Aegean Sea, 35.23N, 26.59E, Morphou Bay to Hamburg, cargo of concentrates. Broken in two, sank, TL.

FORT GLENORA - This was the name given to Fort Mumford after the collapse of the Collins Overland Telegraph Company. Fort Mumford, built in 1863, was moved in 1874 to its new site and given the name Glenora House or Fort Glenora. (See also Fort Mumford.)

FORT GLOUCESTER   7130 gt   5.43   NS   WCSB Vancouver, BC

Nominated manager, (DOC) W.H. Souter & Co. Ltd. Newcastle-on-Tyne.

18.8.44   Damaged by E-boat torpedo near Dungeness, English Channel, in Normandy operations.

1950 *Bedford Prince*   Bedford Overseas Freighters Ltd./I.H. Mathers & Son, Halifax, NS
P.D. Marchessini & Co. Ltd. London

14.6.53   Struck rock, Gulf of Paria. 19.6.53, beached, refloated

24.8.53   Towed to New Orleans. Deemed not worth cost of repairs, CTL, 12.53 scrapped at Baltimore, Maryland.

FORT GLOUCESTER - Otherwise known as Gloucester House, this was a HBC post on Upasheway Lake which fed into the Albany River in Northern Ontario. The first interior fort built by the HBC was Fort Henley or Henley House in 1741. This was 150 miles up the Albany River. In 1774 the master at this post was instructed to choose a suitable site for another fort further inland to compete with the free traders and in 1777-8 Fort Gloucester resulted. Abandoned for several years it was reopened after the HBC-NWC merger of 1821 and then finally closed in 1860.

FORT GOOD HOPE   7130 gt   5.42   NS   BDD/VDD Vancouver, BC

Nominated manager, (WSA) R. Chapman & Son, Newcastle-on-Tyne

11.6.42   Sunk by submarine torpedo 10.19N, 80.16W (Caribbean, off Panama Canal Zone)

FORT GOOD HOPE - This was the most northerly post of the NWC, built on the Mackenzie River in 1804 in the Northwest Territories. In 1823 the newly merged HBC moved the fort one hundred miles downstream at the request of the Loucheux Indians. However, the Indians were averse to going so close to the Esquimaux camps so in 1827 the fort was moved back to the original site where it was still in operation at the time of launching the ship in 1942.

FORT GRAHAME   7130 gt   2.43   NS   NVSR North Van, BC

Nominated manager, (WSA) B.J. Sutherland & Co. Ltd. Newcastle-on-Tyne.

1948   Returned to USMC

1948 *Marco Foscarini*   Soc, Italiana di Armamento (Sidarma), Venice, Italy

1959 *Promina*   Maritenia Shipping Co./Slobodna Plovidba, Belgrade, Yugoslavia

FORT GRAHAME - A HBC post on the east bank of the Finlay River, 60 miles north of the junction with the Peace River in NE British Columbia. This fort was established about 1890 originally as an outpost to Bear's Lake further to the West. It came into prominence in 1898 during the Yukon gold rush, because it was on the route from Edmonton to Dawson City. Fort Grahame was named after the well-known chief commissioner of the company, James Allan Grahame and was still open at the time of launching the ship in 1943.

FORT GRAND RAPIDS completed as CORNISH PARK and then renamed FORT BEAUHARNOIS.

FORT GRAND RAPIDS - Located on the east side of Lake Winnipeg at the point where the Grand Rapids Lake system empties into Lake Winnipeg, Manitoba.

FORT GRANT   7130 gt   6.43   NS   WCSB Vancouver, BC

Nominated manager, (DOC) David Alexander & Sons, Glasgow.

1950 *Commodore Grant*   Northeastern Freighters Ltd. Montreal/J.P. Hadoulis Ltd. London

1961 *Sidon*

1961 *Sidon Star*

1963 *Aethon*

FORT GRANT - This was a post of the NWC on the Assiniboine River on the Saskatchewan side of the present boundary between Saskatchewan and Manitoba. It was built by Cuthbert Grant, one of the leading figures in the NWC, in 1793. Grant was involved in the Red River massacre but later became a loyal HBC functionary. It was also known as Aspin House and at a later point as Fort Aspin. It was one of several posts in the park country north of the Saskatchewan prairies which included Fort Hibernia, Fort Poplar and Fort Carlton. (The latter two are covered by separate entries.)

FORT GREEN LAKE (I) completed as MOUNT DOUGLAS PARK and (II) as BRIDGELAND PARK.

FORT GREEN LAKE - A remote settlement about 180 km NW of Prince Albert, Saskatchewan.

FORT GROUARD	7130 gt	4.43	NS	NVSR North Van, BC

Nominated manager, (DOC) Walter Runciman & Co. Ltd. Newcastle-on-Tyne.
1950 *Sea Crest*   Larix Shipping Co. London/S.G. Embiricos Ltd. London
1952 *Ernest G. Pathy*   Federal Commerce & Navigation Col Ltd. Toronto.
1955 *African Duke*   West Africa Navigation Ltd. Monrovia/Salvatores & Racah SRL, Genoa, Italy
1964   Scrapped at Yokohama, Japan.

FORT GROUARD - Until recent times this was a HBC post at the eastern end of Lesser Slave Lake which is in North Central Alberta. The NWC erected the first fort, at the western end of the lake, before 1802. It was visited by the famous explorer and geographer David Thompson in that year. This post was sometimes called Blondin's Fort. The HBC built a post nearby several years later which was seized by the NWC in 1817. After the 1821 merger the new HBC combined the two forts and in 1900 it was named Fort Grouard in honour of Father Emile-Jean Grouard of Grande Prairie, Alberta.

FORT HALKETT	7130 gt	11.42	NS	BDD/VDD Vancouver, BC

Nominated manager, (WSA) J & J Denholm Ltd. Glasgow
6.8.43   Sunk by submarine torpedo 09.30S, 26.50W (South east of Pernambuco, Brazil).

FORT HALKETT - Following the merger of the HBC and NWC in 1821, the new HBC built Fort Halkett on the left bank of the Liard River at the mouth of the Smith River on the British Columbia side of what is now the boundary between BC and the Yukon. In 1875, Fort Halkett was abandoned and trade transferred to the Toad River post, a little further down the Liard River.

Fort Hall as *Argofax* (Foto-Flite)

FORT HALL	7150 gt	8.43	Vic	NVSR North Van, BC

Nominated manager, (DOC) E.R. Management Co. Ltd. Cardiff
1946 *Argofax*   Argonaut Navigation Co. Ltd. Montreal/Mgr John C. Yemelos/Ass. with A Lusi Ltd.
      London
1959 *Strovili*   Strovili Cia. Nav. Panama/A.Lusi Ltd. London

FORT HALL - The story of this fort is told along with that of Fort Boise. The founder of the fort, N.J. Wyeth of the Columbia River Fishing & Trading Co. returned to Boston and published a book about the west which was of great value to his countrymen. After the abandonment of Fort Boise, Fort Hall was isolated. Communications were no longer possible so men and supplies were moved north to Flathead's House and Fort Hall was abandoned.

FORT HARRISON completed as GOLDSTREAM PARK.

FORT HARRISON - The origins appear to go back to a trading post established by Revillon Freres in 1909, located on the east shore of Hudson Bay at Portland Promontory, Cape Dufferin, at or near the Inukjuak River in Quebec province. The HBC took the post over in 1920 and it was probably named as "Port" Harrison for Benjamin Harrison, brother-in-law of a former Hudson Bay governor. Harrison served as a HBC committeeman from 1807 to 1854. A religious man, Harrison sent more than three dozen missionaries to Rupertsland.

FORT HENLEY	7130 gt	11.43	NS	USY Montreal, QC

Nominated manager, (DOC) Sir R. Ropner & Co. Ltd. West Hartlepool
1950 *Pine Hill*   Halifax Overseas Freighters Ltd./I.H. Mathers & Son. Halifax/Counties S.M.
      Co. Ltd. London

1964 *Newmoat*

FORT HENLEY - Situated on the north shore of the Albany River about 150 miles from its mouth on James Bay, Northern Ontario. For three quarters of a century the HBC had kept rigidly to its policy of making the Indians come with their trade to the forts on Hudson's and James Bays, but the aggressiveness of the French traders forced the HBC to build inland. Fort Henley or Henley House was the first and hundreds followed. It was built in 1741, destroyed by the French in 1760, but rebuilt in 1764 and operated for nearly a century.

FORT HIGHFIELD (I & II) completed as YOHO PARK (I & II)

FORT HIGHFIELD - Originally built by the Russians as Redoubt St. Dionysius in 1834, opposite the mouth of the Stikine River, on the north end of Wrangell Island in what is now Alaska, it was also known as Fort Highfield. From here the Russians were doing an active trade with the Yukon and beyond. When the HBC attempted to send its ship Dryad up the river to establish a post on British territory, the Russians prevented this. The Russians said that any trade through their territory was forbidden, but the HBC circumvented this by obtaining a lease of the strip of Alaskan coastline required to obtain access to the hinterland. With this came possession of Fort Highfield which the HBC renamed Fort Stikine. When Russia sold its Alaska holdings to the United States, Fort Stikine reverted to the US who renamed it Fort Wrangell. (See also Fort Stikine and Fort Wrangell.)

FORT HOWE	7130 gt	11.42	NS	BDD North Van, BC

Nominated manager, (WSA) Frank C. Strick & Co. Ltd. London

30.9.43   Sunk by submarine torpedo 37.19N 06.40 E (Off Bona, North Africa).

FORT HOWE - This fort was built on a high hill above Portland Point at the mouth of the St. John River in what is now the Province of New Brunswick. It was built as the result of appeals made to Halifax authorities to provide protection to the English settlers on the Saint John River after the destruction of Fort Frederick by the Americans in 1775. After it was built its guns never had the opportunity to be fired at an enemy. It was abandoned as a military post in 1821.

Fort Hudson's Hope as *Italvega* (Phil Chandler)

FORT HUDSON'S HOPE	7130 gt	10.42	NS	VMD Victoria, BC

Nominated manager, (WSA) Glen & Co. Ltd. Glasgow

1947		Returned to USMC
1948	*Vega*	Italia Soc. Anon. de Nav (The Italia Line) Genoa.
1950	*Italvega*	Italnavi Soc. di Nav. per Azioni, Genoa, Italy
1951		Converted to diesel
1966	*Bellport*	

FORT HUDSON'S HOPE - Built in 1803 by Simon Fraser for the NWC as a base for Fraser's explorations to the West, it was also known as Rocky Mountain House and was situated on the north bank of the Peace River at the mouth of the Middle River in what is now NE British Columbia. Following the 1821 merger, the new HBC took over Fort Hudson's Hope, but closed it temporarily in 1823 to punish the Indians for the massacre at Fort St. John. The post was moved in 1875 and again in 1880. At the time of launching the ship in 1942, it was still in operation.

FORT ISLAND	7150 gt	4.44	Vic	BDD/VDD Vancouver, BC

Nominated manager, (DOC) Hain Steamship Co. Ltd. London

1946	*Mont Rolland*	Montship Lines Ltd., Montreal/Ass. with Buries Markes Ltd., London and Louis Dreyfus et Cie, Paris.
1949	*Maria Peolina G*	Gestioni Eseroizio Navi, Genoa
1960		Scrapped at Spezia, Italy.

Fort Island (Canadian Forces, Ottawa)

FORT ISLAND - In 1792, Fort George on the North Saskatchewan River was the most westerly of the NWC forts about four and half miles above the mouth of Moose Creek in what is now Alberta. In 1801 a new post was built 18 miles further upstream on an island in the river. Named Fort Island or Isle de l'isle it brought about the abandonment of Fort George. Fort Island had the advantage of being easily defensible, but this in turn guaranteed its demise on account of the difficulty of access and the fact that the NWC in its constant aim of moving further west built a new fort opposite the mouth of the Vermilion River. Thus seven years after its completion Fort Island was abandoned.

FORT JASPER	7130 gt	3.43	NS	NVSR North Van, BC

Nominated manager, (WSA) Common Brothers Ltd. Newcastle-on-Tyne
1948   Returned to USMC. Placed in Reserve Fleet.
1959   Scrapped at Baltimore.

FORT JASPER - This was a HBC post on the upper Athabaska River in what is now western Alberta. It was built in 1799 at the outlet to Brule Lake and first called Rocky Mountain House. In 1801 Jasper Hawes was in charge and moved the fort upstream to the outlet of Jasper Lake and the name changed to Jasper House or Fort Jasper. It was important up to 1861, but by 1875 it was practically abandoned. If the name came from Hawes, which seems likely, it was passed on to the park and its lake. This seems to be one of the few examples of a fort and a major park having received the given name of an individual. (See entry also under Jasper Park.)

FORT JEMSEG	7130 gt	1.43	NS	BDD/VDD Vancouver, BC

Nominated manager, (WSA) Hain Steamship Co. Ltd.   London
23.9.43   Sunk by submarine torpedo, 53.18N 40.24W (South of Cape Farewell, Greenland)

CAPE FAREWELL - This was the first post built by the English on the Saint John River, in present day New Brunswick. It was built by Thomas Temple, Governor of Acadia, as a post to trade with the Indians. In 1667, following the Treaty of Breda, Acadia was returned to France. Temple was succeeded by a French governor, de Grandfontaine, in 1670. In 1674 a Dutch invading force captured Fort Jemseg and proclaimed Acadia to be a Dutch possession which they called New Holland. The New Englanders created many difficulties for the Dutch West Indies Company which tried to carry on an exclusive trade and a Boston force finally dispossessed the Dutch. France regained possession and rebuilt Jemseg, but it was finally abandoned in 1692.

FORT KASKASKIA	7150 gt	9.43	Vic	WCSB Vancouver, BC

Nominated manager, (DOC) Counties Ship Management Ltd. London
1946 *Hants County*   Acadia Overseas Freighters Ltd./I.H. Mathers & Son. Halifax
                        Ass. Counties S.M. Co. Ltd. London
1949 *Tel-Aviv*   Israel America Line Ltd. Haifa/Shoham Sherutey Hayam Ltd. Managers
1961 *Anatoli*
1965 *Sunrise*

FORT KASKASKIA - In 1675 Pere Marquette started a mission for the Kaskaskia Indians near the present day town of Utica, Illinois. Transferred 25 years later to Kaskaskia in the same state, it developed into the first permanent white settlement in the Mississippi Valley. Rich soil and well tilled fields made it the foremost agricultural district between the St. Lawrence and the Gulf of Mexico. For protection against the Indians Fort Kaskaskia was soon built. A Monastery and a college was established by the Jesuits. The Seven Years War brought an end to French rule. In 1778 during the American Revolution, General Rogers Clark captured Fort Kaskaskia for the American side.

Vessel Name:	Tonnage:	Completion date:	Type:	Builder & Yard location
FORT KILMAR	7150 gt	5.44	Vic	BDD North Van, BC

Nominated manager, (DOC) Ellerman & Bucknall S.S Co. London

1947 *Islandside*	Andros Shipping Co. Ltd. Montreal (March Shipping Agency Ltd.)
	Ass. Goulandris Bros. London & New York.
1952 *Catherine M.S.*	Delfin Cia. Nav. SA. Panama/Mgr. Evans Shipping Corp.n. New York
10.2.54	Aground three miles off Nojima Saki, Tokyo Bay, 34.53N 139.55E, CTL, sold for scrap.

FORT KILMAR - This fort was built by the HBC in 1822 about 25 miles from the outflow point of Babine Lake. Fort Kilmar was also known as Fort Babine, it was built to supply dried salmon to New Caledonia. In 1872 those joining the Omineca gold rush opened a new route from the mines to Hazelton on the Skeena. Fort Kilmar was moved to the upper end of Babine Lake to take advantage of the new traffic. Original spelling of Kilmar was Kilmaurs.

| FORT KOOTENAY | 7130 gt | 8.42 | NS | BDD/VDD Vancouver, BC |

Nominated manager, (WSA) J. Morrison & Son Ltd. Newcastle-on-Tyne

1947	Returned to USMC
1948 *Mongioia*	Nav. Alta Italia, S.p.a., Genoa
1950	Converted to turbines with oil firing
1966 *Montjorge*	

FORT KOOTENAY - Built in 1807 for the NWC on the west side of the Columbia River one mile downstream from the north of Windermere Lake, it was the first post erected in what is now SE British Columbia. It was established by David Thompson, one of Canada's greatest explorers who explored the Columbia River from its source to the Pacific Ocean. Following the merger of 1821 the new HBC took over Fort Kootenay.

| FORT KULLYSPELL | 7150 gt | 8.43 | Vic | WCSB Vancouver, BC |

Nominated manager, (DOC) Hall Brothers Ltd. Newcastle-on-Tyne

1947 *Westminster County*	Acadia Overseas Freighters Ltd./I.H. Mathers & Son. Halifax
	Ass. Counties S.M. Co. Ltd. London
1949 *Yaffo*	Israel America Line Ltd. Haifa/Mngd. Shoham Sherutey Hayam Ltd.

FORT KULLYSPELL - Was the third in a series of trading posts built by David Thompson during his service with the NWC and his involvement with the Columbia Basin. In 1809 he erected Fort Kullyspell on a point extending into Pend d'Oreille Lake, between Hope and Clark's Fork Station in the present State of Idaho. Fort Saleesh and Fort Spokane followed. Fort Kullyspell was important chiefly as a headquarters and stopping place for Thompson as he did his work on the Columbia, made surveys of every mile travelled and backed them with astronomical observations. (See Fort Kootenay, Fort Saleesh and Fort Spokane.)

| FORT LA BAYE | 7150 gt | 10.43 | Vic | WCSB Vancouver, BC |

Nominated manager, (DOC) Counties Ship Management Ltd. London

1947 *Digby County*	Acadia Overseas Freighters Ltd./I.H. Mather & Son, Halifax
	Ass. Counties S.M. Ltd. London
1950 *Travelstar*	Cia. Polyna Maritima SA, Panama/Triton Shipping Inc. New York
	C.M. Lemos & Co. Ltd. London
16.10.54	Aground, Bucknor Bay, Okinawa, 26.08N 127.51E
17.10.54	On fire, CTL. Jan. 55 salvage abandoned.

FORT LA BAYE - The French built the first fort on Green Bay, in what is now Wisconsin some time between 1718 and 1721. They called their fort La Baye and it commanded the best portage route to the Mississippi. A period of prosperity followed when Marin took charge until the government suspended fur trading licenses and auctioned off posts to the highest bidder. La Baye was purchased by a large Montreal company which entered into illegal trade with the couriur-de-bois. It was in effect an invitation for abuse and until the return of the license system eight years later, Fort la Baye was burned twice and changed hands three times. In 1749 the government adopted a policy permitting the governor to dispose of the various posts to his favourites. Fort la Baye went to Couterot who was both corrupt and inexperienced. Abandoned by the French it passed to the British following the Seven Years War. (See also Fort Marin and Fort Sakisdac.)

| FORT LA CLOCHE | 7130 gt | 4.44 | NS | MI Sorel, QC |

Nominated manager, (DOC) Buries Markes Ltd., London.

1950 *Akti Hill*	Nova Scotia Marine Enterprises Co. Ltd./Nordic Ship Management Co. Montreal
	Counties S.M. Co. London
1958 *Cape Drepanon*	Merida Cia. Nav. SA, Panama/Mngd. George Nicolau Ltd. London
1.2.61	Aground on Huckleberry Is. Long Island Sound, NY
12.2.61	Refloated, CTL, Sold for scrapping.

FORT LA CLOCHE - This was one of many posts built on the Ottawa River during the latter part of the 18th century. Built in 1790 by the NWC to secure the company's interests on the trail to the north and west. It continued to operate after the HBC -NWC merger of 1821 and records indicate it was still functioning in 1841. The fort takes its name from a large nearby rock which when struck rings like a bell.

FORT LA HAVE 7150 gt 3.44 Vic BDD North Van, BC

    Nominated manager, (DOC) Hain Steamship Co. Ltd. London

1947 *Angusglen*   Lunham & Moore (Canada) Ltd. Montreal/Ass. with E.E. Dean & Co. Ltd. and Simpson Spence & Young Ltd. both of London.

1954 *Cape Melan*   Lyle Shipping Co. Ltd. Glasgow

1955 *Aghios Spyridon*   A.C. Hadjipateras, Athens, Greece under the flag of Costa Rica. Mgr. Harry Hadjipateras Bros. Ltd. London.

27.5.59   Aground and on fire, north coast of Cuba, 22.53N 83.48 W, fire extinguised.

19.6.59   Refloated.

1961   Scrapped at Troon, Scotland.

FORT LA HAVE - Acadia had been returned to the French during the reign of King Charles I of England, the king who later lost his head at the hands of Oliver Cromwell and his roundheads. Charles had wanted to make a financial settlement with the French for the promised dowry of his wife Henrietta-Maria. In 1632 the Treaty of St. Germain-en-Laye returned their old lands, including Acadia, to the French. In turn England received the Queen's dowry. The first French governor was Isaac de Razilly who established his headquarters west of present day Lunenberg, NS at Fort La Have and around it grew a community. After this the fort lapsed into unimportance and was finally burned in 1654.

FORT LA MAUNE 7130 gt 10.42 NS NVSR North Van, BC

    Nominated manager, (WSA) Booth Steamship Co. Ltd. Liverpool

25.1.44   Sunk by submarine torpedo, 13.04N, 56.30E, North East of the Island of Socotra, off the Horn of Africa.

FORT LA MAUNE - This fort was built by Charles Dulhut, Sieur de la Tourette in 1684 at the mouth of the Ombabika River on the NE shore of Lake Nipigon, in modernday Ontario. It was an important link on the route from Hudsons Bay to the Great Lakes. Pierre de la Verendrye was in charge in 1726, but after the cession of Canada in 1763 to the British it was evacuated and the fort destroyed.

FORT LA MONTEE 7130 gt 8.42 NS NVSR North Van, BC

    Nominated manager, (WSA) J & C Harrison, Ltd. London

4.8.43   On fire at Algiers. Forepart blew up, afterpart sunk by gunfire. (See separate account.)

FORT LA MONTEE - Built in 1797 for the NWC, it was situated in the North Saskatchewan River a few miles west of the present City of Prince Albert, SK. Fort La Montée was so named because it was here that canoes were exchanged for horses by traders going to the Beaver River and thence north, west or overland to the South Saskatchewan River. The HBC established their important post at nearby Fort Carlton in 1810. Each of these posts were provision depots for the traders of their respective companies. (See Fort Carlton.)

Fort La Prairie as *Elm Hill* (I.G. Stewart collection)

FORT LA PRAIRIE (II) 7130 gt 11.43 NS USY Montreal, QC

    Nominated manager, (DOC) Common Brothers Ltd., Newcastle-on-Tyne.

1950 *Elm Hill*   Halifax Overseas Freighters Ltd./I.H. Mather & Son, Halifax Counties S.M. Co. Ltd., London

FORT LA PRAIRIE - From 1668 to 1676 this was an Indian fort consisting only of a wooden fence surrounding a settlement of Mohawks who had converted to Christianity. It was situated on the present site of the town of Laprairie on the south bank of the St. Lawrenec near Montreal. In 1687 Gedeon de Catalogne built a strong new fort which served as protection for fifty years. During the night of August 11, 1691, the settlement was attacked by Captain Peter Schuyler leading a small force of New York settlers. The village was burned but the fort was not taken. In 1775 it was temporarily occupied by American troops under Major Brown. The British used it as a blockhouse from 1775 to 1814 and afterwards as an Imperial barracks until 1880. In that year Fort la Prairie caught fire and its remains were finally removed in 1910.

Vessel Name:	Tonnage:	Completion date:	Type:	Builder & Yard location
FORT LA REINE	7130 gt	7.42	NS	BDD/VDD Vancouver, BC

Nominated manager, (WSA) Jos. Constantine & Sons Ltd. Middlesborough

17.8.42   Sunk by submarine torpedo, 18.30N, 75.20W, (North east of Jamaica).

FORT LA REINE - Built in 1738 on the north bank of the Assiniboine River where the town of Portage la Prairie now stands, it was established by Pierre de la Verendrye who was the first recorded white man to reach the great plains. After the death of Verendrye his successor, St. Pierre, made his headquarters at Fort La Reine. It suffered severely as the result of Indian raids in 1752 and 1754 and had to be rebuilt. It was abandoned in 1756 when the French garrison was withdrawn east to fight against the British during the Seven Years War.

FORT LAC LA RONGE	7130 gt	6.42	NS	BDD North Van, BC

Nominated manager, (WSA) Jos. Constantine & Sons Ltd. Middlesborough

3.8.44   Damaged by one man-torpedo 49.22N 00.21W, Towed into Appledore, North Devon.
         Beached and laid up in River Torridge. Sold direct by USMC to British shipbreakers.

FORT LAC LA RONGE - Built in 1781 by Peter Pond, explorer and trader, on the west shore of Lac La Ronge. It was in the heart of the rich beaver and otter country of the English River, afterwards renamed the Churchill, in what is now Northern Saskatchewan. In 1778. Pond while acting for a group of independent cooperative traders found the Methye portage accross the height of land separating the Churchill and Athanaska Rivers. He was thus the first white man to reach the headwaters of the Mackenzie River. With the founding of the NWC in Montreal in 1783 they took over Fort Lac La Ronge, which they operated for several years.

FORT LA TOUR	7130 gt	5.43	NS	MI Montreaal, QC

Nominated manager, (DOC) Stephens, Sutton Ltd. Newcastle-on-Tyne

1951 *Assimina K*   Megantic Freighters Ltd. Montreal/J.P. Hadoulis Ltd. London.
1959 *Jean Baptiste*   Same as above
1960   Scrapped at Blyth, Northumberland, UK

FORT LA TOUR - The story of Fort la Tour is also part of the history of Fort Charnisay,.

FORT LA TRAITE	7130 gt	12.42	NS	WCSB Vancouver, BC

Nominated manager. (WSA) Evan Thomas, and Radcliffe Ltd. Cardiff

1947   Returned to USMC
1948 *Italsole*   Italnavi Soc. di Nav. per Azioni, Genoa
1949   Converted to diesel. This owner was related to the FIAT
         Company and its ships were adapted as car-carriers
1965 *Freeport.*

FORT LA TRAITE - In 1774 the famous fur traders and explorers Joseph and Thomas Frobisher, discovered Frog Passage an important portage over the height of land in Eastern Saskatchewan which separates the drainages of the Churchill and Saskatchewan Rivers. At the northern end they built Fort La Traite. The Frobishers, with others, established the NWC who maintained the post until 1821 and the merger with the HBC. It continued in the service of the new HBC for some years after.

FORT LAJOIE	7130 gt	12.42	NS	BDD North Van, BC

Nominated manager, (WSA) Lyle Shipping Co. Ltd., Glasgow

1.12.43   Damaged by bombs or debris following explosion of an ammunition ship at Bari, Italy
         (see separate story).
1947   Returned to USMC. Placed in reserved fleet.
1959   Scrapped at Mobile, Alabama.

FORT LAJOIE - Built by the French at the entrance to what is now known as Charlottetown, PEI. The island was then known as Isle St. Jean. In 1745 the British captured Fort Louisbourg and in the same year captured Fort Lajoie, but under the terms of the Treaty of Aix-la-Chapelle in 1748 it was restored to France. Governor Bonaventure then erected stronger defences which were augmented by more improvements made by Colonel Francoeur which turned it into a real fort. Lajoie was a base for the French in their attacks on the British during the Seven Years War. With the conclusion of the war and France's withdrawal from Canada the name of the fort became Fort Amherst and the island became Prince Edward Island.

FORT LANGLEY	7150 gt	5.45	Vic	VMD Victoria, BC

Launched as *Montebello Park (II)*
Nominated manager, (DOC) Alfred Holt & Co. Ltd. Liverpool

1945   Finished as a Stores Issuing Ship, renamed *Fort Langley* while in process.
1954   Taken on permanent strength of the Royal Navy.

FORT LANGLEY - Located on the lower reaches of the Fraser River in the lower mainland of British Columbia, Fort Langley dates back to 1827 when it was built by John McMillan for the HBC. Situated on rich fertile land it provided produce for the HBC settlements on the coast and even the Russian settlements in Alaska. Aside from being the first white settlement in BC, it was also the first west of the Great Lakes to export wheat. It exported the first shipment of fish to the Sandwich Islands about 1846, foreshadowing the future commercial centre at Vancouver. The influx of gold-seekers increased its commercial importance further. In 1858 British Columbia became a crown colony and it was here, in effect the first capital of BC, that Governor Sir James Douglas and Chief Justice Sir Matthew Begbie were sworn in.

FORT LAWRENCE 7130 gt 1.43 NS BDD North Van, BC

Nominated manager, (WSA) Frank C. Strick & Co. Ltd. London

| 1948 | Returned to USMC. Placed in Reserve Fleet. |
| 1959 | Scrapped at Mobile, Alabama. |

FORT LAWRENCE - Situated near the shore of Chignecto Bay on the Nova Scotia side of the boundary separating Nova Scotia from New Brunswick, Fort Lawrence was constructed in 1750 by Major Charles Lawrence on orders from Edward Cornwallis, then governor of Nova Scotia. It was from Fort Lawrence that Colonel Monckton with his colonial army from Massachusetts set out to capture nearby Fort Beausejour from the French on June 4, 1755. After a 12-day siege, Fort Beausejour was captured and made into the chief stronghold of the British. Fort Lawrence was evacuated in 1756.

FORT LENNOX 7130 gt 9.43 NS MI Montreal, QC

Nominated manager, (DOC) J & C Harrison Ltd. London.

1948 *Caribou County*	Acadia Overseas Freighters Ltd./I.H. Mathers & Son, Halifax
	Counties S.M. Co. Ltd. London
1950 *Harrow Hill*	Vancouver Oriental Line Ltd. Vancouver/I.H. Mathers & Son, Halifax
	Counties S.M. Co. Ltd. London
1960 *Silver Peak*	

FORT LENNOX - This was one of the largest fortresses built in Canada during the previous two centuries. Situated on the Ile-aux-Noix in the Richelieu River, about 12 miles south of St. Johns, QC, the fortifications were originally built by the French in 1759 to resist the advance of the English from the South. Its surrender in 1760 to an English army under General Haviland was a prelude to the fall of Montreal and the transfer of New France to British rule following the peace terms of the Seven Years War. Fort Lennox fell to an American force under Schuyler and Montgomery in 1775 but was evacuated by the Americans the following year. It was greatly strengthened under orders from the Imperial government in 1782 and again during the war of 1812. The fort was abandoned as a military post in 1870. It served for a while as a prison and is now part of Fort Lennox National Historic Park.

FORT LIARD 7130 gt 9.42 NS VMD Victoria, BC

Nominated manager, (WSA) Chr. Salvesen & Co. Edinburgh.

| 1948 | Returned to USMC. Placed in Reserve Fleet. |
| 1958 | Scrapped at Baltimore, Maryland |

FORT LIARD - The first post on the turbulent Liard and one of the earliest in the vast northern territory. It was built by the HBC in the District of Mackenzie a few miles beyond British Columbia's northern border and did a big trade up the Mackenzie, Slave and Athabaska Rivers. Fort Liard was operated by the HBC for over 140 years at the time of launching the ship in 1942.

FORT LIVINGSTONE 7130 gt 11.42 NS BDD North Van, BC

Nominated manager, (WSA) Wing Line Ltd. Cardiff, Wales

1948	Returned to USMC
1948 *Pietro Orseolo*	Soc. Italiana de Armamento, Venice
1960 *Bor*	

FORT LIVINGSTONE - Most commonly western forts were built for one or other of the trading companies with the North West Mounted Police following to establish a police presence. Fort Livingstone was built expressly for the NWMP. Today the town has grown into Swan River, Manitoba. In 1875 Fort Livingstone became the capital of the North West Territories and headquarters of the NWMP, a distinction it held for two years.

FORT LONGUEUIL 7130 gt 12.42 NS USL Montreal, QC

Nominated manager, (WSA) James Chambers & Co. Ltd. Liverpool

| 19.9.43 | Sunk by submarine torpedo, 10S 68E (approx. position south of the Chagos Islands, roughly midway between Ceylon and Madagascar) |

FORT LONGUEUIL - Built between 1685 and 1690 by Charles le Moyne de Longueuil II, the fort was situated on the south shore of the St. Lawrence River opposite the Island of Montreal on the present day site of the town of Longueuil. In 1775, during the American Revolution, General Richard Montgomery brought his army up the Richelieu in an effort to drive the British from Canada. He occupied Montreal and laid siege to Quebec. In the process Fort Longueuil fell to the Americans. Later it was garrisoned by the British until it was partly burnt in 1792. The ruins were demolished in 1810 and its stones used in the construction of the present Church of Longueuil.

FORT LOUISBOURG   7130 gt   4.42   NS   CVL Montreal, QC

Nominated manager, (WSA) Wm. Thompson & Co. (Ben Line) Edinburgh

20.1.44   Damaged by bombs, Surrey Commercial Docks, London.

1947   Returned to USMC, Place in Reserve Fleet.

3.57   Converted to floating grain storage hulk.

1960   Scrapped at Baltimore, Maryland.

FORT LOUISBOURG - One of the great classic fortresses of North America. Following the Treaty of Utrecht in 1713, Acadia was transferred to the British, but Cape Breton Island was left in possession of the French who built this fort in 1713. It commanded the entrance to the St. Lawrence. In 1745 it fell to a New England force under General Pepperell with the aid of a small British fleet. In 1748 the Treaty of Aix-la-Chapelle gave Louisbourg back to France in exchange for Madras in India which was returned to the British. The Seven Years War broke out in 1756. The first British success was the capture in 1758 of Fort Louisbourg, the first major step in a master plan to oust the French from the continent. This gave them command of the Gulf of St. Lawrence and paved the way for Wolfe's capture of Quebec. Louisbourg is now preserved as an historical site.

FORT MACHAULT   7150 gt   11.43   Vic   BDD North Van, BC

Nominated manager, (DOC) Larrinaga Steamship Co. Ltd. Liverpool

1947 *L'Emerillon*   Papachristidis Company Ltd. Montreal

18.2.49   Aground Sorelles Rocks, 40 miles East of Bona, North Africa at 37.23N 8.33E, TL

FORT MACHAULT - This was a French outpost built by Marin on the site of what is now Franklin, Pennsylvania, near the junction of French Creek and the Allegheny River. Ordered by Duquesne, Governor of New France to strengthen the defences of the Ohio Valley against the British, Marin commandeered a house from a British trader in 1753 and established Fort Machault. After the withdrawal of the French following defeat in the Seven Years War, Fort Machault quickly fell into disuse when the British built nearby Fort Venango. The latter was renamed Fort Franklin when the Americans took possession. (See entry for Fort Venango.)

FORT MACKINAC (I & II) completed as BEATON PARK and DOMINION PARK.

FORT MACKINAC - Established by French explorers in 1634, it was originally known as Fort Michilmackinac and was located on Mackinac Island. There were three distinct military posts that had been built by the French, British and Americans at various times, it remained an American post until 1894 when it was turned over to the State of Michigan to become a state park.

FORT MAISONNEUVE   7130 gt   5.43   NS   USL Montreal, QC

Nominated manager, (DOC) Chellew Steamship Management Co. Ltd. Cardiff.

15.12.44   Sunk by mine near bouy NF11, Scheldt Estuary. (See separate story.)

FORT MAISONNEUVE - On May 18, 1642 a small French party of colonists landed on the Island of Montreal under the leadership of Pierre de Chomedy, Sieur de Maisonneuve. They established themselves at what had previously been Champlain's Place Royale where in 1611 Champlain had started a trading post. Chomedy's party built a stockade for protection against the troublesome Iroquois which was Fort Maisonneuve. The settlement that grew up around it was known as Ville-Marie. It was known later as Hochelaga and in 1701 became officially known as Montreal. (See also Fort Ville Marie.)

FORT MARIN   7150 gt   10.43   Vic   NVSR North Van, BC

Nominated manager, (DOC) E & R Management Ltd. Cardiff

1947 *Argojohn*   Argonaut Navigation Co. Ltd. Montreal/John C. Yemelos, mgr/Ass./A.Lusi Ltd. London

1960 *Kertis*

FORT MARIN - Paul Marin de la Malgue (also recorded as La Marque) was sent south by Duquesne to build a fort on the Mississippi to control the Sioux and increase trading returns from Green Bay. The site chosen was on the west side of Lake Pepin near the present day City of Frontenac, Minnesota. In what might be described as an early form of racketeering, the governor, La Jonquière, granted a monopoly to a chosen few. Marin was granted the Sioux territory, his son received trading rights for La Pointe and the commandant, probably Couterot, at Fort La Baye was compliant. The plan was a financial success for the few, but the effect on the fur trade was disastrous and led to the downfall of New France. The trade monopoly was only broken with the death of La Jonquière and the senior Marin. (See also Fort La Baye)

FORT MASSAC   7150 gt   9.43   Vic   BDD/VDD Vancouver, BC

Nominated manager, (DOC) John Cory & Sons Ltd., Cardiff

1.2.46   In collision off the Sunk lightship, with *Thornaby* (Sir R.Ropner & Co.).

       Sank, TL. 51.53N 01.32.E (Thames Estuary area)

FORT MASSAC - Originally named Fort L'Assumption, this fort was built in 1757 by the commandant in charge at Fort Chartres. It was on the present day site of Metropolis, Illinois, about 120 miles below the mouth of the Wabash River. Named for the Marquis de Massiac following his appointment in 1758, the spelling variation to Massac was caused by a mistake in assuming that Massac alluded to a legendary massacre. In 1765 the Chickasaw Indians attacked and burned the post which remained a ruin until the US Government rebuilt it 1794, retained the name Fort Massac and maintained a garrison there until 1814,

Vessel Name:	Tonnage:	Completion date:	Type:	Builder & Yard location

FORT MATTAGAMI   7130 gt   5.44   NS   MI Montreal, QC

Nominated manager, (DOC) J. Cory & Sons, Cardiff, Wales.

1948 *Haligonian Princess*   Acadia Overseas Freighters (Halifax) Ltd./I.H. Mathers & Son, Halifax Counties S.M. Co. Ltd. London

1950 *Denmark Hill*   Acadia Overseas Freighters Ltd. (Mathers). Vessel renamed when it came under direct management of Counties S.M. Co. from London.

FORT MATTAGAMI - Built in 1673 by de la Tourette, this was a French post situated at the outlet of Lake Piscoutagami on the Frederick House branch of the Abitibi River in present day Ontario. A legend on an old map refers to it as "Little Fort St. Germain which hinders ye Assinipoels to come down to Port Nelson." Fort St. Germain must have been a previous name although this appears to be the only reference to it, but it was also known as Fort Piscoutagami. Probably destroyed by the French when they left Canada, the site was taken up by the HBC who moved Frederick House there, using Fort Mattagami as the name. The post closed in 1794.

FORT MAUREPAS   7130 gt   9.42   NS   WCSB Vancouver, BC

Nominated manager, (WSA) J & C Harrison Ltd. London.

1947   Returned to USMC.

1948 *Rosa Corrado*   Soc. di Nav. Corrado, Genoa

1964 *Tindari*

11.65   Scrapped at Vado, Italy

FORT MAUREPAS - A French fur trading post on the north side of the mouth of the Winnipeg River where it empties into Lake Winnipeg in modernday Manitoba. It was built in 1733 by the eldest son of Pierre de la Verendrye and named after Count Maurepas, minister of colonies in the government of King Louis XV of France. Twice attacked by Indians and destroyed by fire there was no trace of the fort in 1775 when it was passed by Alexander Henry.

FORT McDONNELL   7150 gt   8.44   Vic   BDD Vancouver, BC

Nominated manager, (DOC) Alfred Holt & Co. Ltd. Liverpool

1947 *Cliffside*   Andros Shipping Co. Ltd. Montreal/Ass. Goulandris Bros. Ltd. London

1951 *Cavodoro*   Valedor Cia Nav. SA. Panama/Mgd. Capeside Steamship Co. Ltd. London, the UK subsidiary of Orion Shipping & Trading of New York, both of which in turn were controlled by Goulandris.

1953 *Captain Lukis*   Cia. Europa Commercial y Maritima, Panama/Mgd. D.J. Fafalios, Chios, Greece.

FORT McDONNELL - Established by the NWC in 1784, this NWC post was located at the junction of the Assiniboine and Souris Rivers, in present day Manitoba. This was the principal approach to the Mandan Indians in North Dakota. The HBC saw benefits in this trade also and established two rival posts in the vicinity. When the HBC-NWC merger took place Fort McDonnell, from being a place of prime importance, fell into disuse and was abandoned.

FORT McLEOD   7130 gt   6.42   NS   YAR Victoria, BC

Nominated manager, (WSA) Glen Line Ltd. London

3.3.44   Sunk by submarine torpedo and gunfire, 02.01N 77.06E (East of the Maldive Islands, off West coast of India).

FORT McLEOD - Simon Fraser built this post in 1805 for the NWC. It is situated at the north end of Lake McLeod and was on the early route from Fort Chipewyan on Lake Athabaska, via the Peace and Parsnip Rivers, to Fort St. John, Fort George and Fort Fraser in Central British Columbia. Named after Archibald Norman McLeod who was in charge of the Athabaska district of the NWC, it was taken over by the new HBC in 1821 following the merger with NWC. At the time of launching the ship in 1942, the post was still in operation.

FORT McLOUGHLIN   7130 gt   5.42   NS   BDD North Van, BC

Nominated manager, (WSA) Common Bros. Ltd. Newcastle-on-Tyne

1948   Returned to USMC

1948 *Sebastiano Venier*   Soc. Ital de Arm. "Sidarma", Venice

1952 *Airone*   Marittima Napoletana Soc.di Nav. Naples. Mgd./Giovanni Longobardo

12.65   Scrapped at Vado, Italy

FORT McLOUGHLIN - This fort was built in 1833 by Duncan Finlayson, Donald Manson, and William McNeill for the HBC. It was located on Millbank Sound on the BC coast about half way between Vancouver and Prince Rupert. Named after John McLoughlin, chief factor for the HBC who was in charge of the Columbia District, it operated for ten years and then closed when all operations for the company were concentrated in Fort Camosun on the site of present day Victoria.

FORT McMURRAY   7130 gt   8.42   NS   BDD North Van, BC

Nominated manager, (WSA) Morel & Co. Cardiff

1947   Returned to USMC. Placed in Reserve Fleet

1948 *Pegaso*   Achille Lauro fu Gioacchino & C. Naples, Italy

FORT McMURRAY - The early history of Fort McMurray is that of Fort Fork. After rebuilding and restablishment by the HBC in 1875 the place gradually took on great economic importance and is at the centre of the tar sands developments in Northern Alberta.

FORT McPHERSON   7130 gt   4.43   NS   NVSR North Van, BC

Nominated manager, (DOC) Counties Ship Management Co. Ltd. London

11.6.44 — Damaged by bombs 50.02N 00.36W

26.7.44 — Damaged by flying bomb, Victoria Docks, London

1950 *Labrador* — Waverley Overseas Freighters Ltd./I.H. Mathers & Son, Halifax/Mgd. Fafalios Ltd. London

1956 *Poseidon* — Cia. Filioi di Nav. Panama/D.J. Fafalios. Greece

1960 *Marichristina*

FORT McPHERSON - Was built for the HBC in 1840 by trader John Bell. His explorations to the west were of considerable importance. He explored the Bell River which flows into the Porcupine River and in 1842 went down the Porcupine to the Yukon River in what was then Russian territory but is now Alaska. For many years Fort McPherson was the most northerly post of the HBC, but while it no longer holds that distinction it was still a functioning post for the company when the ship of the name was completed in 1943.

FORT MEDUCTIC   7130 gt   1.43   NS   BDD North Van, BC

Nominated manager, (WSA) J. Morrison & Son, Newcastle-on-Tyne

1947 — Returned to USMC, Placed in Reserve Fleet

1959 — Scrapped at Mobile, Alabama

FORT MEDUCTIC - The date of building is uncertain beyond knowing it was during the 17th century. It was built on the site of what had previously been an Indian fort forty miles up the St. John River from Fredericton. A portage led from Fort Meductic to the Eel River and was the chief route between Acadia and New England. It was much used by raiding war parties who attacked and pillaged the frontier settlements. The fort was also built as a protection for the Acadian Indians who were in dread of the Mohawks. After the Indian dangers had passed the fort was demolished in 1767.

FORT MIAMI   7130 gt   8.42   NS   NVSR North Van, BC

Launched as *Fort Rouge*, completed as *Mount Robson Park (I)*.

Nominated manager, (DOC) Evan Thomas, Radcliffe & Co. Cardiff

1950 *Midhurst* — Rex Shipping Co. Ltd./I.H. Mathers & Son, Halifax, NS/Hadjilias & Co. Ltd. London.

1957 *Andalusia* — Asturias Shipping Co. Panama/Hadjilias & Co. Ltd. London

1964 *Sevilla*

FORT MIAMI - Evidently this was a popular name. The official record of the choice of this name identifies three locations:
1. A French fort built in 1722 on the south bank of the St. Mary's River in present day Indiana.
2. A French fort on the east bank of the St. Joseph River in 1750, in present day Indiana.
3. In 1794 Governor Simcoe built another Fort Miami at the mouth of the Maumee River in present day Ohio. Here the Maumee collected under British protection during General Wayne's western campaign in the Indian wars of the Northwest.
The name derives from the Miami Indians whose territory included the area south of Lakes Michigan and Erie.

FORT MICHIPICOTEN   7130 gt   9.43   NS   MI Montreal, QC

Nominated manager, (DOC) Maclay & McIntyre Ltd., Glasgow.

1950 *Oak Hill* — Halifax Overseas Freighters Ltd./I.H. Mathers & Son, Halifax/Counties S.M. Co. Ltd. London

1964 *Agenor*

FORT MICHIPICOTEN - Built by French fur traders about 1725, it was situated on the North shore of Lake Superior and commanded the route by way of Missinaibi Lake to Moose River and James Bay. When the NWC was formed in 1783 it took over this fort. It became the principal post on the north shore of Lake Superior for the new HBC following the merger with the NWC in 1821. (See note on spelling of Missinaibi, under Fort Missinabie.)

Fort Mingan as *Streatham Hill* (I.G. Stewart collection)

Vessel Name:	Tonnage:	Completion date:	Type:	Builder & Yard location
FORT MINGAN	7130 gt	5.43	NS	DSBR Lauzon QC

Nominated manager, (DOC) E.R. Management Company Ltd., Cardiff
1948 *Haligonian King*   Acadia Overseas Freighters (Halifax) Ltd./I.H. Mathers & Co. Ltd. Halifax
1950 *Streatham Hill*   Acadia Overseas Freighters Ltd. Change of vessel name came when management moved
  directly to London and Counties S.M. Co. Ltd.

FORT MINGAN - This was one of the oldest trading posts in Canada having been established in 1661. Situated on Mingan Island at the mouth of the Mingan River on the north shore of the lower St. Lawrence River opposite Anticosti Island. It was a French forti-fied trading post of the Mingan Seigniory of which François Bissot de la Rivière was the first seigneur. Between 1690 and 1759 the post was destroyed by the British navy on three different occasions. In 1803 the fort was taken over by the NWC and passed to the new HBC following the merger of 1821. The HBC operated it until recent times but prior to 1942.

FORT MISSANABIE	7130 gt	7.43	NS	MI Montreal, QC

Nominated manager, (DOC) Thomas Dunlop & Son, Glasgow
19.5.44   Sunk by submarine torpedo 38.20N, 16.28E, (Off Calabria, Italy).

FORT MISSANABIE - During the 18th Century the HBC built three posts on the Missanabie River which flows through Northern Ontario to its outlet on James Bay. The most southerly of these, Fort Missanabie was erected at the outlet of Lake Missanabie in 1779. It was burned in the following year and immediately rebuilt. The earliest of these forts was Fort Brunswick or Brunswick House dat-ing from 1744. New Brunswick House was built in 1788 nearly 100 miles upstream. It took over the trade of the original Fort Brunswick until it to was abandoned in 1895. After that Fort Missanabie remained the only HBC outlet on the river and was oper-ated by the company until very recent years.
NOTE the spelling variation adopted here compared to the entry under Fort Michipicoten - the first named is believed to be correct in terms of official adoption, but it is a name easily corrupted by phonetic spelling.

FORT MOOSE	7130 gt	10.43	NS	USY Montreal, QC

Nominated manager, (DOC) Larrinaga Steamship Co. Ltd. Liverpool.
1948 *Haligonian Prince*   Acadia Overseas Freighters (Halifax) Ltd./I.H. Mather & Son. Halifax
1950 *Tulse Hill*   Acadia Overseas Freighters Ltd. Vessel name changed when direct management
  moved to London and Counties S.M. Co. Ltd.

1966 *Astronaftis*
FORT MOOSE - Radison and Groseilliers, French traders and explorers in the employ of the HBC built this post on an island in James Bay, in 1671. Originally known as Hayes Island Post, it was the residence of the first Governor of the HBC in the New World. As a result of the struggle for power between France and England it changed hands several times. In 1686 it was captured by the French under d'Iberville. Seven years later the British took it back. The British demolished the fort and the site stood empty until 1730 when the HBC built a new fort on the same island about a half mile further up the Moose River. The name was changed to Moose Factory and it has been in operation ever since. The NWC erected a rival fort at the mouth of the river but this quickly closed, the competition was too intense. Moose Factory was operating at the time of the launch of the ship in 1943.

FORT MUMFORD	7130 gt	12.42	NS	PRDS Prince Rupert, BC

Nominated manager, (WSA) Sir W. Reardon Smith & Co. Cardiff
20.3.43   Sunk by submarine torpedo 10N 71E (Approximate position off the Laccadive Islands,
  Indian Ocean.)
The story of this vessel's loss has been told separately. It remains the most notorious sinking, by enemy action, in the annals of all the merchant ships built in Canada during the Second World War.
FORT MUMFORD - Located on the Stikine River in northwestern British Columbia where the village of Telegraph Creek now stands. The HBC appear to have had a small post at this location some time after 1841, but Fort Mumford was not established until about 1863, the same year that gold was discovered in the Stikine. The Collins Overland Telegraph Company failed, but not before the name Telegraph Creek had been bestowed on the community. Fort Mumford was eventually moved to the vicinity of Glenora and was then often referred to as Glenore House. (See also Fort Glenore and Fort Stager.)

FORT MUSQUARRO	7130 gt	4.44	NS	MI Montreal, QC

Nominated manager, (DOC) Charles Strubin & Co. Ltd. London
1950 *West Hill*   Canadian Tramp Shipping Co. Ltd./Counties Ship Management Co. London
1957 *Rio Doro*   Nestor Cia. Nav. SA Panama/Somerset Shipbrokers Ltd. London, managers
  D.C. & C.D. Georgopoulos
1963   Scrapped in Japan
FORT MUSQUARRO - Established by the French at the mouth of the Musquarro River opposite the eastern end of Anticosti Island in the Gulf of St.Lawrence. It stood on the territory that was granted to the Labrador Company of Quebec in 1780, in whose posses-sion it remained until 1820 when it was leased to the HBC. The name was then changed to Fort Romaine and when the ship was launched in 1944, it was still in operation with a small settlement around the old fort, 334 years later. This was probably a record for a Canadian trading establishment. (See also Fort Romaine.)

FORT NAKASLEY   7130 gt   3.43   NS   WCSB Vancouver, BC

Nominated manager, (DOC) J & J Denholm Ltd. Glasgow, UK

1950 *Argodon*   Argonaut Navigation Co. Ltd. Montreal/A. Lusi Ltd. London

1956 *Union Metropole*   International Union Lines Ltd. Monrovia, Liberia/Mgr. China Union Lines Ltd., Taipei, Taiwan.

FORT NAKASLEY - The history of Fort Nakasley is really the history of today's Fort St. James. No explanation of the unusual name of Nakasley has been found but it was probably the name of an obscure individual trader or officer, but as modern day Fort St. James, it is the oldest continuous settlement in the province of British Columbia. (See also Fort St. James.)

FORT NASHWAAK   7130 gt   2.43   NS   BDD North Van, BC

Nominated manager, (WSA) Dodd, Thomson & Co. Ltd. (King Line Ltd.) London

1947   Returned to USMC. Placed in Reserve Fleet.

1948 *General Artigas*   Oceanic Transport Corp. Monrovia, Liberia/Aristotle S. Onassis, Paris, France.

FORT NASHWAAK - This old French fort was built by Governor Villebon in 1692. It stood on the bank of the Nashwaak River at its junction with the Saint John River in what is now New Brunswick. The fort was 200 ft square with a bastion at each corner on which guns were mounted. Outside was a line of palisades and a ditch, this being a common type of fort in colonial times. At Nashwaak, Villebon was in close touch with the Indians whom he directed in their raids against the New England settlements, One of the most notorious took place in 1694 when many houses were burned and 130 English settlers were killed. After an unsuccessful attack from New England, Fort Nashwaak was abandoned by Villebon in 1698.

FORT NIAGARA completed as LA SALLE PARK.

FORT NIAGARA - Established by the French in 1678 on the east side of the Niagara River at its exit on Lake Ontario. captured by the British in 1759, garrisoned by the Americans from 1796 until, captured by British and Canadian troops in 1813, Fort Niagara was returned to the US in the peace settlement which followed.

FORT NIPIGON   7130 gt   4.42   NS   CVL Montreal, QC

Nominated manager, (WSA) Booth S.S. Co. Ltd. Liverpool

1947   Returned to USMC

1958   Scrapped at Baltimore, Maryland

FORT NIPIGON - This was one of the earliest French trading posts west of Montreal. It was built in 1678 by Charles, Sieur de la Tourette, at the mouth of the Nipigon River. Tourette called his fort, Fort Camanistigoyan, and it became the entrepot for the country between Lake Superior and James Bay. Pierre de la Verendrye was in command in 1728, but about 1785 the NWC took over the post renaming it Fort Nipigon. The new HBC succeeded them to the post in 1821 and maintained it until 1875.

FORT NISQUALLY launched as FORT CARLTON completed as KOOTENAY PARK (I) and then transferred to MOWT as FORT NISQUALLY.

FORT NISQUALLY - Built in 1833 by Archibald Mackenzie for the HBC on a tributary of the Nisqually River close by Puget Sound and the present day state capitol at Olympia. The site chosen was midway on the direct route between Fort Langley and Fort Vancouver on the Columbia River. Due to the pastoral country in which it lay it soon developed into an extensive sheep and cattle ranch which was operated by the Puget Sound Agricultural Company, a subsidiary of the HBC. In 1834 the Snoqualimich (Snoqualmi) Indians attacked, but Nisqually was strong enough to repulse them. In 1946 the United States-Canada boundary was fixed at the 49th parallel and Nisqually and a number of other HBC posts found themselves in the United States. As the HBC did not claim compensation for Nisqually it seems likely that it had been abandoned.

FORT NORFOLK   7130 gt   7.43   NS   USL Montreal, QC

Nominated manager, (DOC) Sir Wm. Reardon Smith & Co. Ltd. Cardiff

24.6.44   Mined and sunk of Normandy while engaged in the Normandy operation.

FORT NORFOLK - In 1798, on the recommendation of Governor Simcoe a survey was made of the high land overlooking Turkey Point on Lake Erie in present day Ontario. This resulted in Charlotteville being laid out as a townsite. By 1813, four buildings had been erected one of which was named Fort Norfolk. In anticipation of the war of 1812 the fort had been garrisoned by a detachment of dragoons. By 1814, Charlotteville had reached its zenith. With the coming of peace Fort Norfolk was abandoned and administrative facilities transferred to Vittoria. Charlotteville went back to sleep as Turkey Point.

FORT NORMAN   7130 gt   10.42   NS   WCSB Vancouver, BC

Nominated manager, (WSA) W.H. Cockerline & Co. London.

9.3.43.   Damaged by submarine torpedo 36.51N 01.09. (NE of Oran, Algeria)

1948   Returned to USMC.

1948 *Al Murtaza Ali*   Muhammadi Steamship Co. Ltd. Karachi Pakistan.

1954 *Amwarbaksh*

FORT NORMAN - This fort was built in 1810 by the HBC. It was situated on the right bank of the Mackenzie River at the mouth of the Great Bear River in what is now the North West Territories. It suffered one move in 1844 when it was moved 30 miles upstream to Old Fort Point, but in 1851 it reverted to its original site. At the time of the ship launch in 1942 it was still functioning as a trading post. Today it is the site of an oil industry based on Norman Wells.

FORT NORWAY completed as MOHAWK PARK (I). Later became FORT SPOKANE.

FORT NORWAY - Norway House or Fort Norman was a HBC post on Playgreen Lake flowing into Lake Winnipeg, Manitoba.

FORT NOTTINGHAM   7130 gt   7.44   NS   MI Montreal, QC

Nominated manager, (DOC) Capper Alexander & Co. Ltd. London
1950 *Alendi Hill*   Nova Scotia Marine Enterprises Co. Ltd./Nordic Ship Management, both of Montreal.
                               Counties Ship Management Co. Ltd.

1960 *Ho Fung*

FORT NOTTINGHAM - The NWC based at Fort Chipewyan had a virtual monopoly over the fur trade of North Eastern Alberta. To compete Peter Fidler built Fort Nottingham in 1802 on the north east shore of Lake Athabaska. The NWC had a very strong hold over the trade and four years later the HBC withdrew, abandoning Fort Nottingham. In 1815 they returned, building a permanent new fort called Fort Wedderburne.

FORT ORLEANS   7150 gt   11.43   Vic   BDD/VDD Vancouver, BC

Nominated manager, (DOC) J. Morrison & Son. Newcastle-on-Tyne
1946 *Mont Sorrel*   Montship Lines Ltd. (Montreal Shipping Co. Ltd.) Montreal/Ass. Buries Markes Ltd. London
1948 *Buys Ballot*   Royal Netherlands Government/A. Veder & Co. Mgrs/The Hague
1949 *Laagkerk*   United Netherlands Navigation Co.
                               Vereenigde Nederlandsche Scheepvaartmaatschappij, NV

FORT ORLEANS - Etienne Veniard de Bourgmand was commissioned by Boisbriand, military commandant of the Illinois country to build Fort Orleans on the route to New Mexico in 1723. Two factors were responsible for its development; to check the Spanish in New Mexico from encroaching on the domain of the King of France and, as a possible post from which to trade with Santa Fe. This was a plan long desired by the French but it was not reciprocated by the Spanish. The venturesome few who crossed the border into Spanish territory always ended in jail in Santa Fe. After years of frustration in dealing with the Spanish the French quietly gave up. Fort Orleans never developed as the French plan proved futile and the fort was abandoned.

FORT PANMURE   7150 gt   10.43   Vic   NVSR North Van, BC

Nominated manager, (DOC) Andrew Weir & Co. (The Bank Line) London.
1948 *Sunvalley*   Saguenay Terminals Ltd. Montreal/Aluminum Company of Canada Ltd., Montreal.
1960 *Kally*
1966   Scrapped at Kaohsiung, Taiwan

FORT PANMURE - The early history of this fort was that of Fort Rosalie, its previous name. The fort, rebuilt after the Natchez massacre of 1729 remained an important French post until 1763 when the Treaty of Paris gave all land east of the Mississippi to the British. In 1764 British troops repaired and occupied the dilapidated Fort Rosalie and renamed it Fort Panmure. In 1779 it was captured by the Spanish who held it until 1798 when it was turned over to the United States following the Pinckney treaty of 1795. It was demolished in 1805. (See also Fort Rosalie.)

FORT PASKOYAC   7130 gt   10.42   NS   NVSR North Van, BC

Nominated manager, (WSA) James Chambers & Co. Ltd. Liverpool.
6.3.43   Damaged by submarine torpedo 36.27N 10.17W
9.43   Damaged Main engine replaced with British made unit by
                               North-Eastern Marine Engineering.
1947   Returned to USMC
1948 *Iran*   Iran Navigation Co. Ltd. Tehran, Iran.
1953 *Hassan*   Royal S.S. Co. Panama
1954 *Tiha*   Cia. de Nav. Phoenix, SA Panama/Ivanovic & Co. Ltd. London
1960 *St. Dunstan*
1962 *Bename*

FORT PASKOYAC - This was a French fur trading post on the Saskatchewan River near the present site of the Pas, Manitoba. Built in 1748 it was one of a chain of posts stretching from Lake Superior to the Saskatchewan River built by Pierre de la Verendrye, his sons and successors. It was built to divert the flow of furs going to the HBC on Hudson Bay and in this it was successful. By now a part of the NWC it forced the HBC to build a chain of inland forts of its own to counter the trade of the NWC. Fort Paskoyac was abandoned prior to 1800.

FORT PELLY   7130 gt   8.42   NS   YAR Esquimalt, BC

Nominated manager, (WSA) Sir R. Ropner & Co. Ltd. West Hartlepool, UK
20.7.43   Bombed and sunk off Augusta, Sicily.

FORT PELLY - In 1790 the HBC built its first fort on the Assiniboine River near the mouth of the Whitesand tributary in what is now the province of Saskatchewan. It was first known as Carlton House or Fort Assiniboine, neither of which should be confused with previous entries above under these names which refer to other posts elsewhere. In 1856-7 the Hon. W.J. Christie built a new fort for the HBC a short distance from the fort of 1790 and the name was permanently changed to Fort Pelly which became one of the main trading posts of the HBC.

FORT PEMBINA 7130 gt 8.42 NS BDD/VDD Vancouver, BC
Nominated manager, (WSA) J.A. Billmeir & Co. London.
1947 Returned to USMC, Placed in Reserve Fleet.
1958 Scrapped at Baltimore, Maryland.

FORT PEMBINA - This fort was built in 1793 for the HBC on the east side of the Red River where St. Vincent, Minnesota now stands. The NWC established their own post nearby. In 1812 the HBC built Fort Daer, a little to the north on the site of the present town of Pembina. Following the HBC-NWC merger, the new HBC then took over the old NWC post. When the first boundary adjustment took place in 1818, Fort Pembina was moved a few miles to the north of the border to remain in Canada.

FORT PERROT 7150 gt 2.44 Vic PRDS Prince Rupert, BC
Nominated manager, (DOC) Headlam & Son, Whitby, Yorks, UK
27.7.44 Damaged by E-boat torpedo 50.50N, 00.44E,
(English Channel, south of Hastings, during Normandy operations.)
1947 *Rockside* Andros Shipping Co. Ltd. Montreal/Mgr, Capeside Steamship Co. Ltd. London
Goulandris Bros.
1952 *Dorion* Imperio Cia Nav. SA Panama/Geo. Hadjilias, beneficial owner
Mgr. Adamanthos Ship Operating Co. SA/A.D. Manthos, New York.
1959 *Apollonia* Imperio Cia Nav. SA. Panama/Adamanthos Ship Operating Co. Inc
(Anthony D. Manthos, New York).
1960 *Antonios S*
1963 Scrapped at Yokohama, Japan

FORT PERROT - In 1685 Nicolas Perrot, commandant of the West under the French regime, followed in Duluth's tracks and journeyed into Wisconsin. In the spring of 1686 he ascended the Mississippi River to Lake Pepin and built Fort Perrot, sometimes known also as Fort St. Antoine, on a site north of the mouth of the Chippewa River. While there he explored the surrounding territory and made allies of the Miami Indians. Arriving back at Fort Perrot he arrived just in time to foil an attack by Fox, Kickapoo and Mascouten Indians. After the massacre of 1689 when the Iroquois fell upon the village of Lachine, Quebec, panic became widespread among the French. Frontenac, who was then governor was determined to quell the hostile tribes and issued orders that all white men trading in distant parts report to Mackinac to aid war expeditions. This order eventually brought peace between the French and the Indians but rang the death knell for Fort Perrot. (See also Fort St, Antoine.)

Fort Pic as *Cassiopeia* (Phil Chandler)

FORT PIC 7130 gt 11.43 NS MI Montreal, QC
Nominated manager, (WSA) J & C Harrison, Ltd., London
1948 *Haligonian Baron* Acadian Overseas Freighters (Halifax) Ltd./I.H. Mather & Son
Asstd, Counties S.M. Co. Ltd. London
1950 *Wembley Hill* Same registered owner as above. Vessel name changed when direct management from
London by Counties S.M. took over.
1957 *Cassiopeia* Transoceanic Finance & Trading Corp. Monrovia/Rethymnis & Kulukundis Ltd. London
1961 *Shankiwan*
1965 *Asia Enterprise*

FORT PIC- Built about 1790 for the NWC, it was situated at the mouth of the Pic River on the north shore of Lake Superior. It was also at the beginning of a canoe route to Long Lake and thence north. This was an old Indian route, via the Albany River, to James Bay which was also used by the French when they were in control of forts on Hudson Bay and James Bay nearly a hundred years earlier. With the HBC-NWC merger of 1821, the new HBC took over Fort Pic and continued its operation until about 1865.

FORT PINE	7130 gt	7.42	NS	BDD/VDD Vancouver, BC

Nominated manager, (WSA) Hall Brothers Ltd. Newcastle-on-Tyne

1947 — Returned to USMC. Placed in Reserve Fleet. Scrapped, year not confirmed.

FORT PINE - This fort was built in 1784 on the north bank of the Assiniboine River below the mouth of the Souris River in present day Manitoba. It was built by the NWC as the chief trading post with the Mandan Indians of Dakota. The NWC abandoned Fort Pine in 1794 when its rival, the HBC, built Fort Souris 20 miles up the river. After the HBC-NWC merger in 1821 the new company reopened Fort Pine for a short period and then abandoned it.

It is of interest to note that Pine either single or in combination appears no less that 50 times in the Canadian Gazette of place names.

FORT PITT	7130 gt	7.42	NS	BDD North Van, BC

Nominated manager, (WSA) H.Hogarth & Son, Glasgow, UK

1948 — Returned to USMC. Placed in Reserve Fleet.

1959 — Scrapped at Mobile, Alabama

FORT PITT - Built in 1831 by the HBC on the south bank of the North Saskatchewan River near what is now the Alberta-Saskatchewan border. Some fifty years earlier a considerable fur trade had been conducted through the posts in this region, but by the time Fort Pitt was established the trade was in decline. The HBC had built the fort primarily as a supply base for dried buffalo meat and pemmican for the posts north and west. It was raided in the rebellion of 1885 and never restored.

FORT POPLAR	7130 gt	10.42	NS	BDD North Van, BC

Nominated manager, (WSA) F.C. Strick & Co. Ltd. London.

1947 — Returned to USMC

1948 *Etrusco* — L'Italica di Nav. S.p.a./Mgr. Ditta Marino Querci

16. 3.56 — Aground near Cedar Point, Scituate, Mass.

22.11.56 — Refloated, CTL, sold and repaired after seven months ashore. High ship values during the Suez crisis of 1956-7 were the probable justification.

1957 *Scituate* — Victor Transport Corp. Liberia/Western Production Co. New York

1961 *Irene X*

8.4.64 — Aground in Gulf of Tonkin, 20.37N 107.12 E

11.4.64 — Refloated in damaged condition.

10.5.64 — Arrived in tow Hong Kong

9.8.64 — Broke moorings in typhoon, beached, suffered further damage.

10.64 — Sold in Hong Kong for scrapping.

This vessel appears to hold a record of sorts among the Canadian Forts and Parks, for the number of incidents in her career after leaving the British flag.

FORT POPLAR - Built by the NWC in 1780 it was situated on the west side of the Assiniboine River near the mouth of the Swan River in present day Saskatchewan. Several forts were built in this beaver and otter country, Fort Poplar being one of the earliest. The HBC established Fort Pelly five miles downstream and in 1803 the XY Company built Fort Hibernia seven miles up the river. This latter post was taken over by the NWC when it absorbed the XY Company in 1804. Fort Poplar did not have a long life. It was attacked by the Indians in 1782, strengthened in 1801, but abandoned at the time when the NWC acquired Fort Hibernia. (See also Fort Tremblant.)

FORT PROVIDENCE	7150 gt	7.44	Vic	BDD/VDD Vancouver, BC

Nominated manager, (DOC) Ellerman & Bucknall S.S. Co. London.

1944 — Completed as a Stores Issuing ship for the Fleet Train.

1948 *Eastwater* — Federal Commerce & Navigation Co. Toronto, later Montreal.

1952 *Duneside* — Andros Shipping Co. Ltd./Capeside SS Co. Ltd. London/Goulandris Bros. London

1953 *Mar Libero* — Franco Maresco fu Mariano. Genoa, Italy.

1959 *Dugiotok* — Jugoslavenska Tankersna, Liberia

FORT PROVIDENCE - In 1786 Leroux who had established Fort Resolution on Great Slave lake for the NWC, in what is now the North West Territories, pressed further north under orders from Peter Pond to establish new connections with the Indians in the region. In 1789 Alexander Mackenzie made his famous trip down the Mackenzie River and took Leroux with him to help establish friendly relations with the Yellowknife Indians at Great Slave Lake. Mackenzie made a promise to the Indians to start a post among them: in 1790 he built Fort Providence at the mouth of the Yellowknife River. Sixty years later this post was moved to the north arm of Great Slave Lake were it was renamed Fort Rae.

Vessel Name:	Tonnage:	Completion date:	Type:	Builder & Yard location
FORT PRUDHOMME	7150 gt	10.43	Vic	BDD/VDD Vancouver, BC

Nominated manager, (DOC) Charlton, McCallum & Co. Ltd.,. Newcastle-on-Tyne.
1946 *Colchester County*   Acadia Overseas Freighters Ltd./I.H. Mather & Son, Halifax.
Counties S.M. Co. Ltd. London
1950 *Corsair*   Cia Nav. Aristomar, Liberia
1954 *Nicolaos*   Livadia Cia. Nav. SA, Panama/S.G. Embiricos Ltd. London

FORT PRUDHOMME- La Salle the great French explorer and trader was imbued with the ambition to reach the Gulf of Mexico, via the Mississippi River. In order to realize this he built ships and gathered together an intrepid group of adventurers one of whom was Pierre Prudhomme. While out hunting Prudhomme became detached from the others. When he was found some time later he was in such a weakened state that he could not carry on with the rest of the party. La Salle built a small stockaded fort in which he could recuperate. Named Fort Prudhomme it stands near the present village of Tiptonville, Tennessee, about 160 miles below the outlet of the Ohio River. Later Fort Prudhomme was used many times by la Salle on his frequent trips through the region.

FORT QU'APPELLE	7130 gt	3.42	NS	BDD/VDD Vancouver, BC

Nominated manager, (WSA) Wm, Thomson & Co. Edinburgh
17.5.42   Sunk by submarine torpedo 39.50N, 63.30W (South of Halifax).

FORT QU'APPELLE - Built by Peter Houris for the HBC in 1864, this fort was located on a flat level of land south of the river in the Qu'Appelle Valley about 40 miles from the City of Regina, Saskatchewan. During the twenty years prior to the coming of the railway, Fort Qu'Appelle became the most important point between the Assiniboine River and the Rocky Mountains. The railway put an early end to the post and in 1885 the HBC discontinued operations.

FORT RAE	7130 gt	9.42	NS	BDD/VDD Vancouver, BC

Nominated manager, (WSA) Glen Line Ltd. London
1947   Returned to USMC.
1948 *Pietro Campanella*   Name change in year of acquisition to
1948 *Clelia Campanella*   Tito Campanella Soc. Nav., Genoa
1960 *Monte Santo*
1964   Scrapped at Vado, Italy

FORT RAE - The early history of this fort was the history of Fort Providence. After its removal, in 1850, to the north arm of Great Slave lake it was renamed Fort Rae after the famous Arctic explorer, Dr. John Rae. It moved a second time a further fifteen miles north to its present location. Fort Rae was still an active trading post at the time of the ship launch in 1942, 156 years after its establishment as Fort Providence.

FORT RAMPART	7130 gt	1.43	NS	WCSB Vancouver, BC

Nominated manager, (WSA) Charlton, McCallum & Co. Ltd. Newcastle-on-Tyne.
17.4.43   Sunk by aircraft torpedo, 36.42N 01.17E (West of Algiers)

FORT RAMPART - In 1842, Trader John Bell of the HBC explored the Porcupine River to its junction with the Yukon River. Although supposedly in Russian territory, the company sent in Alexander Murray who built Fort Yukon at the mouth of the Porcupine in 1847. Not until Alaska became an American possession was the HBC disturbed. It pulled back to the Alaska-Yukon border and established Rampart House or Fort Rampart on Canadian soil in what is now the Yukon Territory.

FORT RELIANCE	7130 gt	9.42	NS	BDD/VDD Vancouver, BC

Nominated manager, (WSA) Allan, Black & Co. Ltd. Newcastle-on-Tyne.
1947   Returned to USMC. Placed in Reserve Fleet.
1959   Scrapped at Bordentown, New Jersey

FORT RELIANCE - This was originally an explorer's house built by Archibald McLeod for Captain George Back, at the mouth of the Lockhart River at the extreme east end of Great Slave Lake in what is now the North West Territories. Fort Reliance was operated as a fur trading post by the HBC for a number of years, but by 1900 it was in ruins. The vicinity is still a prime production area through which a considerable trade with the natives is maintained.

FORT REMY	7130 gt	2.43	NS	USY Montreal, QC

Nominated manager, (WSA) Evan Thomas & Radcliffe Ltd. Cardiff
1948   Returned to USMC. Placed in Reserve Fleet
1958   Scrapped at Baltimore, Maryland

FORT REMY - One of a chain of forts extending along the shore of the Island of Montreal, it was named for the Curè of the Parish, Father Remy. It was built in 1671 by Jean Millot on property he had purchased from La Salle. The fort consisted of a mill of masonry within an enclosure of Cedar posts which also contained a church, presbytery, Millot's house, a barn and the buildings necessary to house the garrison and colonists. When a party of Iroquois approached, cannons were fired to warn the settlers further along the island. After the massacre of Lachine in 1689, Fort Remy fell into disuse but its remains were still standing in the town of Ville Lasalle at the time of the ship launch in 1942.

Vessel Name:	Tonnage:	Completion date:	Type:	Builder & Yard location
FORT RICHELIEU	7130	10.43	NS	MI Sorel, QC

Nominated manager, (DOC) Evan Thomas, & Radcliffe Ltd. Cardiff
1950 *Beech Hill* Halifax Overseas Freighters Ltd./I.H. Mathers & Son. Halifax
Counties S.M. Co. Ltd. London

1964 *Alkon*

FORT RICHELIEU - One of a chain of military forts built by the Government of New France between Quebec City and the Great Lakes to restrict British trade and combat the fierce assaults of the Iroquois. Fort Richelieu was established in 1642 under orders from Governor Montmagny to guard the approaches from the south. Its location was on a point of land formed by the juncture of the Richelieu River and the St. Lawrence. The land was part of the holdings of the seigniory owned by Pierre de Sorel. The site is now modern day Sorel, Quebec.

FORT ROMAINE	7130 gt	9.43	NS	USY Montreal, QC

Nominated manager, (DOC) Hall Brothers, Newcastle-on-Tyne.
1948 *L'Allouette* Papachristidis Company. Montreal
1950 *Montrealer* P & T Steamship Co. Ltd. (Papachristidis & Teryazoa in partnership) Mgr.
Papachristidis Co. Ltd. Montreal
1953 *Everest* Worldwide S.S. Co. Ltd. Panama/Epirotiki S.S. Nav. Co. "George Potamianos," Ltd.
Piraeus, Greece

FORT ROMAINE - The early history of this fort is also that of Fort Musquarro, its previous name. It was built in 1710. The HBC acquired the post in 1820. Today the small settlement consists mostly of fishermen. Buildings other than the fort included a mission house, chapel, school and telegraph station as at 1943 when the ship was launched.

FORT ROSALIE	7150 gt	7.45	Can	USY Montreal, QC

Nominated manager, (DOC) Under Admiralty control.
Completed as an Ammunition Carrier for the fleet train
1947 Transferred to the Admiralty as a permanent addition to Royal Navy strength.

FORT ROSALIE - This fort was built by Bienville in 1716 on the site of the present day City of Natchez, Mississippi. It was named after the wife of the French prime minister, Pontchartrain. The governor of the colony of Louisiana at the time, Cadillac, was desperate over the poverty of his colony, the advance of the British and the hostility of the Natchez Indians. He had an intense dislike of Bienville, but felt the need to subdue the Indians once and for all. He ordered Bienville to defeat the Indians but would only give him 15 men to accomplish the task. Bienville took his orders and his 15 men and built Fort Rosalie and with a plan both brilliant and cunning, defeated the large warlike tribe. His deception of the Natchez only heightened their resentment. This led to the Natchez massacre of 1729 when Fort Rosalie was destroyed and almost its entire garrisoned murdered. Quickly rebuilt it passed into British hands in 1763, then to the Spanish in 1779 and the Americans in 1798. It was demolished in 1805.

FORT ROUGE completed as MOUNT ROBSON PARK (I).

FORT ROUGE - Established by Pierre de la Verendrye at the junction of the Red and Assiniboine Rivers as a French fur trading post. Like most others of the French forts it passed to the NWC upon the cession of Canada to Britain. The original site is the present day location of Portage and Main Streets in modern Winnipeg.

FORT ROUILLE	7130 gt	7.43	NS	USY Montreal, QC

Nominated manager, (DOC) Mitchell, Cotts & Co. Ltd. London
1948 *Ivor Rita* Ivor Shipping Co. Ltd. (Quebec S.S. Lines Ltd.)/Chandris (England) Ltd. London
1956 *Novor Rita* Novor Shipping Co. London
1958 *Rita* Maristrella Nav. SA, Panama/AJ & DJ Chandris, Piraeus, Greece
1.7.60 Aground off Goa, East Coast of India. Broke in two 15.21N 73.47E. TL.

FORT ROUILLE - The first French trading post on the present day site of Toronto was Fond-de-Lac, erected by Douville in 1720 near the mouth of the Humber River. Ten years later this post was abandoned. In 1750 a new post was built on the east bank of the Humber by Chevalier de Portneuf under orders from la Jonquière, governor of New France. Despite the aim of preventing trade between the Northern Indians and the British at Oswego and to control the trade between Lake Ontario and Georgian Bay, trade exceeded all expectations and a new larger fort was built on what is now the site of the Toronto Exhibition Grounds. It was named Fort Rouille after the French Minister of Marine in Paris. At the conclusion of the Seven Years War the French burned it rather than see it fall into British hands. Governor Simcoe seeking a permanent site for the new capital of Upper Canada chose this location in 1793 and named it York.

FORT RUPERT	7130 gt	10.42	NS	PRDS Prince Rupert, BC

Nominated manager, (WSA) Evan Thomas & Radcliffe Ltd. Cardiff
1947 Returned to USMC. Placed in Reserve Fleet
1958 Scrapped at Baltimore, Maryland.

FORT RUPERT - On January 13, 1848, Vancouver Island was granted by Royal Charter to the Hudson's Bay Company on condi-

tion that it developed a colony of British subjects. Therefore when in 1848 coal was discovered a few miles south of present day Port Hardy, the company built Fort Rupert for the protection of the miners who were sent there to open up the coalfield. Difficulties with the Kwakiutl Indians and the discovery of high quality coal further south at Nanaimo sealed the fate of the Susquash coal mining venture as its product was of poor quality. The miners moved to Nanaimo and opened up British Columbia's first large industry. Fort Rupert became an Indian settlement with only one brick chimney stack standing in mute testimony to previous activities.

FORT ST. ANTOINE   7130 gt   12.41   NS   Vic NVSR North Van, BC

Nominated manager, (DOC) H. Hogarth & Sons, Glasgow, Scotland

1948 *Manx Fisher*	Kerr-Silver Lines Ltd. Vancouver
1949	Collided in fog off San Francisco with American tanker,
	Sparrows Point, ran on in fog but arrested by US Coast Guard.
1949 *Al Hasan*	Muhammadi Steamship Co. Ltd. Karachi
5.63	Collision and aground in cyclone at Chittagong, East Pakistan (Bangladesh).
1964	Scrapped at Karachi, Pakistan

FORT ST. ANTOINE - The story of Fort St. Antoine is also that of Fort Perrot. St Antoine might have reflected the zealous interest of the Catholic church and Perrot is said to have bestowed the religious name himself after his own patron saint. Perrot appears to have been the clear choice of at least some of his followers. (See also Fort Perrot)

FORT ST. CROIX   7130 gt   12.43   NS   BDD/VDD Vancouver, BC

Nominated manager, (DOC) United Baltic Corporation Ltd. London

1947 *Argovic*	Argonaut Navigation Co. Ltd. Montreal (John C. Yemelos). Later Mgt. A.
	Lusi Ltd. London
1949 *Vassilis*	Cia. Nav. Coronado, SA, Panama/A.Lusi Ltd. London
1959 *Yiosonas*	Same owner as above.

FORT ST. CROIX - In 1683, Duluth, cousin of the famous explorer Henri de Tonty, travelled into what is now the State of Wisconsin and built the first European structure in its interior. Duluth dreamed of extending New France from the headwaters of the Mississippi to the Pacific Ocean. Having obtained a licence to trade, he arrived to find the Western Indians seething with revolt against the French. Travelling along the Fox River he ascended the Mississippi and made allies of the Sioux. From there he continued to Lake Superior where he built his small trading post on the St. Croix Portage.

FORT ST. FRANÇOIS   7130 gt   12.42   NS   DSBR Lauzon, QC

Nominated manager, (WSA) Counties Ship Management Co. Ltd. London

1948	Returned to USMC, Placed in Reserve Fleet.
1961	Scrapped in USA

FORT ST. FRANÇOIS - This was a French fortified post on the right bank of the mouth of the St. Francis River where it flows into the western end of Lake St. Peter. This lake is a widening of the St. Lawrence River, approximately halfway between Montreal and Quebec City. The fort was established about 1684 to guard a settlement of Abenaki Indians. Although abandoned for a few years it was re-occupied in 1700. The St. Francis River flows through the country south of the St. Lawrence, now known as the Eastern Townships, During the Seven Years War the Rogers Rangers came up from New England and reached Lake St. Peter. Here they came across a village of St. Francis Indians who had settled near the site of the old fort. Rogers took a terrible revenge on them for their massacres of English settlers in the valleys south of Lake Champlain before returning to New England.

FORT ST. IGNACE

An early mission and fort founded by Jacques Marquette in 1690. Situated at the entrance to the Straits of Mackinac, Lake Michigan, the site is in the present State of Michigan. (See also Hastings Park and Tecumseh Park.)

FORT ST. JAMES   7130 gt   1.42   NS   BDD North Van, BC

Purchased outright by the British government, (MOWT) one of two so dealt with.

Nominated manager, Ellerman Wilson Line Ltd., Hull, England

1946 *Temple Bar*	Temple S.S. Co. Ltd./Lambert Bros. Ltd. London
1959 *Nord Sky*	Republic of China
1960 *Hoping Er Shi Chi*	Gov't of the Peoples Republic of China. (Reported to have been on the register
	of China until 1991, although operating condition unknown)

FORT ST. JAMES - Built in 1806 for the NWC, by the famous Canadian fur traders and explorers, John Stuart and Simon Fraser, it was first named Stuart Lake Fort or Fort Nakasley and also called Fort New Caledonia by Fraser. After the HBC-NWC merger in 1821, the new company gave the fort the name Fort St. James which is still in operation. (See also Fort Nakasley.)

FORT ST. JOSEPH   7130 gt   10.43   NS   MI Montreal, QC

Nominated manager, (DOC) Capper. Alexander & Co. London.

1950 *Mavis Hill*	Black Lion S.S. Co./I.H. Mathers & Son. Halifax/Frinton Shipbrokers Ltd. London, a company related to Counties S.M. Co. Ltd. through Basil Mavroleon.
26. 6.52	Ashore near Cape Guardafui, Somalia, Horn of Africa
29.11.52	Refloated 10.2.53 Towed to Suez.
9.53	Scrapped Savona, Italy

FORT ST. JOSEPH - At the request of Governor Denonville of New France, Duluth built Fort St. Joseph in 1686, on the St. Clair River between Lakes Erie and Huron at the present site of modern day Detroit. The fort was erected to intercept the Dutch and English traders who were trying to break the French monopoly of trade with the Northwestern Indians of the Prairies and beyond. In 1688 Fort St. Joseph was abandoned but the site was too important to be left for long. In 1701 Cadillac was sent by the French to build Fort Pontchartrain. Cadillac lost favour and was replaced by Dubuisson. This unhappy move resulted in the violent Fox Wars and a considerable deterioration in trade. Renamed Fort Detroit the fort changed hands several times. In 1760 it fell to the British. In 1796 it was surrendered to the American revolutionaries, In 1814 the Americans replaced it with a new fort which they called Fort Gratiot.

FORT ST. NICHOLAS   7150 gt   9.43   Vic   BDD North Van, BC

Nominated manager, (DOC) John Cory & Son, Cardiff

15.2.44	Sunk by submarine torpedo 40.34N, 14.37E. (Gulf of Salerno, Italy.)

FORT ST. NICHOLAS - Built in 1687 at the mouth of the Wisconsin River, at or near Prairie de Chien in what is now the State of Wisconsin, it was one of the many small posts erected by the famous Nicolas Perrot. Perrot had such influence with the fierce tribes around Green Bay that he was sent in 1685 as the accredited agent of the French government. After building the fort, its life was very short as the result of the Iroquois massacre of Lachine. Frontenac called all white men to report at Michilimackinac to take action against the Indians and with their withdrawal none of the recently built forts in the interior of Wisconsin, including Fort St Nicolas, remained.

FORT ST. PAUL   7130 gt   12.42   NS   MI Montreal, QC

Nominated manager, (DOC) Maclay & McIntyre Ltd., Glasgow.

1951 *Tarsian*	Champlain Freighters Ltd. Montreal/J.P. Hadoulis Ltd. London
1956 *Marika*	Maroios, SA, Panama/J.P. Hadoulis Ltd. London
1958 *Longford*	Republic of China

FORT ST. PAUL - An old French trading post a little west of the mouth of the Eskimo River on the Straits of Belle Isle in what is now the eastern tip of Quebec. It was built before 1701 by Legardeur de Courtemanche within his concession from Kegaska River to the Hamilton River. In 1706 the seigneury was granted to Godefroy de St. Paul. It changed hands several times until a part of it was sold in 1828 to Louis Chevalier who was engaged in the salmon fishery. His descendants operated Fort St. Paul until near the end of the 19th Century.

FORT ST. REGIS   7130 gt   6.43   NS   MI Montreal, QC

Nominated manager, (DOC) Dodd Thomson & Co. Ltd. (King Line) London

1948 *Yale County*	Acadian Overseas Freighters Ltd./I.H. Mathers & Son, Halifax/Counties S.M. Co. Ltd. London
1950 *Sudbury Hill*	Vancouver Oriental Line Ltd./Counties S.M. Co. Ltd. London

FORT ST. REGIS - This fort was situated on the south bank of the St. Lawrence River at the International boundary between what is now the Province of Quebec and the State of New York. A Jesuit mission was founded for the Iroquois in 1752, the first missionary being Father Billard who remained there ten years. In the War of 1812 Fort St. Regis was temporarily captured by an American force advancing on Montreal from Lake Ontario. The garrison led by de Salabarry, in a gallant counter attack, threw off the enemy and recaptured the fort. In 1895 St. Regis was inhabited largely by Indians but is now a town of some size.

FORT SAKISDAC   7150 gt   10.43   Vic   BDD North Van, BC

Nominated manager, (DOC) Hain Steamship Co. Ltd. London.

1946 *Marchcape*	Canadian Shipowners Ltd./March Shipping Agency Ltd. Montreal
1949 *Margo*	Cia. Nav. Panamena Ultramarina SA Panama
1959 *Toula N*	Toula Nav Ltda., Panama

FORT SAKISDAC - This is a name derived from the Sac or Sauk Indians from the Green Bay area of Wisconsin. It was also more commonly known as Fort la Baye and its early history is that of Fort la Baye. During the Seven Years War the French abandoned Fort Sakisdac and in 1761 Lieutenant J. Gorrell took command of the deserted fort for the British and renamed it Fort Edward Augustus, after one of the royal princes. With the removal of the British garrison later in the year, the French started to filter back. Although the territory around Green Bay fell to the British under the terms of the Treaty of Paris, the fur trade in that district remained with the French. (See also Fort la Baye and Fort Marin.)

FORT SALEESH 7150 gt 11.43 Vic NVSR North Van, BC

Nominated manager, (DOC) Evan Thomas & Radcliffe Ltd. Cardiff

1946 *Argomont* Argonaut Navigation Co. Ltd. Montreal/John C. Yelemos mgr./A.Lusi Ltd. London.

1949 *Corfu Island* Cia. de Nav. Zita, SA. Panama/A. Lusi Ltd. London

20.12.63 Aground near Grindstone Light, Magdalen Islands, 47.23N, 61.54W. TL
(Gulf of St, Lawrence)

FORT SALEESH- Late in 1809, a year before the building of forts in the Oregon territory, David Thompson had established Fort Saleesh at the SE end of Thompson Prairie in what is now the State of Montana. Here he carried on a small trade with the Flathead Indians and used the fort as a stopping place on his many travels through the area. Thompson returned in 1811 to find Saleesh in ruins following an attack by Piegan Indians who had been provoked to hostility by the fact that the Flatheads had acquired sufficient arms and ammunition from Thompson to engage in war with the Piegan and inflict a defeat on them. Thompson rebuilt Fort Saleesh but it never regained importance. The name derives from the Saalish Indian tribe who occupied much of the North West in present day Montana, Idaho, Washington and British Columbia.

FORT SANDUSKY (II) 7150 gt 8.45 Can USY Montreal, QC

Completed as a stores issuing ship for fleet train service.

Nominated manager, (DOC) under Admiralty control.

1949 Transferred to Admiralty. Added to the permanent strength of the Royal Navy.

FORT SANDUSKY - In 1740 the Wyandotte Indians were severely routed by the French at the Battle of Detroit. The defeated Indians retreated to the mouth of the Sandusky River which empties into Sandusky Bay. At first known as Sandoski, the Indians allowed the British to build a small fort on the north side of the bay opposite the present city of Sandusky, Ohio. In 1751 the French ousted the British and built Fort Sandusky on the site of the British blockhouse. In 1761 the British built a new blockhouse but it was short-lived as Pontiac and his warriors fell upon it and destroyed it completely. This activity gave rise to a permanent settlement which is now the modern City of Sandusky.

FORT SENNEVILLE 7130 gt 8.42 NS CVL Montreal, QC

Nominated manager, (WSA) J.A. Billmeir & Co. Ltd. London

1947 Returned to USMC. Placed in Reserve Fleet

1949 *Bharatrani* Bharat Line Ltd. Bombay, India

1963 Scrapped at Bombay.

FORT SENNEVILLE - Jacques LeBer built a small windmill at the end of the Island of Montreal in 1686 on land acquired by him from Sieur de Boisbriant. The mill was fortified and surrounded by a stake fence, but in 1691 the Indians pillaged it and burnt everything there to the ground. The following year a more substantial fort was erected on the same site. This time the new Fort Senneville with walls and corner towers of masonry was built and garrisoned by the French in 1701, serving as one of the chain of forts protecting the settlers in Ville Marie from marauding Indians. The fort was captured by an American force under General Arnold in 1776 and after this episode faded from history although the district of Senneville still exists as an enclave of greater Montreal.

FORT SIMCOE

Despite the historical significance of the name Simcoe in Ontario, there is no Fort Simcoe in the province. There was however a Fort Simcoe near Yakima, Washington, built in 1856 by the US military. The name in this case originates from the Yakima Indian word Sim-qu-ee, meaning saddle. (See Elgin Park and Green Hill Park.)

FORT SIMPSON 7130 gt 9.42 NS NVSR North Van, BC

Nominated manager, (WSA) Chellew Navigation Co. Ltd. Cardiff

1947 Returned to USMC.

1948 *Atlanta II* Fratelli, D'Amico, Rome

1949 *Atlanta* As above

FORT SIMPSON - This fort was built in 1820 by the NWC on an island at the juncture of the Liard and Mackenzie Rivers, with the name Fort of the Forks. Following the HBC-NWC merger of 1821 the post was retained by the new HBC and became one of their more famous fur trading posts. The HBC renamed it Fort Simpson in honour of Sir George Simpson, Governor of the Hudson's Bay Company at the time.

FORT SLAVE 7130 gt 10.42 NS WCSB Vancouver, BC

Nominated manager, (WSA) McCowen & Gross, Newcastle-on-Tyne

1948 Returned to USMC. Placed in Reserve Fleet.

1960 Scrapped at Mobile, Alabama.

FORT SLAVE - This fort was built in 1786 by Cuthbert Grant and Leroux for the noted fur trader and explorer, Peter Pond. It was situated on the left bank of the Slave River a few miles from its mouth on Great Slave Lake. The NWC operated the post until 1821 when it was consolidated into the new HBC company following the merger of that year. Fort Slave was then abandoned in favour of the HBC post, Fort Resolution on Great Slave Lake.

Vessel Name:	Tonnage:	Completion date:	Type:	Builder & Yard location
FORT SOURIS	7130 gt	10.42	NS	WCSB Vancouver, BC

Nominated manager, (WSA) B.J. Sutherland & Co. Ltd. Newcastle-on-Tyne.
1948   Returned to USMC. Placed in Reserve Fleet
1961   Scrapped in USA

FORT SOURIS - Built in 1793 on the Souris River near its junction with the Assiniboine River in what is now the SW corner of Manitoba. It was the first HBC post in the region. Within two years there were five posts all competing for the trade of the Mandan Indians. The NWC had built Fort Assiniboine and Fort Ash and in 1794 the HBC had opened Fort Brandon or Brandon House. This meant that Fort Souris was to be short lived as Brandon House quickly became the main HBC post in the district.

FORT SPOKANE	7130 gt	6.43	NS	BDD/VDD Vancouver, BC

Launched as *Fort Norway*, completed as *Mohawk Park (I)*, operated by Park S.S. Company, nominated manager not recorded. In 1944 the ship was transferred to the MOWT and renamed as *Fort Spokane*.
Nominated manager, (DOC) Watts, Watts & Co. Ltd. London.
1951 *La Orilla*   Buries Markes Ltd. London
1952 *Ariella*   Fratelli D'Amico, Rome, Italy
1964   Scrapped at Trieste, Italy.

FORT SPOKANE - In 1810-11 David Thompson had Finan McDonald build this fort for the NWC, at the junction of the Spokane and Little Spokane Rivers in what is now the State of Washington. It soon became the principal distributing and wintering point on the North West Company for the Upper Columbia, Kootenay and Flathead trade. After the HBC-NWC merger of 1821, Fort Spokane was continued for five years. At that time the company chose a new site at Kettle Falls near the confluence of the Colville and Columbia Rivers to which the old fort was moved and renamed Fort Colville.

FORT STAGER	7130 gt	2.43	NS	WCSB Vancouver, BC

Nominated manager, (WSA) Sir R. Ropner & Co. Ltd. West Hartlepool
1948   Returned to USMC. Placed in Reserve Fleet.
1958   Scrapped at Baltimore, Maryland.

FORT STAGER - This fort was situated at the junction of the Kispyox and Skeena Rivers in NW British Columbia. Fort Stager was not important as a trading post, but it is remembered as it accidentally became the terminus of a communications system. The failure of the Atlantic cable of 1858 directed attention to the possibility of a land telegraph from the United States, through British Columbia, Alaska and Siberia to join the continental European systems. While spanning a huge land mass it had the advantage also that there would be only one significant ocean crossing, that of Bering Straits. In 1865-66 the line, known as Collins Overland Telegraph pushed with great speed up the Fraser River to Quesnel and thence across country to Fort Stager. It went no further as in August 1866, the dramatic news came through that the Atlantic cable had been successfully laid. The Collins Overland Telegraph faded quickly and Fort Stager's moment of fame was over.

FORT STEELE	7130 gt	11.42	NS	NVSR North Van, BC

Nominated manager, (WSA) Lyle Shipping Co. Ltd. Glasgow
1948   Returned to USMC, Placed in Reserve Fleet
1959   Scrapped at Baltimore

FORT STEELE - Originally known as Galbraith's Ferry which had been operating since 1860 to take miners across Kootenay Lake to reach Wild Horse Creek, the NWMP built a police post at Galbraith's which they named Fort Steele after Superintendent Sam Steele. Heading "B" Division he led a group of officers and men who were loaned by the Dominion Government to quell an Indian uprising. Fort Steele was also the site of one of the oldest breweries in British Columbia which was functioning until recent years.

FORT STIKINE	7130 gt	7.42	NS	PRDS Prince Rupert, BC

Nominated manager, (WSA) Port Line Ltd. London
14.4.44   Loss by fire and explosion, Victoria Dock, Bombay. What remained was sold for scrap.

FORT STIKINE - The history of this fort is also that of Fort Highfield and Fort Wrangell. The name of this ship will forever be remembered with infamy in the history of Bombay, as it set off the biggest accidental explosion of WWII, rivalling in size and consequences that of Halifax, NS in 1917 (see separate story).

FORT STURGEON	7130 gt	5.43	NS	VMD Victoria, BC

Nominated manager, (DOC) Walter Runciman & Co. Ltd. Newcastle-on-Tyne
1950 *East Hill*   Canadian Tramp Shipping Co. Ltd. Montreal/Counties S.M. Co. Ltd., London.
1957 *Rio Alto*   Nestor Cia. Nav. SA, Panama/Somerset Shipbrokers Ltd. London, DC & CD Georgopoulos
1964 *Aktor*

FORT STURGEON - This was a post of the NWC of Montreal which is reported to have been built by Peter Grant in 1794 at the mouth of the Shell River on the North Saskatchewan River, a few miles west of the present city of Prince Albert. Fort Sturgeon was one of many HBC and NWC posts along the Saskatchewan River trade route. Those that were selected for ongoing operation prior to and following the merger of 1821 often prospered for many years. The rest languished and were quickly abandoned. Fort Sturgeon was one of the latter group. When Alexander Henry Jr. passed this way in 1808 only a few remains were left.

FORT TADOUSSAC   7130 gt   4.42   NS   DSBR Lauzon, QC

Nominated manager, (WSA) Ellerman & Bucknall Steamship Lines Ltd. London.

1947   Returned to USMC, Placed in Reserve Fleet

1959   Scrapped at Mobile, Alabama.

FORT TADOUSSAC - This fort is at the mouth of the Saguenay River, which empties into the St. Lawrence River below Quebec City. It is the oldest fur trading post in Canada and one of the oldest settlements in North America. It was first visited by Jacques Cartier, in 1535, which marks its place in the very beginnings of Canada and for several years after that carried on extensive fisheries. As the fur trade developed, Tadoussac became the chief mart for furs from the west and north. The first trading post was established in 1590. It was visited by Champlain in 1602 after which in 1615, Recollet Father D'Olbeau established the first mission. In 1628 the British under Sir David Kirke seized Fort Tadoussac but it was returned to France four years later. The Jesuits had charge of the mission 1641-1782. After the cession of Canada to Britain in 1763, the fort was leased to several leaseholders, the last being the HBC who discontinued operations in 1859 - a span of 324 years in the history of Canada.

FORT THOMPSON   7130 gt   10.42   NS   BDD/VDD Vancouver, BC

Nominated manager, (WSA) Glen & Co. Ltd. Glasgow

2.11.44   Damaged by submarine torpedo, 48.55N 67.41W.

1948   Returned to USMC. Placed in Reserve Fleet

1959   Scrapped at Beaumont, Texas.

FORT THOMPSON - In 1812 David Stuart built the first fort at the junction of the north and south branches of the Thompson River for the Pacific Fur Company on what is now the site of Kamloops, BC. The NWC of Montreal absorbed the Pacific Fur Company in 1813 and took over Stuart's fort, naming it Fort Thompson after David Thompson. Following the HBC-NWC merger of 1821, the new HBC operated Fort Thompson until 1850 when they constructed a new fort on the opposite bank of the river and changed the name to Fort Kamloops.

FORT TICONDEROGA   7130 gt   12.43   NS   USY Montreal, QC

Nominated manager, (DOC) Chellew Navigation Co. Ltd. Cardiff

10.1.46   Damaged by mine, 12.1.46 Arrived at Trieste

1948 *Ivor Isobel*   Ivor Shipping Co. Ltd./Quebec S.S. Lines, Ltd. Montreal/Chandris (England) Ltd. London

1956 *Novor Isobel*   Novor Shipping Co. Ltd. London/Chandris (England) Ltd.

1958 *Hereford*   Republic of China

FORT TICONDEROGA - Built by the French in 1731, this military fort was originally called Fort Carillon. (Another Fort Carillon existed later, on the Ottawa River, which gave its name to the ship of that name). Renamed Fort Ticonderoga, it lay on the north side of Lake George in what is now upper New York State. During the Seven Years War, Ticonderoga under the command of Montcalm, withstood a British attack under the command of General Abercrombie and inflicted a severe defeat on the British in 1758. The following year Amherst led a fresh attack and this time drove the French out of Ticonderoga who destroyed it as they left for Fort Crown Point. Rebuilt by the British it was captured in 1775 by Ethan Allen leading an American revolutionary force.

FORT TOULOUSE completed as SAPPERTON PARK.

FORT TOULOUSE - the history of this fort is also the history of Fort Alabama.

FORT TREMBLANT   7130 gt   12.42   NS   VMD Victoria, BC

Nominated manager, (WSA) W.H. Seager & Co. Ltd. Cardiff

1947   Legally returned to USMC, but purchased by operator

1947 *Beatus*   Tempus Shipping Co. Ltd. Managers/W.H. Seager & Co. Ltd.Cardiff

1955 *Stanland*   Stanhope Steamship Co. Ltd. Managers/J.A. Billmair & Co. Ltd. London

1963   Scrapped at Hong Kong

FORT TREMBLANT - Built by the NWC in 1780, it was situated on the west side of the Assiniboine River near the source of the Swan River in what is now Saskatchewan. In 1790 the HBC established Fort Pelly, five miles downstream and in 1803 the XY Company built Fort Hibernia seven miles up the river. Hibernia was taken over by the NWC when it absorbed the XY Company in 1804, Fort Tremblant was of short duration. It was attacked by the Indians in 1782, strengthened in 1801, but abandoned about the time the NWC took over Fort Hibernia. Although originally named Fort Tremblant or Poplar Fort, the name was later changed to Fort Alexandria.

Fort Turtle (I.G. Stewart collection)

FORT TURTLE	7130 gt	5.43	NS	PRDS Prince Rupert, BC

Nominated manager, (DOC) Haldin & Phillips Ltd. (Court Line) London.
1950 *Arundel Hill*   Ottawa Steamship Co. Ltd./I.H. Mathers & Son, Halifax/Coulouthros Ltd. London
1957 *Cyprinia*   Andria Nav. SA Panama/Mgr. John A Coulouthros, London
1964 *Ever Health*

FORT TURTLE - This was a post of the NWC situated on the south bank of the Saskatchewan River about one mile below the mouth of Turtle River in what is now Western Saskatchewan. It was built shortly after the formation of the NWC in 1783 to compete with the HBC post established by Mitchell Oman in 1780 known as Buckingham House or Fort Buckingham. So intense was the competition between the two great rivals, it encouraged over trapping, the over building of posts and the ultimate thinning of the resource. So long as the traders could keep on moving further west into untapped trapping territory the volume of furs coming on to the market could be sustained, but Fort Turtle like many others had a short life as the trapping and trading moved past them. Fort Turtle was in ruins by 1800. (See also Fort Buckingham.)

FORT VENANGO	7150 gt	10.43	Vic	BDD/VDD Vancouver, BC

Nominated manager, (DOC) Capper Alexander & Co. Ltd. London
1946 *Colchester County*   Acadia Overseas Freighters Ltd./I.H. Mathers & Son,Halifax/Counties S.M. Co. Ltd. London
1949 *Santa Calli*   Cia de Nav. San George, Panama/Rethymnis & Kulukundis Ltd. London
1952 *Calli*   Marine Transport Co. SA. Panama/Rethymnis & Kulukundis Ltd. London
1958 *August Thyssen*   August Thyssen-Hutte, AG/Frigga AG, Seereederei, Hamburg
1962   Scrapped in Germany

FORT VENANGO - The history of Fort Venango started with the mission of Marin, under orders from Duquesne, to strengthen the defences of the Ohio Valley. Where French Creek joins the Allegheny River in what is now Pennsylvania, Marin hoisted the French flag over what had been the house of an English trader. It was to this house that George Washington came as a very young man and demanded that the French leave British territory. In 1754 the French built an outpost on this site only to abandon it and retire to Detroit five years later. The following year the British built Fort Venango slightly nearer the creek mouth. In 1763 the entire British garrison was captured and murdered by Pontiac's warriors. The fort was not rebuilt until late in the American revolution, in 1788, and was then garrisoned for eight years thereafter. It was given the name Fort Franklin, but that had no bearing on the name of the ship as that vessel was named after Sir John Franklin's fort mentioned above. (See also Fort La Baye and Fort Marin.)

FORT VERCHÈRES	7130 gt	5.43	NS	USY Montreal, QC

Nominated manager, (DOC) Hain Steamship Co. Ltd. London.
1950 *Maple Hill*   Halifax Overseas Freighters Ltd./I.H. Mathers & Son, Halifax/Counties S.M. Co. Ltd. London

FORT VERCHÈRES - The story of this famous fort and its heroine, Madeleine de Verchères is told separately in the preceding chapter 13. It is well known to thousands of school children, particularly in Eastern Canada and Quebec. Some may think it fanciful or exaggerated and it probably has gained something in the retelling over the years.

FORT VERMILLION	7130 gt	10.42	NS	BDD Vancouver, BC

Nominated manager, (WSA)Counties Ship Management Co. Ltd. London.
1948   Returned to USMC. Placed in Reserve Fleet.
1959   Scrapped at Mobile, Alabama

FORT VERMILLION - Built in 1798 on the south bank of the Peace River near the mouth of the Boyer River in what is now Northern Alberta, this fort became an important post for the NWC during the many years that the Peace River afforded a route into the Pacific Territory then known as New Caledonia, but later British Columbia. Following the HBC-NWC merger of 1821, the new company took over what was often called the "Old Establishment" and then built a new outpost transferring its business to the new Fort Vermillion. It was still in operation as such, 144 years later when the ship was launched in 1942.

FORT VILLE MARIE — 7130 gt — 12.41 — NS — CVL Montreal, QC

Nominated manager, (MOWT) T & J Brocklebank Ltd. Liverpool

This was the first ship in the entire Canadian North Sands programs and its successors. It was the only vessel from this fleet that spent its entire war and peacetime career under the one management or ownership. With *Fort St. James*, she was purchased outright upon completion. Nicknamed Vile Mary, within the Brocklebank organization.

| 1946 *Makalla* | T & J Brocklebank Ltd. Liverpool |
| 1963 | Scrapped at Ghent, Belgium. |

FORT VILLE MARIE - The history of Fort Ville Marie is set out more fully under Fort Maisonneuve.

FORT WALLACE — 7150 gt — 2.44 — Vic — BDD North Van, BC

Nominated manager, (DOC) Lambert Brothers Ltd., London

1946 *Vancouver County*	Acadia Overseas Freighters Ltd./I.H.Mathers & Son, Halifax, NS
	Counties S.M. Co. Ltd. London
1950 *Akko*	Israel America Line Ltd./Mgr. Shoham Sherutey Hayem Ltd., Haifa
1954 *Athens*	Athena Shipping Co. Panama/Mgr. Faros Shipping Co. London

FORT WALLACE - This was one of four forts guarding Temple Bay on the Straits of Belle Isle, Labrador. It was built by the British sometime after the fall of Quebec and the simultaneous surrender of Labrador in 1763. This newly acquired strip of seaboard was important chiefly for its fisheries, but hostility on the part of Eskimos made it impossible for the British to approach. Sir Hugh Palliser, Governor of Newfoundland, under whose jurisdiction Labrador then fell, recommended that the fisheries be encouraged and developed and that blockhouses be erected to protect the fisheries, regulate disputes and establish English possessory rights to the whole country. By 1794 there were four forts on Temple Bay of unknown date of build. The one guarding the harbour entrance was Fort Wallace. Even though the French had ceded Canada following the Seven Years War, during the Napoleonic Wars, they periodically launched attacks from the sea against Temple Bay. In 1794 a petition was presented to the new governor of Newfoundland asking that a sloop of war be available to provide additional security when the season's catch was being loaded.

NOTE this is the only time when a Newfoundland and Labrador name was selected in the shipbuilding program, as it was not until 1949 that Newfoundland gave up its independent status and joined Canada. The ship was built by Burrard Dry Dock Company of North Vancouver, a yard owned by the Wallace family. In the Burrard collection held by North Vancouver Museum and Archives, the Wallace family recorded their satisfaction that the name was chosen for a ship built by them, even though they laid no claim to the choice of the name.

FORT WALSH — 7130 gt — 1.43 — NS — VMD Victoria, BC

Nominated manager, (WSA) Larrinaga Steamship Co. Ltd. Liverpool

1947 *Monstella*	Nav, Alta Italia, S.p.a. Genoa.
1951	Converted to turbine propulsion
1965 *Tihi*	

FORT WALSH - This was a NWMP post in the Cypress Hills of SW Saskatchewan, built by Major Walsh in 1875. These hills had long been the home of the Assiniboines, but the influx of other tribes and the demoralizing effect of whiskey peddled by American traders spelt trouble. The NWMP had established Fort McLeod, the year before, in what is now SW Alberta, but it was too far away to have any influence on the Cypress Hills. In 1877, the Sioux chief Sitting Bull, with hundreds of his warriors crossed from American soil to the Canadian side. It was a delicate situation, but Commissioner Irvine and a handful of NWMP were successful in keeping the peace and heading off an outbreak of violence by the Sioux who two years earlier had annihilated an American force under the flamboyant General George Custer.

Fort Wayne as Angusdale (W.S.S. Vancouver Maritime Museum)

FORT WAYNE   7150 gt   9.45   Can   USY Montreal, QC

Nominated manager, (DOC) under Admiralty control.
Completed as a Stores Issuing ship for Fleet train service

1950 *Angusdale*   Angusdale Ltd./Lunham & Moore Shipping Ltd. Montreal/E.E. Dean & Co. Ltd. London
1954 *Cape Adan*   Angusdale Ltd./Lyle Shipping Co. Ltd. Glasgow
1956 *Andora*   Bienvenido S.S. Co. Ltd. Panama/John G. Livanos & Sons Ltd., London

FORT WAYNE - This American fort's place in Canadian history is based on the fact that two previous French forts stood on its site at the headwaters of the Maumee River, overlooking the confluence of the St. Mary's and the St. Joseph Rivers in what is now the state of Indiana. Prior to the building of Fort Wayne the site was known as the Miami Villages because of the Indians of that name who lived nearby. This place was the objective of Major General "Mad" Anthony Wayne's campaign during the Indian Wars of the Northwest. In selecting a site for his fort, Wayne surveyed the region and found traces of the two previous forts. the first stood on the south bank of the St Mary's River and the second was on the east bank of the St. Joseph. It had been built by the French in 1750, but had fallen to the British after the fall of Quebec in 1759 and was soon abandoned. Fort Wayne remained a fully garrisoned American Army post for 25 years and was evacuated in 1719.

FORT WEDDERBURNE   7130 gt   10.42   NS   BDD/VDD Vancouver, BC

Nominated manager, (WSA) Lyle Shipping Co. Ltd. Glasgow

1947   Returned to USMC
1948 *Antonietta Bozzo*   Giuseppe Bozzo, fu Lorenzo, Genoa
1965   Scrapped at Vado, Italy

FORT WEDDERBURNE - Situated on Coal island in Lake Athabaska in what is now the NE corner of Alberta. In 1808 the HBC abandoned the whole of the Athabaska district and left it to the NWC. In 1815 they returned and built Fort Wedderburne, which was the family name of Lady Selkirk, only one mile distant from the NWC post, Fort Chipewyan. The Wedderburne family, in fact had connections with the HBC over more than one generation. Fort Wedderburne was seized by Norman McLeod of the NWC on March 23, 1817, but it was re-established by the HBC the following year. This district was the centre from which Sir George Simpson administered the Athabaska district in 1820-21. It may be said to be the scene where he first displayed the qualities which made him the greatest governor in the long history of the HBC. Following the HBC-NWC merger of 1821, the new HBC took over Fort Chipewyan and Fort Wedderburne was closed.

Fort Wellington as *Muswell Hill* (S.G. Docker)

FORT WELLINGTON   7130 gt   6.43   NS   USY Montreal, QC

Nominated manager. (DOC) Sir R. Ropner & Co. Ltd. West Hartlepool, UK

1949 *Haligonian Queen*   Acadia Overseas Freighters (Halifax) Ltd./I.H. Mather & Son
1950 *Muswell Hill*   Same owner as above, name change came with direct control moving to
                          Counties S.M. Co. in London

FORT WELLINGTON - was built during the War of 1812 on the north shore of the St. Lawrence River where the town of Prescott, Ontario stands today. It was established to keep communications open between the Canadian Great Lakes Naval Base at Kingston on Lake Ontario and Montreal. Its garrison took part in two attacks on the American town of Ogdensburg, directly across the St. Lawrence. The second attack resulted in a British victory and the command of the river at this point. During the Canadian rebellion of 1837-38 when a faction led by William Lyon Mackenzie sought to reform social and political conditions in Upper Canada, the fort was strengthened in anticipation of attack. In 1866 Irish Americans of the Fenian organization invaded Canada in an effort to wrest Canada from Great Britain so Fort Wellington was hastily re-garrisoned. From then on until 1886 it was occupied intermittently by Canadian troops and today stands as a national park.

NOTE - It is a little ironic that while the infant United States was doing its best to thrash the British in Canada in the War of 1812, and generally not succeeding, the Duke of Wellington was inflicting a series of the greatest military defeats ever suffered by Napoleon in Spain which resulted in the invasion of France and the first end of Napoleon's regime at Toulouse in 1813. The final end came at Waterloo in 1815.

FORT WRANGELL | 7150 gt | 12.44 | Vic | BDD/VDD Vancouver, BC

Nominated manager, (DOC) Eastern & Australian S.S. Co. Ltd. (P & 0 Group), London			
1948 *Eastwave*	Federal Commerce & Navigation Co. Ltd. Toronto		
1952 *Lagoonside*	Andros Shipping Co. Ltd. Montreal/Goulandris Bros. London		
1952 *Lagos Ontario*	Cia Armadora San Francisco, Panama		

FORT WRANGELL - Named for Baron Ferdinand Petrovich von Wrangell, governor of the Russian American Fur Company, the history of Fort Wrangell has been covered in that of Fort Highfield and Fort Stikine.

NOTE - it is interesting to note that the name of this one fort in its three different forms was used on three of the Fort ships. It was often the case that a given forts' different names were used twice, but to use the names in three different forms as with Highfield, Stikine and Wrangell was a record of sorts. The only other such example noted has been Forts La Baye, Marin and Sakisdac, although the latter were not necessarily the same structure.

FORT WRIGLEY | 7130 gt | 4.43 | NS | VMD Victoria, BC

Nominated manager, (DOC) Geo. Nisbet & Co. Glasgow. Succeeded later by Dene Ship Mgmt Ltd. London.			
1948 *Pantrooper*	Papachristidis Company, Montreal		
1950 *Royal William*	same owner as above		
1956 *Appulo*	L'Italica di Navigazione, S.p.a./Ditta Marino Querci, Genoa, Italy		
1962	Scrapped in Italy		

FORT WRIGLEY - This fort was built by Chief Factor Camsell for the HBC in 1880 and as at the time of launching the ship in 1943, it was still operating as a trading post. It is situated on the left bank of the Mackenzie halfway between Fort Simpson at the mouth of the Liard and Fort Norman at the mouth of the Great Bear River. Formerly known as Little Rapids, it was later named Fort Wrigley in honour of the Chief Commissioner of the company at the time.

FORT YALE | 7130 gt | 12.42 | NS | BDD/VDD Vancouver, BC

Nominated manager, (WSA) Charlton McCallum & Co. Ltd. Newcastle-on-Tyne.			
8. 8.44	Damaged by mine 49.26N, 00.33W (English Channel).		
23.8.44	Sunk by submarine torpedo 50.23N 00.55W (English Channel).		

FORT YALE - This fort was built in 1848 at the downstream end of the Fraser River Canyon in SW British Columbia. When explorer Simon Fraser descended the Fraser River there was an Indian village on the site. Since 1826 the HBC trade route to the coast had been via the Columbia River, but with the Cayuse war of 1848, between the United States and the Indians, the company was forced to open its trade route via the Fraser. In that year the brigade from New Caledonia, the Thompson River and the upper Columbia, broke its way through the Fraser Canyon to newly established Fort Yale. The canyon route proved too difficult so the following year Fort Hope was built 20 miles downstream and a trail cut over the Cascade Mountain to Kamloops. Gold mining became important in the district and while the fort was demolished about 1880, Fort Yale became an important centre for construction of the Canadian Pacific Railway.

FORT YUKON | 7150 gt | 7.43 | Vic | BDD/VDD Vancouver, BC

Nominated manager, (DOC) Capper Alexander & Co. Ltd. London.			
1947 *Nanaimo County*	Acadia Overseas Freighters Ltd./I.H. Mathers & Son, Halifax		
	Counties S.M. Co. Ltd. London		
1949 *Haifa*	Israel America Line Ltd./Mgr. Shoham Sherutey Hayam Ltd. Haifa, Israel		
1054 *Tarin*	Bozzo & Rollo, Genoa, Italy		

FORT YUKON - In 1847 Alexander Hunter Murray established the most remote of all HBC posts. Murray followed the Porcupine River to its junction with the Yukon River and there built Fort Yukon in what was Russian territory. In 1850 it was visited by Robert Campbell of Fort Selkirk. When Selkirk was destroyed in 1852, Fort Yukon was the only English fur trading post on the Yukon River. After Alaska became an American possession, the HBC withdrew to a new site on the Porcupine River and there erected Fort Rampart in order to continue its Yukon trade.

Vessel Name:	Tonnage:	Completion date:	Type:	Builder & Yard location
FRONTENAC PARK	7130 gt	11.44	Can	MI Sorel, QC

Nominated manager, Constantine Lines Ltd. Montreal.

1946 *Victoria County*	Acadia Overseas Freighters Ltd./I.H. Mathers & Son Ltd./Halifax, NS
1950 *Akron*	Iberia Cia. Mar, SA, Puerto Cortes, Honduras/Mgr. Hadjilias & Co. London
28.3.63	Aground, S of Ras al Ardh, refloated 30.3.63. Towed to Japan for scrapping in 1963.

FRONTENAC PARK -

1. Provincial park located N of Kingston, ON (see also Fort Frontenac).
2. Name of counties in Ontario and Quebec.

GARDEN PARK	7130 gt	3.45	Can	BDD North Van, BC

Nominated manager, Anglo - Canadian Shipping Co. Ltd. Vancouver

1946 *Lake Cowichan*	Western Canada Steamships Ltd. Vancouver, BC
1949 *Annitsa*	Tramp Chartering Corp. S.A. Panama/Constantine J. Carras client of A Lusi Ltd. London
1967	Scrapped in Japan.

GARDEN PARK -

1. Community and Indian Reserve, east side of Ste. Sault Marie, ON. On US - Canada border, situated on the channel connecting Whitefish Bay and Lake Superior to North Channel of Lake Huron.
2. Believed to be an abbreviated and Anglicized version of the name Grande Jardins Provincial Park, which forms part of the western section of Laurentide Park.

Gaspesian Park as *Polyxeni* (Phil Chandler)

GASPESIAN PARK	7130 gt	7.45	Can	PRDS Prince Rupert, BC

Nominated manager, Montreal Shipping Co. Ltd., Montreal

1946 *Mont Gaspé*	Montship Lines Ltd. Montreal/Ass. Buries Markes Ltd. London
1954 *Polyxeni*	Cia, de Nav para Viajes Globales AS, Panama. Costa Rican flag/Mgr. Demosthenes P. Margaronis, Athens, Greece
6.2.65	Grounded on Carapebus Shoal near Vitoria, Brazil. CTL.
8.65	Towed to Valencia, Spain for scrapping.

Note: This vessel was the last to be built by any Canadian yard for the wartime emergency shipbuilding program of 10,000 ton freighters, although some partly built maintenance ships were completed later as merchant vessels.

GASPESIAN PARK - Provincial park located on the Gaspé Peninsula, QC.

GATINEAU PARK	7130 gt	7.42	NS	DSBR Lauzon, QC

Nominated manager, Canadian Pacific Steamships Ltd. Montreal

1946	Transferred to MOWT London.

Nominated manager, (DOC) Aviation & Shipping Co. (Noel Purvis) London

1950 *Alkis*	Cape Breton Freighters Ltd. Montreal/S.G. Embiricos Ltd. London
1964 *Acer*	
1969	Scrapped at Miike, Japan.

GATINEAU PARK - Ottawa area National park covering a large area of the Gatineau Hills.

Vessel Name:	Tonnage:	Completion date:	Type:	Builder & Yard location
GIRDLE NESS	8580 dt	9.45	Vic	WCSB Vancouver, BC

Royal Navy, UK

Built as a Landing Craft Maintenance ship. In 1956 rebuilt as a Guided Missiles Trials ship at Devonport and engaged in various trials for guided missiles. In 1962 reduced to accommodation ship and with *Duncansby Head* formed the accommodation establishment HMS *Cochrane*.

GIRDLE NESS - Headland with lighthouse about a half mile east of the entrance to the harbour of Aberdeen, Scotland. Also marks the northern limit of Nigg Bay.

GLACIER PARK	7130 gt	12.42	NS	MI Sorel, QC

Nominated manager, Cunard White Star Ltd. Montreal

1946 *Wabana*	Dominion Shipping Co. Ltd. Sydney NS/Dominion Steel & Coal Corp. Ltd. Montreal
1964	Transferred to Liberian flag, Same beneficial owner.
1972	Scrapped in Japan

GLACIER PARK - National park close to Mount Revelstoke National Park and the town of Revelstoke, BC.

GOLDSTREAM PARK	7130 gt	11.44	Vic	NVSR North Van, BC

Launched as *Fort Harrison*.

Nominated manager, North Pacific Shipping Co. Ltd. Vancouver

1946 *Cottrell*	Elder Dempster Lines (Canada) Ltd.
1961 *Santagata*	
1971	Scrapped at Blythe, UK

GOLDSTREAM PARK - Located in Metchosin District of Southern Vancouver Island, west of Victoria, BC,

FORT HARRISON - see entry under this name

Grafton Park as *Sunray* (Phil Chandler)

GRAFTON PARK	7130 gt	10.44	Cana	USY Montreal, QC

Nominated manager, Canadian Pacific Steamships Ltd. Montreal

1948 *Sunray*	Saguenay Terminals Ltd. London. UK
1953 *Sunjarv*	Same as above
1961 *Katerina*	
1967	Scrapped at Onomichi, Japan

GRAFTON PARK - Town about 15km ENE of Cobourg, ON.

GREEN GABLES PARK	7130 gt	7.43	NS	NVSR North Van, BC

Launched as *Fort Esperance (I)*.

Nominated manager, Canada Shipping Company, Vancouver

1946 *Papachristidis Vassilios*	Papachristidis Company, Montreal
1949 *Worldtrotter*	Papachristidis Company, Montreal
1953 *Marcos*	Efcarriers Co. Inc. Liberia/Seres Shipping Co. Inc. New York
1964 *Esperanza*	
1964 *Kwong Lee*	
1967	Scrapped at Kaohsiung, Taiwan

GREEN GABLES PARK - National park located on Prince Edward Island. Name inspired by fictional story "Ann of Green Gables." Ann's house is located at Cavendish, within park limits.

FORT ESPERANCE, see entry under this name.

Vessel Name:	Tonnage:	Completion date:	Type:	Builder & Yard location
GREEN HILL PARK	7130 gt	1.44	Vic	BDD/VDD Vancouver, BC

Launched as *Fort Simcoe (I)*.
Nominated manager, Canada Shipping Company, Vancouver.

6.3.45		On fire, exploded at Vancouver, beached off Stanley Park.
12.3.45		Refloated, declared CTL. (see separate account)
1946 *Phaeax II*		Polar Cia de Nav, Ltd.a. Panama/Spyridon Paramythiotis, owner
		Mgr. Union Maritime & Shipping Co. Ltd. London
1956 *Lagos Michigan*		Cia. Armadora San Francisco. SA/Mgr. Salvatores & Racah SRL. Genoa.
1967		Scrapped at Kaohsiung, Taiwan.

GREEN HILL PARK - Provincial park located near New Glasgow, NS. (See also Fort Simcoe.)

Vessel Name:	Tonnage:	Completion date:	Type:	Builder & Yard location
HAMILTON PARK	2895 gt	7.45	Scan/R	ME&D Quebec City, QC

Nominated manager, Saguenay Terminals Ltd., Montreal

1948 *D'Arcy McGee*	
1948 *Stad Dordrecht*	Halcyon Lijn, NV, Rotterdam
1962 *Serena Secondo*	
1962 *Serena II*	
1973	Scrapped in Italy

HAMILTON PARK - Location at Hamilton, ON. A fairly frequent name in the history of Canada which increases the likelihood of other city parks across the land.

Vessel Name:	Tonnage:	Completion date:	Type:	Builder & Yard location
HAMPSTEAD PARK	7130 gt	11.44	Can	USY Montreal, QC

Nominated manager, Canadian Pacific Steamships, Montreal.

1946 *Cheticamp*	Dingwall Shipping Co. Ltd. Halifax
1955 *Carini*	Sicilarma Soc. di Nav. per Azioni, Palermo, Sicily.
10.65	Scrapped at Valencia, Spain.

HAMPSTEAD PARK - Suburb of Montreal between Westmount and Dorval International Airport.

Vessel Name:	Tonnage:	Completion date:	Type:	Builder & Yard location
HARTLAND POINT	8580 dt	7.45	Vic	BDD/VDD Vancouver, BC

Royal Navy, UK
Built as a Landing Ship Maintenance ship.

1956	Commenced conversion to an Escort Maintenance ship
1960	Operational base ship at Hong Kong.
1965	Reserve status at Portsmouth.

HARTLAND POINT - Prominent headland on the north coast of Devon. Marks the westerly point of Bideford Bay. About 20km west of town of Bideford and the shipbuilding centre of Appledore.

Vessel Name:	Tonnage:	Completion date:	Type:	Builder & Yard location
HASTINGS PARK	7130 gt	8.44	Vic	VMD Victoria, BC

Launched as *Fort St. Ignace (II)*.
Nominated manager, Empire Shipping Ltd. Vancouver, BC

1946 *Lake Kamloops*	Western Canada Steamships Ltd. Vancouver.
1950 *Lavadara*	Muhammadi Steamship Co. Ltd. Karachi, Pakistan
1952 *Al Sayyada*	Same owner as above.
1967	Scrapped in Pakistan

HASTINGS PARK - Large city park, east side of Vancouver which used to house the city's main amusement activities and a race track. Popularly known as Exhibition Park, but now in process of reverting to its official name and original use as the entertainment facilities are phased out.

FORT ST. IGNACE (II) - See entry under Tecumseh Park.

HECTOR PARK see separate story and CAMP DEBERT.

Vessel Name:	Tonnage:	Completion date:	Type:	Builder & Yard location
HIGH PARK	7130 gt	7.43	NS	DSBR Lauzon, QC

Nominated manager, Furness Withy & Co. Ltd. Montreal

1946	Transferred to the MOWT,
	Nominated manager, Aviation & Shipping Co. Ltd. (Noel Purvis) London.
1950 *Woldingham Hill*	Falaise S.S. Co. Ltd. Halifax/Counties Ship Management Co. London
1967	Scrapped at Keelung, Taiwan

HIGH PARK - West Toronto park in the suburban area of Swansea

Vessel Name:	Tonnage:	Completion date:	Type:	Builder & Yard location
HIGHLAND PARK	7130 gt	6.45	Can	NVSR North Van, BC

Nominated manager, Montreal, Australia & New Zealand Line, (MANZ) Montreal.
1948 *Sunjewel* — Saguenay Terminals Ltd. London
1960 *Leefoon*
1963 — Scrapped at Hong Kong.

HIGHLAND PARK - A park and district in North Calgary, near Calgary International airport.

HILLCREST PARK	7130 gt	5.44	NS	USY Montreal, QC

Nominated manager, Cunard White Star Ltd. Montreal
1946 — Transferred to the MOWT,
Nominated manager, (DOC) Cunard White Star Ltd. Liverpool
1950 *Bembridge Hill* — Counties Ship Management group London
1957 *Elimarie* — Marproeza Cia. Nav. SA Panama/Bray Shipping Co. Ltd. London
1965 *Tai Fong*
1968 — Scrapped at Kaohsiung, Taiwan

HILLCREST PARK - A city park adjoining Queen Elizabeth Botanical Gardens in Vancouver, BC.

JASPER PARK	7130 gt	9.42	NS	DSBR Lauzon, QC

Nominated manager, Furness Withy (Canada) Ltd. Montreal
6.7.43 — Sunk by submarine torpedo 32.52S, 42.13E in South Indian Ocean (see separate story).

JASPER PARK - National park and resort located in the Rocky Mountains of Alberta, the most northerly of the two main passes through the mountains carrying transcontinental railway lines. This pass carries the CN main lines to Vancouver and Prince Rupert.

KAWARTHA PARK	7130 gt	6.44	NS	MI Montreal, QC

Nominated manager, March Shipping Agency, Ltd. Montreal
1946 — Transferred to MOWT,
Nominated manager, (DOC) South American Saint Line Ltd. Cardiff.
1950 *Haverton Hill* — Counties Ship Management group
1955 *Grande Hermine* — Papachristidis Company Ltd. Montreal
1960 *Canuck Trader* — Canuck Lines/Papachristidis Company Ltd. Montreal
1965 *Eliza* — Quincy Chuang c/o Fuji, Marden & Co. Ltd. Hong Kong
Mgr. Hong Kong Shipowners & Managers Ltd.
1968 — Scrapped at Hong Kong

KAWARTHA PARK - Town on Dummer Lake, 25km NNE of Peterborough, ON. It is at the centre of Peterborough County in an area referred to as the Kawartha Lakes. The park carries the official name Kawartha Highlands Provincial Park.

KELOWNA PARK	2875 gt	7.44	Scan	FM Pictou, NS

Nominated manager, Pickford & Black Ltd. Halifax
1948 *La Petite Hermine* — Seagull Steamship Co. of Canada Ltd. Montreal (connected with Papachristidis Company)
1952 — Transferred to the Indian Navy
1953 — Deleted from the register for non - commercial use
1960 — Commissioned as naval repair ship *Dharini*.

KELOWNA PARK - The largest city in the Okanagan area of British Columbia.

KENSINGTON PARK	2875 gt	10.43	Scan	FM Pictou, NS

Transferred to MOWT, Britain. Nominated manager, not confirmed
1945 *Yersin* — Soc. des Afreteurs Maritimes, Saigon
1948 *Docteur Yersin* — Same as above
14.5.53 — Aground 5km NE of Dong Hoi, near Saigon, TL

KENSINGTON PARK -
1. Town on central north coast of Prince Edward Island
2. Municipal parks in Vancouver and Burnaby, BC

KILDONAN PARK	7130 gt	9.43	NS	USY Montreal, QC

Nominated manager, McLean Kennedy Ltd. Montreal
1946 *Inverness County* — Acadia Overseas Freighters Ltd./I.H. Mathers & Son, Halifax
1954 *Cassian* — San Felicia Cia. Nav. SA. Panama/Marcou & Sons (Shipbrokers) Ltd. London
1967 — Scrapped at Yokosuka, Japan.

KILDONAN - East and West Kildonan, northerly suburbs of Winnipeg, straddling the Red River.

KINNAIRD HEAD see MULL OF GALLOWAY

KITSILANO PARK — 7130 gt — 12.43 — VIC — NVSR North Van, BC

Launched as *Fort Sandusky (I).*
Nominated manager, Empire Shipping Co. Ltd. Vancouver
1946 *Lake Kootenay* — Western Canada Steamships Ltd. Vancouver.
1949 *Phopho* — Comp. Mar. Sampson Ltd.a, Panama
1950 *Harry Lundeberg* — Kaiser Gypsum Co. Redwood City, CA
8.2.54 — Wrecked off Cape San Lucas, Lower California, 22.52N 109.53W, CTL

KITSILANO PARK - City park which once formed part of the route of the CPR through Vancouver suburbs. Once the site of an Indian village of which all trace has disappeared. (See entry under Fort Sandusky (II).)

KOOTENAY PARK (I) — 7130 gt — 8.42 — NS — WCSB, Vancouver, BC

Launched as *Fort Carlton.*
Nominated manager, Canadian - Australasian Line Ltd. Vancouver.
1944 *Fort Nisqually* — Transferred to MOWT
    Nominated manager, (DOC) McCowen & Gross Ltd. London
1950 *Kingsmount* — Kingsbridge Shipping Co. Ltd./Goulandris Bros. Montreal
1957 *Monteplata* — Monteplata Cia. Nav. SA/Camberley S.S. Co. Ltd. London owners, D.L. & N.L. Condylis.
1961 *Ekali*
1965 *Loyal Fortunes*
1974 — Scrapped in Egypt

KOOTENAY PARK - Alberta National park, Alberta. Located in Rockies adjacent to Banff and Yoho National parks. (See also Fort Carlton, Fort Niqually.)

KOOTENAY PARK (II) see MOHAWK PARK (II).

KOOTENAY PARK (III) — 7130 gt — 9.44 — Vic — BDD/VDD Vancouver, BC

Launched as *Mohawk Park (III).*
Nominated manager, Canadian - Australasian Line Ltd. Vancouver
1946 *Seaboard Pioneer* — Seaboard Shipping Ltd. Vancouver, BC
1960 *Pioneer* — Cia. Mar. del Este, SA. Panama/Goulandris Bros. (Hellas) Ltd. Piraeus, Greece
1964 *Atromitos*

KOOTENAY PARK see above.

LAFONTAINE PARK — 7130 gt — 8.43 — NS — USY Montreal, QC

Nominated manager, McLean Kennedy Ltd. Montreal
1946 — Transferred to MOWT, London
    Nominated manager (DOC) Lambert Bros. Ltd. London
1950 — To be renamed *Hazel Hill.* Plans evidently changed.
1951 *Peterstar* — Fairview Overseas Freighters Ltd./Lyras & Lemos Ltd.
    London/Clients of I.H. Mathers & Son, Halifax.
1957 *Aspis*
1957 *Prosperity* — Prosperity S.S. Corp. Liberia/Vlassopulo Bros. Ltd. London
1959 *Polyniki*
1965 *Ivory Neptune*
1971 — Scrapped at Shanghai

LAFONTAINE PARK -
1. Large city park in Montreal.
2. City Park located in central Hull, QC

LAKESIDE PARK — 7130 gt — 4.45 — Cana — VMD Victoria, BC

Nominated manager, Canadian Pacific Steamships Ltd. Montreal
1946 *Lakeside* — Andros Shipping Co. Montreal/Goulandris Bros. London and New York
1952 *Evgenia MG* — Comarc Cia. Nav. SA Panama/Capeside Steamship Co, Ltd. London
    Goulandris Bros. New York
1952 *Theodora* — Cia. Nationale Maritima Dora SA Panama/Lemos & Pateras Ltd. London
25.8.58 — Aground, refloated and beached off Bural Reef 22.30N 69.15E in northern section of the Arabian Sea.
10.9.58 — Broke in two.
14.9.58 — Arrived Port Okha, CTL. Sold to shipbreakers.

LAKESIDE PARK -
1. Provincial park at Grand Lake, NB.
2. City park at Nelson, BC.

Vessel Name:	Tonnage:	Completion date:	Type:	Builder & Yard location
LAKEVIEW PARK	7130 gt	10.44	Cana	MI Sorel, QC

Nominated manager, Furness Withy & Co. Ltd. Montreal
1946 *Halifax County*   Acadia Overseas Freighters Ltd./I.H. Mathers & Son Ltd. Halifax NS
1949 *Canopus*   Soc. Transoceanica Canopus SA. Panama/Rethymnis & Kulukundis Ltd. London
1960 *Ventura Feliz*
1967   Scrapped at Onomichi, Japan
LAKEVIEW PARK - A municipal park located in Vernon, BC

LANSDOWNE PARK	2875 gt	4.43	Scan	DSBR Lauzon, QC

Transferred to MOWT. Nominated manager, not recorded.
1947 *Federal Trader*   Federal Commerce & Navigation Co. Ltd. Montreal.
1951 *Provincial Trader*
1951 *Gander Bay*   Allied S.S. Lines Ltd./Montreal Shipping Co. Ltd. Montreal
1955 *Atlawill*   Plymouth Navigation Co. Liberia
1958 *Caribbean Trader*
6.7.43   Aground on Alacan Reef, north of Progresso, Mexico. TL.
LANSDOWNE PARK -
1. At Richmond, BC. At one time prominent as a horse racing track, but now covered in modern day real estate developments.
2. A city park in Ottawa. Site of the annual Central Canada Exhibition.
The name originates with the Marquis of Lansdowne, Governor General of Canada from 1883 - 1888.

LA SALLE PARK	7130 gt	4.44	NS	USY Montreal, QC

Launched as *Fort Niagara*.
Nominated manager, Cunard White Star Ltd. Montreal.
1946 *Triland*   Triton S.S. Co. Montreal, affiliated with March Shipping Agency/Goulandris Bros.
       London, UK
1957 *Manhattan*   Bahia Salinas Cia. Nav. SA, Panama/Goulandris Bros. Ltd. London
1964 *Eastern Skipper*   Federal Nav. Co. Ltd./First S.S. Co. Ltd. Taipei, Taiwan
LA SALLE PARK - Montreal, city park in the Lachine area, commemorating Rene - Robert Cavalier de La Salle, French explorer, would - be Jesuit, fur trader and intriguer. Greatly romanticized by 19th century historians his main claim to fame was his descent of the Mississippi upon which French claims to the delta lands of that river and what became Louisiana are based. His name was bestowed on towns and universities throughout the region from Quebec down the Mississippi valley, but modern historians recognize that his many shortcomings, including mental instability, produced some disastrous results for his followers which resulted in his assassination in Texas in 1687.

LAURENTIDE PARK	7130 gt	11.42	NS	MI Sorel, QC

Nominated manager, McLean Kennedy Ltd. Montreal
1950 *Winter Hill*   Laurentide S.S. Co. Ltd. Montreal/Nordic Ship Mgmt. Co, Ltd. Montreal
       Counties Ship Management Co. Ltd. London.
1956 *Petite Hermine*   Papachristidis Company Ltd. Montreal
1960 *Canuk Port*   Canuck Lines/Papachristidis Company Ltd. Montreal
1961 *Pantanassa*
1967   Scrapped in Tsingtao, China.
LAURENTIDE PARK - A large provincial park north of Quebec City. Correct spelling is Laurentides.

LEASIDE PARK	7130 gt	1.44	Vic	NVSR North Van, BC

Nominated manager, Anglo - Canadian Shipping Co. Ltd. Vancouver.
1946 *Lake Lillooet*   Western Canada Steamships Ltd. Vancouver.
1948 *Cnosaga*   Cia. Nav. Oceanica, SA, Panama/Michael G. Livanos, Athens, Greece
1967   Scrapped at Kaohsiung, Taiwan.
LEASIDE PARK - Large Toronto area park taking its name from the District of Leaside.

LISCOMB PARK	2875 gt	9.44	Scan	FM Pictou, NS

Nominated manager, Canadian National Steamships Ltd. Montreal
1948 *Saint Malo*   Seagull S.S. Co. of Canada, Montreal/Papachristidis Company, Montreal
1951 *Tapajos*   Panama Shipping Co. Inc. Panama/Booth American Shipping Corp. New York
       Ass. with Booth S.S. Co. and Lamport & Holt Line, Ltd. both of Liverpool UK
1955 *Orland*   A/S Auctor, (Aarnt Haarburg), Bergen, Norway.
1964 *Sagitta*
1972   Scrapped at Trieste, Italy.
LISCOMB PARK - A wildlife preserve established in Nova Scotia in 1928, located S of New Glasgow, NS. Now designated as a game sanctuary.

Vessel Name:	Tonnage:	Completion date:	Type:	Builder & Yard location
LORNE PARK	2875 gt	7.45	Scan/D	FM Pictou, NS

Nominated manager, Canadian National Steamships Ltd. Montreal.

1947 *Canadian Leader*	Canadian Leader Ltd. c/o CNSS, Montreal.
23.11.57	Laid up at Halifax, NS. Sold to Cuba but transfer never completed.
1.65	Scrapped at Aviles, Spain

LORNE PARK - Town between Bathurst and Campbellton, NB, Bay of Chaleur area. The name "Lorne" comes up in a variety of ways across Canada and usually commemorates John Douglas Sutherland Campbell, Marques of Lorne and later Duke of Argyll, governor general of Canada, 1878 - 83.

Vessel Name:	Tonnage:	Completion date:	Type:	Builder & Yard location
LOUISBOURG PARK	7139 gt	2.44	Vic	BDD/VDD Vancouver, BC

Nominated manager, Canadian Transport Company Ltd. Vancouver.

1946 *Harmac Chemainus*	Canadian Transport Company Ltd., Vancouver,
1949 *Bombay*	Eastern Shipping Corp. Ltd./Scindia S.N. Co. Ltd. Bombay, India
1954 *Star of Saurashtra*	Eastern Shipping Corp. Ltd. Bombay
1960	Scrapped at Bombay

LOUISBOURG PARK - Located at Louisbourg, Cape Breton Island, a fortress built by the French, but taken by the British, which was a focal point in the Anglo - French colonial wars. The remains of the fortifications have been preserved and form part of the park.

Vessel Name:	Tonnage:	Completion date:	Type:	Builder & Yard location
MAISONNEUVE PARK	7130 gt	9,45	Scan	ME&D Quebec City, QC

Nominated manager, Canadian National Steamships Ltd. Montreal

1947 *Canadian Highlander*	Canadian National Steamships Ltd. Montreal.
23.11.57	Laid up at Halifax.
1958	Sold to Cuba but sale not completed.
1.65	Scrapped at Bilbao, Spain.

MAISONNEUVE PARK - City park and botanical gardens in Montreal. Name for Paul de Chomedey de Maisonneuve, generally regarded as the founder of Montreal when he established a fort on the Island of Montreal in 1642.

Vessel Name:	Tonnage:	Completion date:	Type:	Builder & Yard location
MANITOU PARK	2875 gt	10.43	Scan	FM Pictou, NS

Transferred to MOWT, no nominated manager recorded.

1946 *Albert Calmette*	Central Supply Co. of Indo - China
1948 *Docteur A. Calmette*	As above - Mgrs. Messageries Maritimes, Marseilles, France
1950 *Darlac*	Denis Freres d'Indochine, SA, Saigon
1955 *Hong Kong Trader*	Hong Kong Navigation & Investment Co.
1958 *Batu Pahat*	Great Southern S.S. Co. Hong Kong
1962 *Sandakan Bay*	
1965 *Luen Tang*	
1971	Scrapped at Kaohsiung, Taiwan.

MANITOU PARK -

1. The town of Manitou is located in the Pembina Hills area of Southern Manitoba,

2. Lac Manitou and the village of Lac Manitou Sud are located in the ski resort area N of Montreal, near southern end of Mont Tremblant Park.

3. There are at least six other lake, river or beach locations carrying the name Manitou, in Ontario, Quebec and Saskatchewan.

Vessel Name:	Tonnage:	Completion date:	Type:	Builder & Yard location
MAYFAIR PARK	2875 gt	6.43	Scan	DSBR Lauzon, QC

Launched as Camp Valcartier, for bareboat charter to MOWT, charter intention cancelled and ship completed as *Mayfair Park*. Managing owner, Park Steamship Company, Ottawa.

Nominated manager not confirmed.

1945 *Siderurgica Quatro*	Cia. Siderurgica Nacional, Rio de Janeiro, Brazil.
1972	Scrapped in Brazil

MAYFAIR PARK -

1. A park and district in Saskatoon, SK

2. Municipal park located on north shore of the Fraser River, at the Port Mann Bridge in Coquitlam, BC. The surrounding area is now named the Mayfair Industrial Park.

Vessel Name:	Tonnage:	Completion date:	Type:	Builder & Yard location
MEWATA PARK	7130 gt	2.44	Vic	BDD North Van, BC

Nominated manager, Canadian Transport Co. Ltd. Vancouver

1947 *Harmac Crofton*	Canadian Transport Company Ltd. Vancouver.
1949 *West Bengal*	Eastern Shipping Corp. Bombay
1954 *Star of West Bengal*	As above
1960	Scrapped in Pakistan

MEWATA PARK - Name of National Defence armouries and property in Calgary, AB.

Vessel Name:	Tonnage:	Completion date:	Type:	Builder & Yard location
MILLICAN PARK	2400 gt	8.44	Lakes/T	CSY Collingwood, ON

Nominated manager, Imperial Oil Ltd. Toronto

1945 *Firbranch*	Branch Lines Ltd. Montreal/Joseph Simard Group of companies which including Marine Industries Ltd.
1970	Scrapped in Sorel, QC

MILLICAN PARK - No explanation as to park location found.

MISSION PARK	7130 gt	10.44	Vic	VMD Victoria, BC

Launched as *Fort Berens* for MOWT

Nominated manager, Canadian Transport Co. Ltd. Vancouver.

1947 *Ottawa Valley*	Montreal Australia New Zealand Line Ltd. (MANZ), a joint venture of Ellerman Lines, Ltd., New Zealand Shipping Co. and Port Line Ltd. (operated by Trinder Anderson & Co. Ltd. London.)
1954 *Rog*	Splosna Plovba,(Gov't of Yugoslavia, Belgrade)
1966 *Mills Trident*	Aries Shipping Company, Hong Kong.
1969	Scrapped at Kaohsiung, Taiwan

MISSION PARK -

1. Mission City, north side of Fraser River, East of Vancouver.

2. At Kelowna, Mission Park shopping centre is located in the southern part of the city.

3. A park known as Mission Creek Sports Fields is located on Mission Creek in the Okanagan Mission District, south of Kelowna.

FORT BERENS - see separate entry under this name.

MOHAWK PARK (I)	7130 gt	6.43	NS	BDD North Van, BC

Launched as *Fort Norway.*

Nominated manager, not confirmed.

1944	Transferred to MOWT as *Fort Spokane.* Nominated manager, (DOC) Watts, Watts & Co. Ltd. London.
1951 *La Orillia*	Buries Markes Ltd. London
1952 *Ariella*	Fratelli D'Amico, Rome, Italy
1964	Scrapped at Trieste

MOHAWK PARK - The Mohawk Indian nation occupied a large area of the N.E. United States and overlapped into Canada, particularly at the Caughnawaga and St. Regis (Akwasasne) reserves which almost certainly inspired the name. There are a number of Mohawk Parks and other locations bearing the name particularly in the U.S. (See also Fort Norway, Fort Spokane.)

MOHAWK PARK (II)	7130 gt	9.44	Vic	BDD/VDD Vancouver, BC

Launched as *Kootenay Park (II).*

Nominated manager, Canadian - Australasian Line, Vancouver

1947 *Manx Sailor*	Kerr Silver Lines Ltd. Vancouver.
1948 *Vistafjord*	Skibs A/S Malmtransport (Norwegian America Line Ltd. Oslo)
1955 *Mar Cheto*	Mariano Maresca & Co., Genoa, Italy
1963 *Daring*	

MOHAWK PARK - as above.

MONTEBELLO PARK (I)	7130 gt	1.45	Cana	WCSB Vancouver, BC

Nominated manager, Cunard White Star Ltd. Montreal.

1946 *Walton*	Dingwall Shipping Co. Ltd. Halifax/Mgr Quebec S.S. Lines, Montreal. Control held by National Gypsum Co. of New York.
1955 *Aci*	Sicilarma Soc. di Nav. per Azioni, Palermo, Sicily.
1966	Scrapped Vido, Spain

MONTEBELLO PARK - Town on the Ottawa river, 45km west of Lachute, Quebec. Park in St. Catharines, ON.

MONTMORENCY PARK	2875 gt	8.43	Scan	FM Pictou, NS

Launched as *Camp Petawawa* for bareboat charter to MOWT.

Nominated manager, on behalf of MOWT not confirmed.

1946 *August Pavic*	Central Supply Co. of Indo - China
1948 *Docteur Angier*	As above
26.10.49	Ashore on Yoronshima Island, Japan, 27.02N 128.28E TL

MONTMORENCY PARK - Town 10km NNW of the City of Quebec, QC.

Vessel Name:	Tonnage:	Completion date:	Type:	Builder & Yard location
MOOSE MOUNTAIN PARK	7130 gt	2.44	Vic/T	WCSB Vancouver, BC

Nominated manager, Shell Canadian Tankers Ltd. Toronto.
1946 *Benoil*   Skibs A/S Excelsior (Einer Rasmussen) Kristiansand, Norway
1951 *Conqueror*   Balearica, Cia Nav. S.A. Panama
1953   Converted to dry cargo
1953 *Patria*   Patria, Cia Nav. S.A. Panama
20.6.54   Ashore one mile NW of East Point, Santa Rosa Island, California. CTL.
1954 *Running Eagle*   St. Augustine SA, Panama
1955 *Patapsco River*
1963   Scrapped at Hirao, Japan
MOOSE MOUNTAIN PARK - Saskatchewan provincial park, 50km SW of Moosomin, SK.

MOUNT BRUCE PARK	7130 gt	12.43	Vic/T	WCSB Vancouver, BC

Nominated manager, Shell Canadian Tankers Ltd. Toronto
1946 *Port Jeromen/a*
1946 *Mosna*   A/S Mosvold Shipping Co./Martin Mosvold, Farsund, Norway
1954   Converted to dry cargo
1954 *Arlesiana*   Insa Soc. di Nav. Genoa, Italy
1963   Scrapped at Spezia, Italy.
MOUNT BRUCE PARK - Bruce County which extends into the Bruce Peninsula, in Georgian Bay, ON.
Provincial park in Nova Scotia.

MOUNT DOUGLAS PARK	7130 gt	6.43	NS	WCSB Vancouver, BC

Launched as *Fort Green Lake*.
Nominated manager, Canadian Transport Co. Ltd. Vancouver.
4.46   Transferred to MOWT.
Nominated manager Hall Bros. Newcastle - on - Tyne.
19.8.46.   Ashore, Preparis Shoal, Coco Islands, Andaman group 14.48N, 93.43 E, TL.
      (see separate account)
MOUNT DOUGLAS PARK - Provincial park located at North end of Victoria. Site of an observatory.

MOUNT MAXWELL PARK	7130 gt	4.44	Vic/T	WCSB Vancouver, BC

Nominated manager, Shell Canadian Tankers Ltd. Toronto.
1946 *Mount Maxwell*   Familoil SS Co. Montreal
1949   Converted to dry cargo
1949 *Buccaneer*   Alba S.S. Co. Ltd. Panama/S.G. Embiricos Ltd. London
1959 *Plate Mariner*   Plate Shipping Co. Piraeus, Greece.
1953   Scrapped at Spezia, Italy
MOUNT MAXWELL PARK - Provincial park located on Saltspring Island, BC. Contains Mount Maxwell.

MOUNT ORFORD PARK	7130 gt	6.44	NS	USY Montreal, QC

Nominated manager, Constantine Lines (Canada) Ltd. Montreal
1950 *Orford*   Orford S.S. Co. Ltd./Ships Finance & Management Co. Ltd. - George Nicolaou, London
1956 *Cape Rion*   Oceanica, SA. Liberia
1964 *Visayan Merchant*   Indian owner
1965 *Mary M*
MOUNT ORFORD PARK - A Quebec provincial park, near St. Denis de Brompton, Eastern Townships.

MOUNT REVELSTOKE PARK	7130 gt	7.43	NS	MI Sorel, QC

Nominated manager, McLean Kennedy Ltd. Montreal
1948 *Laurentian Forest*   Laurentian Marine Co. Ltd. Montreal/Coulouthros Ltd., London/associated also with
      Triton S.S. Co. Montreal/Goulandris Brothers
1957 *Aegean Wave*   Corona Cia. Nav. SA. Panama/Coulouthros Ltd. London.
1959 *Aegean Zephyr*   Same as above
1962 *Southern Star*
1964 *Luzon Merchant*
1965 *Amfiali*
1967   Scrapped at Singapore
MOUNT REVELSTOKE PARK - National park close to town of Revelstoke, BC, and Glacier National park.

Vessel Name:	Tonnage:	Completion date:	Type:	Builder & Yard location
MOUNT ROBSON PARK (I)	7130 gt	8.42	NS	NVSR North Van, BC

Launched as *Fort Rouge.*
Managing owner, Park Steamship Company, Ottawa
Nominated manager, Canadian Australasian Line Ltd. Vancouver

1944 *Fort Miami (III)*	Transferred to MOWT, London
	Nominated manager, (DOC) Evan Thomas & Radcliffe Ltd. Cardiff
1950 *Midhurst*	Rex Shipping Co. Ltd. Halifax/Hadjilias & Co. London/Client of I.H.
	Mathers & Son Ltd. Halifax, NS
1957 *Andalusia*	Asturias Shipping Co. Panama/Hadjilias & Co. London
1964 *Sevilla*	
1969	Scrapped in Japan

MOUNT ROBSON PARK - BC provincial park located around Mount Robson in the Rockies. (See also Fort Rouge, Fort Miami.)

Vessel Name:	Tonnage:	Completion date:	Type:	Builder & Yard location
MOUNT ROBSON PARK (II)	7130 gt	9.44	Vic	WCSB Vancouver, BC

Launched as *Fort Miami.*
Nominated manager, Canadian Australasian Line Ltd. Vancouver.
The names for this ship and the preceding vessel were exchanged simultaneously in what might have been a rare occasion - a moment in time when there were two ships of the same name on the British or Canadian registers. See also *Yoho Park* for the same process.

1946 *Lake Manitou*	Western Canada Steamships Ltd.
1951 *Cliffside*	Andros Shipping Co. Ltd. Montreal/Goulandris Bros. London
1952 *Niki*	
1953 *Star*	Star Steamship Corp. Liberia.
1964 *Nalon*	
1967	Scrapped at Kaohsiung, Taiwan

MOUNT ROBSON PARK - see entry under this name above.

Vessel Name:	Tonnage:	Completion date:	Type:	Builder & Yard location
MOUNT ROYAL PARK	7130 gt	9.43	Vic/T	VMD Victoria, BC

Nominated manager, Imperial Oil Ltd. Toronto.

1946 *Adna*	H.E. Hansen - Tangen, Kristiansand S, Norway
1954	Converted to dry cargo
1954 *Sterling Viking*	Sterling Shipping Corp. London
1956 *Alcyone Might*	Alcyone Shipping Co. Ltd. London/Adelphi Vergottis Ltd. London
1957 *Orjen*	Yugo-Slav Ocean Lines, Kotor, Y - S
1968	Scrapped at Kaohsiung, Taiwan

MOUNT ROYAL PARK - Parc de Mont - Royal, Montreal city park.

Vessel Name:	Tonnage:	Completion date:	Type:	Builder & Yard location
MULGRAVE PARK	2895 gt	4.45	Scan/R	FM Pictou, NS

Nominated manager, H.E. Kane & Co. Ltd. Halifax

1946 *Dun Yu*	
1951 *Nan Hai*	
1983	Condemned in China. Probably scrapped thereafter.

MULGRAVE PARK - Nova Scotia town on Straits of Canso, opposite Port Hawksbury.

Vessel Name:	Tonnage:	Completion date:	Type:	Builder & Yard location
MULL OF GALLOWAY	8580 dt	5.45	Vic	NVSR North Van, BC

Launched as *Kinnaird Head* for Royal Navy
Built as an Escort Maintenance ship

1951	Motor craft maintenance ship
1954	Inshore Minesweeping Flotilla HQ.
1960	Joined HMS *Sheffield* to form new flagship group, Reserve Fleet.
1965	Scrapped at Hamburg.

MULL OF GALLOWAY - Prominent headland at SW tip of Scotland. Stranraer about 34km to the north is the nearest large town.

Vessel Name:	Tonnage:	Completion date:	Type:	Builder & Yard location
MULL OF KINTYRE	8580 dt	10.45	Vic	NVSR North Van, BC

Royal Navy, UK. Unfinished to UK.

1946/9	Completed as an Experimental base HQ ship for target trials
1950	Armament Maintenance ship
1955	Repair and Accommodation ship
1957	Converted to Minesweeper Maintenance ship
1961	Conversion completed

MULL OF KINTYRE - Prominent headland at the S end of the Kintyre Peninsula. It and the outlying Isle of Arran form the westerly shore of the Firth of Clyde.

MULL OF OA — 8580 dt — 12.46 — Vic — NVSR North Van, BC

Royal Navy Maintenance ship. Original projected name *Trevose Head*, name changed to *Mull of Oa*. Work suspended before completion, sold for conversion to merchant ship.

| 1946 *Turan* | Iran Nav. Co. Ltd. Tehran, Iran |
| 1948 *Betty Ryan* | Comp. Argentina de Pesca SA Buenos Aires, Argentina. |

MULL OF OA - Southernmost point of the Island of Islay in the Western Isles of Scotland.

NEMISKAM PARK — 7130 gt — 7.41 — NS — PRDS Prince Rupert, BC

Nominated manager, Empire Shipping Co. Ltd. Vancouver.

1951 *Darton*	Armdale Overseas Freighters Ltd. Halifax/Nomikos (London) Ltd.
1957 *Federal Commerce*	Federal Commerce & Navigation Co. Ltd. Montreal
1959 *Brasilia*	Arbella S.A. Liberia
1959 *Northern Star*	
1960 *Montego Star*	
1960 *Pacific Traveller*	
1961 *Oceanic Express*	
1966	Scrapped at Hikaro, Japan

NEMISKAM PARK - No explanation or source for this name has been identified

NIPIWAN PARK — 2,400 gt — 11.43 — Lakes/T — CSY Collingwood, ON

Nominated manager, probably Imperial Oil Ltd. Toronto

4.1.45	Damaged by submarine torpedo, forepart of ship sunk at 44.30N, 63.00W. Aft part saved, new forepart built at Pictou.
1949	Re - engined
1952 *Irvinglake*	Irving Oil Ltd. St. John NB
1962	Engines removed, cut back to a barge.

NIPIWAN PARK - An example of a number of incorrect spellings, probably caused by the people responsible at Park Steamship Company relying on a phonetic spelling. The correct spelling is "Nipawin". This Saskatchewan park is located directly east of Prince Albert National Park and NW of the town of Nipawin. Since the war years the park has been renamed Narrow Hills Provincial park.

NORANDA PARK — 7130 gt — 9.44 — NS — USY Montreal, QC

Nominated manager, Cunard White Star Ltd. Montreal.

1946 *Oceanside*	Andros Shipping Company, Montreal/Goulandris Brothers, London
1952 *Magdalene*	Broad S.S. Corp. Monrovia, Liberia/Union Maritime & Shipping Co. Ltd. London - John N Vassiliou
1969	Scrapped at Karachi, Pakistan

NORANDA PARK - Located at Noranda, Quebec. The name Noranda derives from the original corporate name of Northern Canada Mines at the time of the mining developments at Noranda - Rouyn in the 1920s.

NORWOOD PARK — 2400 gt — 11.43 — Lakes/T — CSY Collingwood, ON

Nominated manager, Imperial Oil Limited, Toronto.

| 1945 *Elmbranch* | Branch Lines Ltd. Montreal (Joseph Simard group) |
| 1989 | Stranded then scuttled |

NORWOOD PARK - Town 30km ENE of Peterborough, ON.

OAKMOUNT PARK — 2875 gt — 12.44 — Scan — SJDD St. John, NB

Nominated manager, Pickford & Black Ltd. Halifax

1945 *Oakmount*	Atlantic Shipping Agencies Ltd. Montreal
1948 *Makena II*	Cia. Mar. Panamena S.A. Panama
1951 *Sugar Producer*	Silvertown Services Ltd./Managed by R.S. Dalgliesh Ltd. Newcastle on behalf of Tate & Lyle Ltd. London
1956 *Curran*	
1957 *Ocean Fortune*	Bergens Kulkompani A/S Bergen, Norway
1960	Transferred to Indonesian owners

OAKMOUNT PARK - Undoubtedly a local municipal park, but no source or information located.

ORFORDNESS — 8580 dt — 10.46 — Vic — WCSB Vancouver, BC

Royal Navy, UK

Projected Maintenance ship, sold before completion

| 1947 *Rabaul* | W.R. Carpenter & Co. Ltd. Sydney NSW |
| 1947 *Dongola* | Peninsula & Oriental S.N. Co. London |

Vessel Name:	Tonnage:	Completion date:	Type:	Builder & Yard location

1961 *Apj Ashwini*
1965   Scrapped at Bombay, India

ORFORDNESS - A low lying sandy spit formed by the action of the rivers Alde and Ore. It is a less usual example of land building rather than the more common erosion. Situated south of Aldeburgh, County of Norfolk, England

OTTERBURN PARK	2400 gt	5.44	Lakes/T	CSY Collingwood, ON

Nominated manager, not confirmed
1946 *Sprucebranch*   Branch Lines Ltd. Montreal (Joseph Simard group of companies)
1974   Scrapped

OTTERBURN PARK - Park located on Richelieu River opposite Longueuil, Montreal area.

OUTREMONT PARK	7130 gt	9.44	Can	USY Montreal, QC

Nominated manager, McLean Kennedy Ltd. Montreal
1946 *Brazilian Prince*   Furness (Canada) Ltd. (Prince Line Ltd. London)
1958 *Federal Pioneer*   Federal Commerce & Navigation Co. Ltd. Montreal

OUTREMONT PARK - City park in Outremont District of Montreal

PARKDALE PARK	7130 gt	6.44	Vic	WCSB Vancouver, BC

Nominated manager, Canadian Australasian Line Ltd. Vancouver.
1946 *Waikawa*   Canadian Union Line Ltd. (reg, owner), Managed by Canadian Australasian Line, Vancouver
                (A joint venture of Canadian Pacific Railway Co. and Union S.S. Co. of New Zealand.)
1959 *Fulda*   Marine Dev. & Supply S.A. Panama
PARKDALE PARK -
1. Park immediately south of the University of Calgary, AB
2. Community of Parkdale, PEI

POINT PELEE PARK	7130 gt	8.42	NS/T	CVL Montreal, QC

Launched as *Fort Chimo (I)*.
Nominated manager, Imperial Oil Limited. Toronto
1946 *Ranella*   Erling Hansen Rederi, Kristiansand
1954   Converted to dry cargo
1954 *Hudson River*   International Nav. Corp. Monrovia. Liberia
                Tidewater Commercial Co. Inc. Baltimore, Maryland
1960 *Formosan Star*
1961 *Tai Shing*
1964   Scrapped at Ghent, Belgium.

POINT PELEE PARK - National park at south end of Ontario on Lake Erie.

POINT PLEASANT PARK	7130 gt	11.43	NS	DSBR Lauzon, QC

Nominated manager: Furness Withy & Co. Ltd. Montreal
23.2.45   Sunk by submarine torpedo and gunfire at 29.42 S, 0958E, NW of Capetown
                (see separate account)

POINT PLEASANT PARK - Halifax NS park. Once a military establishment with a Martello tower and fortifications command-ing the entrance to Halifax harbour. Now preserved.

PORTLAND BILL	8580 dt	10.45	Vic	BDD North Van, BC

Royal Navy, UK
Built as an Armament Maintenance ship, converted to merchant ship in:
1951 *Zinnia*   Stag Line Ltd./Joseph Robinson & Sons, North Shields. UK
1964 *Chrysopolis*
1965   Scrapped at Kaohsiung, Taiwan

PORTLAND BILL - Prominent headland about 1km due south of Weymouth, Dorset, UK

PORTLAND PARK	7130 gt	11.44	Can	USY Montreal, QC

Nominated manager: March Shipping Agency Ltd. Montreal
1946 *Marchport*   Canadian Shipowners Ltd./March Shipping Agency Ltd. Montreal with connections
                to Goulandris Brothers, London.
1949 *Mont Clair*   Montship Lines Ltd./Montreal Shipping Co. Ltd./controlled by Buries
                Markes Ltd. London/associated with Louis Dreyfus et Cie, Paris.
1954 *Maria Piera*   G.Gestioni Esercizio Navi, Genoa
1960 *Vittorio Veneto*
1969   Scrapped at Spezia, Italy

PORTLAND PARK - District of St. John, NB.

Vessel Name:	Tonnage:	Completion date:	Type:	Builder & Yard location
PORT ROYAL PARK	7130 gt	10.42	NS	MI Sorel, QC

Launched as *Fort Frontenac*.
Nominated manager: Elder Dempster Lines Ltd. Montreal

1946		Transferred to MOWT
		Nominated manager, Tavistock Shipping Co. (Noel Purvis) London
1950 *Fernhurst*		Rex Shipping Co. Ltd. Halifax/Hadjilias & Co. London/connected with I.H. Mathers & Son, Halifax
1958 *Navarra*		Asturias Shipping Co. Panama/Hadjilias & Co. Ltd. London
1963		Scrapped in Holland

PORT ROYAL PARK - At Annapolis Royal, Nova Scotia

Prince Albert Park as *Champlain* (Foto-Flite)

PRINCE ALBERT PARK	7130 gt	6.42	NS	DSBR Lauzon, QC

Launched as *Fort La Prairie (I)*.
Nominated manager, Elder Dempster Lines Ltd. Montreal

1946		Transferred to MOWT, London
		Nominated manager, Tavistock Shipping Co. Ltd. (Noel Purvis) London
1951 *Champlain*		Champlain Freighters Ltd. Montreal/J.P. Hadoulios Ltd. London
25.6.55		Aground during typhoon at Yulan, Hainan Island, 18.17N, 109.33E, TL.

PRINCE ALBERT PARK - National park about 50km NW of Prince Albert, SK. (See also Fort La Prairie.)

PRINCETON PARK	7130 gt	2.45	Can	BDD/VDD Vancouver, BC

Nominated manager: Anglo - Canadian Shipping Co. Ltd. Vancouver

1946 *Lake Minnewanka*		Western Canada Steamships Ltd. Vancouver.
1954 *Santiago*		Cia. Nav. Madraki, SA, Panama/S.G. Embiricos Ltd. London
1960 *Madrakisame*		as above
1969		Scrapped at Sakaide, Japan

PRINCETON PARK - Town 20km ENE of Woodstock, ON.
Town in South Central BC. There has been much mining in the area. It has had an unusual number of prior names including Vermilion, Red Earth Forks, Similkameen and Allisons, the latter after the first pioneer. Renamed Princeton by James Douglas, Lt - Governor in honour of a visit by the Prince of Wales (Edward VII) around 1860.

QUEENS PARK	7130 gt	6.44	Vic	WCSB Vancouver, BC

Nominated manager: Seaboard Shipping Co. Ltd. Vancouver, BC

1946 *Seaboard Queen*		Seaboard Shipping Co. Ltd.
1950 *Queen*		Cia. Mar. del Este SA, Panama/Goulandris Bros (Hellas) Ltd. Piraeus
1960 *Nimos*		
14.1.62		Collision, sank in shallow water Constantza, Roumania.
16.1.62		Refloated
1964 *Mount Othrys*		

QUEENS PARK -
1. City park in New Westminster, BC.
2. The park surrounding the Ontario parliament buildings and the University of Toronto in Toronto ON.

QUEENSBOROUGH PARK 7130 gt 11.44 Vic WCSB Vancouver, BC

Transferred to MOWT while still in shipyard hands for use as a Royal Navy store ship in the fleet train
1945 *Fort Duquesne* Bareboat charter to MOWT
1947 Taken on permanent strength of the Royal Navy without renaming.
QUEENSBOROUGH PARK - Believed to be the parkland surrounding the Queensborough Community Centre, within the City of New Westminster, BC. (See also Fort Duquesne.)

QUETICO PARK 7130 gt 3.44 Vic/T WCSB Vancouver, BC

Nominated manager; Imperial Oil Limited, Toronto
1946 *Donges* Cia. Mar. de Transports de Goudron, Havre, France
1956 *Azure Coast* St. Paul Shipping Corp., Liberia
1962 Scrapped at Vigo, Spain
QUETICO PARK - Ontario provincial park located near Atikokan, ON

RAME HEAD 8580 dt 8.45 Vic NVSR North Van, BC

Royal Navy, UK
Built as an Escort Maintenance ship
1964 In operational reserve at Portsmouth
RAME HEAD - Prominent headland about 6km SW of Plymouth, Devon, marking the entrance to Plymouth Harbour.

RATTRAY HEAD 8580 dt 10.46 Vic NVSR North Van, BC

Royal Navy, UK
Construction halted and placed for immediate disposal
1946 *Iran* Iran Nav. Co. Ltd. Tehran
1948 *Mabel Ryan* Compania Argentina de Pesca SA, Buenos Aires, Argentina
RATTRAY HEAD - A low sandy headland about 15km north of the small port of Peterhead on the east coast of Scotland.

Richmond Park as *Lake Nipigon* (D. Martin-Smith)

RICHMOND PARK 7130 gt 8.44 Vic NVSR North Van, BC

Nominated manager, Anglo - Canadian Shipping Co. Ltd.
1946 *Lake Nipigon* Western Canada Steamship Co. Ltd.
1949 *Pontoporos* La Plata Cia. de Vapores SA, Panama/N.J. Pateras Sons Ltd. London
1955 *Marie II*
1960 *Marie Lemos* C.M. Lemos interests, London.
RICHMOND PARK - 1. Municipal park located in South Burnaby, BC
2. Popular name for Richmond Nature Park in Richmond, BC
3. Richmond Hill, a district of Toronto, ON

RIDEAU PARK 7130 gt 8.43 NS USY Montreal, QC

Managing owner; Park Steamship Company, Ottawa
Nominated manager; Furness Withy & Co. Ltd. Montreal
1950 *Amersham Hill* Ottawa S.S. Co. Ltd. Halifax/Coulouthros Ltd. London/Clients of I.H. Mathers & Son
Ltd. Halifax, NS
1962 *Petalon*
1965 *Alcibiades*
RIDEAU PARK - Ottawa City Park now named Rideau River Park.

Vessel Name:	Tonnage:	Completion date:	Type:	Builder & Yard location

RIDING MOUNTAIN PARK   1875 gt   1905   Government Shipyard, Sorel, QC

ex - *PWD No 1*, ex - *W.S. Fielding*.

A former dredge converted in 1943 to a tanker. Sold in 11.44 to British Ministry of Transport

1945 *Empire Pike*   Ministry of Transport, London.

1947 *Basingford*   Basinghall Shipping Co. London.

1949   Scrapped at Dunston - on - Tyne

RIDING MOUNTAIN PARK - National park in Western Manitoba, about 100km north of Brandon, MN.

Riverdale Park as *Tridale* (W.S.S. Vancouver Maritime Museum)

RIVERDALE PARK   7130 gt   9.43   NS   DSBR Lauzon, QC

Nominated manager; Furness, Withy & Co. Ltd. Montreal

1946 *Tridale*   Triton S.S. Co. Ltd./March Shipping Agency, Ltd. Montreal/Goulandris Bros. London

1957 *Harrier*   Bahia Salinas Cia. Nav. SA Panama/Goulandris Bros. Ltd. London

1964 *Java Steer*

RIVERDALE PARK -

1. Park near mouth of Don River, Toronto, ON

2. One of several adjoining parks north of the Glenmore Reservoir in Calgary, AB

RIVERVIEW PARK   7130 gt   5.43   NS   DSBR Lauzon, QC

Nominated manager; Canadian Pacific Steamships Ltd. Montreal

1946 *Shelburne County*   Acadia Overseas Freighters Ltd. Halifax/I.H. Mathers & Son Ltd./connected with Counties

Ship Management Ltd. London

1954 *Lily*   Fortaleza Cia. Nav. SA, Panama/Rethymnis & Kulukundis Ltd. London.

1960 *Ebro*

1967   Scrapped at Hong Kong.

RIVERVIEW PARK -

1. On south bank of the Petitcodiac river, opposite Moncton, New Brunswick.

2. City park in south side Vancouver, BC

3. Park and zoo in Peterborough, ON

ROCKCLIFFE PARK   2875 gt   7.43   Scan   DSBR Lauzon, QC

Launched as *Camp Aldershot*, for transfer to MOWT, cancelled.

Nominated manager; Canadian National Steamships Ltd. Montreal

1946   Transferred to Government of Newfoundland

1947 *Brigus*   Ministry of Transport (Gov't of Canada) managed by Canadian National Steamships

1955 *Olcat*   Carmelo Cia, Nav. SA. Panama/Andreadis (UK) Ltd. London

1962 *Bay of Bengal*

1972   Scrapped at Bombay, India

ROCKCLIFFE PARK - City park located in Ottawa. Rockcliffe Park is an area of fine homes and the private residences of the prime minister and leader of the opposition.

ROCKLAND PARK — 2875 gt — 6.45 — Scan/R — ME&D Quebec City, QC

Nominated manager; H.E. Kane & Co. Ltd. Halifax
1946 *Liu Kuo*
1961 *Kai Ling*
ROCKLAND PARK - Site of Lieutenant Governor's residence in Victoria, BC.

ROCKWOOD PARK — 2875 gt — 2.43 — Scan — SJDD St, John, NB

Nominated manager; H.E. Kane & Co. Ltd. Halifax
1947 *La Grande Hermine* — Seagull S.S. Co. of Canada Ltd. Montreal/Associated with Papachristidis Company
1951 *Vianna* — Panama Shipping Co. SA, Panama
1955 *Cap Falcon* — Arm. Leon Mazzella & Cie. Oran, Alg.
1963 *Licola*
ROCKWOOD PARK -
1. City park at St. John, NB
2. Town roughly midway between Georgetown and Guelph, ON

ROCKY MOUNTAINS PARK — 7130 gt — 8.43 — NS — MI Sorel, QC

Nominated manager; Elder Dempster Lines Ltd. Montreal
1950 *Wynchwood Hill* — Falaise S.S. Co. Ltd./Counties Ship Management Co. Ltd. London/Assoc. with I.H. Mathers & Son Ltd. Halifax
1959 — Scrapped at Nagasaki, Japan.
ROCKY MOUNTAINS PARK - This relates to Rocky Mountain House. once a trading post but now an important town in Western Alberta.

RONDEAU PARK — 7130 gt — 4.44 — NS — USY Montreal, QC

Nominated manager; Montreal, Australian, New Zealand Line Ltd. Montreal
1950 *Sycamore Hill* — Halifax Overseas Freighters Ltd./Counties Ship Management Co. Ltd. London. Assoc. with I.H. Mathers & Son, Halifax.
1966 — Scrapped at Hong Kong
RONDEAU PARK - Ontario provincial park located on N shore of Lake Erie, ON.

Rosedale Park as *Poplar Hill* (Ian Farquhar)

ROSEDALE PARK — 7130 gt — 5.44 — NS — USY Montreal, QC

Nominated manager; Canadian Pacific Steamships Ltd. Montreal
1950 *Poplar Hill* — Halifax Overseas Freighters Ltd./Counties Ship Management. London/Assoc. with I.H. Mathers & Son, Halifax.
1960 *Shien Foon*
1968 — Scrapped at Hong Kong
ROSEDALE PARK -
1. Toronto city park adjoining Leaside Park.
2. Fraser Valley town, east of Chilliwack, BC.

RUNNYMEDE PARK — 7130 gt — 6.44 — NS — USY Montreal, QC

Nominated manager; Montreal, Australia, New Zealand Line, Montreal (MANZ)
1951 *Lake Michigan* — Runnymede S.S. Co. Ltd. Montreal/Ships Finance & Management Co. Assoc. with G. Nicolaou Ltd. London
1957 *Karaostasi* — Marempressa Cia. Nav. SA. Liberia/Geo. Nicolaou Ltd. London
1964 *Adelphos Petrakis*
1967 — Scrapped at Niihama, Japan.
RUNNYMEDE PARK - From the Runnymede Library in Toronto, ON

Rupert Park as *Lake Okanagan* (W.S.S. Vancouver Maritime Museum)

RUPERT PARK	7130 gt	5.45	Can	BDD North Van, BC

Nominated manager; Empire Shipping Co. Ltd. Vancouver

1946 *Lake Okanagan* Western Canada Steamships Ltd. Vancouver
1949 *Nueva Gloria* Cia. Farallon de Nav. SA. Panama/D.J. Fafalios, Chios, Greece.

RUPERT PARK - All names carrying the name "Rupert" honour or remember Prince Rupert first governor of the Hudson's Bay Company. Not all referred to a park.
1. City park in Vancouver
2. Rupert House at mouth of Riviere de Rupert, Quebec, on east shore of James Bay.
3. Town of Prince Rupert, BC
4. Fort Rupert on Northern Vancouver Island near Port Hardy.

SALT LAKE PARK	7130 gt	10.44	Vic	VMD Victoria, BC

Nominated manager; Canadian Australasian Line Ltd. Vancouver,

1946 *Wairuna* Canadian Australasian Line Ltd.
1960 *Bonna*

SALT LAKE PARK - A specific lake or park which might have featured this name has not been found. However it is safe to say that there are many alkali or salt lakes and marshes formed from a variety of compounds existing across the country. Most of these have been formed as the result of inadequate drainage or other unique physical conditions.

SAPPERTON PARK	7130 gt	1.44	Vic	BDD/VDD Vancouver, BC

Launched as *Fort Toulouse*. Transfer to MOWT, cancelled.
Nominated manager; Canadian Transport Company Ltd. Vancouver.

1946 *Harmac Alberni* Canadian Transport Co. Ltd.
1948 *Royston Grange* Houlder Line Ltd./Furness Withy & Co. Ltd. UK.
1949 *Yiannis* Rio Pardo Cia. Nav SA, Panama/Goulandris Bros. (Hellas) Ltd. Piraeus.
1967 Scrapped at Miihara, Japan.

SAPPERTON PARK - Located in the Sapperton district of New Westminster. So named for the sappers of the Royal Engineers who once garrisoned the lower mainland from their base at this location.
FORT TOULOUSE see separate entry and Fort Alabama.

SEACLIFF PARK	7130 gt	10.44	Vic	BDD/VDD Vancouver, BC

Nominated manager; Canadian Transport Company Ltd. Vancouver

1946 *Harmac Westminster* Canadian Transport Co. Ltd.
1949 *Panaghia* Cia. de Nav. Sappho, SA. Panama/Constantine Hadjipateras & Sons, Athens. Greece
1958 *Bendita* Elcarriers, Inc. Monrovia/Liberia Seres Shipping, Inc. New York.
1966 Scrapped at Hirao, Japan.

SEACLIFF PARK - No park of this name positively identified

SELKIRK PARK	7130 gt	3.45	Can	NVSR North Van, BC

Nominated manager; Johnson Walton Steamships Ltd. Vancouver

1946 *Tahsis* Johnson Walton Steamships Ltd./controlled by the Danish East Asiatic Co. of Copenhagen
1950 *Pelops* Cia Mar. Samsoc. Ltda., Panama/Hermes Steamship Agency Inc. San Francisco, Cal
1959 *Tai Nan*
1964 Scrapped in Taiwan

SELKIRK PARK - Selkirk, Manitoba. The name perpetuates that of Lord Selkirk who led a major colonization effort to settle the area around the present town of Selkirk.

Vessel Name:	Tonnage:	Completion date:	Type:	Builder & Yard location
SELSEY BILL	8580 dt	11.46	Vic	BDD North Van, BC

Royal Navy, UK

Projected as an Armament Maintenance ship. Sold in unfinished condition and converted to:

| 1946 *Waitemata* | Union Steamship Co. of New Zealand. Used from time to time in Trans - pacific trade of Canadian - Australasian Line in which Union SS had a half interest. |

SELSEY BILL - Prominent headland midway between entrance to Chichester Harbour and Bognor Regis, West Sussex, South of England.

| SEVEN OAKS PARK | 7130 gt | 7.45 | Can | VMD Victoria, BC |

Nominated manager; Seaboard Shipping Company Ltd. Vancouver

1946 *Seaside*	Andros Shipping Co. Ltd. Montreal/Goulandris Bros. London
1952 *Rubystar*	Escobal Cia Nav. S.A. Liberia c/o Triton Shipping, New York/C.M. Lemos & Co. Ltd. London
1956 *Lagos Huron*	Cia. Arm. San Francisco S.p.a. Panama/Salvatores & Racah SRL, Genoa.
26.6.60	Pounded against pier during typhoon and sank at Tabaco, Luzon, Philippines. Partly raised,
6.10.60.	Further damaged in a second typhoon and allowed to settle again.
27.3.61	Raised but allowed to sink again on account of a third approaching typhoon.

SEVEN OAKS PARK - Site of skirmish between North - Western and rival Hudson's Bay Companies men in 1816. Governor Semple and 20 other men out of 29 killed. Seven Oaks was in the Selkirk Settlement near Fort Douglas. The park contains the site of the battle.

| SHAKESPEARE PARK | 7130 gt | 11.45 | Scan/R | SJDD St. John, NB |

Managing owner; Park Steamship Company, Ottawa.
Nominated manager; Saguenay Terminals Ltd.

1948 *Sunprince*	Saguenay Terminals Ltd. Montreal
1959 *Salammanna*	Stanhal Navigation Ltd. Liberia
1964	Scrapped at Gijon, Spain

SHAKESPEARE PARK -
1 Town in Ontario, situated 15km east of Stratford, on the Avon River.
2. There is almost certainly a park of this name in Stratford in the heart of Shakespeare country.

| SIBLEY PARK | 7130 gt | 7.44 | NS | USY Montreal, QC |

Nominated manager, Cunard White Star Ltd. Montreal

1946	Transferred to MOWT
	Nominated manager, Cunard White Star Ltd. Liverpool
1950 *Kenilworth*	Waverley Overseas Freighters Ltd. Halifax/Fafalios Ltd. London/Clients of I.H. Mathers Ltd. Halifax
1956 *Aeolos*	Cia. Filiori de Nav. SA. Panama/D.J. Fafalios, Chios, Greece
1964 *Mojkovac*	Yugoslavian owner
1967	Scrapped at Split, Yugoslavia

SIBLEY PARK - Provincial park on the peninsula opposite Thunder Bay and on the east side of the bay of the same name.

| SILVER STAR PARK | 7130 gt | 12.43 | Vic/T | WCSB Vancouver, BC |

Nominated manager, Shell Canadian Tankers Ltd., Toronto.

12.4.45	Run into while at anchor, by *Mangore*, collision and fire, sold in damaged condition. Repaired.
1945 *Santa Cecilia*	Navebras, Rio de Janeiro, Brazil
1951 *Ilha Grande*	Brazilian Navy
9.3.62	Aground on Manoel Luiz Reef, Coast of Brazil, TL

SILVER STAR PARK - Provincial park due east of Spallumicheen, North Okanagan district of BC. Now a popular ski resort.

| SIMCOE PARK | 7130 gt | 4.45 | Can | NVSR North Van, BC |

Nominated manager, Cunard White Star Ltd. Montreal.

1948 *Sunmount*	Saguenay Terminals Ltd. Montreal
1960 *Shun Fung*	
5.9.64	Aground, Hong Kong in typhoon. Back broken. T.L.

SIMCOE PARK - Town in Ontario, 35km south of Brantford, ON

| SPRINGBANK PARK | 2400 gt | 9.44 | Lakes/T | CSY Collingwood, ON |

Nominated manager; Imperial Oil Ltd. Toronto, ON.

1946 *Polarbranch*	Branch Lines Ltd. Montreal/Joseph Simard group
28.11.53	Ashore at entrance to Boca de Cenizas, 3m from Barranquilla. Twice refloated.
13.12.53	Towed to Cristóbal, TL. Vessel purchased by Straits Towing Ltd. towed to Vancouver BC, converted to barge, *Straits Conveyor*. Subsequently lost off BC Coast.

SPRINGBANK PARK - City park in London, ON.

SPURN POINT   7130 gt   12.45   Vic   BDD/VDD Vancouver, BC

Royal Navy, UK.

Built as Landing Craft Maintenance ship, work halted, converted to cargo/passenger liner.

1947 *Lakemba*   Pacific Shipowners Ltd. Suva, Fiji/W.R. Carpenter Ltd. Sydney NSW

SPURN POINT - Better known as Spurn Head, a long narrow spit of sand and shingle, on the Yorkshire side of the river, jutting into the estuary of the River Humber, east coast of England.

Stanley Park (D. McMillan collection)

STANLEY PARK   7130 gt   7.43   NS   MI Montreal, QC

Nominated manager; Elder Dempster Lines Ltd. Montreal.

Transferred to MOWT.

Nominated manager, Dalhousie Steam & Motorship Co, Ltd. (Nomikos & Co.)London

1948 *Haligonian Duchess*   Acadia Overseas Freighters (Halifax) Ltd./Rethymnis & Kulukundis Ltd. London.
                     Clients of I.H. Mathers & Son. Halifax

1950 *Malden Hill*   Acadia Overseas Freighters Ltd. under Counties Ship Management group, London.

1964 *Newmoor*   Trafalgar S.S. Co. Ltd./Tsavliris (Shipping) Ltd. London

1969   Scrapped at Spezia, Italy.

STANLEY PARK - The largest and most spectacular of Vancouver's city parks at the seaward gateway to the Port of Vancouver, Named for Governor General Lord Stanley at the time of dedication by way of the lease of the land in perpetuity to the City of Vancouver.

STRATHCONA PARK   7130 gt   9.43   Vic   BDD North Van, BC

Nominated manager; Furness Withy & Co. Ltd. Montreal

1946 *Cabano*   Elder Dempster Lines Ltd. Montreal

1960 *Happy Voyager*

1964 *Hitaka*

STRATHCONA PARK - Large provincial park located on Vancouver Island in the vicinity of Campbell River, BC.

SUNALTA PARK   7130 gt   9.44   Can   USY Montreal, QC

Nominated manager; Montreal Shipping Company Ltd. Montreal

1946 *Mont Alta*   Montship Lines Ltd. Montreal/Associated with Buries Markes Ltd. London.

1955 *Georgian Flame*   Cia. Gloriana de Nav. SA Liberia/Pateras Shipbrokers Ltd. London

1962 *Bonifacio*

1963 *President Laurel*

1968   Scrapped at Hirao, Japan

SUNALTA - City park located on the Bow River, west central side of Calgary, AB.

SUNNYSIDE PARK   7130 gt   4.44   Vic   WCSB Vancouver, BC

Nominated manager; Canadian-Australasian Line Ltd. Vancouver

1946 *Waitomo*   Canadian-Australasian Line Ltd.

1963 *Blue Shark*

1967   Scrapped at Kaohsiung, Taiwan

SUNNYSIDE PARK - City park in Vancouver, BC.

SUNSET PARK 2895 gt 11.44 Scan/R FM Pictou, NS
Managing owner; Park Steamship Company, Ottawa
Nominated manager; Canadian National Steamships Ltd.
1945 *Siderurgica Cinco* Cia. Siderurgica Nacional, Rio de Janeiro, Brazil.
1968 Scrapped in Brazil

SUNSET PARK - A common name believed repeated in many places across Canada.

SUTHERLAND PARK 2960 gt 5.45 Scan/D FM Pictou, NS
Nominated manager; Canadian National Steamships Ltd.
1947 *Canadian Conqueror* Canadian National Steamships Ltd.
7.57 Placed in lay - up at Halifax, NS
1958 Sold to Cuba but sale not finalized
1965 Scrapped at Bilbao, Spain

SUTHERLAND PARK - District of the City of Saskatoon, SK.

TABER PARK 2875 gt 8.44 Scan FM Pictou, NS
1944 Transferred to the MOWT, nominated manager not confirmed
13.3.45 Sunk by midget submarine 52.22N, 01.53E, SE of Yarmouth, East coast of England.
(see separate account)

TABER PARK - Located at Taber, AB.

TARBET NESS 8580 dt 5.45 Vic WCSB Vancouver, BC
Royal Navy, UK
Projected as a Maintenance ship. Type not indicated. Sold before completion.
1947 *Lautoka* Pacific Shipowners Ltd. Suva, Fiji/W.R. Carpenter & Son Ltd. Sydney, NSW.
1947 *Devanha* Peninsula & Oriental S.N. Co. London
1961 *Fortune Canary*
1964 *Wing An*

TARBET NESS - Prominent headland at the easternmost tip of Easter Ross peninsula separating Dornoch and Moray Firths on the East coast of Scotland.

TARONGA PARK 2875 gt 4.44 Scan SJDD St. John, NB
Transferred to the Commonwealth Government of Australia
1947 *Federal Ranger* Federal Commerce & Navigation Co. Ltd. Montreal
1948 *Marie Toft* Jens Toft A/S, Copenhagen, Denmark
1951 *J.E. Manne* A/B Helge, Gothenburg, Mgr. Claes Manne.
1956 *J.E.M. Naess* Ingvar Jansen, Fjosanger, Bergen, Norway
1963 *Hermes Leader*

TARONGA PARK - Famous city park and zoo located at Sydney, NSW, Australia

TECUMSEH PARK 7130 gt 10.43 Vic WCSB Vancouver, BC
Launched as *Fort St. Ignace (I)*, transfer to MOWT cancelled.
Nominated manager; Canadian Transport Company Ltd.
1947 *Argovan* Lunham & Moore (Canada) Ltd. Montreal
1959 *Cardamilitis* Strovili Cia. Nav. SA, Panama/A.Lusi Ltd. London.
1967 Scrapped at Shanghai, China

TECUMSEH PARK -
1. Calgary city park. Named for Chief Tecumseh of the Shawnee Indians who was prominent in the War of 1812 on the British side. He was killed at the Battle of the Thames in Southern Ontario.
2. City park in South Vancouver, BC. (See also Fort St. Ignace.)

TEMAGAMI PARK 7130 gt 2.44 Vic NVSR North Van, BC
Nominated manager; Anglo-Canadian Shipping Co. Ltd. Vancouver.
1946 *Lake Pennask* Western Canada Steamships Ltd., Vancouver
1954 *Cygnet* Bahia Salinas Cia. Nav. SA, Liberia/Goulandris Brothers Ltd. London.
1958 *Cresta* Villaviosa Cia Nav. SA Panama/Ormos Shipping Co. Ltd. London
Believed to be related to the Goulandris interests.
1970 Scrapped at Shanghai, China

TEMAGAMI PARK - Provincial park in the Temagami Lakes region of Quebec. A high grade copper/gold mine was located in the park until it was mined out in the 1960s.

Tipperary Park as *Table Bay* (Phil Chandler)

TIPPERARY PARK 7130 gt 2.44 Vic BDD/VDD Vancouver, BC

Nominated manager; Anglo - Canadian Shipping Co. Ltd. Vancouver
1946 *Lake Shawinigan* Western Canada Steamship Co. Ltd. Vancouver
1950 *Table Bay* Western Canada Steamship Co. Ltd./Managed by Lyle Shipping Co. Ltd. Glasgow
1957 *Rumija* Yugoslav Ocean Lines, Kotor, YS
TIPPERARY PARK -
1. There are indications of early Indian occupation of a site on Tipperary Creek, Saskatoon, SK. This was followed by Cree settlement with Sioux at nearby Moose Woods. Later Metis settled here. White settlement commenced in 1882 when the site was chosen for a location by a Toronto settlement society.
2. City park south side of Vancouver, BC

TOBIATIC PARK 7130 gt 9.44 Vic BDD North Van, BC

Nominated manager; Seaboard Shipping Co. Ltd. Vancouver
1946 *Seaboard Trader* Seaboard Shipping Co. Ltd.
1954 *Trader* Bahia Salinas Cia Nav. SA, Panama/Goulandris Bros. Ltd. London
1966 Transferred to Taiwan
1967 Scrapped at Osaka, Japan
TOBIATIC PARK - A Nova Scotia provincial park located NW of Liverpool and now designated a wildlife management area. The correct spelling is "Tobeatic" – an example of occasional spelling inconsistences between the ship and its namesake.

TUXEDO PARK 7130 gt 7.44 Vic WCSB Vancouver, BC

Nominated manager; Empire Shipping Co. Ltd. Vancouver
1946 *Angusdale (1)* Lunham & Moore (Canada) Ltd. Montreal
1948 *Point Aconi* Navitrans Corp. Panama/Mgr. Piero Ravano, Genoa
1965 *Phopho Xila*
1968 Scrapped at Hong Kong
TUXEDO PARK -
1. Park at Regina, SK
2. Location, Tuxedo district of Winnipeg, MB.

TWEEDSMUIR PARK 7130 gt 5.43 NS MI Sorel, QC

Nominated manager; McLean Kennedy Ltd. Montreal.
1946 Transferred to MOWT
  Nominated manager, Aviation & Shipping Co. Ltd. (Noel Purvis) London.
1950 *Bedford Queen* Bedford Overseas Freighters Ltd. Halifax/P.D. Marchessini & Co. Ltd. London.
  Clients of I.H. Mathers & Son Ltd. Halifax, NS
1955 *Lord Tweedsmuir* Glenrock Shipping Co. Ltd. Montreal/J.P. Hadoulis Ltd. London
1961 Scrapped at Kinoe, Japan
TWEEDSMUIR PARK - Large provincial park in Central BC named for John Buchan, Baron Tweedsmuir, famed novelist, historian, publisher, diplomat and politician. Lord Tweedsmuir was Governor - General of Canada for 1935 - 1940.

VICTORIA PARK 2875 gt 4.43 Scan FM Pictou, NS

Nominated manager; Johnson Walton Steamships Ltd. Vancouver.
1946 *Tatuk* Johnson Walton Steamship Ltd./Danish East Asiatic Company, Copenhagen
1948 *Kalo* Damps. Bothnia/Mgr. Christian Jensen, Copenhagen, Denmark

Vessel Name:	Tonnage:	Completion date:	Type:	Builder & Yard location

1957 *Ester*   Panaghia S.S. Corp. Liberia
1964 *San John P.*
1965 *Ramsdal I*
1966 *Rio Atrato*
1982   Scrapped in Colombia

VICTORIA PARK - Provincial park located near Victoria, PEI. There are also city parks Truro NS, Regina SK, Charlottetown PEI, Quebec City, Sherbrooke, QC and London ON. There are no doubt a number of others in other cities and smaller centres.

Wascana Park as *Cargill* (D. McMillan collection)

WASCANA PARK   7130 gt   8.43   Vic   BDD/VDD Vancouver, BC
Nominated manager; North Pacific Shipping Co. Ltd. Vancouver
1946 *Cargill*   Elder Dempster Lines Ltd. Montreal
1960 *Marine Navigator*
1962 *Marine Ace*
1966   Scrapped at Hirao, Japan.

WASCANA PARK - A popular name in Regina derived from the Cree Indian meaning a "pile of bones". It was effectively the first name for Regina and today is the large tract of parkland that surrounds the Saskatchewan legislature and University of Regina.

WAVERLEY PARK   7130 gt   3.45   Can   WCSB Vancouver, BC
Nominated manager; Constantine Lines (Canada) Ltd. Montreal
1946 *Dingwall*   Dingwall Shipping Co. Ltd. Halifax/Quebec S.S. Lines. Montreal and
                           National Gypsum Co. Buffalo, NY
1955 *Rayo*   Comp de, Nav Gaviota, SA, Panama and Lugano, Switzerland.
1960 *Maripindo*
1969   Scrapped at Vado, Italy

WAVERLEY PARK -
1. Established in 1926 as a park and game sanctuary in Nova Scotia, a short distance NE of Halifax, NS
2. City park in Port Arthur, ON. (now Thunder Bay)

WELLINGTON PARK   7130 gt   11.44   Can   USY Montreal, QC
Nominated manager; Cunard White Star Ltd. Montreal
1948 *Sunwhite*   Saguenay Terminals Ltd. Montreal
1960 *Ceres*
1970   Scrapped at Osaka, Japan.

WELLINGTON PARK -
1. Preserved site of Fort Wellington, near Prescott, ON
2. Land surrounding Wellington Barracks which were destroyed in the Halifax explosion in 1917.
3. Town in Prince Edward County, ON. 20km S. of Belleville,
4. North and South Wellington, small colliery towns in the Nanaimo Coal Field, central Vancouver Island.

WENTWORTH PARK	2875 gt	10.44	Scan	FM Pictou, NS

Nominated manager; Saguenay Terminals Ltd. Montreal
1948 *Sundial* — Saguenay Terminals Ltd. Montreal
1958 *Celeste* — Carga Maritima SA, Liberia
1961 *Nadine*
1965 *Azar*
1968 — Wrecked, total loss
WENTWORTH PARK - City park at Sydney NS.

WESTBANK PARK	7130 gt	3.44	Vic	NVSR North Van, BC

Nominated manager; Seaboard Shipping Company Ltd. Vancouver
7.10.45 — Ashore west side of Baja Peninsula, Lower California, near Magdalena Bay, (see separate account) TL
WESTBANK PARK - Located at community of Westbank on the west side of Okanagan Lake, BC

WESTDALE PARK	2895 gt	8.45	Scan.D	ME&D Quebec City, QC

Nominated manager; Canadian National Steamships Ltd. Montreal
1946 *Canadian Observer* — Canadian National Steamships Ltd.
1958 — Laid up at Halifax. Sold to Cuba, but sale not completed.
1956 — Scrapped at Bilbao, Spain
WESTDALE PARK - No satisfactory explanation or location for this name found.

WESTEND PARK	7130 gt	7.44	Vic	BDD North Van, BC

Nominated manager; North Pacific Shipping Co. Ltd. Vancouver
1947 *Triberg* — Triton S.S. Co. Ltd. Montreal/Connected with Goulandris Bros. London
1954 *Sevilla* — Nueva Sevilla, Cia Nav. SA, Panama/N.J. Goulandris Ltd. London
1960 *Naxos*
1962 *Stevo*
1971 — Scrapped in Yugoslavia
WESTEND PARK - There are several small parks in the West end of Vancouver as there often are in other larger cities. The name chosen could be a generalized name to cover parks generally associated with west ends, but no specific location identified.

WESTMOUNT PARK	7130 gt	9.43	NS	USY Montreal, QC

Nominated manager; Furness Withy & Co. Ltd. Montreal.
1946 — Transferred to MOWT
— Nominated manager, Andrew Crawford & Co. Ltd. Glasgow
1950 *Nordicstar* — Fairview Overseas Freighters Ltd. Halifax/C.M. Lemos & Co. Ltd./Clients of I.H. Mathers & Son. Ltd. Halifax
27.12.56 — Disappeared at sea. Last reported 44N 38W west of Ushant. 23.1.57 Posted missing.
WESTMOUNT PARK - Located in the fashionable district of Westmount, Montreal

WESTON PARK	7130 gt	10.44	Vic	WCSB Vancouver, BC

Nominated manager, North Pacific Shipping Co. Ltd. Vancouver
1946 *Lake Sicamous* — Western Canada Steamship Co. Ltd. Vancouver
1953 *Archipelago* — Panedo Cia. Nav. SA. Panama/John C. Hadjipateras & Sons. Ltd. London
1960 *Silver Valley* — Silver Star Shipping Corp. Liberia
15.3.63 — Aground on the River Douro Bar, off Oporto, Portugal
16.3.63 — Broke in two, TL
WESTON PARK -
1. Southern Ontario town, outside Toronto, ON
2. City park in Winnipeg, MB.

WESTVIEW PARK	7130 gt	10.44	Vic	PRDS Prince Rupert, BC

Launched as *Fort Beaver Lake*, transfer to MOWT not completed.
Nominated manager, Seaboard Shipping Co. Ltd. Vancouver, BC.
1946 *Seaboard Enterprise* — Seaboard Shipping Co. Ltd. Vancouver
1957 *Doric* — Doric S.S. Corp., Liberia/Ormos Shipping Co. Ltd. London

1964 *Patagonia*
1965 *Mary F*
1969   Scrapped in Shanghai, China
WESTVIEW PARK -
1. The prime residential area of the industrial town of Powell River on the BC coast, NW of Vancouver
2. City park in Winnipeg, MB. (See also Fort Beaver Lake.)

WHITEROCK PARK   7130 gt   10.44   Vic   NVSR North Van, BC
Launched as *Fort Daer,* transfer to MOWT not completed
Nominated manager; Johnson Walton Steamships Ltd. Vancouver
1946 *Tantara*   Johnson Walton Steamships Ltd. Vancouver
1951 *Pelopidas*   Cia. Mar. Samsoc Ltd.a. Panama/Hermes S.S. Agency, San Francisco,
1956 *African Count*   West African Nav. Co. Liberia
1963   Scrapped in Japan
WHITEROCK PARK - City south of Vancouver at US border. So named for prominent highly visible white rock on the beach.
Correct spelling separates the words as in "White Rock." (See also Fort Daer.)

WHITESHELL PARK   7130 gt   4.44   NS   USY Montreal, QC
Launched as F*ort Beauharnois* (I). Transfer to MOWT not completed
Nominated manager; Canadian Pacific Steamships Ltd. Montreal
1946   Transferred to MOWT.
                         Nominated manager, (DOC) Novocastria Shipping Co. Ltd.
                         Stott Mann & Fleming Ltd. Newcastle
1950 *Fir Hill*   Halifax Overseas Freighters Ltd. Halifax (Counties Ship Management Co. London).
                         Clients of I.H. Mathers & Son Ltd. Halifax.
1964 *Universal Trader*
1968   Scrapped at Hirao, Japan
WHITESHELL PARK - Provincial park located approximately 105km E of Winnipeg MB. (See also Fort Beauharnois.)

WILDEWOOD PARK   7130 gt   1.44   Vic/T   WCSB Vancouver, BC
Nominated manager; Imperial Oil Ltd. Toronto
1947 *Irvingdale*   Irving Oil Ltd. St. John, NB.
1961   Scrapped at Valencia, Spain.
WILDWOOD PARK - Town located W. of Ottawa, ON. Note a typical variation as the town does not have an "e" in its spelling.

WILLOW PARK   2895 gt   12.44   Scan/R   DSBR Lauzon, QC
Transferred without change of name to the MOWT
Nominated manager, not confirmed
1946 *Docteur Roux*   Centre for Supply. Saigon, Indo - China.
1955 *Danakil*   Trans. Mar. de l'Afrique Occidentale Francaise, Konakri, French Guinea/Mgr. Chargeurs Reunis
1960   Seized by the Republic of Indonesia
WILLOW PARK - There are at least 11 locations containing the name "Willow" in Ontario, Saskatchewan, Alberta and BC.

WILLOWDALE PARK   7130 gt   3.44   Vic/T   WCSB Vancouver, BC
Nominated manager, Imperial Oil Ltd., Toronto
1946 *Georgia*
1955   Converted to dry cargo
1957 *Sao Paulo*
1959 *Matija Gubec*
WILLOWDALE PARK - Town in Ontario.

WINDERMERE PARK   7130 gt   11.43   Vic   WCSB Vancouver, BC
Launched as *Fort Miami (I)*. Transfer to MOWT not completed.
Nominated manager; Anglo - Canadian Shipping Co. Ltd. Vancouver
1946 *Lake Sumas*   Western Canada Steamship Co. Ltd. Vancouver
1949 *Katherine*
1961 *Nagos*
WINDERMERE PARK - At Windermere on Windermere Lake, opposite Invermere, BC. (See also Fort Miami.)

Vessel Name:	Tonnage:	Completion date:	Type:	Builder & Yard location

WINNIPEGOSIS PARK   7130 gt   11.43   Vic   PRDS Prince Rupert, BC

Launched as *Fort Aspin (I)*. Transfer to MOWT not completed.
Nominated manager; Seaboard Shipping Co. Ltd.
1947 *Bayside*   Andros Shipping Co. Ltd. Montreal/Ass. Goulandris Bros. London
1949 *Aghia Anastasia*   Guardia Cia. Nav. SA, Panama.
22.6.50   Aground off Drew Bank, West Tobago. Refloated 25.6.50. Sank 11.04N 60.56W. TL
WINNIPEGOSIS PARK - Located on or near Lake Winnipegosis, MB. The name derives from Cree, meaning "little murky waters"
FORT ASPIN (I) - see entry under Fort Aspin (II).

WINONA PARK   7130 gt   12.44   Can   WCSB Vancouver, BC

Nominated manager; Canada Shipping Co. Ltd. Vancouver.
1944 *Lake Tatla*   Western Canada Steamship Co. Ltd. Vancouver.
1950 *Walvis Bay*   Western Canada Steamship Co. Ltd./Sir R. Ropner & Co. Management Ltd.
                          Darlington, Yorkshire, UK
1957 *Andros Halcyon*   Andros Shipping & Trading Co./Goulandris interests, Greece
1957 *M.A.S. Primo*   Maritima Anon. Siciliana, Palermo/Mgr. Pasquale Mazzella, Naples, Italy
1959 *Kirlangiclar*   Kirlangiclar Silepoilik, Istanbul
1973   Scrapped at Kaohsiung, Taiwan
WINONA PARK -
1. Town or village of Winona, Ontario.
2. City park in Vancouver, BC .

Withrow Park as *Kingsbridge* (Foto-Flite)

WITHROW PARK   7130 gt   7.44   NS   USY Montreal, QC

Nominated manager; McLean Kennedy Ltd. Montreal
1946   Transferred to MOWT.
                          Nominated manager, (DOC) South American Saint Line, Cardiff
1950 *Kingsbridge*   Kingsbridge Shipping Co. Ltd./Goulandris Bros. London
1960   Scrapped at Hong Kong
WITHROW PARK - Alberta town about 30km E of Rocky Mountain House.

WOODLAND PARK   2875 gt   12.43   Scan   FM Pictou, NS

Transferred to MOWT without change of name
1946 *Huynh Khuong An*   Centre for Supply, Saigon, Vietnam
1948 *Dr. Pham hun Chi*   Same as above
1952 *Vimy*   Charles Audibert, Monaco.
1955 *Dimitris*   D.J. Papadimitriou Sons, Alexandria, Egypt
29.9.56   Aground near Orresgrund, near Kotka. Refloated, CTL, wreck sold, repaired becoming:-
1957 *Dimitrakis P*
1960 *Elli*
1964 *Aspasia*
WOODLAND PARK - Location about 10km, SW from Edmonton city limits.

Yamaska Park as *Yamaska* (Foto-Flite)

YAMASKA PARK   7130 gt   7.44   NS   MI Sorel, QC
Nominated manager; Furness Withy & Co. Ltd. Montreal
1946   Transferred to MOWT
                                            Nominated manager, Novocastria Shipping Co./Stott, Mann & Fleming Ltd. Newcastle-on-Tyne
1951 *Yamaska*   Yamaska S.S. Co. Ltd. Montreal/Ships Finance & Management Co. Ltd.
                                            Ass. with G. Nicolaou Ltd. both of London.
1959 *Gunn*   Republic of China
Still listed in 1992, but existence doubtful.
YAMASKA PARK - Location town and river Yamaska, Eastern townships area of Quebec.

YOHO PARK (I)   7130 gt   7.43   NS   VMD Victoria, BC
Nominated manager; Canadian Australasian Line Ltd. Vancouver
In a switch of names similar to the two *Mount Robson Parks*, simultaneously with *Yoho Park (I)* becoming *Fort Highfield (I)*.
Fort Highfield (II) became *Yoho Park (II)*. It was the means whereby the older ship was transferred to the MOWT.
1944 *Fort Highfield*
Nominated manager, (DOC)
1951 *Darfield*   Windsor Overseas Freighters Ltd. Halifax, NS/Nomikos (London) Ltd. managers
1954   Aground in fog off Flat Iron Point, 10m north of Los Angeles, CA. Refloated, towed to
                                            Los Angeles, CTL, scrapped at Terminal Island, CA
YOHO PARK - National park located on the BC side of the border with Alberta, in the Rockies, adjacent to Banff and Kootenay
National Parks.

YOHO PARK (II)   7130 gt   7.44   Vic   NVSR North Van, BC
Launched as *Fort Highfield,* see preceding remarks
Nominated manager; Canadian - Australasian Line Ltd. Vancouver
1946 *Lake Winnipeg*   Western Canada Steamship Co. Ltd. Vancouver, BC
1953 *Americana*   Altos Mares Cia. Nav. SA. Panama/A.Lusi Ltd. London
YOHO PARK - as above. (See also Fort Highfield.)

Bibliography

Brewer, L.R.   *The Last Voyage of S.S. Westbank Park.* San Jose, CA: Privately published by the author.

Burrell, D.C.E.   *Scrap & Build.* Kendal, U.K.: The World Ship Society, 1983.

Carroll, Olive.   *Deep Sea Sparks: A Canadian Girl in the Norwegian Merchant Navy.* Vancouver: Cordillera Publishing, 1993.

Cowden, James E.   *The Elder Dempster Fleet History.* Mallett & Bell Publications, 1986.
and John O.C. Duffy.

Cowling, Bill.   *1413 Days: In the Wake of a Canadian DEMS Gunner.* Calgary AB: William A. Cowling, 1994.

Darlington, Robert,   *The Canadian Naval Chronicle,* 1939-1945. St. Catharines, ON: Vanwell Publishing, 1996.
and Fraser McKee.

Dover, Victor.   *Handbook of Marine Insurance.* Sixth Edition. London: Witherby Ltd., 1962.

Fraser, Doug.   *Postwar Casualty: Canada's Merchant Navy.* East Lawrencetown, NS: Pottersfield Press, 1997.

Gray, James W.   *Financial Risk Management in the Shipping Industry.* Fairplay, 1986.

Green, Jim.   *Against the Tide: The Story of the Canadian Seamen's Union,* Toronto: Progress Books, 1986.

Gripaios, Hector.   *Tramp Shipping.* London: Thomas Nelson & Sons, 1959.

Halford, Robert. G.   *The Unknown Navy: Canada's World War II Merchant Navy.* St. Catharines, ON: Vanwell Publishing, 1995.

Hawes, Duncan.   *Merchant Fleets - Ellerman Lines.* TCP Publications, 1989.

Heal, S.C.   *Across Far Distant Horizons: The Life and Times of a Canadian Master Mariner.* Vancouver: Cordillera Publishing, 1995. With references to *Mount Robson Park I & II.*

Heal, S.C.   *Conceived in War, Born in Peace: Canada's Deep Sea Merchant Marine.* Vancouver: Cordillera Publishing, 1992.

Heal, S.C., with   *Full Line, Full Away: A Towboat Master's Story.* Vancouver: Cordillera Publishing, 1991.
James E. Wilson.   With references to the master of *Jasper Park.*

Hunter, Harry,   *The British Merchant Shipbuilding Programme in North America, 1940-42.* Eleventh Andrew
and R.C. Thompson.   Laing Lecture. London, 1943.

Hutcherson, W.   *Sparks in the Parks.* Privately published by the author.

Infield, Glen.   *Disaster at Bari.* MacMillan, 1972; Bantam 1988.

Jones, Herbert G.   *Portland Ships are Good Ships.* Portland, Maine: Machigonne Press, 1945.

Kaplan, William.   *Everything That Floats: Pat Sullivan, Hal Banks and the Seamen's Unions of Canada.* Toronto: University of Toronto Press, 1987.

Lane, Frederic C.   *Ships for Victory: A History of Shipbuilding Under the United States Maritime Commission in World War II.* Baltimore: The Johns Hopkins Press, 1951.

Martin-Smith, David.   *South to the Southern Capes; The Maiden Voyage of the S.S. Beaton Park.* Victoria, BC: Galleon Crown, 1997.

Mattox, W.C.	*Building the Emergency Fleet.* Cleveland: Penton Publishing , 1920; New York: Library Editions, 1970.
Metaxas, B.N.	*The Economics of Tramp Shipping.* Athlone Press/University of London, 1971.
Miller, Nathan.	*War at Sea: A Naval History of World War II.* Oxford and New York: Oxford University Press, 1995.
Patterson, Donald, and Hill Wilson.	*Roll of Honour: Canadian Seamen Lost or Missing During World War II.* Privately published by the authors.
Reid, Max	*DEMS at War.* Ottawa: Commoners' Publishing Society, 1990.
Sawyer, L.A., with W.A. Mitchell.	*Empire Ships of World War II.* Liverpool: Journal of Commerce & Shipping Telegraph, 1965. Sawyer, L.A. with W.A. Mitchell. *The Liberty Ships.* Cornell Maritime Press, 1970.
Sawyer, L.A., with W.A. Mitchell	*The Oceans, The Forts, & The Parks.* Liverpool: Journal of Commerce & Shipping Telegraph, 1966.
Slader, John.	*The Fourth Service, Merchantmen at War, 1939-45.* Wimborne Minster, UK: New Era Writer's Guild (UK) Ltd., 1995.
Smith, Peter C.	*Task Force 57:The British Pacific Fleet, 1944-45.* Wm. Kimber, 1969; Crecy Books, 1994.
Stanton, John.	*Life & Death of a Union: The Canadian Seamen's Union, 1936-49.* Toronto: Steel Rail Educational Publishing, 1978.
Stewart, Ian G.	*British Tramps: The History of British Tramp Shipping.* Rockingham Beach, Australia: Ian Stewart Marine Publications, 1998.
Stewart, Ian G.	*Liberty Ships in Peacetime And Their Contribution to World Shipping History.* Rockingham Beach, Australia: Ian Stewart Marine Publications, 1992.
Tull, Peter.	*Cromwell Park; Voyages 1, 2 and 3, 1945-46.* Richmond, BC: privately published by the author, 1997.
Tull, Peter.	*Harmac Vancouver, ex-Cromwell Park, Voyages 4-9, 1946-48.* Richmond, BC: privately published by the author, 1998.
Tull, Peter.	*The Amaryllis, ex-Harmac Vancouver, ex-Cromwell Park: The Story of the Ship's Loss.* Richmond, BC: privately published by the author, 1996.
Walton, Thomas.	*Know Your Own Ship.* London: Chas. Griffin & Co. 1924.
Wilson, Hill.	*A School of Seamen, A Pride of Ships: St Margaret's Sea Training School, 1942-46.* Victoria, BC: privately published by the author, 1993.
————	*A History of Shipbuilding in British Columbia.* Marine Retirees Association of the The Marine Workers and Boilermakers Industrial Union, 1977.
————	*British Merchant Vessels Lost or Damaged by Enemy Action during the Second World War.* HM Stationary Office, 1947.
————	*Lloyds Confidential Index.* Various yearly editions. London: The Corporation of Lloyds of London.
————	*VJ: The Final Victory.* DPR (Navy) Ministry of Defence, UK.
Winser, John de S.	*The D-Day Ships.* Kendal, UK: World Ship Society, 1994.

INDEX

As the complete Fleet List is in alphabetical order, none of the items listed therein are included in this index.